Critical Theory
—— and the ——
Human Condition

Studies in the
Postmodern Theory of Education

Joe L. Kincheloe and Shirley R. Steinberg
General Editors

Vol. 168

PETER LANG
New York • Washington, D.C./Baltimore • Bern
Frankfurt am Main • Berlin • Brussels • Vienna • Oxford

Critical Theory —and the— Human Condition

FOUNDERS AND PRAXIS

EDITED BY
Michael Peters, Colin Lankshear,
and Mark Olssen

PETER LANG
New York • Washington, D.C./Baltimore • Bern
Frankfurt am Main • Berlin • Brussels • Vienna • Oxford

Library of Congress Cataloging-in-Publication Data

Critical theory and the human condition: founders and praxis /
edited by Michael Peters, Colin Lankshear, and Mark Olssen.
  p. cm. — (Counterpoints; vol. 168)
Includes bibliographical references and index.
1. Critical pedagogy. 2. Postmodernism and education.
I. Peters, Michael (Michael A.). II. Lankshear, Colin. III. Olssen, Mark.
  IV. Counterpoints (New York, N.Y.); vol. 168.
    LC196 .C78   370.11′5—dc21   00-048770
          ISBN 0-8204-5168-1
          ISSN 1058-1634

Die Deutsche Bibliothek-CIP-Einheitsaufnahme

Critical theory and the human condition: founders and praxis /
ed. by: Michael Peters....
–New York; Washington, D.C./Baltimore; Bern;
Frankfurt am Main; Berlin; Brussels; Vienna; Oxford: Lang.
(Counterpoints: Studies in the Postmodern Theory of Education. Vol. 168)
          ISBN 0-8204-5168-1

Cover design by Joni Holst

The paper in this book meets the guidelines for permanence and durability
of the Committee on Production Guidelines for Book Longevity
of the Council of Library Resources.

© 2003 Peter Lang Publishing, Inc., New York
275 Seventh Avenue, 28th Floor, New York, NY 10001
www.peterlangusa.com

All rights reserved.
Reprint or reproduction, even partially, in all forms such as microfilm,
xerography, microfiche, microcard, and offset strictly prohibited.

Printed in the United States of America

For Maxine Greene

CONTENTS

Acknowledgments — ix

Introduction: Critical Theory and the Human Condition — 1
MICHAEL PETERS, COLIN LANKSHEAR, AND MARK OLSSEN

PART 1 — CRITICAL THEORY: LABORS OF THE DIALECTIC

1. Critical Theory, Critical Pedagogy and the Possibility of Counter-Education — 17
ILAN GUR-ZE'EV

2. Down Sudden Vistas: Walter Benjamin and the Waning of Modernity — 36
ROBERT A. DAVIS

3. On Having and Being: The Humanism of Erich Fromm — 54
COLIN LANKSHEAR

4. Marcuse and the Quest for Radical Subjectivity — 67
DOUGLAS KELLNER

5. "What rough beast . . .": On Reading Arendt after the Twin Towers — 84
JAMES C. CONROY

6. Marx, Wittgenstein, and the Problem of Consciousness — 101
GRANT GILLETT

7. Habermas's Postmodernism — 114
ROBERT YOUNG

8   Admitting "A Perhaps": Maxine Greene and the Project of Critical Theory   130
DEBORAH P. BRITZMAN AND DON DIPPO

PART 2 — CRITICAL THEORY: PROJECTS AND MOVEMENTS

9   Pedagogy of the Depressed: Beyond the New Politics of Cynicism   143
HENRY A. GIROUX

10   Knowledge, Dialogue, and Humanization: Exploring Freire's Philosophy   169
PETER ROBERTS

11   Critical Race Theory in Education: Possibilities and Problems   184
LAURENCE PARKER

12   Critical Multiculturalism   199
STEPHEN MAY

13   The Grotesque Body as a Feminist Aesthetic?   213
ERICA MCWILLIAM

14   Critical Theory and British Cultural Studies   222
TOM STEELE

15   Critical Theory and the Environment   238
TIMOTHY W. LUKE

References   251

List of Contributors   277

Index   283

ACKNOWLEDGMENTS

The editors are grateful for permission to reproduce in this text previously published work as follows: *College Literature* for "Pedagogy of the Depressed: Beyond the New Politics of Cynicism," by Henry Giroux (Chapter 9); the *Journal of Educational Thought* and Bergin & Garvey/Greenwood Press for "Knowledge, Dialogue and Humanization: Exploring Freire's Philosophy," by Peter Roberts (Chapter 10).

We also acknowledge our indebtedness to the colleagues who have generously contributed to this volume. They all have many demands made on their time and energies, and requests to contribute essays to edited collections come on top of already exacting workloads. We want them to know that their generosity is greatly appreciated, and we hope that the volume as a whole is one they can feel pleased to have contributed to.

As always, our friends and colleagues at Peter Lang Publishing have made the task of putting the book together as enjoyable and trouble-free as possible. We particularly thank Joe Kincheloe, Shirley Steinberg, and Chris Myers for supporting this project. To Valerie Shea and Phyllis Korper we owe a big debt of editorial gratitude. We also thank the members of Lang's production and marketing teams and hope the book repays their efforts.

Michael Peters
Colin Lankshear
Mark Olssen

Michael Peters, Colin Lankshear, and Mark Olssen

INTRODUCTION: CRITICAL THEORY AND THE HUMAN CONDITION

Students of the social sciences and humanities who have entered the academy since the advent of "post everything" are often subjected to glib and dismissive versions of pre-Foucauldian social and political theory. It has become common for students to be informed that there is little or no thought still relevant prior to poststructuralism—that any theory coming in the guise of a grand narrative is ideological, and that with the possible exception of Nietzsche, the only theory that speaks to the present and future began with Foucault or, perhaps, Derrida. As a result, many contemporary students have missed out on receiving a sound history of social and educational theory. No single tradition of Western thought has suffered more in recent times than critical theory. Foucault himself comments to the effect that had he been introduced to and allowed to read the Frankfurt School, it would have saved him a lot of work. Indeed, in one interview Foucault locates himself in the tradition of critical theory that he traces to Max Weber and the Frankfurt School.

In our view, a great disservice has been done by a surfeit of such myopic theoretical work in undergraduate courses. Today we find ourselves in the midst of a host of massive social and educational issues that many of those who have invested in the "theory since Foucault" view have little or no ken of, and where the best contemporary theorizing is being done by people who *do* have a strong grounding in earlier traditions including, above all, critical theory. Accordingly, this collection is thematized and organized around major issues that impact on social and educational practices and institutions, and it establishes the value of a critical theory perspective to these issues. We recognize the historical specificity of the Frankfurt School but also the wider tradition of critical philosophy, stretching back to Kant and Hegel, and in sociology to Weber, and also the ways in which the term has recently been appropriated to apply to aspects of contemporary thought, including the innovations of structuralism, semiotics, and poststructuralism.

Many commentators have observed differences between the reading preferences of today's students and students of earlier generations, for whom the printed word constituted the main source of information. Faced with serious competing media, the book is being required to adapt its form and structure in order to be taken up by "screenage" students. This generates a worthy challenge for academics with a good grasp on their theoretical specialisms: to cut quickly and in engaging ways to the heart of stances, concepts, and issues. Hence, this book is conceived as one that covers a wide range of theorists and issues, but does so by way of essays of varying length, and where the contract for meaning-making is shared fairly between author and reader.

In the remainder of this introduction, first, we provide some background in terms of the influence of Hegel on the tradition of critical theory; second, we investigate the relationship between critical theory and orthodox Marxism; third, we comment on the twin concepts of rationalization and bureaucratization; fourth, we take up the question of the relationship between Hegel and poststructuralism before, finally, commenting on the structure and organization of the book.

Hegel and the Tradition of Critical Theory

Critical theory emerged in Germany in the 1920s with the establishment of the Institute for Social Research at Frankfurt am Main in 1923. Known as the Frankfurt School, the group became exiled to France, then to the United States in the early 1930s until 1941 when it closed down. According to Löwenthal (1989, p. 141), the decision to emigrate from Germany was made as early as 1930 as a consequence of the rise of the Nazis to political power and the increasingly difficult situation faced by a group of intellectuals that was predominantly Jewish. Among its members were Max Horkheimer, Theodor Adorno, Herbert Marcuse, Frederick Pollock, Franz Neumann, Leo Löwenthal, and Eric Fromm. In 1934 the group were given permission to establish their Institute at Columbia University in New York. After the war, in 1950, it was reestablished in Frankfurt, where it attracted new members such as Jürgen Habermas and Alfred Schmidt.

Although informed by multiple perspectives, the work of the Frankfurt School began primarily as a Marxist critique of capitalist society. This moved away from orthodox economistic versions of Marxism toward a reinstatement of Hegelian Marxist themes that resurrected the "young Marx" with his emphasis on philosophy, ethics, dialectics, alienation, consciousness, and the human subject as the self-realization of history and as the basis for the critique of bourgeois society.

Initially conceived as a Marxist critique of capitalist society, the theoretical base of critical theory was soon to broaden, incorporating ideas drawn selectively from Nietzsche, Marx, Weber, Heidegger, Lukacs, Korsch, and Hegel. These influences were increasingly incorporated as critical theory sought to challenge the traditions of modernity, a core theme with which it had been concerned from the start in its opposition to the forces of modernization and representations of modernity, which saw it as a purely positive force linked to the development and progress of science, technology, and industry. While, like Marx, the members of the Frankfurt School saw modernity as comprising both positive and negative influences, in representing modernity as the product of capitalism, they sought to revise and update Marxist theory by focusing attention on the irrational and oppressive features of modernity and on its totalitarian tendencies. In this regard they developed theories of consumerism and culture, as well as science and technology, as new forms of social control linked to changing patterns of individual social development. During the 1930s and 1940s their research projects included topics such as the family, aesthetic theory, the critique of culture, the causes and origins of Nazism, and the nature of authority relations under capitalism.

The term "critical theory" was originally coined and used by Horkheimer in 1937 to describe the theoretical program of the school. Horkheimer became director of the school in 1930, succeeding Carl Grunberg, and directed it away from its initial emphasis on orthodox, scientific Marxism. Under Horkheimer's influence, the Institute's journal *Zeitschrift für Sozialforschung* became the mouthpiece for a more humanistic, philosophical Marxism, shifting the frame of reference away from a focus on the economy and exploitation toward a critique of culture and a concern with alienation.

In his article "Traditional and Critical Theory," first published in 1937, Horkheimer explains that the term derives from the critical function of Marxist theory as a form of opposition to bourgeois society. This in fact was the crucial dividing line between traditional and critical theory. Whereas traditional theory sought to reproduce the relations of capitalist society, critical theory sought to subvert or undermine them. In this it was fashioned to expose or bring to light the fundamental intrinsic contradictions by critiquing the processes of reproduction from the outside. Horkheimer (1972, p. 221) maintains that critical theory has no specific content but comprises simply a philosophical orientation "whose business is to hasten developments which will lead to a society without injustice." As he continues (1972, p. 227, n.20), "critical theory maintains: it need not be so, man can change reality, and the necessary conditions for such a change already exist." In this it attempts "to go beyond the prevailing social ways of acting" (Horkheimer, 1972, p. 209).

In addition, critical and traditional theory embodied two different *Erkenntnisweisen*, or modes of cognition. While the modes of cognition of traditional theory derived from the natural sciences, those of critical theory focused on "men as producers of their own historical way of life in its totality" (Horkheimer, 1972, p. 244). In this it compares the existing pattern of civilization with the inherent possibilities of men as conscious producers. One of the central issues here was whether the methods of the natural sciences could be extended to the social domains. Horkheimer held that they could not. Thomas McCarthy (1994, p. 14) notes that the "axis on which the contrast turns is the reflexivity . . . of social enquiry." He continues:

4 CRITICAL THEORY AND THE HUMAN CONDITION

> The social sciences, in modelling themselves after the natural sciences, were attempting to position themselves centrally in an industrial society increasingly dependent on monitoring and managing key socio-economic variables. By promoting a positivistic image of themselves of just "telling it like it is," they could claim to offer a "view from nowhere" with all its rights and privileges, other approaches thereby became marginalized as prescientific, ideological, self-interested, or the like. One of the first tasks of critical theory was to challenge the privileged "non-position" of social-scientific knowledge by analyzing the modes of its production, the roles it played in society, the interests it served, and the historical process through which it came to power. (McCarthy, 1994, pp. 14–15)

The methods of the natural sciences thus misrepresented the human world by absolutizing knowledge. Science thus failed to understand both the reflexivity and contingency of social truths. In addition, because it was based on an atomistic metaphysic, it failed to theorize the holistic, or contextualized, character of social existence. Critical theory for Horkheimer, on the other hand, sought to explicate the nature of the relations between part and part, and parts and whole, revealing in addition its own embeddedness in the social matrix from which it arises and operates. In this sense, critical theory incorporates a constructionist dimension not only in that it sees itself as part and parcel of the social reality it seeks to comprehend, but also in that social actors and realities are produced and shaped by historical forces and processes. Although the representation of truth as the outcome of specific social situations introduces the specter of relativism, Horkheimer, departing from writers like Mannheim, sought to maintain a distinction between the true and the false independent of the historically constructed and conditioned nature of existing states of affairs. Horkheimer believed that reason could be maintained through sustained critique that preserved rather than displaced the fundamental ideas of truth, freedom, and justice. In fact, such normative ideas were integral to critical theory, in that it sought the liberation of humans from their oppressed conditions and the realization of a socialist society. In an epistemological sense, Horkheimer maintained that an interest in the improvement of the human conditions of existence was intrinsic to the very capacity of reason and the ability to utilize its capabilities. In this sense, the driving force of critical theory was practical, and linked as a moral-political system to the improvement of the human condition and, as with Kant, the realization of freedom through reason.

In relation to method, Kellner points out that from the beginning to the present, critical theory has disregarded divisions between existing disciplines, stressing the interconnectedness between them. In Kellner's words:

> Critical Theory is distinguished from traditional mainstream social science through its multidisciplinary perspectives and its attempts to develop a dialectical and material social theory. This project represents a collective, supradisciplinary synthesis of philosophy, the sciences and politics, in which critical social theory is produced by groups

of theorists and scientists from various disciplines working together to produce a Critical Theory of the present aimed at radical socio-political transformation. (Kellner, 1989, p. 7)

This "supradisciplinary" approach, says Kellner (1989, p. 7), involves not just collaboration between researchers from different disciplines but the criticism of "the validity claims of the separate disciplines." In this sense critical theory provides an overarching approach to the present age that links philosophy, politics, and economics in its critique of bourgeois culture and philosophy. Linking theory and practice, it seeks to isolate and expose the relationships between cultural elements, economic and social processes, and the historical context. Adopting the viewpoint of oppressed social groups, it expressly seeks to become an agent in the promotion of social change and transformation.

Critical Theory and Orthodox Marxism

At the time of critical theory's development in the 1920s, the orthodox version of Marxism was that of Kautsky, Plekhanov, and Hilferding, who were members of the Social Democracy movement. The version of Marxism to which they subscribed tended toward reductionist determinism, which interpreted the dynamics of history primarily in terms of economic effects of the economic base as it acted on the superstructure of society. Economism acted both synchronically, in that the economic base shaped the overall character of the culture, and diachronically, as an explanation of the laws of movement of the society in history.

Horkheimer and his colleagues followed Lukacs and Korsch who, in the early decades of the twentieth century, represented the main opposition within Marxism to the sterile economism of the Social Democrats. Lukacs and Korsch stressed human praxis and the central importance of the human subject as an active history-shaping force. Central to their approaches was the reinstatement of Hegel's philosophy at the center of Marxism, together with an emphasis on the concepts of reification, alienation, subjectivity, spontaneous action, dialectical method, and totality, as well as a representation of history as the self-realization of freedom through the exercise of historical praxis.

The crisis of Social Democracy was hastened by a number of important historical events, such as the First World War, the ill-fated 1918 German Revolution and, ultimately, the rise of Nazism and fascism, events that reinforced for Horkheimer and his group the fact that economistic Marxism of the Social Democrats focused only on the objective determinants of revolution but failed to consider the subjective factors such as consciousness, praxis, subjectivity, culture, and ideology.

Lukacs's book *History and Class Consciousness,* as well as Korsch's *Marxism and Philosophy,* challenged the conception of Marxism as a scientific treatise concerning the inevitable destruction of capitalism and its abandonment of Hegelian dialectic at the center of Marxism. To represent Marxism as a scientific theory that sought to explain the inevitable trajectory of capitalism's path as the consequence of purely objective contradictions internal to economic development was to neglect an activist orientation to history by which one sought to change history through intervening to transcend the present state of affairs. Although not a movement that was practically linked in any way to the working class, the Frankfurt School took up much of Lukacs's approach, based as it was in Hegel's philosophy. As Horkheimer (1972, p. 239) put it, Hegel's philosophy "constructs a developing picture of society as a whole." In this approach history is viewed as one all-embracing process in which the human species realizes itself in history. Although existing capitalist society was such that self-realization could not be attained in the present, internal to the human essence and manifested in the will and through struggle is the quest for a more rational form of existence reflecting man's inherent possibilities. Hence the possibility of transcending the present state of life is inherent in the human essence that progressively links the structure of thought to that of reality.

It is through this affinity to Hegel that critical theory becomes linked to German Idealism. For in "Critical and Traditional Theory," Horkheimer asserts a conception of truth as metaphysically residing in the essence of human activity in the sense that, as he puts it (1972, p. 251), "the thrust towards a rational society . . . is really innate in every man." For Hegel the notion of totality demonstrated that reality is not ascertainable through empirical senses but can be revealed only through philosophical analysis. Through the conception of totality all possible contradictions and oppositions must be comprehended to operate within the unity of the system where conflict provided the mechanism of progress toward history's ultimate goal. Thus Hegel's view of history holds out the promise of freedom premised on the march of reason through history.

In that Hegel envisaged history as the reconciliation of idea and reality, the inversion of the system by Marx saw historical progress through the transformation of reality. By turning Hegel "on his head" the dialectic comes to serve as the instrument for change, and as the "algebra of revolution," as Herzen put it. What became important was dialectic of whole and part, which conformed to the actual structure of reality as a dialectical process of interaction and movement whereby all things unfold in a pattern of transcendence (or self-transcendence) to a higher unity.

For Marx, Hegel's dialectical method was to function as a method of radical criticism and in seeing history as the unfolding of man's inner essence. The theme that Marx incorporated in his doctoral thesis, and in his early writings, was that the world was to be transformed not by an appeal to a historical principle, but by the progressive redistribution of its essence—freedom. With Hegel, and the Enlightenment thinkers such as Kant and Rousseau, Marx believed freedom to be the inner essence of man, which man seeks to realize by acting on the world and transforming it. Although he criticized Hegel's conservatism for his equation of thought with reality in Mind or Spirit, what he shared with Hegel was the notion that history has an objective meaning and development. While for Hegel this is embodied in the progressive evolution of Mind toward freedom, for Marx it is incorporated in man's mastery over nature and himself. For both thinkers, the historical process was equivalent to the whole. For both, history is the process of the self-realization of humanity. Yet, while for Hegel it was a change in Mind or reason in relation to the world, for Marx it was the transformation of the conditions of existence in accordance with man's inner potentialities.

Rationalization and Bureaucratization

Horkheimer and the members of the Frankfurt School reinstated a method of critique as an immanent process based on Hegel and the early Marx whereby existing actual appearances, affirmed often as universal laws, are questioned as ideological representations in favor of a dialectical understanding of society in terms of historical evolution and the future development of society. In this sense, critical theory is concerned with unraveling the contradictions between ideological representations and real states of affairs. Yet while, in this sense, critical theory aimed at being an emancipatory discourse, Horkheimer and the Frankfurt thinkers had less faith than Marx or Lukacs in the proletariat as a force for change, believing that the "general intellectual level of the great masses is rapidly declining" (Horkheimer, 1972, p. 238) as a consequence of an increasingly bureaucratized and rationalized mass culture, based on corporate capital, which rendered the comprehension and opposition by the masses as increasingly difficult to achieve.

The increasing commodification of culture and life was a theme central to Horkheimer and Adorno's *Dialectics of Enlightenment* (1947/1972), as well as Marcuse's *One-Dimensional Man* (1964). Believing that the economy could not itself provide an adequate explanation of modern capitalism, the Frankfurt scholars were to focus on mass culture, mass consumption, and the growth of new technologies of advertising and entertainment as vehicles by which mass indoctrination was achieved, introducing new forms of domination. Whereas practices such as art and music had, before the era of mass culture, performed a critical function, often negating or expressing opposition to dominant forms, the rise of mass radio, television, and print culture eroded such possibilities and encroached on the liberties of the private sphere with new "manipulated pleasures and wants" (Horkheimer & Adorno, 1972, p. 277). Although Horkheimer and Adorno argue that Enlightenment thought had emerged as a criticism of traditional feudal life, it lost its critical capacity by being driven by capitalist designs, through which it was turned into a form of instrumental reason concerned exclusively with maintaining the functioning of the ongoing order. Hence, for the Frankfurt School, the "culture industry" undermines the capacity for criticism or opposition, and led, in Horkheimer's (1974) view, to an "eclipse of reason."

For Adorno and Marcuse as well, the post-World War II development of mass media, together with the colossal growth of international capitalism, introduced the specter of a society where opposition was a defeated logic, a society characterized by "total administration" and "total integration." Drawing off Weber's thesis concerning rationalization and bureaucratization of life under capitalism, they held that such a development eclipsed the possibilities for social transformation or change on behalf of dispossessed groups. The rise of welfarism further concealed the exploitative nature of capitalist relations, eliminating further the possibilities of negative thinking, criticism, or opposition.

In the 1960s Marcuse emerged as the leading left-Hegelian Frankfurt academic, arguing in *One-Dimensional Man* (1964) that the new technical and cultural capacities of capitalism defeated the possibilities of opposition or protest right down to the commodification of private mental space, now constituted according to the logic of market exchange, which shapes the character of the individual.

From Hegel to Poststructuralism

The effect of Hegelianism on the theoretical orientation of the Frankfurt School can be adduced more accurately in historical retrospect, especially in the light of Althusserian and poststructuralist criticisms of Hegel. Of central importance is the conception of totality. For Hegel this was an expressivist notion, where society expresses the inner essence of its subject in a process of continuous unfolding by which reason realizes itself in history. As a consequence, for critical theory, every aspect of capitalist society—every institution, social form, or relationship—becomes an expression of the inner essence. For Lukacs, reification and alienation manifest the essence of capitalism. The essence manifests its appearance in different ways at different times, becoming more exposed in the process of history. Much of Horkheimer's early approach can be saddled with a totalizing concern with the realization of reason through history, carrying as Hoy and McCarthy (1994, p. 13) have put it, a number of "left-Hegelian formulae . . . [which] have a disagreeably totalizing ring to them." These emphases include:

> [h]is tendency to conceptualize society as at least potentially a unified subject with a unified will and, hence, to marginalize considerations of social, cultural, and political pluralism; his over-reliance on Marxian political economy, particularly class analysis, in identifying the causes and conditions of injustice in existing social orders; his subscription to a philosophy of history or "grand metanarrative" that underplayed the roles of contingency, locality, and identity in struggles against oppression. (Hoy and McCarthy, 1994, p. 13)

In his later works Horkheimer claimed that critical theory could not be labeled as totalizing or utopian, but must be seen as relativistic and temporary. In this he concurred with Adorno, who in *Negative Dialectics* rejected Hegel's emphasis on oneness, unity, and the possibility of achieving truth in history, stressing the nonidentical relationship of discourse to the world, which manifested itself in fragmentation, diversity, and multiplicity of perspectives. In this Adorno denies the possibility of universal history or truth. The prospect of historical progress based on theoretical self-reflection appeared remote and utopian. A philosophy that held that universal history could progress toward liberation and progress became replaced by an emphasis on historical discontinuity, the accidental, and historical arbitrariness. Historical necessity is thus replaced by an emphasis on discontinuity and incommensurability, representing, as Hoy and McCarthy (1994, p. 119) put it, "a partial critique of Hegel, one that is inspired initially by Nietzsche and practiced later by Michel Foucault." In this retreat from Hegelianism there exists a possible convergence between Frankfurt critical theory and French poststructuralist theories such as those of Foucault and Lyotard. The latter similarly reject an emphasis on totality and integration, focusing instead on the contingent, local, and particular nature of discursive phenomena rather than the universal. By this they mean, on the one hand, that there is no single theory of the real, as for instance exists in Marxism, or positivist or empiricist science, that can encapsulate the real and do justice to it, for, as Foucault (1994, p. 20) expresses it, "the attempt to think in terms of totality has in fact provided a hindrance to research." On the other hand, the retreat from Hegelianism rejects the teleological possibility of unified conception of the real in terms of which history unfolds or evolves in some linear or consistent fashion. The introduction of a nondeterministic sense of necessity is to "prefer Hegel without the absolute" (Hoy and McCarthy, 1994, p. 122). Necessity is no longer historical or sequential-teleological process but contextual or configurational and shot through with randomness and chance. Horkheimer and Adorno, like the poststructuralists, reject Hegel's insistence on a single teleological process of historical development, thus rejecting the conception of necessity in history whereby truth emerges from falsity in a process of successive approximations toward a more real understanding of the world. For Adorno in *Negative Dialectics,* giving up on absolute knowledge meant that dialectical thought must be concerned only with a "negative" or "critical" function and resign itself to the fact that no method can provide insight into truth or absolute certainty or as to how social change can be effected. In this sense Adorno posits an incommensurable gap between thought and the real and attempts to refrain from positing utopian goals. Such a theorization defeats the possibility of "identity thinking" in Adorno's view. The processes of signification and the objects they describe are never perfectly synchronized but remain inevitably incommensurable. Although there is an attempt here by the Frankfurt scholars to reject Hegel's absolute, tensions remain linked to the fact that to reject any conception of history as universal or tending toward progress is to commit oneself to an acceptance of the status quo, or at least to giving up the Marxist hope for the realization of a classless society. Such a tension was only finally surpassed with poststructuralism, where the idealized conception of progress toward a better state of the world is finally abandoned.

The Future of Critical Theory

In this section we follow the recent thoughts of Thomas McCarthy, who offers a series of important reflections on the current status of critical theory and its future.

McCarthy has played a major role in the dissemination and translation of Habermas's thought, especially in the 1970s. While he concedes to being "more pragmatic" than Habermas, he constitutes one of the most perceptive commentators on the future of critical theory. McCarthy makes a series of observations for the revitalization of critical theory.

First, he suggests that it is important for critical theory to get back in touch with its Marxist roots:

> "Iron laws" of political economy are emerging again as a central issue, this time at a global level, as in the period of national industrialization. This presents enormous problems of social dislocation, cultural degradation, political disempowerment, and just plain misery. Once again, "all that is solid again melts into air, all that is sacred profaned" and so on. What critical theory needs most now is something like a new Marx and I do not think we can think of Habermas in that way. What is more likely in the present organization of intellectual life is a new tradition of critical political economy. But that is not likely to be accomplished by philosophers. (McCarthy, 2001, pp. 420–421)

The error of much twentieth-century critical theory has been its almost exclusive cultural focus—it was always much better on culture and politics than on economics. McCarthy emphasizes the role of an understanding of economics in a new tradition of internal political economy that can begin in a systematic way to make sense of the emerging social and economic patterns of inequality. In the context of the need for a new international political economy, McCarthy does not think that Habermas can fulfill the role of the new Marx, for Habermas nowadays supports a mixed economy. McCarthy, however, agrees with Habermas that

> we have to learn to live with markets and bureaucracies and that the task is to domesticate them, to get as much democratic control of them as we can, even if sometimes only by indirect means. What we need to get from Marx, I think, is a refocusing of theoretical energies on the workings of the global economy. (423)

Habermas has given up on the idea that a "direct democratization of *all* politically relevant social institutions, including economic ones," is possible in large, complex societies. This means that against Marx's original expectations, Habermas believes that it is not possible to do away with markets and state administrations. Habermas believes that we have to learn to tame them, and with this realization he moves closer to the traditional concerns of liberal constitutionalism.

> The question now becomes how best to secure a full schedule of basic rights for everyone, how to secure political institutions and processes so that individuals and groups have a say in the decisions that affect them, and how to design distributive and redistributive mechanisms to ensure that all have adequate resources to exercise their

rights and pursue their life projects. This is to be sure, less radical a project than the Marxian vision, but it provides a critical perspective on all actually existing forms of political liberalism. (425)

Second, McCarthy turns to the role of reason in critical theory. He makes the point that critical theory has been too confident about its reach and not enough concerned with its limits. For instance, he suggests that the idea of emancipation, represented as a realization of reason and understood as forms of self-determination and self-realization, is somewhat overblown. The privileged role granted reason in human affairs, a hangover from the confidence of Enlightenment thought and culture, often blinds us to "what deconstructivists refer to as 'the other side of reason'":

> So one lesson that can be learned is to attend carefully to what is inevitably left out of any conceptualization. But there are more particular lessons to be learned as well, especially from Foucault, whose methodologically diverse forays—archaeological, genealogical, ethical—suggest a multiplicity of models for critical-theoretical research. There is no need to employ them in any one-sided negative way as he typically does. Often it is the ambiguity of rationalization processes that has to be articulated. (423)

For McCarthy it is a matter of "detranscendentalizing" reason and of understanding how deeply it is implicated in "history and tradition, language and culture, body and desire, practices and institutions." This realization about the limits of reason forecloses on the possibility that "there will be one right answer to ethical and political questions." This means that not "anything goes" but that we should expect "reasonable disagreement" as a matter of course. Reason does not prescribe in unambiguous terms the "proper course of action, the right policy, the best program": this is a matter for public debate and there will not miraculously appear the one right answer determined through the application of reason, but different positions, all reasonable (423–424).

Third, McCarthy explains that critical theory has been too closely tied to academic work carried out in universities or research institutes, which seal off the working lives of critical theorists from the lived forms of oppression as they are experienced by groups of the population. McCarthy suggests that we must try to resist the pressure of disciplinary specialization on the one hand, while attempting to maintain contact with the progressive social movements of the day. He remarks:

> Feminist theory, race theory, gay and lesbian studies, postcolonial studies and the like have recently been better at this than critical social theory—though they too have had their problems with too much distance from the lived forms of oppression they theorize. The Marxian tradition has been tied primarily to class politics, and in many industrialized countries, that form of politics has waned. In any case, new forms of politics have arisen and there is a need constantly to develop critical theory so as to articulate the concerns of new social movements. (428)

Responding to the question: "What do you see as the main challenges facing critical theory today?," McCarthy answers:

> The main challenges, I think, come from the general sense of social and cultural exhaustion that pervades both theory and practice today, the general skepticism about theory in anything stronger than its ironic or deconstructive forms, and the general feelings of helplessness in the face of impersonal forces and the fragmentation of life. These things mitigate any kind of renewal of the enlightenment project, let alone one with the utopian impulses of critical theory. I don't think there's much one can do here as a theorist, except to try to understand and theorize these forces, and to relate them to the actual political concerns of the day. (428–429)

McCarthy's critical theory is a mix of influences from the Frankfurt School and American pragmatism. As James Bohman (2001, p. 87) argues, he wants "to overcome the opposition between deconstruction and reconstruction through a 'critique of impure reason' that affirms both the transcendence and situatedness of reason, in its 'ideals and illusions.'" He, thus, focuses on developing a "pragmatics of communicative reason," a mixture of critical theory and pragmatism where truth is "deabsolutized" and reason is "detranscendentalized." Such an account gives up on the God's-eye point of view to defend a methodological and social pluralism, where we seek to critique and reflect on a range of different standpoints, each reasonable in its own way. We might call this a critical perspectivism or pluralism, which is characteristic of modern complex societies where there are competing political and ethical claims. Given that "no one perspective or theory may lay claim to epistemic, moral or rational superiority in advance," the reconciliation or mediation of these claims, as Bohman (2001, p. 89) argues, thus becomes the central issue for critical theory. Critical theory as "the pragmatic theory of democracy as a mode of inquiry" becomes "a distinctive mode of inquiry of practices of democratic deliberation." Bohman (2001) puts the case for a pragmatic critical theory in the following way:

> Critical social science is distinctive, not because of the type of knowledge it employs as such, but because it does something with social scientific knowledge. It is reflexive social inquiry into the practical knowledge (i.e., the knowledge of practical knowledge) that is needed for effective social agency and freedom in the social world. This sort of practical knowledge, I argue, is tied up with the capacities of agents to adopt and to relate to a variety of social perspectives. Such a practical account of social inquiry has much in common with pragmatism, old and new. (89)

Yet for some readers this intimate alignment of critical theory with pragmatism may bring it into line with Rorty's version of liberalism, or with accounts of liberalism offered either by Rawls, who invokes a notion of "overlapping consensus," or by Habermas, who talks of the consensus-formation inherent in the ideal speech situation. Certainly, when Bohman (2001, p. 90) defines critical inquiry as the "attempt to unite various perspectives by engaging in a form of reflective inquiry that crosses among them," then it is not clear the extent to which critical theory has been assimilated into a kind of pragmatism that has become wedded to versions of American liberalism. But then if we are to pluralize the possibilities of critical theory in the postmodern condition, clearly the pragmatist version of critical theory has to be one of the major alternatives. Yet this version does seem to rob critical theory of its original critical intent or to tame it, recasting it as a method of inquiry in the service of democracy.

Organization of the Book

The book contains two parts. Part 1 addresses Critical Theory: Labors of the Dialectic, essays on the foundation thinkers of critical theory. Part 2 deals with Critical Theory: Projects and Movements, that is, various movements that have taken root as a result of critical theory, including critical pedagogy, critical multiculturalism, critical environmentalism, and the like.

This edited collection comprises a series of readable and thematically compact essays on the founders, projects, and future of critical theory. It is aimed at audiences from education as well as wider areas of social science, with an emphasis on undergraduates. The book is meant to function as a "reader" for students seeking an informed entrée to critical theory.

Part 1 is a thematically organized historical treatment of critical theory. This opening thematic essay, written by the editors, is meant to provide an intellectual and historical context for understanding the contributions of the most distinguished critical thinkers of the twentieth century and the implications of their thought for educational theory. Since its establishment in the 1920s, critical theory has operated as a critique of both "traditional" (or positivist) theory and bourgeois society, engendering a form of Western Marxism, which came to prominence and maturity as a school with Max Horkheimer and Theodor Adorno. Critical theory has passed through a number of generations: The first generation took shape under Carl Grunberg with the establishment of the *Institut für Sozialforschung* in 1923; the second generation was shaped into a school under Horkheimer and Adorno, and involved the participation of Herbert Marcuse, Eric Fromm, Wilhelm Reich, and others; the third generation, it could be argued, is represented in the work of Jurgen Habermas and Claus Offe, although their work no longer constitutes a school. The existence of fourth and fifth generations can plausibly be identified, based on the migration of critical theory abroad—to the United States, Britain, and Australasia—based around journals like *Telos* and *Thesis Eleven*. In this section there are essays by a range of international scholars on some of the most prominent thinkers we customarily refer to collectively as critical theorists: Adorno, Horkheimer, and Marcuse (Gur-Ze'ev), Benjamin (Davis), Fromm (Lankshear), Marcuse (Kellner), Arendt (Conroy), Marx and Wittgenstein (Gillett) and Habermas (Young). This first section concludes with an essay on Maxine

Greene (Britzman and Dippo), whose life and work have involved a sustained, imaginative, and inspiring engagement with the spirit, contradictions, and possibilities inherent in critical theory, and their potential for envisaging expansive educational vistas.

Part 2 divides the high point of modernist narrativizing from the poststructuralism and postmodernism that was to follow. This period, roughly from the mid-1960s until (in some cases) the late 1980s (the collapse of the eastern bloc and the onset of "end of history" temperaments provide a convenient, if none-too-original cutoff point) is an interesting phase. It is treated here mainly in terms of critical theory themes and issues being taken up as educational and social *praxis*—examples of social and educational projects being enacted within applied domains of life.

This section moves "critical" themes from the level of theory into some applied level of pedagogical struggle ("pedagogical" in the broad sense) and into the everyday sites of social life and practice. During the "watershed" period we find numerous examples of praxis producing changes in the world consistent with values and priorities associated with the tradition of critical theory—from mass social programs like literacy and health campaigns, civil rights, feminist programs, and the like to more modest and localized efforts at the level of schools, communities, and classrooms. By the end of the 1980s, however, "postmodern sensibility" (à la Lyotard) joins forces with the global trend-shifts (from end of cold war to neoliberal reform initiatives) of the '70s-'90s and missiles us into "new times." Chapters in this section deal with projects and "movements": critical pedagogy (Henry Giroux), critical literacy (Peter Roberts), critical race theory (Laurence Parker), critical multiculturalism (Stephen May), critical feminism (Erica McWilliam), critical cultural studies (Tom Steele) and critical environmentalism (Timothy Luke).

PART 1
Critical Theory: Labors of the Dialectic

I   *Ilan Gur-Ze'ev*

CRITICAL THEORY, CRITICAL PEDAGOGY AND THE POSSIBILITY OF COUNTER-EDUCATION

The direct and indirect influences of critical theory on the current philosophy of education are immense. The manifestations of these influences go far beyond the horizons of critical pedagogy as the concrete realization of critical theory in the schooling process. Even within the limited concept of education as schooling, feminist pedagogies, multicultural and post-colonial theories of education, cultural studies, as well as critical literacy or aesthetic education are all seen to be influenced by the ideas of Theodor Adorno, Max Horkheimer, Herbert Marcuse, Walter Benjamin, Erich Fromm, and the other members of the Frankfurt School. Some of the influences of critical theory are more obvious and explicitly acknowledged by central educational thinkers such as Paulo Freire, Peter McLaren, Henry Giroux, and Kathleen Weiler, and some are less explicit and are subterranean or are realized indirectly.

It is not uncommon that some of these influences are dressed in postmodern garb and are offered—how ironic—as an alternative to the modernity of critical theory and the Enlightenment's arrogance and self-defeating educational project.

The main argument below is that the foremost philosophers of education who were explicitly and even enthusiastically influenced by critical theory were influenced by the work of Herbert Marcuse and by the first stage in the development of Adorno and Horkheimer's thought. According to this argument, the second stage in the development of Adorno and Horkheimer's thought was disregarded by most philosophers of education and did not illumine the paths chosen by the various versions of critical pedagogy.

When the main version of critical pedagogy became defensive and apologetic in face of the critique of the academic left, it turned to the postmodern alternatives for help.[1] This was instrumental in allowing the development of original, influential, and progressive educational theories such as those of Giroux, McLaren, Weiler, Aronowitz, and Ellsworth. It was most unhelpful, however, for the task of establishing a reflective counter-education. For all its importance, it also contributed to the establishment of repressive properties and uncritical trends within critical pedagogy itself. The thoughts of Adorno and Horkheimer in the second stage of the development of their critical theory, I argue, could have been and still are potentially open to the creation of a genuine counter-educational struggle—of the kind that went beyond the prospects of hegemonic critical pedagogy.

The part in critical theory that was not ignored and was even praised by most educational theoreticians was fundamentally optimistic, revolutionary, and positive, at least on first sight. Its Marxist birthmarks were still very present at this stage. In the tradition of critical pedagogy, this part of the work of Horkheimer and Adorno was conceived in a manner that deprived critical theory of its self-reflection and its dialectical dimension. The thinkers of critical pedagogy normally underestimate Adorno and Horkheimer's anti-utopianism and self-reflection. On the one hand, they overemphasize their optimism about the possibility of the constitution of a theoretical and educational framework that will enhance a praxis that, on the other hand, will overcome the logic of capitalism and other forms of oppression.

The third issue of the sixth volume of *Zeitschrift für Sozialen Forschung*, the official journal of the Frankfurt School, which was published in 1937, can serve as a vivid manifestation of the complexity of the smilingly explicit anti-utopian commitment of Horkheimer of that time. In "a contribution" to Marcuse's main article in that issue he goes out of his way to criticize "those who call themselves critical theoreticians"—namely, Marcuse—whose utopianism "contradicts genuine Critical Theory" (Horkheimer 1985, V, p. 224). He criticizes Marcuse's "philosophical utopianism," likening it to other dangerous versions of utopianism. He especially targets the liberal version—for manifesting "saintly egoism," which ultimately opens the way to nihilism and National Socialism, and the orthodox Marxist version, which is "mechanistic and non-dialectical" (ibid., p. 223). Already in 1931 when the theologian Paul Tillich described capitalism as "the devil," both Adorno and Horkheimer were quick to criticize him for the kind of utopianism that constituted this unworthy critique (Horkheimer, 1985, XI, p. 410). The two colleagues attacked those intellectuals who attempted to find a philosophical ground for the revolution. They criticized those who saw capitalism as "the ultimate kingdom of evil, the bad form of human togetherness" and who "expect the ultimate truth on earth" (Horkheimer, 1985, XI, p. 264) to be realized in actual history. Their evaluation and critique of the ideological dimensions of hegemonic knowledge, in that period, were still guided by the Marxist claim of anti-idealism and antitranscendentalism, founded on materialist reality, class interests, and economic developments. At the same time Adorno and Horkheimer of that period favored the possibilities of a proletarian revolution and more than once even found themselves siding with the kind of utopianism they so strongly opposed. It was Horkheimer himself who wrote then, "Maybe they are right. Maybe socialism does bring with it the kingdom of the millennium and the prophecies of the old testament's prophets will be realized after all" (Horkheimer, 1985 XI, p. 226).

The standard position of the critical theory thinkers of this period is, however, that theory is never neutral—and this is valid in respect of critical theory itself. The very foundation of critical theory is not justified merely on theoretical grounds: "a vision of a worthier human reality guides it" (Horkheimer, 1985, III, p. 105). And yet, with all its explicit anti-utopian commitment, already in his 1935 "Notes for Philosophical Anthropology" one encounters other trends, whereby critical theory commits itself to the mission of "a happier humanity" (Horkheimer, 1985, III, p. 266). In 1936 Horkheimer explicitly speaks of the possibility of "future circumstances [in which] efficiency and consciousness will constitute a common interest for human beings; 'the destruction drive' will no longer disturb them" (Horkheimer, 1985, III, p. 86). This trend is visible even in "Traditional and Critical Theory," probably the most important publication of critical theory in its first stage of development (1937/1972). Critical theory is here explicitly presented as "a moment" of revolutionary praxis toward "new social forms." While still founding his perspectives for future society on materialist grounds and not on philosophical speculations Horkheimer speaks here of the importance of the idea of a future free human community ("as much as it is allowed by the technical conditions"). At the same time, however, he develops a vision of the realization of reason and overcoming of alienation between thinking and reality, rationality and sensuality; in an almost Marcusian spirit he even speaks of "future freedom and spontaneity." This positive utopian trend is manifested also in "Montaigne and the Function of Skepticism" (1938/1988). Here critical theory is presented as directed to nothing less than "the establishment of a brand new world" (Horkheimer, 1985, IV, p. 289). At this period both Horkheimer and Adorno offer a promising, progressive, revolutionary theory of knowledge and of overcoming oppressive social realities and ideological manipulations. While doing very little in the field of actual educational theory, their critical theory is of much relevance for criticizing established leftist and rightist pedagogical theories, and they draw the framework for a possible revolutionary pedagogy. In this respect Paulo Freire, Peter McLaren, Henry Giroux, Patti Lather, Ira Shor, Kathleen Weiler, and other teachers of critical pedagogy are not totally mistaken in their implementation of critical theory as critical pedagogy. Still, as I will show by referring to Giroux as a representative of this attempt, the project is far from being unproblematic.

The pedagogical project of the early Giroux serves as a model for an educational project that almost disregards Adorno and Horkheimer's later work. At the same time it makes productive use of the other, less optimistic and less foundationalist, dimensions, even in the first stage of the development of critical theory (Gur-Ze'ev, 1998, pp. 463–486). Giroux expressly notes that his educational project is founded on critical theory. The revolutionary potential of critical theory is of special importance in the early stage of the development of his thought (Giroux, 1983, p. 19). In another place he says that a precondition for a worthy pedagogical work is a reading of the work of the critical theory thinkers (Giroux 1981a, p. 81).

Here Giroux draws on the positive utopianism of early critical theory, and following Freire he develops his project in accordance with the requirements of an optimistic revolutionary pedagogy.

According to Giroux, in the critical theory of the Frankfurt School every thought and theory is bound to a specific interest in the development of an unjust society (Giroux, 1983, p. 19). Of special importance for Giroux, as for other thinkers in critical pedagogy, is to present Ideology Critique—which challenges hegemonic knowledge and its claims—as a fundamentally unproblematic tool, a tool for emancipatory education. As a prima facie Critical-Theory-in-action, critical pedagogy, in this sense, becomes a transformative process, controlled in a more humane future (Aronowitz & Giroux, 1985, p. 103). Giroux speaks here explicitly of critical theory as a transcendental power within which critical thinking becomes a precondition for human freedom (Giroux, 1983, p. 19).

The central trend in critical pedagogy as here represented by Giroux contradicts not only the central message of late critical theory as manifested by later Adorno and Horkheimer, but even the central commitments of its first stage, as laid down in the works of Benjamin, the early Adorno, and the early Horkheimer. Actually, Giroux follows Herbert Marcuse and ignores the reservations of Adorno and Horkheimer concerning Marcuse's easygoing revolutionary project (Gur-Ze'ev 1996, p. 160).

In the following I will show that in the second stage of the development of critical theory Adorno and Horkheimer not only abandoned their positive utopianism, they forcefully cast aside its philosophical foundations and historical justifications. They rejected the entire tradition, which supported and manifested optimism about the possibility of a nonrepressive revolution and about an unproblematic emancipatory critique.

This is the theoretical arena out of which they developed their later negative Utopia. It was based on the tradition of philosophical pessimism, which they elaborated into a transcendental dimension within their negative utopianism. Since they refused to give up the utopian axis they founded it in a most original way on philosophical pessimism (Gur-Ze'ev, 1996). This later work, as will be argued, is of vital importance in any attempt to develop current possibilities for countereducation in a postmodern era; critical pedagogy was deprived of such possibilities since it ignored the mature part of critical theory. Nevertheless, when developing his critical pedagogy on critical theory's foundations, following Marcuse and avoiding the work of later Adorno and Horkheimer, Giroux offered an important contribution to the development of a progressive critical pedagogy that emphasized "possibilities" without neglecting "critique."

According to Giroux's critical pedagogy, when evaluating the schooling process it is wrong to disconnect the school curriculum and its other texts from its cultural and social contexts. In this sense school is a prima facie political arena, which plays an indispensable part in the production of discourses, meanings, identities, and subjects, and allows efficient control of their manipulated representation, distribution, and consumption. Following critical theory, critical pedagogy reveals the powers, interests, and ideologies beyond the *Maya* curtain of the school's declared commitment to the distribution of true/relevant knowledge/information. It critically reconstructs the abundant ways by which schools reflect and serve central social interests. This structural role of the school determines its function as a space dedicated to the organization of canonic knowledge, the control of time, body, consciousness, and conscious, and even the constitution of "valid" evaluation apparatuses, validating the "relevant" interpretive strategies. In this sense school functions as one of the cultural, social, and economic reproduction apparatuses in service of the dominant group and/or the hegemonic master signifiers and their realm of self-evidence.

In contrast to the hegemonic pedagogical rhetoric, which is committed to depoliticizing the predicates and the sources of the representations of schooling, Giroux—following Adorno, Horkheimer, and Marcuse—acknowledges that at the present stage of capitalistic development there is no level or terra in society that is free of the presence of the hegemonic ideology.

Giroux presents ideology in two very different contexts: of distortion and perversion on the one hand, and as elaboration and enlightening power on the other. On the one level, ideology becomes hegemonic as the distortion of true deciphering of reality and as a prevention of true dialogue. On the second level, ideology contains a reflective moment and becomes a precondition for a dialogical process that leaves room for conscious and social emancipation. Giroux notes that given its enslavement to a conservative sociocultural context, which does not search for contradictions and the invisible powers and interests, the reflective potential of ideology is very limited and prevents it from being a foundation for emancipation (ibid., p. 67). In light of this reconstruction, following critical theory in its first stage of development, Ideology Critique becomes for Giroux a central emancipatory educational apparatus (ibid., p. 159). This is because he conceives the human subject as autonomous and open to critical overcoming of the social and ideological manipulations that limit his or her horizons. This is where his educational language of "possibilities" and "transformation" is situated.

Giroux explicitly identifies his critical pedagogy with the work of Marcuse, and commits himself to realizing this work in the field of education in order to develop a radical new pedagogical theory (ibid., 2). Within this project, the Marcusian work is interpreted as a call for intellectual activism for teachers and students in the school arena. Teachers are called upon to become "transformative intellectuals" in schools and in society in general. As deeply committed intellectuals, they are obliged to develop every aspect of the formal educational process into an active and "popular" clash with the hegemonic order of society (Giroux, 1988, p. 37).

In the middle of the 1980s Giroux made a turn, and postmodern influences became central to his critical pedagogy. This has not only conceptual manifestations, it becomes clear even in other respects. It is not surprising, therefore, that in Giroux's 1981 book *Ideology, Culture and the Educational Process* Marcuse is explicitly referred to in twenty-two pages, Adorno is mentioned in ten, and Horkheimer in four. In

Giroux's *Border Crossings* (1992), however, Adorno is mentioned only four times, and so is Horkheimer. Marcuse, from then on, is not mentioned at all. Michel Foucault, who was mentioned only once in the text of 1981, has now become the hero of the reformulated critical pedagogy and is cited more than any other philosopher. It is not only that Giroux, like McLaren, Weiler, Lather, Shor, and other prominent American thinkers in the tradition of critical pedagogy—and to a certain degree also Paulo Freire—disregarded the mature work of Adorno and Horkheimer. Even within the part of critical theory that they did relate to they selected the more optimistic and foundationalist parts, especially in the work of Marcuse. They disregarded the complementary, skeptic-pessimistic-antifoundationalist aspects of critical theory, which is of vital importance even for the understanding of the immanent dialectic of critical theory in its first stage of development. The inner dialectics between these two dimensions is the gateway to understanding critical theory and its educational implications (Gur-Ze'ev, 1996).

This dialectic is present not only in the work of Adorno, Horkheimer, and Benjamin (Gur-Ze'ev, 1998, pp. 119–155). It is there even in Benjamin's utopianism, which was challenged along with that of Marcuse, even if for contrasting reasons (ibid.).

The dialectical dimension between optimism and pessimism and between positive and negative utopianism is essential also for the work of Marcuse, whose supposed optimistic revolutionary project has been celebrated for more than thirty years now among leftist intellectuals and many of the 1968 generation. This misunderstanding of Marcuse, and certainly of the work of the other members of the Frankfurt School and their critical theory, is of special importance. It becomes a constitutive element in establishing critical pedagogy's educational optimism in respect of developing its central concepts such as "empowerment," "dialogue," "Ideology Critique," "transformative education," "agency," "possibilities," and "praxis education."

The limits of critical pedagogy were challenged both within the tradition of critical pedagogy and outside, by critics such as Elizabeth Ellsworth (Ellsworth, 1989). These difficulties, however, were not met by an attempt to rearticulate critical pedagogy in light of a new reading of critical theory as a first step in countering new critical theories and trends within postmodern, postcolonialist, feminist, multiculturalist, and queer theories and discourses. The effort to rearticulate critical pedagogy was made in an explicit attempt to be in line with the last fashions in current critical rhetoric (Giroux 1996, p. 51). Among the very few prominent critical pedagogy thinkers who were not swallowed up by this trend one should mention McLaren. But he too did not respond to the limits of critical pedagogy by rethinking his conceptions of critical theory. He has preferred to rearticulate orthodox Marxism in light of the current capitalistic globalization processes and in face of the dehumanization and the suffering it brings along with the "prosperity" it offers its elected ones (McLaren, 2000, pp. 25–33). To show how avoiding the essentials of critical theory, even in the first phase of its development, became a constitutive element for critical pedagogy is not difficult. It is easily demonstrated by reference to the silence of the critical thinkers in the field of education in face of the challenges of philosophical pessimism and the implications of skepticism in the works of Benjamin, Adorno, and Horkheimer. Far harder, however, is to show these elements in the work of Marcuse, who was the most influential thinker of the Frankfurt School among the 1968 generation's revolutionary students. This is the best reason for responding first to the Marcusian challenge, before proceeding to the later philosophy of Adorno and Horkheimer.[2]

For the Marcusian project the utopian dimension was of vital importance. In Marcuse's thought there is no potential for the critique of culture and society that is disconnected from the utopian axis as a sources of hope and as a total moral responsibility to resist injustice. This claim is valid in respect of immanent critique as well as of critique as the heart of transcendence. Art and art criticism were essential for Marcuse's utopian project. This is because only in art did bourgeois society tolerate its own ideals and present them as a general demand. What is conceived as utopian, fantasy, or an unforgivable revolt against the world of facts, in art is conceived as legitimate (Marcuse, 1968, p. 114). Concepts such as "otherness" or "the totally other," which challenge the current world of "facts" and the "not-yet" — concepts that are so vital for the project of the Frankfurt School's critical theory — are realized in the work of Marcuse in respect of the category of beauty. "Beauty," says Marcuse, "is nothing less than the sudden appearance of another truth to the heart of the established reality" (Marcuse Archive, 406.00). Marcuse is very clear about his understanding of "otherness." In a still unpublished fragment in the Marcuse Archive he refers to the urge toward or the manifestations of the trinity of "the beautiful, the good and the just" (Marcuse, 1936). Here Marcuse and Adorno are very close. Adorno too understood that it is art that is to approach "the very target of rationality" by its very structure or aim. Marcuse and Adorno are closer on this point to Heidegger (Heidegger, 1996a, pp. 340–341) than to Horkheimer (Gur-Ze'ev, 2002).

In his *One-Dimensional Man* and in many other texts Marcuse manifests historical pessimism, which is very different from Benjamin's, Adorno's, and Horkheimer's philosophical pessimism. It is, however, of vital importance for the educational implications of his work. Central to the Marcusian constitution of an emancipatory epistemology and to the critique of culture and society are a practice and theory of art within which "the aesthetic form of beauty" is manifested in sublimation (Marcuse, 1971, p. 78).

Marcuse, however, came to the conclusion that as part of the historical success of the repressive desublimation of the capitalist Culture Industry, this potentially transcending dimension of Western culture was being demolished by the omnipotence of the realization of the logic of capitalism. The traditional gap between art (and that which it points to) and the "factual" order of things that artistic alienation traditionally contained was vital for the emancipatory potential of art and for critical theory. However, Marcuse concluded that alienation itself was being impaired in the current technological society as an element of the total irrational rationalization of human space.

As part of this process, according to Marcuse, there was diminishing room for "the grand refusal" or indeed for any moral resistance or meaningful critique. No less devastating for the critical mind, according to Marcuse, was that the otherness, or "the other dimension," was being swallowed, and—after being castrated of its antagonistic potential—reproduced, as part and parcel of the present order (Marcuse, 1971, p. 68). The cultural reality of late capitalism, according to Marcuse, presents an ever more efficient attack on the very possibility of transcendence and the very possibility of an immanent critique. After neutralizing the antagonistic dimensions in the culture and after deconstructing the possibilities for transcendence, this society targets human inwardness as a potential source for immanent autonomy and courageous critique. It transforms the human psyche and its strivings. It domesticates the psyche until it becomes an unproblematic dweller of current hegemonic one-dimensionality (Marcuse, 1971, p. 80).

While suggesting the possibility of the continuation of art as the only possible source of hope (Marcuse, 1976, p. 18) Marcuse himself is very clear about the implications of his work: The words and the concepts that until recently allowed the presentation of a possible free society have lost their meaning today. They can no longer serve to introduce the human condition into a worthier society (ibid.).

A critical reconstruction of Marcuse's *One-Dimensional Man* reveals two conceptions of progress in his work, one of which is conceived as "genuine" or "good," while the other is nothing less than the sophistication and progress of evil. And it is the latter, according to Marcuse, that is being realized unhampered in present postindustrial society (Marcuse, 1971, pp. 20, 32). In an unpublished text Marcuse presents this kind of progress, within which the productive powers are to be understood as representing "productive destruction" within a process that is "irreversible" (Marcuse 1979a). Summarizing this point in another unpublished text, Marcuse concludes: "Western industrial society has no future" (Marcuse Archive, 569.00). And in still another unpublished text he says in this light, "being today a realist is to become a pessimist" (Marcuse Archive, 406.00, 36).

This neglected side in Marcuse's thought conceives pessimistically the presence of the idea of reason in its present historical setting. Today, the idea of reason, which was central to the concepts of progress in humanistic projects of Kant, Hegel, and Marx, says Marcuse, "became itself an illusion, like the prejudices that it was aimed to replace" (Marcuse, 1964, p. 12). "Rationality itself," he concludes, "became a repressive apparatus" (ibid., 11), cultural progress becomes less and less rational (ibid., 13) or, in other words, the irrational reality becomes rational and the resistance to it becomes irrational. This is the triumph of what he calls "irrational rationality" (ibid., p. 14). The resistance as well as the critique of this historical progress becomes, accordingly, "unrealistic" and the identification with the alternatives to the present order becomes a matter of mere "personal preferences."

How then are we to understand Marcuse's identification with the student revolt, with guerrilla warfare, and with the radical reeducation of the people within the framework of critical theory and its Ideology Critique? And how are we to understand in this light the founding of optimistic critical pedagogy on his thought while ignoring these essential parts of his philosophy?

Any reply to this challenge should, to my mind, address the dialectical tension between the positive-utopian and the pessimist dimensions in Marcuse's work. Such an attempt was not made by his disciples, such as the early Giroux, or by his numerous opponents. Entering this gate will afford us the possibility of seeing Marcuse as a sophisticated educator, of the kind of Marx and Lenin.

Neither Marx nor Lenin was content with reliance on a genuine understanding of the explicit educational role of their texts by the oppressed. They allowed themselves to be manipulative and consciously to deceive their disciples. This was within the Jesuit pedagogical framework of the goals justifying the means. So they tried to use "only" the didactics that would make the oppressed think what they ought to think and want what they ought to want, if only for them to become free to recognize their own interests or meet their authentic/true self, identity, or consciousness.

In acting as arch-educators whose "lessons" endure not hours or days but generations, Marx and Lenin behaved like servants or media for the human historical process as educators, as presented by Lessing and the other heroes of the Enlightenment.[3] In this they followed the deepest eschatological trends in the Jewish and Christian traditions, which the Enlightenment secularized under the flag of the emancipatory project (Funkenstein, 2000, pp. 4–9). So in the name of the eschatological logic of historical progress as the genuine educator and as the realization of the humanist Messianic commitment to future human lasting happiness, Marx, Lenin, and Marcuse trusted that they were allowed, even obliged, to conceal from the yet-unredeemed their real conclusions, ideas, and erotic imperatives. They did so with no qualms of conscience, like so many caring parents do with their beloved young children.

As a self-appointed arch-educator, Marcuse understood, like Marx at the time of the Paris Commune, that in the concrete historical conditions the students' revolt could not gain the upper hand. Yet he did not challenge the students' optimism and openly supported and encouraged them. How may we understand this in terms of realizing his responsibility as an arch-educator?

Within the framework of a one-dimensional society, what remained to Marcuse as an educator was to do everything to keep alive the very idea of resistance as a master signifier for a totally different reality and for a totally different relationship among humans, symbolic intersubjectivity, and history. He reflects how a mystic can become an effective magic and really change reality, if not presently, then in future generations. As such, his historical role, as a devotee of the concealed and defeated master signifier of emancipation, was of utmost importance. Especially in the days when "the grand refusal" or the very idea of transcending the affluent society had become irrelevant, naive, or even ridiculous. As a master of magic in the field of normalizing education within the framework of radical social philosophy, and as a person responsible to the future stages of the struggle for human emancipation, Marcuse understood that the students' failure, if grandiose and tragic enough, would become an important educational lesson for future generations of revolutionaries. For an essentialist such as Marcuse this historically educational lesson was actually an ontological sign, a sign of the presence of a positive Utopia that one day might be realized. Keeping alive the very possibility of negation and the dream of a more humane reality became part of the awakening process of the defeated idea of the redemptive process itself. What could be more important than fulfilling this educational responsibility to the historical teleological imperative itself?

Marcuse's positive utopianism was articulated within a linear, progressive concept of history. His non-optimistic conclusions were not founded, as were those of Adorno and Horkheimer, on philosophical pessimism. This is very relevant to his understanding of historical impasses and their educational implications. He understood the historical barriers to human progress as fundamentally historical, temporary in nature. They were therefore also historically to be overcome—when conditions changed and if humanistic-oriented intellectuals like him responded to the call of history and realized their educational duty.

As will be shown in the following, critical pedagogy, as formulated by Giroux—which was explicitly founded on critical theory—disregarded the most important educational aspects of Adorno and Horkheimer. It even misunderstood the central elements of Marcuse's educational implications. In this respect it could not justify its claim to being the pedagogical realization of critical theory. Maybe these, and not the reasons presented by Ellsworth (1989), are the main reasons for the shortcomings of critical pedagogy.

In the following I try to show that the most important implications of critical theory are beyond the scope of the inner dialectics in the work of Marcuse. They are to be found in the work of Benjamin or in the second phase of the work of Adorno and Horkheimer.

In the first stage of critical theory both Adorno and Horkheimer interlaced the goal of critical theory with the Marxian revolutionary project. In the second stage the turn away from Marx's main theses is evident. Marx's project was regarded as an element in the positive utopian position, which by then they both rejected. Horkheimer expressly declares that it is a trend from the Marxian thought to that of Schopenhauer and the tradition of philosophical pessimism (Horkheimer 1985, VII, pp. 339–340).

In the second stage of the development of Horkheimer's thought he is explicitly antirevolutionary. It is the nature of the revolutionary, every revolutionary, according to later Horkheimer, to become an oppressor (Horkheimer, 1985, VII, p. 418). Every revolution, especially a "successful" one, is a manifestation of power. And justice, when it becomes powerful, is realized only at the cost of its transformation into oppression (ibid., p. 341). In contrast to the Marxian tradition, it is now conceived that as long as even some remnants of freedom survive, violence will flourish (Horkheimer, 1989, XIII, p. 247). "In the end, whatever hopes Marx did hold on behalf of true society, apparently they seem to be the wrong ones, if—and this issue is important to critical theory—freedom and justice are interrelated in mutual opposition. The more justice there is, freedom will diminish accordingly" (Horkheimer 1989, XIII, p. 340).

The historical reconstruction of the Culture Industry with its limitations, about which Giroux was aware and articulated important implications in his critical pedagogy, is conceived here within the framework of philosophical pessimism. For Adorno, "space is nothing but absolute alienation" (Adorno, 1970b, X, p. 205). For him this is the framework for viewing the whole historical reality of advanced technological society, in which everything has become "consumption," and life, with all its layers and dimensions, is nothing but "a fetish of consumption" (Adorno, 1970a, III, p. 243).

In their *Dialectics of Enlightenment* Adorno and Horkheimer do not target the capitalistic logic and its realization in itself, or the other representations of totalitarianism, such as the National-Socialist or the Stalinist. Ultimately they target culture itself: "Culture has developed with the protection of the executioner.... All work and pleasure are protected by the hangman. To contradict this fact is to deny all science and logic. It is impossible to abolish . . . terror and retain civilization. Even the lessening of terror implies a beginning of the process of dissolution" (Adorno & Horkheimer, 1988, p. 255). The conception of revolution and critical theory within the framework of historically progressing human emancipation is conceived within a double-layered philosophy of history, one linear, the other circular.

From the viewpoint of a circular conception of time there is no room for progress in the Kantian, Hegelian, or Marxian sense, which made possible the optimism of critical pedagogy.

According to Benjamin, there is no document of culture that is not at the same time a document of a barbarity (Benjamin, 1972, p. 696). For Adorno and Horkheimer all substantive levels of "progress" manifest an oppressive regression. In this sense, "adaptation to the power of progress involves the regression of power. Each time anew 'progress' brings about those degenerations. They manifest not the unsuccessful but successful progress to be its contrary" (Horkheimer & Adorno, 1988, p. 42).

On the other level of "progress," the explicitly historical one, unless an unpredictable interference occurs, the good intentions and progressive talents of educators devoted to revolutionary education are of little use in halting the enhancement and sophistication of barbarism. The instrumentalization of rationality is reconstructed as representing and serving the growing needs of technological progress and economic development. Instrumental Rationality becomes "a magic essence." Instrumental Rationality is conceived here as a metaphoric revolt of instrumentalized nature, as a return of *mythos,* whose overthrow was the essential mission of Enlightenment. Mythical thought gave birth to Enlightenment as overcoming *Bildung* and human emancipation. This is the reason that today, for its part, in its most "progressive" form Enlightenment returns to a more dangerous type of mythical thought (Horkheimer, 1974, p. 22) within what Horkheimer calls "the fully-administered world" (Horkheimer, 1985, VIII, p. 328).

In such a reality there is no room for nonrepressive "progressive," positive utopianism, or for an objective, justifiable education and praxis for resistance and overcoming the present reality (Horkheimer, 1974, p. 26). Does this mean that Adorno and Horkheimer abandoned Utopia altogether, that they gave up the essential commitment of critical theory, or ended their transformative-educational imperative? Not at all. On the contrary, they became devoted more than ever to the Utopian call.

Adorno and Horkheimer gave up the Marxist conception of progress, and in this sense their optimism as to a social revolutionary change, and even the goal, and to a certain degree also the means of critique. But they did not abandon the utopian project and the essential imperatives of critical theory as an emancipatory dimension and political praxis. However, their definition of emancipation and the stance of realization of intellectual autonomy as praxis changed dramatically to become more in line with its early Jewish eschatological sources in the Qumran sect and other Jewish and Christian members of the Messianic tradition.

In Horkheimer's work, the change from a Marxian critical theory to a pessimistic philosophy is paralleled by an articulation of critical theory as a new, Jewish, Negative Theology. Adorno's Negative Dialectics follows the same path, attempting to present counter-education, attempting to face the present absence of the quest for and the awaiting for the human stance of readiness to be called upon, a seriousness toward that which is being called "redemption" in Christian theology.

In the second stage of the development of their work, both thinkers offer a counter-educational praxis whose religiosity is fertilized by the alarming recognition of the impossible realization of the imperative of human advance toward God, absolute Spirit, or Reason; toward the progressing true knowledge of genuine human interests and realization of their potentials. The current work of Slavoj Žítzek, who writes that "the paradox of self-consciousness is that it is possible only against the background of its own impossibility" (Žítzek, 1993, p. 15) is very close to this later work of Horkheimer and Adorno. In this sense the later work of critical theory becomes prima facie counter-educational, even if the word "education" is rarely mentioned and schooling is hardly tackled at all.

At the same time, both Adorno (1971) and Horkheimer (VIII, 361–456) referred to education and to schooling and academic education quite specifically and explicitly, in more popular texts and radio interviews. On these occasions another aspect of their work is expressed that is less sophisticated, less negativistic, and less utopian-pessimist. There is a permanent gap, sometimes an unbridgeable abyss, between these popular references to education in its narrower sense and the deeper aspects of their formulated Negative Dialectics and Negative Theology as a path to counter-education. Here I concentrate on their more refined and deeper elaborations and on their educational implications.

Adorno and Horkheimer's treatment of the challenge of modern historical progress, especially in the twentieth century, assigns a special place to technological progress and its implication for human life. They contend in a profound and courageous manner the challenge of current dwindling possibilities for human autonomy, solidarity, and elevation. On this level they are surprisingly close to Heidegger—much closer than to Marcuse (Gur-Ze'ev, 1996, p. 83). The elaboration of the present state of technology and its implications is realized here within a critical reconstruction of Western metaphysics, since technology is understood by them as the zenith and the essence of Western metaphysics.

According to the later Horkheimer, in the modern world everything is enslaved for the ennoblement and advancement of technological progress under the control of Instrumental Rationality. Within this process nature has lost its own meaning and humans have lost their transcendental mission. Only one aim is still valid, namely self-preservation: egoism, which ultimately is revealed as serving omnipotent mythical powers within and as part and parcel of the totally administered world (Horkheimer, 1974, pp. 101–102). Within this process of post-industrial society and its Culture Industry there is no room for the autonomy of the individual. This conception is vital for the understanding of Horkheimer's perspective on education in its narrower and its wider manifestations.

The big challenge for the critical mind and for humanistic education is not the fruit of alienation but the disappearance of (the consciousness of) alienation within the totality, which is governed by Instrumental Rationality. This quest for alienation and the challenges of the exile of Spirit make the difference between orthodox Marxist Ideology Critique and Horkheimer and Adorno's conceptions. Governing Instrumental Rationality leaves no room for nonefficient and nonpragmatic considerations, and drives out the concepts, ideals, and traditions that allowed speculation and critique of the self-evident and offered transcendence from the oppressive practices of all master signifiers. Instrumental Rationality is responsible for the current reality in which the more progressive the processes of dehumanization become, the more efficient becomes the concealment of the oppression of present Culture Industry (Adorno, 2000, p. 233). The exile of Spirit and the overcoming of the abyss between substance and subject are trivialized, and Spirit is again presented after being equalized with the governing representations as "reality," "normality," and (given or promised) pleasure machine, which normalizing education is quick to introduce.

The seeming political freedom, free opinion, and tolerance within this society conceal and actually serve the process of totalistic dehumanization. "Not only does the mind mould itself for the sake of its marketability, and thus reproduce the socially prevalent categories. Rather, it grows to resemble ever more closely the *status quo* even where it subjectively refrains from making a commodity of itself. The network of the whole is drawn ever tighter. . . . It leaves the individual consciousness less and less room for evasion, performs it more and more thoroughly, cuts it off as it were from the possibility of differentiating itself as all difference degenerates to a nuance in the monotony of supply" (Adorno, 2000, p. 198).

Within this process traditional Marxist Ideology Critique cannot be of much use since culture itself "has become ideological" (Adorno 2000, p. 206). "Today," he says, "ideology means society as appearance . . . ideology is not simply reducible to partial interest" (Adorno, 2000, p. 207). However, since ideology is no longer conceived as a socially necessary appearance that veils the "facts," Ideology Critique can no longer offer an emancipatory deciphering of "reality" and cannot claim to empower humanistic-oriented resistance to social oppression and to manipulative representations of histories, identities, and realities, as critical pedagogy claims to offer in the name of critical theory. Adorno offers a view that does not allow this kind of optimism, since "ideology today is society itself in so far as its integral power and inevitability, its overwhelming existence-in-itself, surrogates the meaning which that existence has exterminated" (Adorno, 2000, p. 207).

Horkheimer is on the verge of acknowledging that there is no more justification for a critical theory. In a personal letter to Adorno he says that nowadays "reflection [has become] senseless. Actually the world to which we saw ourselves as belonging is destroyed" (Horkheimer Archive, VI, 13, p. 511). Elsewhere he writes that serious talk itself has become senseless and that those who refuse to listen—to the attempts to save meaning—are not totally wrong (Horkheimer, 1978, p. 129). Truth in this context is not absent, it is rather reviled in and swallowed by the present reality. It can, however, offer only technological and scientific advance—not meaning, direction, or responsibility to resist injustice. The issue at stake here is not solely truth or justice but the very quest for truth and the commitment to justice, or, in other words, the possibility of transcending from meaninglessness and the Same—from the mere thingness of being.

In the work of later Adorno and Horkheimer, two very different conceptions of truth emerge. One is of the kind of the existing world of facts, which ultimately represents "power" (Adorno & Horkheimer 1988, p. 236). Here human existence in its essence is revealed at its full price: practical involvement, within which ideals transform into oppression (Adorno & Horkheimer 1988, p. 224). The implicit negation of any optimistic positive emancipatory educational project is mercilessly manifested here.

In an imaginary conversation between the philosopher—an implicit reference to the masters of critical theory themselves—and the practical man, the philosopher is the one on the defensive, and not his practical interlocutor. The genuine philosopher is introduced by Adorno and Horkheimer not as a promising educator, but as a neurotic, who manifests his refusal to be cured when insisting on continuing his project of curing normal, realistic-oriented, sane people (Adorno & Horkheimer, 1988, p. 255). Facing these conclusions one should ask: What, if any, is the justification for critical theory and for critical pedagogy as emancipatory education in action, under conditions in which "serious philosophy has come to its end" (Horkheimer 1985, VII, p. 404)?

The texts of the later Adorno and Horkheimer reconstruct a cultural moment that resembles an Arab story about a vicious magician who poisoned the well whence all the tribe drew its water. Everyone drank from the well—and went mad. Only the king did not drink. It took no time before the rumor spread all over: "How sad, our beloved king has gone crazy." The king, who was a wise man, asked his servants to hurry as fast as they could and bring him water from the poisoned well, and when left alone he drank from it. In no time a new rumor spread all over:

"How wonderful, our beloved king has come back to his senses." And so, according to the story, the tribe was saved.

Adorno and Horkheimer present us with a diametrically opposite vision. It is a vision of a philosopher who refuses at all cost to integrate, to be normalized, and as a neurotic, within impossible conditions, keeps his commitment to his counter-educational mission, which nothing in reality can justify.

The later Horkheimer presents mature critical theory as a Jewish Negative Theology. This change carries major educational implications. Following Benjamin, it was for him of vital importance that Judaism did not present God as a positive absolute. Following Benjamin, and in contrast to Marcuse, the negativity of this utopianism is constituted from two elements. The first is rejection in principle of the possibility of a positive realization of any Utopia. He refuses to imagine a positive picture of future society prior to its realization (Horkheimer, 1985, VII, p. 382). The second is his commitment to confront critical theory with its own negativity. He refuses any philosophy that leads to consensus, synthesis, and the end of dialectics and worthy suffering. And at the same time he refuses to abandon the quest for the Messiah or human emancipation. The quest as a Messianic tension is central here, not its "successful" fulfilment. That is why Judaism is so important for him. He sees in Judaism "a non-positive religion"; it was "a hope for the coming of the Messiah" (Horkheimer, 1988, p. 331). Judaism, within this framework, is a symbol, not a reality, a symbol for solidarity, a nonviolent solidarity of the powerless (ibid., p. 140). As a Jewish Negative Theology, critical theory expresses, in his view, "a refusal to recognize power as an argument for truth" (Horkheimer 1985, VIII, p. 158).

The conception of being in the continuum of ontological Diaspora was vital for presenting late critical theory as a Jewish Negative Theology. The uniqueness of Judaism lies in its permanent demand for justice, emerging out of a hope with no real historical anchor: "Jewry was not a powerful state, but the hope for justice at the end of the world" (Horkheimer, 1978, p. 206). The idea that the demand for justice essentially cannot obtain power, and that justice can be realized only at the cost of its transformation into its opposite—injustice—is central to the educational implications of this version of critical theory.

It implies that genuine education must not attempt to transcend negativism; it is committed to antidogmatism and it must resist any manifestation of the self-evident, even that of the oppressed and the persecuted. It must resist popularization and political victories, while at the same time its Messianism is directed to resisting actual injustices in the present reality as the only manifestation of the quest for truth and justice. This version of Negative Theology as a mature critical theory in Horkheimer's thought complies with Adorno's concept of Negative Dialectics.

It was not in opposition to the view of the philosopher as a neurotic who refuses to be cured, but in compliance with this vision that Adorno articulated the "categorical imperative of philosophy" (Adorno, 2000, p. 53). There he concludes: "It does not hold the key to salvation, but allows some hope only to the moment of concept followed by the intellect wherever the path may lead" (ibid.). Actually, he presents critical theory as a path to salvation after all. This, however, is within a negative framework that leaves no room for any positive Utopia or actual salvation in the sense that traditional positive utopias or optimistic-oriented critical pedagogy can promise its disciples.

Regardless of its situation, according to Adorno, philosophy has not concluded its mission. However, it does not have any foundation, self-evidence, social strata, or pain on which to establish its critical education: "Philosophy offers no place from which theory as such might be concretely convicted of the anachronisms it is suspected of, now, as before" (Adorno, 2000, p. 55). Adorno, in accordance with Benjamin and Horkheimer, and contrary to Marcuse, presents another kind of dialectics, a Negative Dialectics. Note, however, that his position stands in contrast to the orthodox Marxist concept of dialectics and its version of Ideology Critique[4] (as an emancipatory overcoming of alienation and false consciousness, and as a precondition for a revolutionary praxis). As a genuine counter-educator he refuses any concept of dialectics, which promises victory, emancipation, or peace.

According to Adorno, "contradiction is not what Hegel's absolute idealism was bound to transfigure it into. . . . It indicates the untruth of identity, the fact that the concept does not exhaust the thing conceived" (Adorno, 2000, p. 57). Adorno and Horkheimer are united here in refusing any manifestations of the absolute, the totality, the truth, or a positive justice on earth. Adorno grounds his concept of negativity in what in another philosophical tradition is called "the essence of being."

This is why even dialectics is not in peace with itself, nor brings appeasement or truth. "The name of dialectics," he says in his *Negative Dialectics,* "says no more, to begin with, than that objects do not go into their concepts without leaving a reminder, that they come to contradict the traditional norm of adequacy" (Adorno, 2000, p. 57). The gap will never be bridged, no theory will fully and adequately represent its object.

The very presence of the object separated from its representation apparatuses is problematized here in a manner that leaves no room for easygoing promises of "understanding," "empowerment," or "emancipation." Surely not of collectives, as critical pedagogy never tires of promising the oppressed and the marginalized in the name of critical theory.

Adorno is very much aware of the contradictions in the heart of his project. The important philosophical and educational view of his rests here, on these contradictions precisely, as a way of overcoming meaninglessness and self-evidence of various kinds, including the revolutionary kind. "The work of philosophical self-reflection consists in unraveling that paradox. Everything else is signification, secondhand construction, pre-philosophical activity" (Adorno, 2000, p. 60). What then remains for philosophy to do, if there is still a mission it can devote itself to?

Adorno, like Horkheimer, constituted his utopian thought on his philosophical pessimism, so Negative Dialectics becomes the last way to save the struggle to challenge the self-evident and to transcend meaninglessness. "To change this direction of conceptuality, to give it a turn toward nonidentity, is the hinge of Negative

Dialectics. Insight into the constitutive character of the nonconceptual in the concept would end the compulsive identification, which the concept brings unless halted by such reflection. Reflection upon its own meaning is the way out of the concept's seeming being-in-itself as a unit of meaning" (Adorno, 2000, p. 63). In this sense, and solely in this sense, "philosophy can make it after all" (Adorno, 2000, p. 60).

Philosophizing, in this respect, becomes the only way to resist the process of destruction of the autonomy of the human subject (Adorno, 1999, p. 5). It becomes the only manner of resistance to being overwhelmed by the one-dimensional functionality and thingness of the system (Adorno. 2000, p. 234) and its deceiving message of freedom in accordance with the laws of the market and the current world of facts (Adorno 2000, p. 198). As such, within its negativity, it incubates an alternative to the hegemonic educational message propagated by the Culture Industry. In so doing, it offers the possibility of refusal of the present process of subjectification or resistance to the reality of constructing the dehumanized agent. As such, philosophy offers a kind of thinking that allows hope of overcoming the current educational reality, of which critical pedagogy is an important part (Adorno, 2000, p. 238)

The later work of Adorno and Horkheimer is indispensable in the present historical moment of Western culture. In face of the exile of Spirit it represents an uncompromising quest for Utopia. Western Eros is not being destroyed but consumed and reproduced as part of the one-dimensional reified diversity of the preset cultural moment, which in some respects is already beyond the horizons of the Culture Industry that was challenged by critical theory.

In face of the current postmodern conditions, which are accompanied by modernist and even premodernist ones, the later work of Adorno and Horkheimer is of special value, and not solely as a theoretical and educational challenge to postmodern ideologies and educational alternatives. It is also important as an alternative to normalizing education and the Same itself, for which some postmodern sensitivities and articulations can be of much importance.

Later critical theory struggled for the very possibility of sensitivity to alienation, for worthy suffering, and for containing the pursuit for "the totally other." Within this attempt, and only within it, are we to understand its refusal to abandon the imperative of responsibility to the yet unrealized human potentials. To this imperative, as to the presence of hope out of worthy suffering, it offered only one possible way: that of religious negation.

The message here is the messianic impulse, or the commitment for transcendence from any consensus, or the self-evident, into a struggle to overcome meaninglessness in a Godless world. In this sense any possible educational "implication" should be negative, if true to itself. And in this sense later Adorno and Horkheimer are so important in the attempt to keep alive the quest and the actual appearance of counter-education as a concrete Utopia in a postmodern condition.

Counter-education, if true to itself, cannot be, like critical pedagogy wants us to believe, an attempt to implement any "theory," as sophisticated or well-intentioned as it may be. If true to itself, counter-education must challenge any theoretical, ideological, or political "home," any master signifier, dogma, or ethnocentrism as manifestations of the Same, of the thingness in Being, which human beings are called to guard and transcend (Heidegger, 1962, p. 234). Counter-education, in this sense, must be at once Messianic and negative at any cost. This means that it cannot satisfy itself even with identification with the negation of self-evident, with the resistance to the ethnocentrism of the oppressed, and it cannot identify itself with the "worthier" violences they actualize against their own "internal" and "external" Others.

If faithful to itself, counter-education must concentrate on overcoming itself; negating its own theoretical assumptions, procedures, and conclusions.

A special role is reserved here for a critical reintegration of ethics, aesthetics, and interdisciplinary critical scientific work in its cultural and social context. Its negativity must avoid being abstract and one-dimensional, and love is essential to its realization.

It must turn to realize solidarity in actual dialogical situations and make room for love and generosity in actual life situations. As a concrete Utopia, counter-education must acknowledge this world and the presence of politics and power relations. And in this sense there is some affinity between it and critical pedagogy. However, it should not see itself as of this world, and it should refuse reduction to power relations, group interests, and implications of politically correct vocabularies. It acknowledges itself as a religious work *(avodat kodesh)*, and only as such also as an involvement in the political space.

Counter-education speaks only from the perspective of the Exile, as a homeless one who challenges the meaninglessness of the celebrated truths, values, and pleasures. It is enabled by the possible appearance of grace in a Godless world. For such a project the later work of Adorno and Horkheimer is certainly not the sole source but it is a worthy point of reference, and a relevant erotic experience. As an alternative to normalizing education, of which critical pedagogy is part and parcel, mature critical theory has "educational relevance": as a manifestation of counter-education and as a link in a worthy tradition that has not yet said its last word.

Only after developing these aspects is it worth reconstructing the later texts of Adorno on education after Auschwitz (Adorno, 1971, pp. 88–104) and Horkheimer's conceptions of higher education as the last barrier against the new barbarism enhanced by the culture industry (Horkheimer VIII, 1985, pp. 409–419). Such work has not yet been done. That is why its initiation must pay special attention to the overcoming of the worthier parts of Adorno's Negative Dialectics and Horkheimer's Negative Theology.

Notes

1. In this chapter I do not prove this claim. I try to show its validity only by referring to Henry Giroux, who is undoubtedly one of the central figures in this field.

2. This is still a much missing element in the critique of Marcuse's work. Here I offer only the main argument with brief references to its textual justifications. The dialectic between his philosophical pessimism and positive utopianism is extensively analyzed in: Ilan Gur-Ze'ev, *The Frankfurt School and the History of Pessimism,* Jerusalem 1996 (in Hebrew).
3. Ephraim Gothold Lessing, *On the Education of the Human Kind*. Lessing's small book is only an example. Schiller's *On the Education of Man in a Series of Letters* belongs to the same tradition. My argument is that even works that did not present themselves explicitly as representatives of this tradition, such as those of Karl Marx, should be considered, at least partially, as members of this tradition, to which Marcuse also belongs. The parallels between the historical process as the educator of humanity and the personal approach to maturity within the tradition of the *Bildungsroman* are of a real significance here.
4. This is the kind of Ideology Critique that is fundamental to hegemonic Critical Pedagogy.

DOWN SUDDEN VISTAS: WALTER BENJAMIN AND THE WANING OF MODERNITY

> It is by words and the defeat of words,
> Down sudden vistas of the vain attempt,
> That for a flying moment one may see
> By what cross-purposes the world is dreamt.
> —Richard Wilbur, "An Event"

> "Every angel is terrible."
> —Rainer Maria Rilke, *Duino Elegies:* Elegy II'

In his monumental work of historical melancholy, *The Waning of the Middle Ages,* first published in 1919, the great medievalist Johan Huizinga drew a fleeting and ironic distinction between the epoch he sought to elegize and the period glimpsed on its distant horizon:

If in all that regards the things of this world there is no hope of improvement and of progress, however slow, those who love the world too much to give up its delights, and who nevertheless cannot help aspiring to a better order of things, see nothing before them but a gulf. We will have to wait till the eighteenth century — for even the Renaissance does not truly bring the idea of progress — before men resolutely enter the path of social optimism; only then the perfectibility of man and society is raised to the rank of a central dogma, and the next century will only lose the naivete of this belief, but not the courage and optimism which it inspired. (Huizinga, 1971, pp. 36–37)

The vigilant attentiveness of Walter Benjamin offers critical witness to the progressivist allure of the modern, which Huizinga characterized in such subtle contrast to the pessimism of the Middle Ages. The gaze of Benjamin's *flaneur* discerns hope, possibility, concentrated energies of vast and permanent renewal in the contours of modernity. Simultaneously, however, Benjamin is the magus of this transformed vista of human civilization, unmasking its traps and deceptions, exposing its genealogies, revealing its complicity with the cultural forms it purports to have surpassed; alert to the paradoxical patterns of decline and decay that are its central sustaining narratives. In some of his most important writings, therefore, Benjamin returns us to an imagined melancholy close to that of Huizinga's fantasy of medieval belatedness, where those who aspire to embrace the fragmentary delights of modernity experience them obscurely as a protracted fading or falling away from unitary tradition; as if the sense of waning were not only an effect of the final phase in the late history of the modern but its very condition.

"A total absence of illusion about the age and at the same time an unlimited commitment to it" (Benjamin, 1999a, p. 733) is Benjamin's pugnaciously engaged disposition toward the ambiguity of living in the modern in his mature essay of 1933, *Experience and Poverty*. A number of popular responses to the modernist "destruction of tradition" (Benjamin, 1999a, p. 732) epitomized by the First World War are presciently identified and interrogated in the essay, ranging from nostalgia for the occult through to the dreamfactory escapism of Walt Disney. Each is seen as an inadequate form of compensation for bridging the gulf of history—the specifically modernist transformation of experience that demands a much more radical reconfiguration of perception and of action in the world than contemporary mass culture holds forth. *Experience and Poverty* develops Benjamin's emergent understanding of a usable politics of the modern first referred to in the inchoate *Theologico-Political Fragment* of 1921 as the "method . . . called nihilism" (Benjamin, 1979, p. 156), and there quite deliberately equated with Nietzsche's "active nihilism" (Eagleton, 1981). The actively nihilistic temper disclosed in figures such as Einstein, Loos, or Le Corbusier exploits the potential of the modern for "opening up" experience to new and unprecedented epistemologies, while recognizing that such endeavors are inescapably contaminated by the collapse of the tradition out of which they originally arose. Le Corbusier's glass architecture points to a new organization of urban space founded on utopian transparency: "objects made of glass have no 'aura.' Glass is, in general, the enemy of secrets. It is also the enemy of possession" (Benjamin, 1999a, p. 734). The new architecture not only reflects a change in experience; it helps to create it. Similarly—if still more far-reaching in its implications—the breach with tradition in the fabric of the modern redefines the function of language as "No technical renovation . . . but . . . mobilisation in the service of struggle or work—at any rate, of changing reality instead of describing it" (Benjamin, 1999a, p. 733).

This statement in *Experience and Poverty* about the relationship of language to modernity is only superficially Marxian. Benjamin is here completely consistent with his core philosophy of language, which argued from its beginnings that language did not describe or reflect a pre-existing reality but constituted a means of intervening in it. In his early Bern doctoral thesis on *The Concept of Criticism in German Romanticism* (1919), Benjamin brilliantly set out to challenge the "epistemological presuppositions" (Benjamin, 1996, p. 116) of the Kantian concept of experience by showing how Romantic theory and artistic ambition broke the boundaries of the Kantian critique:

> Through Kant's philosophical work, the concept of criticism had acquired for the younger generation an almost magical meaning; in any case, the term explicitly connoted not the sense of a merely discerning, unproductive state of mind; rather, for the Romantics and for speculative philosophy, the term "critical" meant objectively productive, creative out of thoughtful deliberation. To be critical meant to elevate thinking so far beyond all restrictive conditions that the knowledge of truth sprang forth magically, as it were, from insight into the falsehood of these restrictions. (Benjamin, 1996, p. 142)

Like Hamann before him, Benjamin saw in the dialectical extremities of high Romantic art an interventionist practice that drew out from Kantian philosophy a species of "speculative critique" ultimately fatal to the Kantian project and its transcendental version of experience (Ferris 1992). The departure from Kantian idealism enables the irruption of the absolute into the spatial and temporal structures of intuition and the logocentric categories of understanding. Eschewing the Kantian split of experience from the absolute, and the coercive continuities of Hegel's "mysticism of brute force" (Scholem and Adorno, 1994, p. 113), Benjamin gradually articulated an enhanced and textualized concept of experience in which spatiotemporal structures and logocentric systems admit the illocutionary realization of the absolute in their surface discontinuities, disruptions, and chaotically concealed patterns of meaning. In this revisionist account of the Kantian critique of judgment, the productions of modern culture assume the status previously reserved for abstract philosophical reasoning. The absolute is "immanent" in the critical supplement of material production, and the supplement is itself revealed in the performance of a critical reading that is always subsequent to the work of culture yet without which the work of culture remains incomplete:

> This is the structure of the work for which the Romantics demand an immanent criticism.... The immanent tendency of the work and, accordingly, the standard for its immanent criticism are the reflection that lies at its basis and is imprinted in its form. Yet this is, in truth, not so much a standard of judgement as, first and foremost, the foundation of a completely different kind of criticism—one which is not concerned with judging, and whose center of gravity lies not in the evaluation of the single work but in demonstrating its relations to all other works and, ultimately, to the idea of art. (Benjamin, 1996, p. 159)

The recasting of Kant's account of experience, which in effect replaces philosophical enquiry with critical theory, gives rise in Benjamin's thought to a decisive methodological innovation. Immanent criticism demands a radical shift from the application of judgment to the "unfolding" of the possibilities for transformation in the work of art and the historical processes in which its meaning is circulated. Immanent criticism is "an experiment on the artwork, one through which the latter's own reflection is awakened, through which it is brought to consciousness and knowledge of itself" (Benjamin, 1996, p. 151). The work of art enters the discursive zones of the self-conscious historical continuum which, through criticism, become incorporated into its formal possibilities and validate its aesthetic afterlife. "Folded" within each of the productions of culture lies an infinite set of possible appropriations that, when activated by critique, reestablish a commerce between past and future, tradition and modernity. As Benjamin demonstrated in a much later comment on Baudelaire, it is one of the functions of immanent criticism to "complete" the artwork by discerning its implicit critical future in its present complex negotiations with the recalcitrant materials of history and social power:

> It is an illusion of vulgar Marxism that the social function of a material or intellectual product can be determined without reference to the circumstances and bearers of its tradition. . . . The tradition of Baudelaire's work is a very short one, but it already bears historical scars which must be of interest to critical observers. (Benjamin, 1983, p. 104)

Reference to the "historical scars" of tradition highlights the potential contained in immanent criticism for the violent realignment or even destruction of the products of culture. Criticism can move toward a convulsive closure of the artwork as well as its open expansion, because it "earnestly dissolves the form in order to transform the single work into the absolute work of art." This, indeed, is what Benjamin terms "the task of the objective tribunal in art, of criticism." In their interactions with criticism, the works of culture attain completion through "the destruction of the work." Their meanings are actualized in time only through a loss of an originary integration with the material circumstances and historical sensibilities that created them: "Criticism sacrifices the work totally for the sake of the single sphere of connection" (Benjamin, 1996, pp. 163–164).

When fully historicized, the dialectic of completion and destruction in the critical engagement with culture constitutes the axis of Benjamin's messianic materialism, the uneasy synthesis in his thought of a speculative critique of experience with an eschatological longing for the "messianic cessation of happening" (Benjamin, 1996, p. 182). In *The Concept of Criticism,* Benjamin goes to great lengths to distinguish the messianism he sees as the mainspring of the Romantic consciousness of historical time from the "modern misunderstanding" that equates it with "the . . . term 'progress'." The modern ideology of progress consists "in seeing progression as a mere function of the indeterminate infinite of the task, on the one hand, and the empty infinity of time, on the other." The Jewish messianic conception of history rejects homogeneous accumulation and succession in favor of endless intensification and "an infinite process of fulfilment." It is therefore not "a progress into the void" but "a continually more comprehensive unfolding and enhancement of poetic forms." Borrowing a term from Schlegel, Benjamin insists that this messianic "cessation" is the Romantics' "fundamental stand on the ideology of progress" (Benjamin, 1996, p. 168) and supplies the underlying critical position from which to dispel the self-authenticating illusions of modernity (Wohlfarth, 1989).

The messianic form of thinking in Benjamin's major writings presupposes neither a teleological structure within history nor a mystical epistemology breaking in upon it. Messianism serves an allegorical and heuristic function for Benjamin, albeit an apocalyptic one. The objective is to show how aesthetic awareness and historical intelligence are empowered by extreme and unconditional theological commitments. The method historicizes messianism as active anticipation of the provisionality of all historical configurations without the ontological or religious loyalties that normally accompany such antinomian attitudes to time and eternity (Handelman, 1991). Insofar as the immanent criticism participates in such a system, it will reflect an absolute experience symbolically rendered in the allegorical context of language. The messianic fusion of the historical, the theological, and the epistemological therefore results in a constantly shifting foundation for the work of critical practice. Justified by the existence of an allegorical world, however, the problematic synthesis of Marxian materialism and messianic Judaism offers for Benjamin a temporary standpoint from which to overcome the mythology of progress and the fallacies cast up by modernity's extended sociopolitical catastrophe. In the final analysis, modernity threatens to remain, for all its technological accomplishments, a disastrously desiccated condition denied any meaningful intercourse with a realizable tradition. The famous image of Klee's painting of the *Angelus Novus* dramatizes the conflict between messianic alertness to the transformative potential of the every moment and the disabling determinism of the doctrine of progress. For Benjamin in the *Theses on the Philosophy of History,* the Klee painting "shows an angel looking as though he is about to move away from something he is fixedly contemplating":

> His face is turned toward the past. Where we perceive a chain of events, he sees one single catastrophe which keeps piling wreckage upon wreckage and hurls it in front of his feet. The angel would like to stay, awaken the dead, and make whole what has been smashed. But a storm is blowing from Paradise; it has got caught in his wings with such violence that the angel can no longer close them. This storm irresistibly propels him into the future to which his back is turned, while the pile of debris before him grows skyward. This storm is what we call progress. (Benjamin, 1992, p. 249)

The "modern misunderstanding" of unlinear progress, already subverted by the experience of World War I and the rise of Fascism, is here contested in the name of a materially transfigured view of history. In the messianic critique that the *Angelus*

Novus adumbrates, every element of the past becomes open to redemption on the messianic Day of Judgment. "Nothing that has ever happened should be regarded as lost for history. To be sure, only a redeemed mankind receives the fullness of its past—which is to say only for a redeemed mankind has its past become citable in all its moments. Each moment it has lived becomes a citation *a l'ordre du jour*—and that day is Judgement day" (Benjamin, 1992, p. 254; Jennings, 1987, pp. 56–58). A secularized apocalypse reintroduces an emancipatory point of reference in contradistinction to the totalitarian appropriation of history that is the "single catastrophe" modernity has made of the works of humanity in bleak fulfillment of the Enlightenment ideology of progress. Such a view places new responsibility on the artist and the critic; Benjamin was aware that "the task of history is not only to give the oppressed access to tradition, but also to create it" (Benjamin, 1992, p. 255). Interpreted pessimistically, the Angel of History bears witness to the retributive destruction of the endlessly deferred messianic moment (Lowy, 1992). He also just possibly gestures, however, to the promise of a new type of "citability" in which apocalyptic consummation gives way to instauration. This is the future-oriented glimmer of renewed faith in time, change, memory, and history of the kind first suggested by Benjamin in the 1921 fragment *The Meaning of Time in the Moral Universe:* "In order to struggle against retribution, forgiveness finds its powerful ally in time." Here, a different storm presses the wings of the Angel of History, one "in which the voice of the evildoer is drowned," and where "time not only extinguishes the traces of all misdeeds but also—by virtue of its duration, beyond all remembering or forgetting—helps, in ways that are wholly mysterious, to complete the process of forgiveness, though never of reconciliation" (Benjamin, 1996, pp. 286–87). Messianic eschatology is for Benjamin never simply an aesthetic of vengeance or redress. It remains part of the materialist strain of "active nihilism" in his thought, which does not merely mourn modernity or long narcissistically for its promised annihilation, but which searches out in its marginal spaces, episodic utterances, and glittering surfaces ephemeral witness to new forms of postmessianic "becoming" that perform the miracle dreamt of in historical materialism of abolishing the self-deceptions of progress (Serres, 1995, pp. 242–245; 295).

Benjamin's pervasive concern with "becoming" shows that, throughout his work, his awareness of the waning of modernity was neither nostalgic nor fatalistic but strategic and enabling. Recognition of the attenuated character of modernity as a fundamental property of its relationship to its technology, politics, culture, and history is mainstreamed into an immanent critical practice that reconfigures the interstitial persistence of tradition and valorizes the foreshadowings of futurity contained in the present crisis. At the outset of *The Origin of German Tragic Drama* (1928), the idea of "becoming" is mobilized within the semantic and temporal potential of the term "origin" itself:

> Origin, although an entirely historical category, has, nevertheless, nothing to do with genesis. The term origin is not intended to describe the process by which the existent came into being, but rather to describe that which emerges from the process

of becoming and disappearance. Origin is an eddy in the stream of becoming, and in its current it swallows the material involved in the process of genesis. . . . There takes place in every original phenomenon a determination of the form in which the idea will constantly confront the historical world, until it is revealed fulfilled, in the totality of history. (Benjamin, 1998, pp. 45–46)

There lies in this definition a superficial resemblance to Nietzsche's concepts of origin and eternal recurrence as expressed in *The Birth of Tragedy* and *The Gay Science*, and equated by Heidegger with Nietzsche's later conception of "Becoming stamped with the character of Being" from *The Will to Power* (Heidegger, 1987, p. 200). Benjamin, however, categorically rejected this aspect of Nietzsche's transcendentalism as at odds with "the essence of this empirical reality" (Benjamin, 1998, p. 36) because of its lingering attachment to the mythic refusal of history. The analysis of origin is for Benjamin part of the practical task of immanent criticism, and its "unfolding" of the pattern of meaning within the experience of time and human action. If it rejects the doctrine of progress, it does not replace it with a surrender to the totalizing primitivism Benjamin ominously saw as European fascism's reactionary response to the contradictions of modernity.

Origin, in fact, endeavors to investigate the seemingly remote and abstruse mentality of the German baroque *Trauerspiel* or "mourning play" (the term now preferred to the confusing "tragedy" of the standard translation) in order to advance Benjamin's immanent critique of the condition of modernity. The mourning play is seen by Benjamin as a conflicted site for actualization or "stage-setting" of the early modern attitude to time, to history, and the disclosure of human destiny, reoriented under the pressure of the Protestant Reformation, the scientific revolution, and the emergent capitalist polity. Read symptomatically, the mourning play can be seen to ossify history into a series of endlessly repeated dramatic gestures that accrue only the most diminished and narrowed sense of *telos,* or time as meaningless succession: "The constantly repeated drama of the rise and fall of princes . . . appeared to the writers less as a manifestation of morality than as the natural aspect of the course of history, essential in its permanence" (Benjamin, 1998, p. 88). Baroque drama reduced the philosophy of history to "the manner of a chronicle," where dramatic action is evacuated of all moral content or volition and presented as nothing more than "the painstaking analysis of the calculations of political intrigue" (Benjamin, 1998, p. 89). The plays of von Lohenstein, for example, obstruct ethical reflection of the sort seen in *Hamlet* (which retains its affiliations with the saturated time-sense of the medieval worldview) by repeated recourse to a language that deterministically equates the historical and the natural, the work of character and the body of destiny, thus "resolving historical and ethical conflicts into the demonstrations of natural history" (Benjamin, 1998, p. 90; Cohen, 1993, pp. 235–237).

The "dehistoricization of history" emblematized in the mourning play is partially explained by Benjamin in terms of the deeply influential secularization hypothesis championed at the end of the nineteenth century by Weber and Lowth

(Weber, 1993). Benjamin's account of secularization is much more far-reaching than that of his predecessors and anticipates the "archaeological" method of Michel Foucault in its concern with the context of secularization in the broad outworking of the disciplinary structures of rationality and power in the modern era (Foucault, 1970). Secularization is an effect and not a cause. The loss of the sense of historical symbolic intelligibility in the early modern period, "the total disappearance of eschatology," is signaled in the dramatic organization of the mourning play where "history merges into setting" and there is depicted on the desacralized enclosure of the stage "the transposition of the originally temporal data into a figurative spatial simultaneity" (Benjamin, 1998, pp. 90–92). This is the heart of Benjamin's analysis of modernity concentrated into the exposure of a single historical and artistic moment. The aesthetics of the mourning play issue in a theatrical practice that breaks irrevocably with the sacred, hierarchical, messianic *telos* of medieval religious drama—with its free, collective cooperation of human and divine agency toward a consummation of historical time—while also sundering itself from the individualized, self-contained, and completed action of Renaissance tragic heroism. Symptomatic of its status as a cultural production of the "late," or even "waning," Renaissance, the mourning play inscribes its unique inclination toward history as petrifaction and repetition (Bouwsma, 2001), replacing classical symbolism with the distinctively modern trope of allegory:

> Within the decisive category of time . . . is permitted the incisive, formal definition of the relationship between symbol and allegory. Whereas in the symbol destruction is idealised and the transfigured face of nature is fleetingly revealed in the light of redemption, in allegory the observer is confronted with the facies hippocratica of history as petrified, primordial landscape. . . . This is the heart of the allegorical way of seeing, of the baroque, secular explanation of history as the Passion of the world; its importance resides solely in the stations of its decline. (Benjamin, 1998, p. 166)

In allegory, the potent semiotic of the symbol is flattened into a finitude of fixed significations. Where the symbolic showcases the transcendent erotic radiance of the ordinary object and the messianic vulnerabilities of time, the allegorical materializes all meaning as subject to the disembodied controlling sovereignty of shifting but ubiquitous ideological regimes—intellectual, political, religious, scientific. The literary form of the mourning play, its "principle of construction," is a passive set of equally frozen structural oppositions (Sovereign/Intriguer; law/anarchy; eternity/transience) in the repetition of which the genre expresses and laments the spatialized modalities of the early modern worldviews that implicitly sustain it. "Spatialization" of the temporal is inaugurated in this critical historic phase of the late Renaissance as the defining and normalizing rationality of modernity, and of which nascent secularization is but an institutional and cultural reflex: "If history is secularised in the setting, this is an expression of the same metaphysical tendency which simultaneously led, in the exact sciences, to the infinitesimal method. In both cases chronological movement is grasped and analysed in a spatial image" (Benjamin,

1998, p. 92). Throughout *Origin,* the "spatialization" typified by the mourning play announces modernity's falling away from the imagined authenticity of tradition into an absolute amnesiac linearity of grids, networks, surfaces, and flattened discursive experiences. This is the totalizing *mathesis* of modernity that denies true subjectivity, enthrones the despotism of an antidemocratic politics, and universalizes in language the subordination of the performative to the constative (Pickstock, 1999, pp. 81–89).

The "nihilistic" method exists to contest the ascendancy of the *mathetic* commodification of reality and to "unfold" the spatial allegories of modernity through the countersigns of difference (sexual, political, ethical), ontology, expectation, intersubjectivity, and the pure gift of narrative (Deleuze, 1993, pp. 28–35). In the culminating *aporia* of the mourning play, Benjamin finds that the genre's stylized characterization is disempowered by the repeated utterances of mechanistic metaphors—such as that of the moving clock hand—which cumulatively repress the impulse to moral action and tragic authority in the lives of the protagonists until an apparently irresistible cloud of inertia descends on the stage. There nonetheless exists in the recesses of the dramatic plotting a residual persistence or "memory" of the symbolic in the form of agonistic submission to the influence of "fate," which results, paradoxically, from the finality of the genre's empty arithmetic metaphors and which is manifest in its spectral catalogues of ghosts, madmen, and premonitory dreams. "Fate is not purely a natural occurrence—any more than it is purely historical.... It is the elemental force of nature in historical events, which are not themselves entirely nature, because the light of grace is still reflected in the state of creation" (Benjamin, 1998, p. 129). The recourse to fate is the marginal location in the drama where it is momentarily "opened out" to "transcendental phenomena whose dimension is temporal, in contrast to the immanent, predominantly spatial phenomena of the world of things" (Benjamin, 1998, p. 134). The presence of fate is not a gap for the admission of regressive theologies of eventual redemption, nor a triumphant return of the *deux ex machina* of the symbolic, but it does stress that "the subject of fate cannot be determined" (Benjamin, 1998, p. 132), and extends the possibility of a new dialectical interaction of the allegorical and the symbolic—one that is finally enabled to embrace the modern condition as the only viable context for human affirmation. The work of mourning in the mourning play confronts the trauma of the loss of the symbolic and the remedial relationship to temporal meaning that it once described, recognizing that there is no conceivable return of the symbolic in either the waxing or the waning of modernity (Sacks, 1985, pp. 15–18). The allegorical bears the inconsolable weight of this loss, but carries also the compensatory memory of its prior dialectical attachment to the symbolic as the renovated ground or endlessly deferred "origin" of a new kind of engagement with the modern:

> Ultimately, in the death-signs of the baroque, the direction of allegorical reflection is reversed; on the second part of its wide arc it returns, to redeem.... This solves the riddle of the most fragmented, the most defunct, the most dispersed. Allegory, of

course, thereby loses everything that was most peculiar to it: the secret privileged knowledge, the arbitrary rule in the realm of dead objects, the supposed infinity of a world without hope. All this vanishes with this one about-turn, in which the immersion of allegory has to clear away the final phantasmagoria of the objective and, left entirely to its own devices, re-discovers itself. (Benjamin, 1998, p. 232)

The internal structural tensions, which place a typically baroque artwork such as the German mourning play under such extreme stress, are simultaneously displayed and contained by the genre's hypertrophied literary ornament of repetition and duplication. Repetition of this sort is a decadent evasion of dialectical progression and signals the dominance of "an inner world of feeling that bears no relationship to the cosmos" (Benjamin, 1998, p. 119). Mourning symptomizes the obsessive revisitation of the scene of primal loss, once again wholly differentiated from the vitality of individual confrontation and sublimity characteristic of classical and Renaissance tragedy. Enthralled to the decisively modern repetition compulsion—which is nothing more than the psychological reaction formation to the arithmetic calculus of modernity—the mourning play laments its dissociation from the temporal inimitability of the "here and now." Repetition, duplication, reproduction are tropes sustained by the spatialized thematics of early modern technological innovations such as printing, manufacture, and urbanization. Within the organized energies of art they carry the "marks" or "historical scars" of both the breach with tradition and the onset of the ideology of progress. Such progress is equated not with dynamic growth but with accumulation, quantification, and uniformity—Enlightenment principles that colonize all cultural meaning even as the material technologies on which they depend, and that created them, become the universalized matrix of social consciousness and action (McCole, 1993, pp. 140–143). The melancholy attraction of the mourning play derives its power from the liminal cultural location at which the genre is situated: on the early modern cusp of the era of "mechanical reproduction," pointing both backwards and forwards. The project of immanent criticism, Benjamin states, henceforward must resist collusion with the nostalgic poetics of the alluring cultural forms haunting this imaginary threshold. Speculative critique ought to seek out, instead, the temporal authenticity and dialectical discontinuity of those works of art that definitively inhabit the circumstances of modernity, even if by their adversarial existence they contest some of modernity's deepest assumptions about human flourishing.

What radically distinguishes the modern artwork from the premodern in this philosophical scheme is the shifting and unresolved valences of representation, and these valences constitute the motivating preoccupation of Benjamin's deservedly famous essay *The Work of Art in the Age of Mechanical Reproduction* (1939). In an earlier essay, *Painting, or Signs and Marks* (1917), Benjamin highlights a distinction of "*enormous* metaphysical significance" between the "absolute mark" and the "absolute sign." The absolute sign is another strapline of modernity, and Benjamin is quick to identify it with the technology of inscription as "printed on something," and with a "spatial relation" to what it represents. In contrast to the absolute mark—which exists in "a medium," "is more temporal," and which "emerges from" reality—the sign is inscribed on a surface as a cut or division or split, with the purpose of separating one thing from another. The mark belongs with the "mythical" past, the "sign" with the "historical" present (Benjamin, 1996, p. 84). Benjamin's fragmentary observations suggest a slippage between modes of representation of great significance for the modern engagement with artistic meaning and production, the implications of which he goes on to explore in *The Work of Art*. In the half-concealed genealogy of the artwork in Benjamin's evolving thought, the essential informing element in the identification of the "absolute mark" or the "symbolic" is temporal presence. This is effaced and neutralized in modernity as a result of wide-ranging theological and technological change, which sees the religious *image* become a secular *re-presentation* (most militantly in the Calvinist assault on the Catholic doctrine of transubstantiation) and which encloses dialogic meaning in visible inscription.

Like Benjamin, Walter Ong closely equates this alteration in thought with the arrival of the processes of print and their intrinsic "sense of closure and completeness" (Ong, 1982, p. 132). Print divides even as its signifies. It embeds the word in the logic of manufacturing, and in so doing commodifies text. It fixes words in defined space, abandoning the immanence of the voice and fulfilling both the material promise (distance) and threat (control) of writing. Print relegates the symbolic to atemporal exposition and affords allegory the potentially fixed surface of the blank page for which it has always longed. In its enthronement of duplication and copying, print turns all "marks" into fragments and all texts into commentaries on a perpetually irretrievable original or vanished logocentric wholeness. Print intensifies the modern perception of re-presentation as itself a state of waning or falling away. The image becomes, as Rodolphe Gasche has argued, the "re-mark" (Gasche, 1986, p. 225), signifying a condition of pervasive duplication where one representation is added to another until the proximity of originary presence is infinitely distanced. The Latin particle *re-*, originally read as "again"—meaning a renewed access to, or reiteration of, the singular image—is made subject to "the logic of *re-*," which makes everything readable under a general theory of duplication. Copying vitiates presence, until there is limitless separation between the signifier and its multiply recapitulated re-presentations. The gulf between history and tradition, which this fundamental reorientation of meaning seems to betoken, may be another name for that *mise-en-abyme* in which some contemporary postmodernists affect to delight. This is the point where, as Rosalind Krauss has commented, the foregrounding of representation on absence is "the very condition of the sign," and (post)modernity's late spatialization of the temporal is shown to be nothing less than the final reification of absence itself, "suspended between the symbolic and the real decay of matter" (Krauss, 1983, p. 33).

One of Walter Benjamin's major achievements in *The Work of Art in the Age of Mechanical Reproduction* is to embrace the "tremendous shattering of tradition which is the obverse of the contemporary crisis and renewal of humanity" (Benjamin, 1992, p. 213). As his phrasing suggests, one of the overriding intentions of the essay is to negotiate the impasse between the perceived dislocation of traditional understandings of the meaning and value of the artwork—and of representation generally—and the blind consumerist affirmation of mass reproduction and obsolescence. "Crisis and renewal" remain cardinal and complementary points of reference throughout the essay. For Benjamin, the solution to the aesthetic, political, and ethical stand-off between tradition and modernity lies in a revised understanding of technology and its impact on the metaphysics of presence. Interestingly, for Benjamin, "print is merely a special, though a particularly important, case" in the difficult genealogy of representation. "The liquidation of the traditional value of the cultural heritage" (Benjamin, 1992, p. 213) is a serious consequence of technology's encounter with the lineage of representation, but it opens up ("unfolds") new possibilities for the interaction of art and modernity, not all of which are constrained by modernity's political limitations and aggressive moral appropriations:

> One might generalise by saying: the technique of reproduction detaches the reproduced object from the domain of tradition. By making many reproductions it substitutes a plurality of copies for a unique existence. And in permitting the reproduction to meet the beholder or listener in his own particular situation, it reactivates the object produced. (Benjamin, 1992, p. 215)

The advance of technology does not stand in opposition to the claims of the traditional artwork. It is not reproached by it, but neither is it unaffected by it. Technology fulfils the goals of the Enlightenment project, but these goals are themselves altered radically by their engagement with the experience of art (as the Romantics foresaw), and art in turn is brought into a new symbiosis with technology that reanimates the power of invention in hitherto unimaginable forms. Technology irreversibly penetrates every feature of the human and draws new boundaries between nature, culture, and manufacture. There is consequently no vantage point outside of the technological reality from which to maintain the separation of art as a privileged category of experience. Far from demeaning art, however, this state of affairs invests it with unparalleled relevance. It vindicates the method of immanent criticism by requiring that the work of art be read as always already inscribed with its subsequent technological reproductions, which are then read back into its essential "authenticity." The focus of critique is neither abstract formalism nor the cruder historical mimesis Benjamin saw in the ideas of some of his Marxist contemporaries. The relationship between the work of art and everything that surrounds it is one of circulation, exchange, and negotiation, and not detached transcendence or social reflection. The existence of technological reproduction deepens discursive appreciation and underlines the uniqueness of the work of art "inseparable from its being embedded in the fabric of tradition" (Benjamin, 1992, p. 217).

The paradox of technology leading to the recovery of tradition remains rigorously compatible with Benjamin's sense, in *The Work of Art,* that technological reproduction initiates a decisive break with past uses of art. Benjamin outlines three separate historical stages in the genealogy of the artwork in Western culture and its relation to tradition (Caygill, 1998, pp. 93–97). In the first, the artwork is inherently cultic and articulates its presence through magic and religious ritual. In the second, early modern phase, the artwork sheds religious value but acquires the fetishistic status of "authenticity," explicitly associated with originality and autonomy in post-Kantian German idealist aesthetics. Benjamin cleverly sees in this apparently far-reaching shift the continuing "trace" of the art object's former cultic cache. At the third, modern stage—essentially that of mechanical reproduction—the archaic connection to ritual and cult is finally relinquished, to be replaced by an uncompromising rootedness in the sociopolitical and ethical textures of history. Mechanical reproduction strips all posthumous disguise and mystification from the artwork and foregrounds the modern material relations of creation and reception:

> For the first time in world history, mechanical reproduction emancipates the work of art from its parasitical dependence on ritual. To an ever greater degree the work of art produced becomes the work of art designed for reproducibility . . . Instead of being based on ritual, it begins to be based on another practice—politics. (Benjamin, 1992, p. 218)

The cancellation of art's affiliations with ritual and aesthetics does not imply another damaging rupture in the fabric of modernity. One of Benjamin's most remarkable insights into the condition of modernity comes in his suggestion that the advent of mechanical reproduction offers a healing of the division of the temporal and the spatial, and, indeed, prompts a recognition of its ontological illusoriness. His invocation in *The Work of Art* of the concept of "aura" is his most polemical statement of this. "Aura" and the "auratic" start off in the essay as spatiotemporal references to the artwork's uniqueness and "authenticity": "Even the most perfect reproduction of a work of art is lacking in one element: its presence in time and space, its unique existence at the place where it happens to be" (Benjamin, 1992, p. 214). Denying the ontological primacy of the original, the essay nonetheless proposes "that which withers in the age of mechanical reproduction is the aura of the work of art" (Benjamin, 1992, p. 215). The nimbus of plastic, imaginative expression that adhered to the singular, elevated art object of tradition is steadily displaced by reproductive actions that carry it through history, whether these be subtle alterations in its physical condition, changes of ownership and consumption, or the instrumental uses to which it is put. The nuances drawn from the term "reproduction" when it is discussed in the context of the art object's elusive "aura" reflect an important development in the conceptual range of the essay. "Reproduction" comes to refer not just to tangible replicas of a hallowed original, but to every conceivable intervention of the artwork in history and every potential inclusion of history in the artwork. Reproduction occurs everywhere and every time the art object makes its presence felt because the "unique existence of the work of art determined the history to which it was subject throughout the time of its existence" (Benjamin, 1992, p. 215). The art object's future history is already inscribed on its originary condition, and reproduction simply makes explicit the basis of all of its possible representations, whether realized or not. These are then retroactively incorporated into any and all critical engagements with the art object and become inseparable from its completion and its spatiotemporal "authenticity": "The authenticity of a thing is the essence of all that is transmissible from its beginning, ranging from its substantive duration to its testimony to history it has experienced" (Benjamin, 1992, p. 215). The authentic dimension of a work was once thought of as its unattainable, hieratic essence, exempt from the measure of even the most apophatic criticism. For Benjamin the liberating advent of mechanical reproduction reveals that "authenticity" resides in precisely the opposite of this: in the limitless capacity of the art object to generate its own representation and to make itself subject to the pleasures of interpretation.

The emphasis in *The Work of Art* on "transmissibility" sharpens Benjamin's already acute sensitivity to the potential future histories of art being unlocked by the definitively modern technologies of photography and film. Film, especially, stimulated Benjamin because of its ambitious nontranscendental collapse of the tension between the spatial and the temporal, the symbolic and the allegorical. As even its name implies, film is the ultimate infinitely flattened cultural form, projected onto pure surface, which nonetheless commands privileged access to depth, movement, interdisciplinary hybridity, mass appeal, and reproducibility. It also aspires to these artistic freedoms from a highly dependent base in the complex layering of modern technology. Near the end of *The Work of Art,* Benjamin identifies film, with astonishing foresight, as the modern art form most attuned to the needs of mass audiences, and most likely to reconcile the rival demands of elite culture and popular entertainment in a "progressive" aesthetic. Precisely because of its roots in the boundless potential of industrial technology, film possesses the capacity to push back the limits of modern experience and probe the recesses of the new forms of consciousness emerging in the late capitalist polity. This last claim Benjamin supports with insightful reference to Freud's *The Psychopathology of Everyday Life,* which he uses to strengthen his prophetic assertion that film "extends our comprehension of the necessities which rule our lives." It

> manages to assure us of an immense and unexpected field of action. Our taverns and our metropolitan streets, our offices and furnished rooms, our railroad stations and our factories appeared to have locked us up hopelessly. Then came the film and burst this prison world asunder by the dynamite of the tenth of a second, so that now, in the midst of its far flung ruins and debris, we calmly and adventurously go travelling. (Benjamin, 1992, p. 229)

The whole artistic apparatus of film—its technological generic procedures and its resultant narrative and representational techniques—permit it to imagine and re-imagine, with psychological acuteness and grand specular ambition, the characteristically modern zones of our lived experience. The capacity of film for "awakening ... unconscious optics" breaks down the disabling intuitive polarities of the spatiotemporal impasse of late modern culture (Benjamin, 1992, p. 230). In its acts of re-imagining, film dispels the obliviousness of modern life and "replaces" "an unconsciously penetrated space" with "a space consciously explored by man" (Benjamin, 1992, p. 230). It is the art form that, by virtue of its reproducibility, recaptures the temporal energies of tradition and reconnects them intact to the spatialized sensibilities of modern consciousness.

In its concluding passages on the participatory aesthetic of film, *The Work of Art* succeeds in overcoming the specular *aporia* visible in *Origin*'s melancholy account of early modern spectator art, while at the same time moving into the terrain of the most intrinsically collective and voyeuristically observed experience in all of modernity: the city. The impedimenta of film's habitual visual subject matter—streets, offices, railroad stations, factories—paraphrase the city, which steadily emerges in Benjamin's mature thought as the "lens" through which all of the contradictory imagery of modernity is to be refracted. Accordingly, the presentation of the conditions for the possible imagined experience of urban modernity in Benjamin's final unfinished work, *The Arcades Project,* entails a critique of the reconfiguration of spatiotemporal experience in late capitalism that borrows heavily from the empowering insights and critical practices of film. The relationship between *The Arcades Project* and *The Work of Art* is sustained by the key claims made in the earlier work about the potentially mobilizing properties of the reproducible artwork when its full engagement with history is recognized and affirmed. *The Arcades Project* advances a series of interlocking articulations of urban modernity in which the registering consciousness of the artist-critic exploits the technological processes of montage, derealization, and the proxemic image pattern uniquely associated with the operations of film as the new critical methods for grasping the dispersed experiences of the city. The promise contained in film's generic disposition toward experience is tested by the fissiparous topologies of the city, which otherwise defeat tradition and exhaust all efforts to accord them the formal coherence of art.

By placing the "arcade"—the futuristic shopping malls of mid nineteenth-century Paris—at the center of his critical audit of the city, Benjamin aligns his most ambitious undertaking with the documentary gaze of the camera, which eschews the conventionally political and hierarchically conceived histories of urban identity in favor of what is revealed at the incidental edges and margins of the metropolis (Gilloch, 1997, pp. 139–148). "These arcades, a recent invention of industrial luxury, are glass-roofed, marble paneled corridors extending through whole blocks of buildings.... Lining both sides of these corridors, which get their light from above, are the most elegant shops, so that the arcade is a city, a world in miniature" (Benjamin, 1999b, p. 31). The arcades' imagery of light and glass is the signature of the city's spectral identity, in contrast to the anthropological or social terrain of the "street." The street is the "exterior" place of reason and political organization, the arcade the "interior" landscape of capitalism's imaginary life; its unconscious of the fetishized commodity where the material processes of production and consumption are mystified and made holy. The arcades are, for Benjamin, "temples": "the dream-house of the arcades is encountered again in the church. Encroachment of the architectural style of the arcades on sacred architecture" (Benjamin, 1999b, pp. 37, 408). They represent the capitalist acumination of modern commodified and linearized space, yet they also harbor the longing for a refurbished experience of the symbolic and the temporal, and by their once extraordinary material resources come close to its realization. They are the conflicted precincts of loss and attainment in capitalism's profligate narratives of manufacture, scarcity, and consumption.

Part of the appeal of the arcades as the fragmented master text of modernity's secret history is, for Benjamin, forensic. They are, to all intents and purposes, ruins. By the time of Benjamin's writing the Paris arcades had long fallen into neglect and near-abandonment. This makes them "citable" as indices of the waning of a modernity whose meaning is decoded only at the point of its dissolution and whose unravelling mocks the pretensions of progress. Such a reading of the arcades has led some critics to see the whole project of Benjamin's last years as fundamentally melancholic in outlook (Buck-Morss, 1989, p. 79). There is certainly merit in this viewpoint. Dialectics may have been Benjamin's preferred mode for reconstructing the lost possibilities within the arcades phenomenon, but in his overarching theory, the particular details of its history are neither fully amenable to transcendent intervention nor sufficiently situated within material contradictions projecting determinate "emancipatory possibilities" of the kind championed by *The Work of Art*. What is to be done with the arcades except the mourning of the fading histories of acquisition and deprivation ("civilisation" and "barbarism") trapped within them? Benjamin always presupposes the transcendent potential of the material object, in messianic fashion. Existing in an allegorical universe, where each element of the past is always messianically recoverable in the "here and now," the signification of the arcades appears directly in relation to that of the other products of capitalist culture that the massive undertaking of *The Arcades Project* explores. Even in their dereliction, allegory supplies the arcades with signification and with the endless possibility of transformation, just as it subverts the concerns of historical materialism with determinacy and mediation and the traces of real human suffering. By the same token, however, dealing with such concerns robs the arcades of their alleged allegorical transcendence. While the need for a concrete appropriation makes an allegorical interpretation impossible, the emphasis on allegorical transcendence undercuts the ability of any interpretation of the arcades to offer a fully materialist means of appropriating its object. This conundrum, it could be argued, paralyzes the act of immanent reading without which the arcades possess only an antiquarian value.

Benjamin's solution to this series of problems emerges most directly in his theory of "the dialectical image," which attempts to make a significant advance on the already liberating principle of reproducibility. Within the logic of reproducibility it would be imperative to read the arcades as an art object, discerning the future history already impregnated in their seemingly superannuated originality. The ironic reinvention of the arcades as the twentieth-century shopping mall of postwar mass consumerism would be an example of just such an active unfolding of their "authenticity" into history. The "dialectical image" advances on this position by suggesting that the image that constitutes the object of immanent critical inspection forms an instantaneous interface in the act of reading between lost past tradition and the present yearning for intelligibility:

> The dialectical image is an image that emerges suddenly, in a flash. What has been is held fast—as an image flashing up in the now of its recognisability. The rescue that is carried out by these means—and only by these—can operate solely for the sake of what in the next moment is irretrievably lost. In this connection, see the metaphorical passage . . . concerning the prophetic gaze that catches fire from the summits of the past. (Benjamin, 1999b, p. 473)

The critical formulation of the image at work in Benjamin's attempt to make sense of the diverse simultaneity of the amnesiac metropolis and its subjugation to linear concepts of progress borrows directly from the materialist messianism of his much earlier view of history. History is always, we recall, about to be interrupted by the terrible angel of temporal accountability. The anarchic energies of the city are not resolvable into the cultural salience of the commodified art object. The city is simply too cacophonous, too crowded with difference. But the city of late modernity can nevertheless be comprehended by an immanent criticism that avoids the traps of externality, whether temporal or spatial. The pervasiveness of technology confirmed the boundless horizon of history. There is no view from nowhere. The city must be read or unfolded from the inside, where tradition is always already breaking in wherever the potentialities of the image are recognized and embraced:

> It is not that what is past casts its light on what is present, or what is present its light on what is past; rather, image is that wherein what has been comes together in a flash with the now to form a constellation. In other words, image is dialectics at a standstill. For while the relation of the present to the past is a purely temporal, continuous one, the relation of what-has-been to the now is dialectical: is not progression, but image, suddenly emergent. (Benjamin, 1999b, p. 462)

Seen in the flaring light of the dialectical image, the Paris arcades can be read as the syntax of the capitalist unconscious. Like some Rosetta Stone of immanent criticism, the disused arcades are the keys to unlocking the polysemous narratives of the city, and, by implication, of modernity as a fractured whole. They afford critique a language of imagery and allegorical explication through which a commerce with tradition can be intermittently rearticulated at the heart of modernity. Down the sudden vistas of the contemporary urban landscape that the dialectical image momentarily illuminates, the "new *flaneur*," the critic—who is modernity's true wandering magus—finds in architecture, topography, cinema, fashion, books, music, law, prostitution, transport, shops, photography, food, money, crime, domesticity—all of the disposable phantasmagoria of the polyglot metropolis that *The Arcades Project* vainly aspires to encompass—fragmentary witnesses to the forgotten possibilities and abandoned futures of a dreaming civilization. The messianic obligation of the urban critic is therefore what it always has been in Benjamin's major writing: to proclaim that "the Now of recognizability is the moment of awakening" (Benjamin, 1999b, p. 486), and to herald the end of modernity's enchanted sleep of oblivion, when its catastrophic fantasy of progress is brought abruptly face-to-face with the wreckage of history (Santer, 2001, pp. 56–60).

The waning of modernity—which is the prophetic, emancipatory message that immanent criticism ultimately discovers in the disused arcades—represents for Benjamin the oncoming disintegration of the spatialized understanding of time and the corresponding melodrama of progress. As modernity slips into what may be its final, terminal phase, relentlessly propelled to a new threshold of change by a vertiginously accelerating technology of actual flattened surfaces and virtual imaginary depths, then in each of its constructs can now be read with increasing transparency the spectral palimpsest of repressed pasts and unbounded futures ideology strives vainly to recuperate. The skylines of today's great cities rise and fall with a violence even Benjamin would have been hard-pressed to anticipate, and every disenchanted edifice conveys with a fluency and volubility no monumental order can repress the many competing and complementary narratives coexisting behind its impotent mythic façade. Whether we decipher in the contemporary representations of a passing age flashing evanescently before us from a thousand glassy surfaces the brutal discourses of globalization, the clash of civilizations, or just the sum of human lives melting into air, the legacy of Walter Benjamin helps us to recover all of these texts from behind the mystifying veil of modernity's melancholy and forgetful tears.

ON HAVING AND BEING: THE HUMANISM OF ERICH FROMM

> *The less you* are, *the less you express your life, the more you* have, *the greater is your* alienated *life and the greater is the saving of your alienated being.*
> —Karl Marx (in Fromm, 1961, p. 144)

Introduction

Erich Fromm was born in Frankfurt am Main in 1900 into an orthodox Jewish family. He practiced the faith of his parents until he was 26. Fromm studied the Old Testament closely as a young man and studied the Talmud with rabbis in Frankfurt and Heidelberg prior to and during his university years. As a university student he studied jurisprudence, philosophy, psychology, psychiatry, and sociology, completing his doctoral study on the sociopsychological structure of three Jewish Diaspora communities in 1922 (Funk, 2000). His reading of Marx resonated with his strong interest in the radical humanism he found in the messianic vision of the Old Testament prophets Amos, Isaiah, and Hosea (ibid.). After completing his doctorate he further studied psychiatry and psychology in Munich and during 1928 to 1930 was trained in psychoanalysis in Munich and Berlin.

Shortly after cofounding the South German Institute for Psychoanalysis in Frankfurt in 1930, Fromm joined the Institute for Social Research at Frankfurt University, from which the "Frankfurt School" of critical theory emerged. Recognizing Fromm's expertise in psychoanalysis, Max Horkheimer invited Fromm to membership in the Institute's four-member core group and to become a life associate. Fromm accepted and worked with the school in its German, Swiss, and U.S.

incarnations until 1939, when he parted—following attacks by Horkheimer and Marcuse on his particular appropriation of Freud.

Throughout his life Fromm drew on three main intellectual influences—Freud, Marx, and religious-theological currents (principally Judaic, Christian, and Buddhist)—to develop a socialist humanist ideal based on "a dynamic analysis of the economic, political, and psychological forces that form the basis of society" (Fromm, 1970, p. 21). It is important to delineate Fromm's humanism (and that of Marx before him), which views humanity as part of nature (human nature), from the highly anthropocentric tradition of humanism characteristic of late Scholasticism (Southern, 1995). The latter has tarnished humanism as the basis for social theory among influential contemporary groups interested in transformative social practice. For Fromm and Marx alike, humanity—human nature—is part of nature more generally. From the standpoint of socialist humanism, what humans *are* and how they *be* are intimately related to the nonhuman world.

Fromm's humanism was based on the idea that the human unconscious "represents the entire person . . . and all of humanity" (Funk, 1997, p. 10). In Fromm's view, human cultures and individuals have diverse potential for what they *may* become. What they *do* become, however, depends largely on "which possibilities are cultivated and which are hindered and repressed" (ibid.). This in turn depends greatly on the kind of society an individual lives in, since all humans can exist only as social beings. They must be socialized to want to do and be what they must do and be in order for the society to function. Hence, according to Fromm, "social necessities become transformed into personal needs, into the 'social character'" (Fromm, 1964a, p. 76). Consequently, "our conscious mind represents mainly our own society and culture, while our unconscious represents the universal [human being] in each of us" (Fromm, 1964b, p. 93; Funk, 1997, p. 10).

Among Fromm's many publications, his best known include *Escape from Freedom* (1941), *Man for Himself* (1947), *The Sane Society* (1955), *The Art of Loving* (1956), *Marx's Concept of Man* (1961), *The Heart of Man* (1964), *The Anatomy of Human Destructiveness* (1973), and *To Have or to Be?* (1978). Fromm died in 1980.

Overview

In this chapter I want to focus on the distinction Fromm developed in his final major published work between *having* and *being,* as two fundamental human orientations toward the self and the world. In explicating this distinction, Fromm built creatively on ideas advanced by Marx in his *Economic and Philosophical Manuscripts,* where Marx (1844/1961) observed that

> [p]rivate property has made us so stupid and partial that an object is only *ours* when we have it, when it exists for us as capital or when it is directly eaten, drunk, worn, inhabited, etc., in short, *utilized* in some way. . . . [A]ll the physical and intellectual senses have been replaced by the simple alienation of *all* these senses; the sense of

having. The human being had to be reduced to this absolute poverty in order to be able to give birth to all his [or her] inner wealth. (144–145)

I will try to show why Fromm believed that the having mode, which prevails under (post)industrial capitalism, is destructive, debilitating, and dangerous for the prospects of human fulfillment and mutual well-being. On the basis of this account, I will then try to show by means of a specific case how the having mode "gets into" even the most ordinary aspects of everyday lives. This case involves participation in the eBay.com (would-be) *community*. It provides a microcosm of what can happen when new aspects of human relatedness come under the logic of the having mode of experience and existence.

Human Propensities: The Human Condition, Human Nature, and the Social Structure

To Have or to Be? proved to be Fromm's final major work in his long-term study of selfishness and altruism as basic human character orientations. He believed that pursuing a viable future for people and their world depended on reversing the powerful socially encouraged tendency toward selfishness evident throughout the "advanced" (post)industrial capitalist world. This, he argued, called for renouncing ways of life lived under the *having* mode of existence and moving progressively toward ways of life lived under the *being* mode of existence. Such a renunciation would require changes at both the individual and societal levels.

Fromm presents two opposing accounts of human nature and the human condition. These provide a useful entry point to his ideas about having and being. Fromm believes the first account provides key ideological underpinnings for industrial capitalism and, in our own time, informational or knowledge capitalism. It follows from this view that *having* is the natural and inevitable human orientation toward self and world. The second account is the view Fromm promotes. It maintains that *being* (and altruism) is an entirely open option for humans and, moreover, that it is the only option that enables self-actualization, fulfillment, and abiding peace.

According to the first account, the aim of human life is happiness, which consists in *pleasure* defined as satisfaction of the wants and needs we feel. From this perspective, egotism and self-interest are seen as leading naturally to harmony. Each person pursuing their own interests within recognized legitimate limits in a market of satisficers (goods and services) that is kept as unregulated as possible is, allegedly, the best guarantee of conditions under which humans can realize their life aims. Fromm notes that a particular view of human nature accompanies this conception of the human condition. It presumes that humans are "basically lazy [and] passive by nature" and that they "do not want to work ... unless driven by the incentive of material gain" or else coerced by hunger or fear of punishment (Fromm, 1978, p. 103). It is the view of human nature that underpins neoclassical and neoliberal theories of political economy.

Against this view, which he claims dominates consciousness in contemporary modern Western societies, Fromm presents a second account of the human condition and human nature. According to this view, the human condition and human nature are characterized by two crucial features. One is "the biological urge for survival." This tends to predispose human beings toward the *having* mode. The other feature is the *species* character unique to human beings, which combines "minimal instinctive determination" with "maximal development of the capacity for reason" (ibid., p. 107). As a result of this unique species structure, humans have "lost [their] original oneness with nature." Other animals remain "submerged" or "immersed" in nature. But having consciousness—including consciousness that they are alone, or *individuated*—humans have the capacity to experience existential aloneness (see also Fromm, 1941). As a result, says Fromm, "in order not to feel utterly isolated" humans need to establish "a new unity: with our fellow beings and with nature" (Fromm, 1978, p. 107). Humans can effect this unity or relatedness in very different ways, however. For example, we can seek unity in relations with others of domination or submission (authoritarian forms) or by relating equally with them (dialogical or loving forms). We can seek unity through acts of sadism toward others, at one extreme, and by "acts of utter solidarity" at the other (ibid.). In short, we can pursue unity in so many ways through *having* other people or nature, or through *being* with them. On the basis of this account Fromm concludes that "both the having and the being modes are potentialities of human nature" (ibid., p. 103).

> Our biological urge for survival tends to further the having mode, but . . . selfishness and laziness are not the only propensities inherent in human beings. [In addition] human beings have an inherent and deeply rooted desire to be: to express our faculties, to be active, to be related to others, to escape the prison cell of selfishness. (ibid.)

In other words, both tendencies—to *have*, expressed in possessive individualism, and to *be*, expressed in sharing, giving, and even sacrificing—are "present in human beings" (ibid., p. 108). These opposed and opposing tendencies owe their strength to different aspects of human nature and the human condition. That is, so far as *human constitution* is concerned, we are "set up" with the potential to orient ourselves to self and world in either the having or the being mode. Given this, Fromm concludes that whichever orientation prevails within a society will be shaped by "the social structure, its values and norms" (ibid.).

> Cultures that foster the greed for possession, and thus the having mode of existence, are rooted in one human potential; cultures that foster being and sharing are rooted in the other potential. (ibid., p. 108)

Fromm claims that a crucial consideration for every society has to do with what quality of relatedness—the kind of union and solidarity—it fosters between persons, and between persons and nature/the world, "and the kind it *can* further" under the "given circumstances of its socioeconomic structures" (ibid.). What are the possibilities for becoming otherwise? How might people start acting in their everyday lives, or start to refrain from acting, in order to resist and seek to transform socioeconomic structures that foster *having* at the expense of *being*?

To Have or to Be? Human Orientations Toward Self and World

Having laid out some key elements of Fromm's argument for the view that having and being are both potential orientations for human beings toward self and world, but that in modern (post)industrial societies the having mode predominates, it is time now to spell out just what these two modes are. What *is* the option framed by the question "To have or to be?" ?

Fromm claims that having and being constitute two fundamental (underpinning) modes of experience and existence. They are two different kinds of orientation toward the self and the world. We can think of them as two different kinds of *character structure* within which people do and be in specific ways at myriad points in their lives. People whose characters and cultures are structured around *having* do and be (albeit with variations in detail from person to person) in different kinds of ways from people whose character and cultures are structured around being. People manifesting these different character structures "think, feel and act in different ways" (ibid., p. 33).

The distinction runs deep in ordinary language and, in many cases, may seem insignificant until we follow the logic further. In language, for example, we readily say "I have a headache." This, says Fromm, "transforms an experience [the sensation of feeling sore in the head] into something I possess." The "*I* of experience is replaced by the *it* of possession" (ibid., p. 31): that is, the "is-ness" of experience is replaced by the "thing-ness" of possession. The experience of the headache, which is part of the life-in-process that is *me* at a given time, is objectified as some separate (or alien thing) that I happen to possess. In the *having* mode I enter into a property relationship with the headache and relate to it as property (shall I get rid of it and, if so, what other sort of thing do I need as a mediator to divest myself of it?). The difference is between a state that I am experiencing — something I an actively doing or *being* — and a thing that I *have*. According to Fromm, when people are in the *having* mode, their relationship to the world and to themselves "is one of possessing and owning," where they "want to make everything and everybody — including themselves — their property" (ibid., p. 33). When they are in the being mode, by contrast, they are "alive" to the world and "authentically related" to it — directly, and as expressions of what they are as human beings, not indirectly or in an alientated way mediated by way of relationships of property.

By considering some other everyday examples we can see more tellingly the extent to which *being* sore in the head and *having* a headache underwrite different modes of existence and experience, and what is at stake between these modes.

Fromm looks at activities like learning and knowing in the *having* and *being* modes respectively. In the case of learning, students in the *having* mode attend classes, hear what is said (or what they are to read), make notes, and convert these into forms that can be used for passing exams or writing assignments. They become owners of collections of statements made by somebody else (ibid., p. 37). These are stored, guarded, or memorized, in order to be cashed in, exchanged, or capitalized on at appropriate times. In contrast, students who learn in the *being* mode have previously thought about the issues or problems involved in the course. When they hear or read what teachers and authors are saying they *respond* in active ways, producing new ideas, questions, or perspectives as they listen or read. They *produce* in the moment. This new production becomes both the moment and the *point or purpose* of learning. Learning in this mode becomes a process of putting one's capacities to work in dialogue with stimuli from the world, then and there, in order to be changed and to be challenged—a process of responding and doing, not accumulating, storing, and deferring (ibid., pp. 37–39).

In the case of knowledge, knowing in the *having* mode is an accumulative act of "taking and keeping possession of available knowledge (information)" (ibid., p. 47). Optimizing knowledge involves "having more knowledge" (ibid., p. 48). In the *having* mode, people acquire (buy, commission, contract, download) knowledge in order to have access to truth or better information—often to get a competitive edge over their potential colleagues. They do not need to actively generate this knowledge themselves. It is easier, and often more convenient, to "get it in," as one might a delivery pizza. Knowledge becomes a commodity that one can own, acquire, guard, and use as one would any other aspect of one's private property. In the *being* mode, learning is a process of knowing, meant here as critically reasoning to try and understand aspects of the world more deeply. In the *being* mode, learning is an affirmation of one's human capacity for critical reasoning. It is to be curious and intelligent, to experience ourselves relating to or interacting with some aspect of the world. The point is not to try and *get* something (like certainty) that will make us more secure in our grip on the world, or to give us an edge over our fellow humans. Not knowing something is equally attractive to the knower in the *being* mode, because it presents a further opportunity to learn. Learning becomes a matter of seeking to know more, and more deeply, which is always possible in the being mode—as opposed to "getting some knowledge in" as a pristine finished product.

For knowledge workers, like researchers, the difference between working under the two modes can be palpable. Under a *having* regime, the knowledge worker is a hired hand whose critical capacities are turned to whatever the knowledge contractor wants knowledge about. Rather than our knowing faculties being exercised for their "use value"—to affirm our being as humans and to satisfy authentic purposes that we envisage—they are made into a commodity production unit with exchange value. They are made subservient to other people's demands that may not interest us, and that we may actually find abhorrent. What passes as knowledge under such conditions can become an intensely alienating experience.

This, of course, applies to work in the *having* mode more generally, which is alienated work from the outset.

It is important to see clearly what is at stake here. When Fromm talks about the *being* mode in terms of being "alive to the world" and "authentically related to it," he has in mind processes like knowing in the *being* mode. Humans are rational creatures, with the ability to reason, to express, and to actualize. In processes of affirming this capacity by knowing because we are "moved" to know something, we authentically express who and what we are as a species. We actualize or realize what, in a very deep sense, we *are*. This is not a zero sum game. In the being mode, one person's pursuit of knowledge does not compete with or infringe that of others. Moreover, it is absolutely compatible with individuals collaborating with one another in expressing what they are as "knowers." Living as human *beings* becomes an end in itself, and this option is open to all. In the *having* mode, by contrast, there is no need at all to affirm our *being* in the process of acquiring the thing-like *[dingliche]* facts of knowledge. Moreover, knowledge readily becomes a resource that we can use to advantage ourselves over others. The point of one person knowing in the *having* mode may be precisely to prevent others knowing or getting access to "their" knowledge. Knowing becomes competitive and exclusionary, and divides people into "haves" and "have-nots." Destroying other people's knowledge, or their access to it, can become (almost) as good as having knowledge oneself. This logic is buttressed by all sorts of mechanisms designed to discourage people from thinking they can know. Only some knowledge is "genuine," "legitimate," "authoritative." This becomes a way of robbing humans of their species capacities, precisely by telling them they do not have them, thus forcing people to acquire their innate capacities from a market, or to "get" the necessary training.

A parallel example here, which shows how much is at stake in the difference between the modes, concerns *work*. In the *being* mode, work means applying our physical and mental powers to some aspect of the world in order to do something. All humans have these powers, hence all can work whenever they choose. In working they affirm their species being (as in knowing, which can be seen as a form of work), they express themselves, and experience a sense of engagement and realization. In the *having* mode, work means having a job, and applying our physical and mental powers to some aspect of the world that someone else has designated. In the *having* mode, if one does not *have* a job one is not considered to be working. Under market conditions of less-than-full employment, for one person to have a job necessitates that another does not. When income is tied to having jobs, things can become dangerous. People without jobs believe they *cannot* work, have no worth, and may become passive and debilitated, or frustrated and destructive, and so on. They are robbed of the capacity to do what humans innately do because they are not permitted to see their life activities as work, and may hence lose the incentive to engage and affirm their human capacities.

Finally, for present purposes, we may consider identity from the respective standpoints of *having* and *being*. Fromm discusses identity in the *having* mode in relation to *ego,* in the sense of perceiving our ego as something we possess, and where this thing is the basis for our sense of identity. According to Fromm,

> Our ego is the most important object of our property feeling.... [I]t comprises many things: our body, our name, our social status, our possessions (including our knowledge), the image we have of ourselves and the image we want others to have of us. (ibid., p. 77)

In the *having* mode we feel our ego as *a thing we possess:* the ego we *have* that becomes the basis for the identity we have, or need to get and, having got it, to defend, invest in, build up, shore up, and so on. In this mode the ego is not just something I have, but something I can *build and add to* by having "it." Thus "I have X" (an object, a reputation, a CV, a certain status) becomes the definition of an "I." In the statement "I have X," says Fromm, "the subject is not *myself*." Rather, it is *"I am what I have,"* since "my property constitutes myself and my identity" (ibid., p. 82). Furthermore, because "I" depends on having "it" then "it has *me*" (ibid., p. 83). Subjecthood is destroyed and relegated to the realm of dead matter. The *having* mode makes *things* of subject and object alike. Take the "it" away and the "I" collapses. In the remaining sections of this chapter we will see just what this can mean in concrete instances.

In the *being* mode we are what we express and enact in our relationships with others and the world. We do not *have* an ego and an identity based on it. Rather, we *be,* moment by moment, in the ways we affirm our specifically human nature, which comprises "activity, critical thinking, [and] faith in life" (ibid., p. 85). In the *being* mode individuals are indeed *identifiable* and "identitied." But identity is simply not an issue for them as it is in the *having* mode. A *having* identity is constructed as a possession we are encouraged to invest in and draw upon. Beings who are continually and actively engaged in affirming their capacities have no need to possess an identity, not least because they are not in competition with others for scarce resources (prestige, status, power, possessions) out of which to carve the things of identity, which may in turn be drawn upon for investment in an identity. They can just get on with living, as do others around them. In this way they are able to cooperate, share, enter egalitarian relationships, help, encourage, and support others because *being* is not a zero sum game.

Fromm argues that the having mode, or

> the attitude centered on property and profit, necessarily produces the desire—indeed the need—for power... In the having mode, one's happiness lies in one's superiority over others, in one's power, and in the last analysis, in one's capacity to conquer, rob, kill. In the being mode it lies in loving, sharing, giving. (ibid., pp. 86–87)

In this context it is important to note that when he talks about *having* as a mode of existence and experience, Fromm is talking about what he calls *characterological* having, not what he calls *existential* having. Humans, as material beings, need to have certain things in an existential sense: food, shelter, and clothing, for example. That is, Fromm does not confuse "simple possession" with private property relations (cf. Marx 1844/1961). It is not the same thing as *having to have* in the sense of a character structure—the need to live through property relations and acquisition. Rather, what has happened in the "developed" West is that we have created a world of practices and institutions whereby existential having is now *predicated* on characterological having, to the point where it is hard to see the distinction, and hard to contemplate the former without the latter. Yet they are conceptually and ontologically distinct modes of relating with the world, and the relationship between them is contingent. In the "developed" world, however, we have learned to live the relationship as though it were necessary.

Ratings@eBay.com

What does all this mean "on the ground" and, more specifically, in the context of an emerging knowledge society and knowledge capitalism?—bearing in mind here that Marx and Fromm developed their respective distinctions between having and being under industrial capital? How can we put concrete instances to the idea that humans have a propensity for either mode but that social structure—social patterns of thought, feeling, and behaving (Fromm, 1978, p. 83)—shape the mode we are most likely to take up? How might these patterns change? To answer these questions, I want to consider an increasingly common everyday practice within societies with ready access to the Internet. This involves online buying and selling and, in this specific case, the pursuit of personal ratings as buyers and sellers within the eBay.com online trading community (netgrrrl ☆ (12) and chicoboy26 ★ [32] 2002).

eBay was among the first person-to-person auction venues to go online and is presently the world's most popular trading community (Friedman, 2000; Multex.com, 2001). By mid-2001 eBay had twenty-two million registered users buying and selling on average a million items daily from a list of three million in three thousand categories—and growing. (In August 2002 it was claiming forty-nine million users.)

Friedman (2000, p. 202) identifies eBay as a "shaper": an agent shaping up activities within a globalized world of networked coalitions and practices. Friedman sees eBay as a leader in creating a whole new marketplace and instigating an entirely new set of "interaction protocols for buyers and sellers on the World Wide Web" (ibid.).

At the heart of eBay's business process is a simple rating scale and feedback system through which buyers can rate and respond to the effectiveness of sellers, and vice versa. This has changed relations between buyers on the Internet. It has also, however, elevated to prominence in the identity-shaping behavior of many participants the practice of pursuing a positive ratings profile. eBay uses a three-point rating scale—positive, neutral, and negative—and stands as a public judgment of the reputation, trustworthiness, and reliability of a person. Once an auction transaction has been completed, the buyer can leave feedback about the seller and vice versa. Only the buyer and seller are authorized to comment on a particular transaction. Feedback comprises the actual rating (positive, neutral, negative) and a written recommendation.

eBay reminds participants that "[h]onest feedback shapes the community" (eBay, 2001a). The higher their positive ratings the more "trustworthy" and "reliable" participants are in eBay terms. eBayers are clear about the importance of their ratings. Many go to extraordinary lengths to obtain positive ratings and construct elaborate processes aimed at ensuring as many positive feedback statements and ratings as possible:

> I have a spreadsheet that i use to keep track of my items, buying and selling and there is a space for me to check off that i have left feedback for a buyer/seller. When the buyer/seller leaves feedback for me in return, i circle the check mark, letting me know the transaction has come full circle. when i sell something, i include a thank you card with the item number listed, the item name listed, my ebay name and a note stating that i have left positive feedback for them and would appreciate the same in kind and i still have problems getting them to leave me feedback! So every month, i go down the spreadsheet and e-mail those who have failed to leave feedback asking them why they have not done so and if there were problems i was not aware of. this is very time consuming but it has worked on most of the delinquents. it more or less embarrasses them into leaving feedback. (eBay, 2001b)

From a different standpoint, participants often prefer to be "duped" by buyers than risk negative feedback. *Bea1997* explained:

> Sometimes I lose money from customers who break an item and ask for money back. I just don't want to risk having my good reputation ruined for a few lousy bucks so I just take the blame and send their money back. (e-mail interview, 25/09/2000)

This tallies with others reported elsewhere. Erick Sherman (2001) recounts:

> Both buyers and sellers get burned from time to time, but usually not badly. Shamus remembers someone who bought a $25 trading card from him on eBay then returned it, but with a corner newly bent. "He said, 'That's what you sent me,'" says Shamus, who didn't argue because the amount was too small and negative feedback would hurt his future sales. (63)

Exchanges on the feedback discussion board can get heated, with little evidence of the kind of tolerance expected in a community of the kind eBay aims to foster:

> . . . and i agree if you knew the answer why bother asking? i get lots of people asking stupid ? [trans: questions] like what does it measure? when it is already posted on my

auctions . . . i tell them to go back and read the description. i don't find that to be rude. (discussion board, 2001)

Two people responded as follows:

- not rude? must be why you have so many successful transactions. Why not just answer the question and accept that stupid people make up a big percentage of customers?
- The guy's sarcastic, not rude. Read his very limited, posted feedback for a good laugh.

The references to the first person's "successful transactions" and "very limited posted feedback" are snide comments on his beginner status: one positive rating. These kinds of reactions indicate that ratings are read as integral to people's public reputation and also as an indicator of "wisdom" and knowledge in matters eBay.

Within this milieu a new lexis is rapidly emerging. It includes items like "feedback bombing," "feedback extortion," and "retaliatory negative feedback." In one version of feedback bombing, two or more people gang up on someone, purchase products, then leave negative feedback. Feedback extortion involves demanding some action from a fellow user that he or she is not required to do, at the threat of leaving negative feedback. Retaliatory negative feedback occurs when a negative feedback rating is given to one person in a transaction by the other and the first responds with a negative rating, regardless of the quality of service received. This often goes with "feedback hostage taking" (e.g., "I was really unhappy with this transaction but can't leave feedback until the other party does because I want to leave a negative feedback but am worried that if I leave it first then the person I'm dealing with will give me a negative feedback in response!").

Having and Being Had

The data presented in the previous section can be read as a sad and sorry, but not unfamiliar, tale of social practices in the *having* mode. Participants hang so much on possessing positive ratings that they will go to almost any length to get them and to deny them to others. Possibilities of spontaneous, decent, person-to-person trading interactions are seemingly undermined by what might initially look like a good idea: public evaluations of people's interactions. Under the *having* mode, this becomes a pretext for building status, bolstering ego, acquiring elements of an identity. Acting in good faith becomes alienated. We end up with the precise opposite of the idea expressed by the thirteenth-century theologian Meister Eckhart, cited approvingly by Fromm:

"People should not consider so much what they are to do as what they are . . . Thus take care that your emphasis is laid on being good and not on the number or kind of things to be done. Emphasise rather the fundamentals on which your work rests." Our being is the reality, the spirit that moves us, the character that impels our behaviour; in contrast, the deeds of opinions that are separated from our dynamic core have no reality. (Fromm, 1978, p. 70)

The data reported above betrays a perversion of human possibility. We find precisely those things Fromm associates with the *having* mode that are inimical to mutual human well-being. We find recourse to power and various forms of manipulation (extortion, retaliation, bombing, hostaging, coercion, bribery) in order to try and get/have more positive ratings. We find acts of destruction and animosity directed toward other people who have unwittingly made themselves vulnerable to these. It is hard to fathom the quiet depth of malice involved in bending the corner of a card and returning it with the charge that the seller, who was acting in good faith, was the perpetrator of a dishonest act. This, however, is not too far removed from all manner of destructive and power-tripping practices associated with *having*. Examples like damning colleagues with faint praise, or damning them outright behind privileges of anonymity within reviewing or refereeing situations readily come to mind within academic contexts. Readers will be able to produce countless examples from their own walks of life.

From a different angle, we see all too clearly examples of the *having* mode destroying subjecthood and making *things* of subject and object alike. The "it" of ratings has "me" to the extent of my dependence upon "it" for ego and identity. "It" has "me" so strongly that I will spend hours devising and trawling spreadsheets in order to "more or less embarrass delinquents" into providing positive feedback.

Finally, it is interesting to return to Marx's idea of "inner wealth"—the wealth that is realized through humanizing relationships to other humans and to nature, through which we actualize our "species character"—wealth that is born of *need* for meaningful human relatedness with the *other* (Marx, 1844/1961, p. 138). Our inner wealth is constituted precisely through meaningful relations like trust, love, reciprocity, caring, and so on. In the light of the kind of data presented above—which, of course, are replicated in diverse social practices constituted within contemporary discourses like "accountability" and "quality assurance"—we may well ask whether trust and reciprocity and fidelity are now "things" that "can be quantified and 'had' in [the] new realm of exchanges" within the eBay community (Phil Graham, personal communication). The incorporation of virtual spaces into heartlands of e-capitalism and a knowledge economy intensifies the potential for alienating our inner wealth, just as relations of private property integral to early and industrial capitalism had previously and ever more intensely alienated our "outer wealth."

Much more could be said by way of analysis of the data here, but that might run the risk of taking perversions too seriously. The point, rather, has to do with how easy it is to find concrete instances of the negation of human(izing) potential almost anywhere we care to look once we apply the kind of critique Fromm makes possible through his account of "having." Equally sobering is the corresponding relative difficulty of finding bona fide examples of *being* within vast tracts of our lives as institutionally regulated participants in the (post)industrial capitalist dream. To this extent, Fromm's critique of having and being, which is forged within the context of a larger humanist project, provides rich and ready clues as to where and how we might practice transformative action within the most ordinary routines of our everyday lives in pursuit of a better world.

Note

I want to thank Phil Graham for his insightful reading of the original version of this text. I am also indebted to Michele Knobel for collaborating with me in the work on eBay.com.

4

Douglas Kellner

MARCUSE AND THE QUEST FOR RADICAL SUBJECTIVITY

The past decades have witnessed a relentless philosophical assault on the concept of the subject, once the alpha and omega of modern philosophy. Materialists have decried the idealist and essentialist dimensions of the traditional concept of the subject in its various Cartesian, Kantian, and other philosophical forms. More recently, poststructuralist and postmodern theorists have attacked the universalizing pretensions of subject discourse, its positing of a (false) unity, its assuming a centered and grounded status as a linchpin for philosophical systems or knowledge-claims, and its transparent self-certainty from Descartes' cogito to Husserl's phenomenology. Following Nietzsche, poststructuralists have seen the subject as an effect of language, constructed in accord with the forms of grammar (i.e., subject/predicate) and existing linguistic systems, or, with Deleuze, have privileged the flux and flow of bodily experience over more idealist conceptions of consciousness and the self.

For traditional philosophy, the subject was unitary, ideal, universal, self-grounded, asexual, and the foundation for knowledge and philosophy, while for the poststructuralist and postmodern critique the human being is corporeal, gendered, social, fractured, and historical with subjectivity radically decentered as an effect of language, society, culture, and history. Yet if the construction of the subject in language, the social, and nature is the key mark of a poststructuralist or postmodern conception of subjectivity, then the Frankfurt School analyses are not antithetical to such conceptions. The entire tradition of critical theory—which draws on Hegel, Marx, Nietzsche, Freud, and Weber—posits the historical and social construction of the individual, and members of this tradition can be read as providing aspects of theorizing the social construction of subjectivity in language, social interaction, and culture in specific historical contexts. Habermas in particular has followed this motif and has attacked the philosophy of the subject, while proposing replacing its subject/object model with an ego-alter model that is based on the ideal of communicative reason.[1]

In this chapter, however, I want to pursue Herbert Marcuse's sharp critiques of the rationalist subject of modern philosophy, which he counterposes to notions of libidinal rationality, eros, and the aesthetic-erotic dimensions of an embodied subjectivity. Marcuse is part of a historicist tradition of critical theory that rejects essentialism and sees subjectivity developing in history, in interaction with specific sociopolitical conditions. Following Adorno and Horkheimer and the earlier Frankfurt School tradition, Marcuse also sees dominant forms of subjectivity as oppressive and constraining, while challenging us to reconstruct subjectivity and to develop a new sensibility, qualitatively different from the normalized subjectivity of contemporary advanced industrial societies. In particular, Marcuse was engaged in a lifelong search for a revolutionary subjectivity, for a sensibility that would revolt against the existing society and attempt to create a new one.

Hence, I will argue that Marcuse and the Frankfurt School contribute important perspectives for criticizing the traditional concept of the subject and for rethinking and reconceptualizing subjectivity to develop conceptions potent enough to meet poststructuralist, postmodern, materialist, feminist, and other forms of critique. Crucially, the assault on the subject has had serious consequences, for without a robust notion of subjectivity and agency there is no refuge for individual freedom and liberation, no locus of struggle and opposition, and no agency for progressive political transformation. For these reasons, theorists from diverse camps, including feminists, multiculturalists, and poststructuralists who have had second thoughts about the all-too-hasty dissolution of the subject, have attempted to rehabilitate constructive notions of subjectivity and agency, in the light of contemporary critique.

My argument is that Marcuse anticipates the poststructuralist critique of the subject, that these critiques suggest that the traditional concept of the subject contains too much philosophical and political baggage, and that we need a reconstructed notion of subjectivity, which Marcuse and the Frankfurt School helped initiate and enabled us to further develop. In drawing on Nietzsche, Freud, and aesthetic modernism, Marcuse posits a bodily, erotic, gendered, social, and aestheticized subjectivity that overcomes mind-body dualism, avoids idealist and rationalist essentialism, and is constructed in a specific social milieu. Moreover, Marcusean subjectivity is challenged to reconstruct itself and emancipate itself from limited and oppressive forms and to pursue the project of cultivating a new sensibility. In delineating Marcuse's reconstruction of subjectivity, I'll first offer a rereading of *Eros and Civilization* to demonstrate how it anticipates the poststructuralist critique of the subject and offers an alternative conception of subjectivity. Then I pursue some of the contributions to rethinking subjectivity in Marcuse's later writings, focusing on his notion of the new sensibility and aesthetic education. At stake is developing a reconstructed Marcusean theory of subjectivity that emphasizes the need for a transformation of the affective dimension, the sensibility, and our very notion of subjectivity to help create new conceptions of subjectivity and to provide conceptions of the subjective conditions for radical social change and of agency in order to promote individual and social transformation.

Rereading *Eros and Civilization*

In *Eros and Civilization* (1955/1997; hereafter *E&C*), Marcuse draws on Freud to depict the social construction of subjectivity in the dramatic clash between the pleasure principle and the reality principle. For Freud, the instincts are originally governed by the pleasure principle: They aim solely at "gaining pleasure; from any operation which might arouse unpleasantness ('pain') mental activity draws back" (*E&C*, p. 13). From early on, however, the pleasure principle comes into conflict with a harsh environment and after a series of disciplinary experiences, "the individual comes to the traumatic realization that full and painless gratification of his needs is impossible" (*E&C*, p. 13). Under the tutelage of the reality principle, the person learns what is useful and approved behavior, and what is harmful and forbidden. In this way, one develops one's rational faculties, becoming "a conscious, thinking *subject*, geared to a rationality which is imposed on him from outside" (*E&C*, p. 14).

For Marcuse, then, rationality is a social construct and subjectivity is a product of social experience. Thus, like Foucault, Marcuse sees subjectivity not as a natural and metaphysical substance, preexisting its social gestation, but as a product of societal normalization, whereby the individual is subjected to rationalizing forms of thought and behavior. According to Marcuse's conception, the reality principle enforces the totality of society's requirements, norms, and prohibitions, which are imposed upon the individual from "outside." This process constitutes for him a domination of the individual by society that shapes thought and behavior, desires and needs, language and consciousness. In Marcuse's words: "neither his desires nor his alteration of reality are henceforth his own: they are now 'organized' by his society. And this 'organization' represses and transsubstantiates his original instinctual needs" (*E&C*, pp. 14–15).

Marcuse employs Freud's theory to produce an account of how society comes to dominate the individual, how social control is internalized, and how conformity ensues. He concludes that "Freud's individual psychology is in its very essence social psychology" (*E&C*, p. 16), and he repeatedly emphasizes that Freud's psychological categories are historical and political in nature. Hence, Marcuse boldly fleshes out the "political and sociological substance of Freud's theory" to develop what I call a *critical theory of socialization*. Whereas most theories of socialization stress its humanizing aspects by claiming that socialization makes individuals more "human"—and thus legitimate dominant social institutions and practices—Freud exposes the repressive content of Western civilization and the heavy price paid for its "progress." Although industrialization has resulted in material progress, Freud's analysis of the instinctual renunciations and unhappiness it has produced raises the question of whether our form of civilization is worth the suffering and misery (*E&C,* pp. 3ff). In Marcuse's view, Freud's account of civilization and its discontents puts in question the whole ideology of progress, productivity, and the work ethic, as well as religion and morality, by "showing up the repressive content of the highest values and achievements of culture" (*E&C,* p. 17).

Thus Marcuse, like Foucault, stresses the social construction of subjectivity and the ways that subjectification (i.e., the ways of producing a socially submissive subject) are involved in a process of domination. But whereas Foucault and many poststructuralists call for resistance to domination, they often have no theoretical resources to construct a notion of agency that would efficaciously resist repression and domination.[2] For Marcuse, however, there is a "hidden trend in psychoanalysis" that discloses those aspects of human nature that oppose the dominant ethic of labor and renunciation, while upholding "the tabooed aspirations of humanity": the demands of the pleasure principle for gratification and absence of restraint (*E&C,* p. 18). He argues that Freud's instinct theory contains a "depth dimension" that suggests that our instincts strive for a condition in which freedom and happiness converge, in which we fulfill our needs and strive to overcome repression and domination. For Marcuse, memory contains images of gratification and can play a cognitive and therapeutic role in mental life: "Its truth value lies in the specific function of memory to preserve promises and potentialities which are betrayed and even outlawed by the mature, civilized individual, but which had once been fulfilled in the dim past and which are never entirely forgotten" (*E&C,* pp. 18–19).

Marcuse subtly reformulates the therapeutic role of memory stressed in psychoanalysis. In Freud's theory, the suppression of memory takes place through the repression of unpleasant or traumatic experiences, which are usually concerned with sexuality or aggression; the task of psychoanalysis is to free the patient from the burden of repressed, traumatic memories—whose repression often produces neurosis—by providing understanding and insight that would enable the individual to work through painful experiences of the past and to dissolve neurotic behavior. Although Marcuse preserves the psychoanalytic linkage between forgetting and repression, he stresses the liberating potentialities of memory and recollection of pleasurable or euphoric experiences, as well as the unpleasant or traumatic experiences stressed by Freud.

In his reconstruction of Freud, Marcuse suggests that remembrance of past experiences of freedom and happiness could put into question the painful performances of alienated labor and manifold oppressions of everyday life. These memories are embedded in individual experiences of a happier past and historical conditions that offered more and better freedom, gratification, and happiness. Marcuse will link these emancipatory dimensions of memory with phantasy and will argue that both human beings and their cultural tradition contain resources that can be mobilized against suffering and oppression in the present.

Memory for Marcuse thus re-members, reconstructs, experience, going to the past to construct future images of freedom and happiness. Whereas romanticism is past-oriented, remembering the joys of nature and the past in the face of the onslaught of industrialization, Marcuse is future-oriented, looking to the past to construct a better future.[3] Marcuse's analysis implies that society trains the individual for the systematic repression of those emancipatory memories, and devalues experiences guided solely by the pleasure principle. Following Nietzsche in the *Genealogy of Morals,* Marcuse criticizes "the one-sidedness of memory-training in civilization: the faculty was chiefly directed towards remembering duties rather than pleasures; memory was linked with bad conscience, guilt and sin. Unhappiness and the threat of punishment, not happiness and the promise of freedom, linger in the memory" (*E&C,* p. 232).

Marcuse claims that for Freud "phantasy" is a crucial mode of "thought-activity" that is split off from the reality principle (*E&C,* pp. 14, 140ff). For Freud, phantasy "was kept free from reality-testing and remained subordinated to the pleasure principle alone. This is the act of *phantasy-making (das Phantasieren),* which begins already with the game of children, and later, continued as *daydreaming,* abandons its dependence on real objects" (*E&C,* p. 140). Building on this conception, Marcuse suggests that "phantasy—in day-dreaming, dreams at night, play, and its embodiments in art—can project images of integral gratification, pleasure, and reconciliation, often denied in everyday life.

Hence, along with memory, Marcuse argues that phantasy can imagine another world and generate images of a better life by speaking the language of the pleasure principle and its demands for gratification. He stresses the importance of great art for liberation because it refuses "to accept as final the limitations imposed upon freedom and happiness by the reality principle" (*E&C,* p. 149). Art for Marcuse practices the "Great Refusal," incarnating the emancipatory contents of memory, phantasy, and the imagination through producing images of happiness and a life without anxiety. In Marcuse's view, phantasies and hopes embody the eruption of desires for increased freedom and gratification. The unconscious on this account contains the memory of integral gratification experienced in the womb, in childhood, and in peak experiences during one's life. Marcuse holds that the "psychoanalytic liberation of memory" and "restoration of phantasy" provide access to experiences of happiness and freedom that are subversive of the present life. He suggests that Freud's theory of human nature, far from refuting the possibility of a nonrepressive civilization, indicates that there are aspects of human nature that are striving for happiness and freedom.

In defending the claims of the pleasure principle, Marcuse believes that he is remaining true to a materialism that takes seriously material needs and their satisfaction, and the biological "depth-dimension" of human nature. In his view, defense of the validity of the claims of the pleasure principle has critical-revolutionary import in that Freud's analysis implies that the human being can tolerate only so much repression and unhappiness, and when this point is passed the individual will rebel against the conditions of repression. Freud's theory thus contains elements of an *anthropology of liberation* that analyzes those aspects of human nature that furnish the potential for radical opposition to the prevailing society.

Marcuse concludes that Freud's theory contains implications that have been covered over, or neglected, and that he wishes to restore in their most provocative form. He argues that this requires a restoration of Freud's instinct theory, preserving his claims for the importance of sexuality and acknowledgment of its vital and explosive claims. Neo-Freudians who deny the primacy of sexuality have, in Marcuse's view, repressed Freud's deep insights into human sexual being by relegating sexual instincts to a secondary place in their theory (*E&C,* pp. 238ff). Marcuse believes that Freud's theory discloses the depth and power of instinctual energies that contain untapped emancipatory potential. He describes these instinctual energies that seek pleasure and gratification as "Eros." A liberated Eros, Marcuse claims, would release energies that would not only seek sexual gratification, but would flow over into expanded human relations and more abundant creativity. The released Eros would desire, he suggests, a pleasurable aesthetic-erotic environment requiring a total restructuring of human life and the material conditions of existence.

In addition, Marcuse also accepts Freud's concept of Thanatos, the death instinct, as well as the Freudian notion of "the political economy of the instincts," in which strengthening the life instincts enables Eros to control and master Thanatos, and so to increase freedom and happiness, while diminishing aggression and destruction. Thus, surprisingly, Marcuse adopts a rather mechanistic concept of the instincts, building on Freud's biologistic energy-instinct model—which has been sharply criticized and rejected within various circles of psychoanalytic theory, as well as within critical theory (Habermas and his students) and poststructuralism. I believe, however, that one can construct a Marcusean theory of subjectivity without deploying the problematic aspects of Freud's instinct theory.

The key to Marcuse's reconstruction of the concept of subjectivity, I would suggest, is the "Philosophical Interlude" in *E&C* in which he develops a critical analysis of the presuppositions of Western rationality and its concept of the philosophical subject. Marcuse claims that the prevalent reality principle of Western civilization presupposes an antagonism between subject and object, mind and body, reason and the passions, and the individual and society. Nature is experienced on this basis as raw material to be mastered, as an object of domination, as provocation or resistance to be overpowered (*E&C,* p. 110). The ego in Western thought is thus conceptualized as an aggressive, offensive subject, fighting and striving to conquer the resistant world. Through labor, the subject seeks continually to extend its power and control over nature. The Logos of this reality principle is, Marcuse argues, a logic of domination that finds its culmination in the reality principle of advanced industrial society, the performance principle. The performance principle is hostile to the senses and receptive faculties that strive for gratification and fulfillment. It contains a concept of repressive reason that seeks to tame instinctual drives for pleasure and enjoyment. Its values, which are the governing norms of modern societies, include:

> profitable productivity, assertiveness, efficiency, competitiveness; in other words, the Performance Principle, the rule of functional rationality discriminating against

emotions, a dual morality, the "work ethic," which means for the vast majority of the population condemnation to alienated and inhuman labor, and the will to power, the display of strength, virility. (*M&F*, 1974, p. 282)[4]

This hegemonic version of the reality principle has been challenged, Marcuse argues, from the beginning of Western philosophy. Against the antagonistic struggle between subject and object, an opposing ideal of reconciliation and harmony has been formulated, in which the individual strives for fulfillment and gratification. This "Logos of gratification," Marcuse suggests, is found in Aristotle's notion of the *nous theos* and Hegel's ideal of spirit coming to rest and fruition in absolute knowledge (*E&C*, pp. 112ff). In these philosophical conceptions, the human being is to attain a condition of reconciliation after a process of struggle, suffering, and labor, in which alienation and oppression are finally overcome. Schopenhauer advocates a similar idea of the restless, ever-striving "will" seeking peaceful Nirvana. In addition, Marcuse finds a logic of gratification and different conception of subjectivity in Nietzsche's emphasis on the body, the passions, joy, and liberation from time and guilt (*E&C*, pp. 119ff). The values affirmed in this reality principle would be the antithesis of the repressive performance principle and its dominating subject and would affirm

> receptivity, sensitivity, non-violence, tenderness, and so on. These characteristics appear indeed as opposites of domination and exploitation. On the primary psychological level, they would pertain to the domain of Eros, they would express the energy of the life instincts against the death instinct and destructive energy. (*M&F*, p. 284)

This alternative reality principle and conception of subjectivity also find expression in Freud's notion of the Nirvana principle, which holds that all instincts aim at rest, quiescence, and the absence of pain (*E&C*, pp. 5ff and 124ff). In addition, Marcuse draws on Schiller's conception of aesthetic education and play, arguing that in aesthetic and erotic experience, play, and fantasy, the conflict between reason and the senses would be overcome so that "reason is sensuous and sensuousness rational" (*E&C*, p. 180). Operating through the play impulse

> the aesthetic function would "abolish compulsion, and place man, both morally and physically in freedom." It would harmonize the feelings and affections with the ideas of reason, deprive the "laws of reason of their moral compulsion" and "reconcile them with the interest of the senses." (*E&C*, p. 182)

In the language of poststructuralism, Marcuse thus envisages an embodied subjectivity in which the opposition between reason and the senses, central to the modern philosophical concept of the subject, is deconstructed. For Schiller and Marcuse, the play impulse is connected with the aesthetic function, which would mediate between the passive, receptive "sensuous impulse" and the active creative "form impulse," thus reconciling reason and the senses. The play impulse aspires to a condition of freedom from restraint and anxiety, involving "freedom from the established reality: man is free when the 'reality loses its seriousness' and when its necessity 'becomes light'" (*E&C*, p. 187). This "freedom to play" and to create an "aesthetic reality" requires liberation of the senses and, as both Schiller and Marcuse called for, "a total revolution in the mode of perception and feeling" (*E&C*, p. 189).

The resultant conception of an aestheticized and eroticized subjectivity preserves the connotation of *Sinnlichkeit* as pertaining to sensuality, receptiveness, art, and eros, thus redeeming the body and the senses against the tyranny of repressive reason and affirming the importance of aesthetics, play, and erotic activity in human life. Hence, against the rational and domineering subject of mastery, Marcuse advances a notion of subjectivity as mediating reason and the senses, as seeking harmony and gratification. Thus, he affirms an intersubjective ideal of a libidinal subjectivity in harmonious and gratifying relations with others and, one might add, with nature itself. Instead of controlling and dominating objects, Marcusean subjectivity seeks gratifying and peaceful relations with others and with the external world.

Moreover, Marcuse proposes a new concept of reason, which he describes as "libidinal rationality" (*E&C*, pp. 223ff). In this conception reason is not repressive of the senses, but acts in harmony with them, helping to find objects of gratification and to cultivate and enhance sensuality. Marcuse rejects the dominant philosophical paradigm, which sees reason as the distinctly human faculty and the senses as disorderly, animalic, and inferior. The concept of reason operative in this model, Marcuse suggests, is repressive and totalitarian and does not adequately allow for aesthetic-erotic gratification and development (*E&C*, pp. 119ff), due to its embrace of the mind-body split. Marcuse's ideal is a form of human life in which reason becomes sensuous, protecting and enriching the life instincts, and whereby the unity of reason and the senses helps create a "sensuous order" (*E&C*, pp. 223ff). He assumes that as more restrictions are taken away from the instincts and as they freely evolve, they will seek "*lasting* gratification" and will help generate social relations that will make continual gratification possible. In this way, "Eros redefines reason in its own terms. Reasonable is what sustains the order of gratification" (*E&C*, p. 224). This could make possible freer, more fulfilling human relations and could create a social order and community based on freedom, gratification, cooperation, and rational authority. Then, "repressive reason gives way to a new *rationality of gratification* in which reason and happiness converge" (*E&C*, p. 224).

The New Sensibility, Emancipation, and Revolution: The Late Marcuse

Hence, against the notion of the rational, domineering subject of modern theory, Marcuse posits a subjectivity that is libidinal and embodied, evolving and developing, while striving for happiness, gratification, and harmony. Such subjectivity is always in process, is never fixed or static, and is thus a creation and goal to be achieved and is not posited as an absolute metaphysical entity. Marcusean subjectivity is corporeal, gendered, oppositional, and struggles against domination, repression, and oppression, and for freedom and happiness. There is thus nothing essentialist, idealist, or metaphysical here. Instead, Marcuse's conception of subjectivity is both materialist and socially mediated, while active in cultivating the aesthetic and erotic dimensions of experience as it strives for gratification and harmonious relations with others, nature, and itself. Marcuse's radical subjectivity is also political, refusing domination and oppression, struggling against conditions that block freedom and happiness and for a freer and better world.

There is widespread agreement today that we need the discourse of subjectivity and agency for ethics, for politics, and for the positive reconstruction of self and society. Within this context, I have argued that Marcuse's perspectives on subjectivity stand up to at least aspects of the poststructuralist and other critiques of the subject, as well as providing resources for reconstructing the concept of subjectivity in the contemporary era. It is important to note that for Marcuse the reconstruction of subjectivity, the creation of eroticized rationality, and the development of a free creative self can take place only through practice and the transformation of social relations and activity. Marcuse argued that the existing society is organized precisely to prevent such a reconstruction of subjectivity and new social relations, prescribing instead a regime of domination, authority, repression, manipulative desublimation, and submission. Especially in *One-Dimensional Man* (1964; hereafter *ODM*), but throughout his work, Marcuse presents a critique of hegemonic forms of subjectivity and domination and a challenge to overcome the one-dimensional, conformist, and normalized subjectivity of the advanced technological society.

Throughout his later writings, Marcuse was vitally concerned to discover and theorize a "new sensibility," with needs, values, and aspirations that would be qualitatively different from subjectivity in one-dimensional society. To create a new subjectivity, there must be "the emergence and education of a new type of human being free from the aggressive and repressive needs and aspirations and attitudes of class society, human beings created, in solidarity and on their own initiative, their own environment, their own *Lebenswelt*, their own 'property.'"[5] Such a revolution in needs and values would help overcome a central dilemma in Marcuse's theory—sharply formulated in *One-Dimensional Man*—that continued to haunt him: "How can the administered individuals—who have made their mutilation into their own liberties and satisfactions . . . liberate themselves from themselves as well as from their masters? How is it even thinkable that the vicious circle be broken?" (*ODM*, pp. 250–251).

In order to break through this vicious circle, individuals must transform their present needs, sensibility, consciousness, values, and behavior while developing a new radical subjectivity, so as to create the necessary conditions for social transformation (*EL*, p. 67). Radical subjectivity for Marcuse practices the "great refusal" valorized in both *E&C* and *ODM*. In *E&C* (p. 149f), the "Great Refusal is the protest against unnecessary repression, the struggle for the ultimate form of freedom—'to live without anxiety.'" In *ODM* (pp. 256ff), however, the Great Refusal is fundamentally political, a refusal of repression and injustice, a saying no, an elemental oppositional to a system of oppression, a noncompliance with the rules of a rigged game, a form of radical resistance and struggle. In both cases, the Great Refusal is based on a subjectivity that is not able to tolerate injustice and that engages in resistance and opposition to all forms of domination, instinctual and political.

In the late 1960s, Marcuse argued that emancipatory needs and a "new sensibility" were developing within contemporary society. He believed that in the New Left and counterculture there were the beginnings of "a political practice of methodical disengagement and the refusal of the Establishment aiming at a radical transvaluation of values" (*An Essay on Liberation*, 1969, hereafter *EL*, p. 6) that was generating a new type of human being and subject. The new sensibility "expresses the ascent of the life instincts over aggressiveness and guilt" (*EL*, p. 23) and contains a "negation of the needs that sustain the present system of domination and the negation of the values on which they are based" (*EL*, p. 67). Underlying the theory of the new sensibility is a concept of the active role of the senses in the constitution of experience that rejects the Kantian and other philosophical devaluation of the senses as passive, merely receptive. For Marcuse, our senses are shaped and molded by society, yet constitute in turn our primary experience of the world and provide both imagination and reason with its material. He believes that the senses are currently socially constrained and mutilated and argues that only an emancipation of the senses and a new sensibility can produce liberating social change (*EL*, pp. 24ff and *CR&R* [*Counterrevolution and Revolt*, 1972], pp. 62ff).[6]

Instead of the need for repressive performance and competition, the new sensibility posits the need for meaningful work, gratification, and community; instead of the need for aggression and destructive productivity, it affirms love and the preservation of the environment; and against the demands of industrialization, it asserts the need for beauty, sensuousness, and play, affirming the aesthetic and erotic components of experience. The "new sensibility" translates these values and needs into "a practice that involves a break with the familiar, the routine ways of seeing, hearing, feeling, understanding things so that the organism may become receptive to the potential forms of a non-aggressive, non-exploitative world" (*EL*, p. 6). This total refusal of the dominant societal needs, values, and institutions represents a radical break with the entirety of the society's institutions, culture, and lifestyle, and supplies prefigurations of a new culture and society.

The new sensibility would be developed, Marcuse claimed, by an aesthetic education that would cultivate imagination, fantasy, the senses, and memory. The new sensibility would combine the senses and reason, producing a "new rationality" in which reason would be bodily, erotic, and political. Far from being an irrationalist, Marcuse always argued that the senses and reason need to be mediated, that reason should to be reconstructed, and that critical and dialectical thinking are an important core of the new sensibility. He maintained that aesthetic education constituted a cultivation of the senses and that theory and education were essential components of transformative social change.[7]

In his writings of the late 1960s, Marcuse believed that the new sensibility was embodied in the liberation movements of the day, the counterculture, and the New Left (see, especially, *EL*). Of course, he was disappointed that the new sensibility did not become the agent of revolutionary change that he envisaged; he was also dismayed that the New Left and counterculture fell prey to the seductions of the consumer society, or were repressed and fragmented (see *Counterrevolution and Revolt,* 1972, for a poignant account of Marcuse's failing hopes and continued attempts to theorize emancipation and radical social change). In the 1970s, however, he sought precisely the same values and subjectivity in new social movements, in particular feminism, the environmental movement, the peace movement, and various forms of grassroots activism that came to be described as "new social movements."

In the 1974 lecture on "Marxism and Feminism," Marcuse notes for the first time the constitutive role of gender, while theorizing the differences between men and women in terms of his categories in *Eros and Civilization*. It is notable that his conception of the feminine is associated with the traits he ascribes to the new sensibility, while the masculine is associated with the features of the Western ego and rationality of domination that Marcuse long criticized, thus anticipating "difference feminism" that would also valorize the feminine and maternal against the masculine.[8] In this article, which generated significant debate, Marcuse argues that "feminine" values and qualities represent a determinate negation of the values of capitalism, patriarchy, and the performance principle. In his view, "socialism, as a qualitatively different society, must embody the antithesis, the definite negation of aggressive and repressive needs and values of capitalism as a form of male-dominated culture" (*M&F,* p. 285). Furthermore:

> Formulated as the antithesis of the dominating masculine qualities, such feminine qualities would be receptivity, sensitivity, non-violence, tenderness and so on. These characteristics appear indeed as opposite of domination and exploitation. On the primary psychological level, they would pertain to the domain of Eros, they would express the energy of the life instincts, against the death instinct and destructive energy. (*M&F,* pp. 285–286)

Marcuse was, however, criticized by women within the feminist movement and others for essentializing gender difference, although he insisted the distinction was a historical product of Western society and not an essential gender difference. Women, he argued, possess a "feminine" nature qualitatively different from men because they have been frequently freed from repression in the workplace, brutality in the military, and competition in the public sphere. Hence, they developed characteristics that for Marcuse are the marks of an emancipated humanity. He summarizes the difference between aggressive masculine and capitalist values as against feminist values as the contrast between "repressive productivity" and "creative receptivity," suggesting that "increased emancipation of feminine qualities in the established society" will subvert the dominant masculine values and the capitalist performance principle.

During the same decade, Marcuse also worked with Rudolf Bahro's conception of "surplus consciousness." He argued that just as Bahro claimed that in the socialist countries a new consciousness was developing that could see the discrepancy between "what is" and "what could be" and was not satisfied with its way of life, so too was such oppositional consciousness developing in the advanced capitalist countries.[9] "Surplus consciousness," in the Bahro-Marcuse conception, is a product of expanding education, scientific and technical development, and refinement of the forces of production and labor process. On this account, contemporary societies are producing a higher form of consciousness and create needs that cannot be satisfied in the labor process or everyday life, producing resentment and the potential for revolt. In effect, Bahro and Marcuse are arguing that critical consciousness is produced by the very social processes of the technological society and that this subjectivity comes into conflict with existing hierarchy, waste, repression, and domination, generating the need for social change. This position maintains that existing social processes themselves are helping produce a subjectivity that demands participation and fulfillment in the labor process and sociopolitical life, as well as increased freedom, equality, and opportunities for advancement and development. If these needs are not satisfied, Bahro and Marcuse suggest, rebellion and social transformation will be generated.

Curiously, precisely this process happened in the socialist world, in which rebellion against irrational and repressive bureaucratic social forms led to an overthrow of what Bahro termed "actually existing socialism."[10] The critiques of Marxism in the 1970s and 1980s in the increasingly hegemonic discourses of poststructuralism and postmodern theory among the radical intelligentsia, connected, I believe, with the collapse of "actually existing socialism" and helped produce a rejection of Marxism, while defaming revolution as utopian and, in many cases, deconstructing concepts of oppositional subjectivity and politics. Such extreme versions of poststructuralism and postmodernism,[11] however, vitiate the project of emancipation and social reconstruction and undermine efforts to develop oppositional politics and alternative conceptions of society, culture, and subjectivity—alternatives found in the work of Herbert Marcuse, who I believe continues to provide important resources for theory and politics in the contemporary era.

The postmodern/poststructuralist conception of subjectivity that stresses decentering, fragmentation, and flexibility reproduces aspects of the crisis of contemporary subjectivity overwhelmed by big corporations, new technologies, seductive media culture, and the complex and contradictory forces of globalization. Many postmodern critiques of traditional notions of the subject or subjectivity thus end with fragmentation, crisis, decentering, and dispersal, which they either cynically affirm without hope of reconstruction or valorize positively as conditions of the possibility of more flexible subjects that can be in turn rejected, reconstructed, and recreated at one's will and whim. Another possibility, however, is to call for a reconstructive concept of subjectivity and agency in the face of theoretical critique and practical fragmentation and dissipation. This is the position of Marcuse and much of critical theory, which begins by recognizing theoretical flaws in the modern concept of the (rational, unitary, ideal) subject, as well as the crisis of subjectivity in contemporary society.

Critical theory is dialectical, resisting both claims to the primacy of structure or agency, thus overcoming both determinism and idealism. Marcuse problematizes subjectivity and agency, recognizes the force of domination, and yet militates for liberation and transformation. Opposing mechanistic theories of history without agency and subjectivity, as well as idealist notions that see history as the development of humanity or subjectivity (i.e., the subject, spirituality, God, etc.), critical theory seeks to overcome unproductive dichotomies and to produce more sophisticated and transformative perspectives.

This problematization of subject and history discloses an intersection between critical theory and postmodern theory and significant differences between some of the versions. Both unveil the abstractness and mythological constitution of the subject; both reject a universal subject and the equation of the subject with metaphysical rationality. On the whole, critical theory is more reconstructive, with theorists like Adorno, Marcuse, Fromm, and Habermas offering quite different perspectives on the reconstruction of subjectivity and agency, while many postmodern theorists either revel in difference and heterogeneity (Lyotard), cynically reject any possibility of reconstruction and transformation (Baudrillard), or assume neutral and/or micrological perspectives that eschew ambitious theoretical or political reconstruction (followers of Foucault, Rorty in some moods, and postmodern camp followers who don't yet see its transformative potential); other postmodern theorists, however, urge reconstruction of subjectivity and agency à la feminism and critical theory, and thus present supplementary positive reconstructive positions to critical theory.

Hence, some versions of postmodern theory reproduce liberal reformism and pluralism in their emphasis on difference, reform, and rejection of broader perspectives of social transformation. There is also a tendency for fragmentary, aleatory, and nomadic postmodern subjectivity to replicate the self-centered, competitive, yet interactive subjectivity of contemporary capitalism.[12] Yet in view of the complex and contradictory development of contemporary capitalist culture and subjectivity, the sort of critical and oppositional perspectives offered by Marcuse are needed more than ever. As in Marcuse's day, the ambivalent unity of the positive and negative, of production and destruction, continues to operate in the global restructuring of capitalism, with its technological revolution and seductions, growing discrepancies between the haves and the have nots, and increasingly powerful forces of domination and destruction. Now, more much than ever, critical consciousness and oppositional subjectivity are needed to counter the forces of domination that appear more in the guise of the seductions of AOL and Time Warner, the machinations of Microsoft, and the global maneuvering of near-invisible forces like the WTO, IMF, and World Bank than in the boots and repression of Big Brother.[13]

Some Concluding Comments

In retrospect, the critiques of the subject launched by the Frankfurt School, feminism, poststructuralism, postmodern theory, and others have enriched our thinking on subjectivity by challenging us to rethink the problematics of the subject and agency, and have helped us think through and conceptualize various dimensions of experience and action neglected in traditional accounts, as well as to envisage alternative possibilities for thought, action, and everyday life. While traditional and modern conceptions of the subject were excessively rationalist, essentialist, idealist, and metaphysical, I have argued that the contemporary critiques of the subject provide the impetus and occasion to develop more critical and creative conceptions of postmetaphysical subjectivity.

But often discussions of the "crisis of the subject" conflate contemporary critique and rejection of the concept of a metaphysical unitary subject with the fragmentation, decline, or dispersal of subjectivity and agency under the sway of powerful social forces like the compulsion to work and consume, seduction of the media, or disciplinary agencies. I would argue that while critiques of problematic theoretical concepts of the subject are generally salutary, critical theory needs to respond reconstructively to evocations of decline of agency, the will to resist and struggle, and the eclipse of politics in the present era. Marcuse always attempted to ground his conception of radical subjectivity in existing struggles, movements, and tendencies. He was aware that oppositional subjectivity, and the movements and revolts in which it was grounded, were fragile, subject to dispersion and defeat, or absorption and cooptation. Moreover, he was aware of the contradictions of oppositional subjectivities and movements that on one hand reproduced tendencies of the existing capitalist societies, while opposing other aspects and seeking alternatives.

Hence, subjectivity for Marcuse, whether the dominated subject of advanced capitalism or the oppositional subjectivity that he sought in first the New Left and counterculture and then new social movements, was historical, and always full of contradictions and ambiguities. Marcuse was more aware than most in the Marxian tradition of the need for a robust theory of subjectivity to generate the subjective conditions for change, and he was deeply interested in theory, culture, and social experience that would help create a new subjectivity. Hence, his attempts to reconstruct subjectivity are grounded in his political desire for radical social change and preservation of the individual.

In his sometimes tortured attempts to generate new perspectives on subjectivity and an alternative society and politics, during his last decade of work in the 1970s, Marcuse privileged cultural revolution and the cultivation of a new sensibility as crucial catalysts for social change, as he (unsuccessfully) sought new social movements to embody his oppositional subjectivity and politics.[14] While this work provides important theoretical impulses to rethink radical politics, subjectivity, and culture in the contemporary era, we must move beyond Marcuse in a new historical situation, drawing on the best resources of the most advanced critical theories of our time.

Hence, in conclusion, I would like to make some comments contrasting Habermasian perspectives on subjectivity with Marcusean ones to indicate the specific contributions, strengths, and limitations of Marcuse's position. I have suggested that Marcuse offers a notion of a corporeal subjectivity with an emphasis on its aesthetic and erotic dimensions, while Habermas's communicative reason lacks a body, grounding in nature and materiality, and the aesthetic and erotic components. That is, while Habermas's conception of subjectivity contains a grounding in sociality and ego-alter relations, he does not offer a notion of aesthetic, erotic, and embodied and sensual subjectivity as in Marcuse's conception. There is also not as strong a critique of the tendencies toward conformity and normalization as in Marcuse's conception, nor is there as forceful a notion of transformation and emancipation. Nor does Habermas offer a notion of revolutionary subjectivity.

There are, on the other hand, problems with Marcuse's conceptions of subjectivity. I have downplayed the extent of Marcuse's dependence on questionable aspects of Freud's instinct theory because I believe that a Marcusean conception of subjectivity can be produced without dependence on Freud's conception of the political economy of the instincts, the death instinct, and the somewhat biologistic notion of Eros that Marcuse draws from Freud. Yet while Marcuse's focus on the corporeal, aesthetic, erotic, and political dimensions of subjectivity constitutes a positive legacy, there are omissions and deficiencies in his account. Crucially, he underemphasizes the ethical and arguably, concerning the political, does not adequately develop notions of justice and democracy. Since notions of ethical, just, and democratic subjectivity are not cultivated in Marcuse's writings, Habermas's analyses provide a necessary complement. Habermas's primary focus on the ego-alter relation and his subsequent treatises on morals and moral development, democracy and law, and the social obligations and constraints on subjectivity offer an important correction to Marcuse's analyses. Hence, both perspectives on subjectivity by themselves are one-sided and require supplementation by the other.

While I have been primarily concerned in this chapter with interrogating Marcuse's resources for the rethinking and reconstruction of subjectivity, I would argue that no one thinker has *the* answer to the question and that we would thus be well advised to draw on a wealth of thinkers to rehabilitate and reconstruct subjectivity in the contemporary moment. Within the Frankfurt School, Adorno, Benjamin, Fromm, Habermas, Marcuse, and others make important contributions, and outside of the tradition many feminist theorists, poststructuralists, and others also advance the project.[15] Marcuse and other critical theorists provide many important contributions to our understanding of subjectivity and agency, while challenging us to further rethink the problematics of subjectivity in relation to the socioeconomic developments and political struggles of our own turbulent period. In this way, the contemporary critiques of the subject challenge us to come up with better conceptions and to develop new resources for critical theory and practice.

Notes

1. See, in particular, Jurgen Habermas (1984 and 1987a).
2. This is true of the Foucault of texts like *Discipline and Punishment* and *The History of Sexuality;* the late Foucault, however, like Marcuse, was engaged in a search for a stronger conception of agency. I would argue, however, that Marcuse offers a more robust account of resistance and agency than Foucault. On Foucault's later quests to develop a theory of subjectivity and resistance and its limitations, see Steven Best and Douglas Kellner (1991), Couze Venn (1997).
3. This conception might be contrasted with Walter Benjamin who in his "Theses on the Philosophy of History" claims that "images of enslaved ancestors rather than that of liberated grandchildren" drive the oppressed to struggle against their oppressors (1969, p. 260). Benjamin's conception is similar to Freud's, who holds that past traumas enslave individuals, and argues, in a different register than Benjamin, that working through the source of trauma can free individual from past blockages and suffering. A dialectical conception of memory merging Marcuse and Benjamin might argue that both remembrances of past joys and suffering, happiness and oppression, can motivate construction of a better future if oriented toward changing rather than just remembering the world.
4. I am quoting from Marcuse's 1974 lecture on "Marxism and Feminism" here to suggest that he continued to hold to many key ideas in *Eros and Civilization* through his later work and that his strong adherence to feminism was deeply rooted in some of his fundamental ideas; I take up "Marxism and Feminism" later in this study.
5. Herbert Marcuse (1969).
6. In *CR&R*, pp. 63ff., Marcuse connects his notion of the new sensibility with the analysis of the early Marx on the liberation of the senses; his conception is also influenced by Schiller's idea of aesthetic education.
7. For a systematic study of Marcuse's perspectives on art and education, see Charles Reitz (2000).
8. For an argument parallel to mine developed through an engagement with French feminism and poststructuralism, see Kelly Oliver (1998). Oliver provides an extended argument that we can talk about subjectivity (and agency) without presupposing or needing a subject, claiming that subjectivity does not necessarily imply a "subject" and that we are better off without such a concept. She develops notions of subjectivity as relational and intersubjective at its "center" and contrasts varying discourses and forms of masculine and feminine subjectivity. This project is parallel, I suggest, to Marcuse and the Frankfurt School, disclosing a provocative affinity between Critical Theory, French feminism, and poststructuralism.
9. Herbert Marcuse (1979). See also Marcuse's (1980) reflections on Bahro.
10. One could, of course, argue that the Marxist-Leninist-Stalinist systems overthrown in the late 1980s were not really Marxist or socialist at all, but constituted a bureaucratic deformation of Marxian socialism. This is indeed Bahro's and Marcuse's position, which continues to have force in explaining the collapse of Soviet-style communism; see my analysis in Kellner (1995b).
11. For fuller summaries of the varieties of postmodern theory, similarities and differences with critical theory, and reflections on productive and problematic versions of postmodern politics, see Steven Best and Douglas Kellner (1991, 1997, and 2001).
12. Such a conception of postmodern subjectivity is found in a highly developed form in Sherry Turkle (1995).

13. For an argument that Huxley's *Brave New World* and Marcuse's *One-Dimensional Man* provide more salient perspectives on contemporary global capitalism than Orwell's *1984*, see Douglas Kellner (1990). For my perspectives on globalization, see Douglas Kellner and Ann Cvetkovich (1996) and Kellner (1998).
14. See, in particular, his previously unpublished studies "Beyond One-Dimensional Man," "Cultural Revolution," and "The Historical Fate of Bourgeois Democracy," which I will publish in the forthcoming Herbert Marcuse, *Toward a Critical Theory of Society*, the second volume of *The Collected Papers of Herbert Marcuse* that I am editing for Routledge Press.
15. This essay was first presented in a panel at SPEP (Denver, 1998) in which my colleagues David Sherman and Pierre Lamarche presented the contributions of Adorno and Benjamin in rethinking subjectivity. See, in addition, Oliver's account of the contributions to refiguring subjectivity in poststructuralism and feminism, Note 8.

Bibliographic Note

Abbreviations for the works of Herbert Marcuse cited in this chapter are as follows.

R&R: *Reason and Revolution*
E&C: *Eros and Civilization*
ODM: *One-Dimensional Man*
EL: *An Essay on Liberation*
CR&R: *Counterrevolution and Revolt*
M&F: *Marxism and Feminism*

"WHAT ROUGH BEAST . . .": ON READING ARENDT AFTER THE TWIN TOWERS

> Turning and turning in the widening gyre
> The falcon cannot hear the falconer;
> Things fall apart; the centre cannot hold;
> Mere anarchy is loosed upon the world,
> The blood dimmed tide is loosed, and everywhere
> The ceremony of innocence is drowned;
> The best lack all conviction, while the worst
> Are full of passionate intensity.
> . . .
> The darkness drops again; but now I know
> That twenty centuries of stony sleep
> Were vexed to nightmare by a rocking cradle,
> And what rough beast, its hour come round at last,
> Slouches towards Bethlehem to be born.
> —W. B. Yeats, "The Second Coming"

Introduction

As I was working on this essay a colleague knocked on my door and informed me of the "breaking" news about the suicide attack on the World Trade Center in New York and the Pentagon in Washington on 11 September 2001. As I surfed the net and "hopped" the television, images of carnage and devastation vied for attention with those of Yeats's poem, "The Second Coming." No doubt essays of all kinds penned around this time will reverberate with the shock waves created by these events and there will be much analysis of the "how":

How did it happen? How were they allowed to? I suspect that rather less attention will be paid to the "why." This does not imply that there will be an insufficiency of journalistic inquiry (much of it well intentioned, some of it malign) into the relationship among the politics of the Middle East, the political power of the Anglo-American model [1] of the globalized market, and the theological roots of Islamic fundamentalism. But none of this will even stir the why question (and I pen this before the recriminations begin!). Phrases of condemnation and high rhetoric arrived thick and fast in the wake of this tragic news. While understandable as deeply human reactions, it is likely that much of this will merely obscure the more fundamental questions not just about these events but about what it means to be human in the world of this moment.

To begin the task of reflection it is necessary to ask what it was that was attacked. Was it trade or commerce or defense or government, or even democracy? In a banal sense it was all of these or at least it was all of these viewed through a particular ideological prism: that of the dominant social and economic discourse. It was also, of course, an attack on individuals and their families. Behind the grand political narrative lie a multitude of "little" stories; stories of terrible tragedy for certain but also stories of hope and comedy and absurdity and the trivial. In addition, and perhaps above all these, it was an attack on the "dream of happiness"; the "dream" so poignantly articulated in Arthur Miller's *Death of a Salesman*. Tales of happiness sit uncomfortably in the midst of such a quagmire of political and personal sadness, and there is a pervasive quality to our attempt to disassociate the personal and the political with respect to personal happiness. Much contemporary philosophical and political thought has sought to create separate domains of public goods and private happiness, ignoring their mutuality. Such elision merely serves to mask some of the deeply entrenched political difficulties and, some might suggest, the "madness" of late capitalism. Difficulties about which Hannah Arendt was acutely aware.

Miller's play exposes the hollowed out "inscape" of the "American dream"[2] and the inability of the modern person to confront the self in its nakedness. One of Miller's characters, Happy Loman, whose name is hardly without resonance, remains blind throughout the play to the bankruptcy of his father's life, his brother's life, and his own life. Despite his brother's failure as a football player, his father's failure as both a parent and a salesman and consequent suicide, despite his mother's oppression and his own rather trivial existence, he still manages to imagine the dream. At the end of the play, his brother, Biff, emerges into something approaching self-awareness but both his mother Linda and Happy continue to give sanctuary to that self-deception which is the American dream: the pursuit of happiness. Biff claims that his father had "the wrong dreams, All, all, wrong." Happy is ultimately forced to reply: "gonna show you and everybody else that Willy Loman did not die in vain. He had a good dream. It's the only dream you can have—to come out number-one man. He fought it out there and this is where I'm gonna win it for him" (Miller, 1949, pp. 110f).[3] Happy has condemned himself to relive his father's false dream.

All this might seem a far remove from the thought of the German-Jewish political philosopher and commentator Hannah Arendt, her place in the development of critical thought in the third quarter of the twentieth century, and her enduring legacy. So significant are the events of 11 September 2001 to our understanding of Western liberal political life and ethical life, and so profoundly have they shaken the foundations of our generally benign view of the global markets,[4] that it would have been difficult to pen an essay on Arendt without refracting it through such a lens. This is because Arendt was a remarkably prescient commentator on ontology, ethics, and political philosophy in late modernity. In opting for this approach I trace a path through selected insights, connecting them as I go. This carries the disadvantage of placing to one side much of her work and many of her insights. This is not a chronological journey beginning with Arendt's earliest work but focuses on a number of her texts, especially *The Human Condition* and *On Revolution*, in the attempt to understand that the attacks on New York and Washington were indeed attacks on a particular atelic notion of happiness that has its roots in the "stories" of the American and French revolutions.

To fully understand how "happiness" has come to the fore in the social life of Western democracies it is necessary first to have some insight into three key features of Arendt's thought: life as appearance, her conception of being, and her understanding of the narrated self. Understanding the individual self is a necessary prolegomenon to understanding the political, and "happiness" as constructed in modern liberal democracies is itself deeply political. The exploration of Arendt's concept of happiness requires some understanding of her deeply held conviction that the doing of philosophy was not an activity of the abstracted self but a political and ethical action.

Philosophy as a Political Act

Arendt's place in the world of political and critical theory is fissured with ambiguity—metaphysical, ontological, and epistemological. On the one hand she eschewed the meta-theoretical, if by this it is intended to communicate the construction of a systematic and comprehensive doctrine of how things "are" or "ought to be" or a singular philosophic method to get to the *deep-downness*[5] of things. On the other hand she developed a coherent ontology—knowing how the world is and acting within the world may not be disentangled in Arendt's work precisely because she regarded philosophizing about the world as an action of the being who enters into it. The reason for her reluctance to develop a meta-theory is hinted at throughout her work but only fully emerges in her return to her existential roots in the posthumously published *The Life of the Mind*. With more than passing similarities to Jasper's[6] understanding of appearance she opines,

> The everyday common-sense world, which neither the scientist nor the philosopher eludes, knows error as well as illusion. Yet no elimination of errors or dispelling of

illusions can arrive as a region beyond appearance. *"For when an illusion dissipates, when an appearance suddenly breaks up, it is always for the profit of a new appearance which takes up again for its own account the ontological functions of the first.... The dis-illusion is the loss of one evidence only because it is the acquisition of another evidence."* ... That modern science in its relentless search for the truth behind mere appearances will ever be able to resolve this predicament is, to say the least, highly doubtful, if only because the scientist himself belongs to the world of appearances although his perspective on this world may differ from the common-sense perspective. (Arendt, 1971; see also Hinchman & Hinchman, 1994, pp. 143–150)[7]

Another significant existentialist influence on her position that it was not necessary to meta-theorize was Kierkegaard, whose anti-Hegelianism (1941) offered radical subjectivity as a *modus operandi* in the world. This depended not on a historically driven schema but on the decision of the acting self. Arendt's early intellectual career was significantly affected by this trope in Kierkegaard's thought[8] (Young-Bruehl, 1982, p. 45)[9] and by the perception that, while Hegel was of course concerned with human action, this concern took the form of contemplation (Arendt, 1963a, p. 52).

Thus for Arendt, the effort of philosophical thought and political being (for the two are, in important respects, one) and engagement can only be understood in relation to each other in the public world of appearance. In this she reacts against what she perceived to be the solipsistic timber of Heidegger's[10] early philosophy. As she perceived matters, he left the burning issue of twentieth-century philosophy—the political—unexplored. In his early work Heidegger sets his face against the political, regarding *Dasein* as standing on its own with no requirement that it be set against any other public criteria, including politics. He observes that "To say that it is 'illuminated' *[erleuchtet]* means that as Being-in-the-world it is cleared *[gelichteit]* in itself, not through any other entity, but in such a way that it is itself the clearing" (Heidegger, 1962, p. 171).

Arendt's reaction to Heidegger was not purely philosophical. It was also personally motivated by her experiences of anti-Semitism, National Socialism, and the events of the Second World War, so deeply embedded in her writings. These gave rise to her passion to engage with what she perceived to be the problems of the world, but problems that were also deeply personal. The unfolding of *Dasein* was not enough for Arendt, who had, after all, lived in the midst of the political as a German Jew and who had explored the identity of the Jew as both parvenu and pariah. There was no escape from the political if one were a German Jew in nineteenth- and early twentieth-century Europe. The options open to Jews were to either remain socially and politically invisible, always the outsider, or be assimilated. But assimilation could only happen where one distinguished oneself from the "mass" of Jewry and became, it might be said, an honorary non-Jew. Even then full political and social recognition would not be afforded the parvenu. "Assimilation, in the sense of acceptance by non-Jewish society, was granted them only as long as they were clearly distinguished exceptions from the Jewish masses even though they still shared the same restricted and humiliating political condition. . . . Society . . . made it quite clear that none of its classes was prepared to grant them social equality" (Arendt, 1979, pp. 56ff).

Additionally, Arendt's own Jewishness, that is, her incarnate story and her philosophical background, ensured that her political philosophy would become deeply entrenched in the narratival structure of human *being*. Most of her work has such a quality to it, and *Men in Dark Times* offers testament to the importance of what Wojtyla referred to as "the Acting Person" (Wojtyla, 1979). In her essay on Lessing[11] in this collection of essays on those she regards as figures of illumination in a period of human darkness she suggests that

> we who for the most part are neither poets nor historians are familiar with the nature of the process of narration which opens up our past and allows for our involvement and ultimate reconciliation [dealing with it] from our own experience of life, for we too have the need to recall the significant events in our own lives by relating them to ourselves and others. . . . Thus we are constantly preparing the way for poetry. . . . No philosophy, no analysis, no aphorism, be it ever so profound, can compare in intensity and richness of meaning with a properly narrated story. (Arendt, 1968, pp. 21ff)

For Arendt then the structure of philosophizing is to be rooted in the stories that emanate from people and events. It is not, I think, that she subscribed to the great men theory of history, rather that to understand what is transacted in the public spaces it is necessary to understand the stories. A history that has emptied itself of the story(ies) is in actuality an ideology since "ideologies are never interested in the miracle of being" (1973, p. 469).[12] The narrative understanding of human existence is embedded in natality; the raw fact of being born whereby we are born and in turn can bring into being another self. The possibilities of freedom are not the result of a gift but inhere in the very structure of bringing the self into being (Arendt, 1958, pp. 7–10; see Kristeva, 2001, pp. 45ff). It is in sharing the issue of the possibilities of freedom in public with the other that the narration takes effect.

The attack on New York can be understood as a clash of ideologies, and undoubtedly that is part of the story in Arendtian terms.[13] Those who perpetrated an act of barbarism and those who respond with similar acts of barbarism embody distinct ideologies that, in their different ways, are concerned to obliterate difference and individual behavior, preferring singularity to plurality. It is ideological to the extent that the human natality of the other is in some fundamental way denied; there is no story to be shared as if there were some kind of public space where each side could sit down and *communicate* about each other's story. This denial of the other is not just a matter of speaking a different language or even having different sets of beliefs. It is, as Wittgenstein saw matters, that the one would not necessarily know what was to count as a belief within the other's frame. For example, Wittgenstein asks, "Suppose someone is ill and he says: 'This is a punishment,' and I say: 'If I'm ill, I don't think of punishment at all.' If you say: "Do you believe the opposite?"—you can call it believing the opposite, but it is entirely different from what we would normally call believing the opposite" (Wittgenstein, 1966, p. 55). Wittgenstein's account offers us nothing more or less than an account of the incommensurability of the stories. Much of this incommensurability arises out of the very particular way in which modern liberal democratic states have evolved. It is also an interior incommensurability.

Labor, Work, and Action

For Arendt the modern liberal state has seen the reversal of the historic preeminence of the *vita contemplativa* over the *vita activa* (1958, p. 289). Contemplation, once the means to enter the wonder of being (ibid., p. 303f), is no longer seen as an appropriate aspiration and has long been made redundant.[14] Its redundancy has been brought about by the "discovery of the Archimedian point and the concomitant rise of Cartesian doubt" though the process began with the Greeks. In order to understand the *vita activa* and its role in the narratives that arise out of our natality, Arendt developed a tripartite classification: labor, work or fabrication, and action. Labor is that which enables us to experience our being alive; in this particular sense it is intimately tied up with our natality. In being born we are given to labor as the activity that sustains us. Just as a lion has to labor to eat and sustain itself and its offspring, so too human beings have to labor to a similar end. It is in this sense that labor is a prehuman activity but one that enjoys a certain blessedness. We labor to keep alive. As that which is concerned with the maintenance of life, labor finds its sphere of operation located within the private space of the *oikos* (household).[15] Arendt distinguishes labor from work in that the latter is about the "work of one's hands" rather than the "fruits of one's labour." Work then is about making or fabricating and is consequently not centrally concerned with surviving or putting food on the table or clothing one's family. Insofar as it is about creating, making, or producing it is a reflection of the desire to form and control our environment; shaping it to our desires and placing into nature our own regulatory capacities. With the passing of time, work loses its early creativity and gives way to artifice and reification. "From the viewpoint of nature, it is work . . . that is destructive, since the work process takes matters out of nature's hands without giving it back to her in the swift course of the natural metabolism of the living body" (ibid., p. 100). Labor emerges out of our encounter with the world, whereas work draws from nature and shapes it into manageable elements. What might be said to begin as encounter ends as rape.[16] *Homo faber* represents the attempt to retreat from the unpredictability of acting into the world. This sense of the durability of the created object emerges out of the perception that it is relatively independent of its own creator; a thing that stands over and against its maker. Thus it offers something approximating stability. "From this viewpoint, the things of the world have the function of stabilizing human life, and their objectivity lies in the fact that—in contradistinction to the Heraclitean saying that the same men can never enter the same stream—men, their ever-changing nature notwithstanding, can retrieve their sameness, that is, their identity, by being related to the same chair and the same table" (ibid., p. 137).

The original contours of labor as "encounter"[17] and work as creation have given way to what Pickstock (1999, pp. 103ff) would term the polity of death in late capitalist society[18] where both labor and work have been transmuted through the ages from their original state. The former has changed from oneness to alienation through the mechanization and routinization of labor, which has itself been, so to speak, distanced from the soil; the latter has replaced creativity with objectification and disposability. In neither case can these activities help us deal with the conditions of late modernity, since they have become expressions of our failed attempt to either retreat from the world into the private sphere of labor or reduce our public spaces to locations for trading the work of our hands. While work does indicate our capacity for thought, it cannot itself offer a location for it. This is why Arendt posits the third category in the *vita activa*, action.

Action is the engagement that takes place between people and between people and the world and is freighted with danger and uncertainty. It is, *par excellence,* that which truly makes us human, giving shape to our individuality. To act or speak (speech being itself an action) is the means by which we distinguish the self from the other and assert our individual being. It is the *hoi logos* of John's Gospel, a kind of self-initiation borne not out of physical "necessity like labor . . . [nor] prompted by utility, like work" (Arendt, 1958, p. 177). Neither is it the consequence of the other but is the act of the initiating self who brings into being some word or deed. But such action is always subject to risk since it "is in the nature of beginning that something new is started which cannot be expected from whatever may have happened before" (ibid., pp. 177ff). It is through action that the individual appears in the world. It is, in this sense, the activity of the public spaces. Because it has as its source the beginning of the individual it has the characteristic of independence. In its independence it opens up and challenges the closure that has accompanied the routinization of labor and the utilitarianism of fabrication. Thus, the fullest expression of the human life is neither labor (which is prehuman) nor work, which is fundamentally a violent act (a violation of nature), but action; the means by which we encounter[19] the other and disclose the self in the public space. Action, which includes speech acts, is power, but power in Arendt's sense is only "actualised where word and deed have not parted company" (ibid., p. 200).

Too often word and deed do part company, ruptured by the disassociation of initiation from completion. The blame for this disassociation is laid squarely at the feet of Plato, who reframed *archein* and *prattein*. Prior to Plato's intervention the former signified the beginning or initiating of some action, activity, or project and the latter its completion. When I initiated something it was with a mind to completing it. Beginning and completion were complementary, but this complementarity was compromised by Plato so that *archein* dissolved into rules and *prattein* constituted the activity of completion according to the rules.[20] So it was that the creation of the rules governing activity and the activity itself came to be lodged in different hands; the rulers "speaketh" the instructions; the doers followed. For Arendt, the consequence of this change has been the elision into *behavior*. Behavior is a feature of the social realm, which she distinguished from the political or public,[21] believing that it had made a significant contribution to the twentieth-century trauma that was the Holocaust. What Arendt understood with greater percipience than almost any commentator, philosopher, or psychologist in modernity was that evil and wickedness were not to be situated in a class of uniquely wicked Mephistophelian characters but were rooted in the behaviors of those very "ordinary" souls who incarnated the rules. Behavior (possibly a synonym for behaving oneself) finds its completion in the story of National Socialism and the outworkings of the Holocaust. Arendt recognized, as Yeats did, that "twenty centuries of stony sleep / Were vexed to nightmare by a rocking cradle." Despite the ethical claims of the incarnation to act out of love for both the other and for the world, evil could easily lodge itself in the "souls" of humans because they were rule followers and behavers. In "Eichmann in Jerusalem" she carefully, if controversially,[22] analyzed Eichmann's "being" in the world of Nazism, recognizing that he had feelings and was not, in any meaningful sense, a monster but a quite ordinary man who had perfectly embodied an ideal and who had learned to live by behaving according to the commands of the situation and speak only its clichés. As an idealist he would subordinate all other considerations in order to hold fast to the ideal, so much so, as Arendt points out, that he would have sent his father to his death. As the perfect idealist "like everybody else [he] had of course his personal feelings and emotions, but he would never permit them to interfere with his actions if they came into contact with his 'idea'" (1963b & 1992, p. 42). It is true that the things that Eichmann did as a representative of Nazism were not simply against the law but served rather to annihilate it. Nevertheless, in Arendt's analysis, this annihilation was not the most awful feature of the whole affair. Indeed, she suggests that "one cannot extract any diabolical or demonic profundity from Eichmann" (ibid., p. 288). Maybe the fact that there is no such straightforward lesson to be extracted from its awfulness is itself the most disturbing element of the Holocaust.

Behavior inevitably removes the self from the immediacy of the encounter with the world, locating the self not as a *sui generis* creation and actor but as one of the mass. Behavior is the activity of those who have been denuded of their capacity to act. In part this is caused by the erosion and eventual loss of the public space, within which one could act politically and corporately. The loss of the public space, as a place to act, creates both political isolation and social loneliness. Totalitarian regimes create this emptiness in the public spaces, enmassing the people as they roll out their pernicious philosophies. Arendt predicated her understanding of the enmassing of society on her analysis of Russian and Nazi totalitarianism, and of course totalitarianism is a very particular form of mass society. Scholars such as Benhabib take issue with her conflation of these two forms of totalitarianism, seeing very different forces at work in each case (Benhabib, 1996, pp. 62–69).[23] So the question must be asked, "Does her analysis of the loneliness of the enmassed individual have any contemporary purchase in the light of the Twin

Towers catastrophe?"[24] I wish to suggest that while the origins of her work emerge out of no particular methodological insight, which might be easily transferred to a different context, nevertheless the trenchancy of her analysis continues to serve us. Political isolation and social loneliness cannot be grafted onto architectural decision making in some simplistic way. Nevertheless, this building may be seen as a metaphor for more than the success of a particular (market capitalism) form of political economy. It also acts as a metaphor for the domination of the individual by the idea of the globalized and incorporated mass. Such corporatism (the very word having a somewhat ironic twist) creates an illusion of humans acting together because they inhabit a particular space while they actually engage in the behaviors redolent of the mass. Modern liberal democracies may not reasonably be bracketed with totalitarian or fundamentalist religious movements, which obliterate all distinction, but the gradual displacement of action by behavior is a central feature of late modern capitalism (see Conroy, 1999). The loss of the acting self is also, I wish to suggest next, at the root of Happy Loman's dream, which is simultaneously that of the isolated individual and of the enmassed society devoid of a true political forum (Berlin, 1996). As "things fall apart" and the center is "unable to hold," the dream of individual success *appears* to offer some sort of amelioration of the crisis precipitated by the loss of the "acting self."

The American Dream

To understand Arendt's place as a pivotal figure of the twentieth century who enhances our understanding of the attack on the Twin Towers as one directed to the heart of the Loman dream it is necessary to do two things. The first is to draw out Arendt's understanding of how "happiness" came to inhere in the very notion of a modern liberal democracy. The second is to illuminate the way this atelic happiness has become manifest in mass culture. One of Arendt's best known works is *On Revolution,* which is a genealogical exploration of revolution centered primarily on the history of the French and American Revolutions. I do not propose to examine the distinctions between these revolutions or why Arendt thought that the American version was rather more successful than the French. Nor do I wish to either examine the relationship between power and authority in the establishment of constitutions or provide further discussion on a comparative reading of her modernist as opposed to the Derridean postmodernist interpretation of the coherence of the foundations of constitutional democracies (see Ingram, 1996, pp. 221–250). Instead I wish to concentrate on a single strand of Arendt's "dig" into the foundations of modern liberal democracy—her unearthing of happiness as an economic category that displaced freedom in the aftermath and subsequent outworking of the American Revolution. I believe that this concept is central to our understanding of how the radical potential of the thought of Rousseau, Paine, Jefferson, Adams, Robbespierre, and other "revolutionaries" of the eighteenth century was subordinated to privatized mass culture. It will also help explain why the attack on the Twin Towers is to be construed above all as an attack on the dream of happiness.

In a vital sense the modern age emerges out of the progressive loss of political authority vested in tradition and religion. These pillars, which had historically provided stability to social and political relations, were shaken to their foundations by the emergence of the Enlightenment emphasis on human rationality as the court of last resort. By the mid-twentieth century they are a "veritable rubble heap" (Arendt, 1968a, p. 10). As the old order gradually disintegrated and the structured constancy of the monarchy across Europe lost even its rhetorical force, something had to replace it lest "mere anarchy [be] loosed upon the world." That "something," in both Europe and America, was a passion for involvement in public affairs. Because of the existence of "town hall" meetings, assemblies and corporations, or bodies politic,

> what was a passion and "taste" in France clearly, was an experience in America, and the American usage which, especially in the eighteenth century, spoke of "public happiness," where the French spoke of "public freedom" suggests this difference quite appropriately. The point is that the Americans knew that public freedom consisted in having a share in public business, and that the activities connected with this business by no means constituted a burden but gave those who discharged them in public a feeling of happiness they could acquire nowhere else. (Arendt, 1963, p. 119)

The possibility of involvement in public affairs arises out of the particular construction of that freedom which itself issues from the "rationally rooted" "eclipse of the transcendent world" (Arendt, 1968b, p. 69) with its inherent religious framing. Men were freed to engage in the political because the religious no longer offered either a superstructure within which human decision-making was contained, or a dominant political position of power that could *ipso facto* determine meaning, purpose, and process. Religion was eliminated from public life. If happiness had been located in acting in accordance with the will of God and anticipating eternal happiness, the dislocation of the religious from the political opened up alternative possibilities for existence in the public spaces. As construed by John Adams and others, happiness emanated from the exercise of a kind of liberty afforded the individual in virtue of both the possibility of, and the participation in, the governance of his own life. This experience of freedom in America was also an aspiration for the French *hommes de lettres* after they began to refocus their leisure on the ancients and their political forms out of a sense that they were somehow "on the edge" of politics and marginalized by the *ancien regime*. "It was their search for political freedom, not their quest for political truth, that led them back to antiquity, and their reading served to give them the concrete elements with which to think and dream of such freedom. . . . Had they known in actual experience what public freedom meant for the individual citizen, they might have agreed with their American colleagues and spoken about public happiness" (Arendt, 1963a, p. 123). While it's often supposed that the French Revolution was founded not on happiness but on the "social question" of poverty, which Arendt herself discusses at some length (ibid., Chap. 2), and while it's true that the immediately postrevolutionary period was etched with violence and factional hatred (Schama, 1989), it is equally the case that the intellectuals who orchestrated the French Revolution, such as Lafayette, were deeply committed to the American construal of rights. In a letter to his wife, Adrienne, quoted by Schama, Lafayette made it clear that the happiness of liberty was his aim in supporting the Continental army.

> Defender of that liberty which I worship, utterly free in my own person and going as a friend to offer my services to the most interesting of Republics, bringing to the service only my candour and goodwill without ambition or ulterior motive. Working for my own glory will become working for their happiness. (ibid., p. 27)

Clearly, Lafayette, a man of action and a political leader, was persuaded by the notion that happiness was the fruit of free political participation as much as were *les hommes de lettres*. This congruence between representation, the political activity of the free individual, and the sense of happiness provided the roots for the American Constitution. Importantly, this happiness was also tied to visibility. What the French *philosophes* and the *sans-culottes* shared was their invisibility in the public realm. To the extent that decisions about their well-being were taken elsewhere the Americans were also absent from any meaningful legislative visibility. Happiness then is a public state—it manifests itself not in the private sentiments of the individual but in the ability to deliberate, contest, and enact in the public realm. Arendt is careful to distinguish this affirmative possibility from the "easily . . . mistaken . . . [and] perhaps much more vehement, but politically sterile, passionate hatred of masters, the longing of the oppressed for liberation" (Arendt, 1963a, p. 125).

Public happiness is then a positive engagement of the individual citizen in the public political space. Now, "the very fact that the word 'happiness' was chosen in laying claim to a share in public power indicates strongly that there existed in the country," Arendt suggested, "prior to the revolution, such a thing as 'public happiness,' and that men knew they could not be altogether 'happy' if their happiness was located and enjoyed only in private life" (ibid., p. 127). But, pursuing Jefferson's thoughts, Arendt traced the gradual confusion of the public and the private with respect to happiness, which arose largely because a number of the Founding Fathers failed to recognize the politically radical way in which the term *happiness* was being used. The displacement and banishment of happiness to the private realm mirrors the gradual reduction of the import of the public spaces in political life from Aristotle on. In *The Human Condition,* Arendt established a persuasive case for seeing the *polis,* originally the space where deliberation as to the good life and concomitant political reflection was conducted, as having given way to the *oikos,* originally the space for deliberation about the conditions of physical and material survival and well-being, as the place of "meaningful" activity. Here she offers a substantive account of how the defining charcteristics of even the most public of events, revolution, are ultimately rehoused in the privacy of the home—a space within which the public cannot make any claim.

Constitutionally, this move can be seen in the ways in which the emphasis shifted almost at once from the contents of the Constitution, that is the creation and partition of power, and the rise of a new realm where, in the words of Madison, "ambition would be checked by ambition." And, as Arendt (1963a) goes on to stipulate, this ambition was

> to excel and be of "significance," not the ambition to make a career—to the Bill of Rights, which contained the necessary constitutional restraints upon government; it shifted, in other words, from public freedom to civil liberty, or from a share in public affairs for the sake of public happiness to a guarantee that the pursuit of private happiness would be protected and furthered by public power. (135)

This particular notion of private happiness does two things. First, it enables the individual to prescind from public engagement; such engagement is no longer necessary because one's individual or family drive to pursue certain kinds of goods deemed to "make one happy" has been constitutionally vouchsafed. In her essay on Lessing, Arendt makes the related point that "more and more people in the countries of the Western world, which since the decline of the ancient world has regarded freedom from politics as one of the basic freedoms, make use of this freedom and have retreated from the world and their obligations within it" (1968a, p. 4). This sense of retreat is shared by other liberal philosophers such as Berlin (1996, Chap. 2) and by and large welcomed by a number of influential contemporary philosophers who would claim that how one should conduct oneself is a matter of private disposition and not public interest. The forum would be reserved for only those things about which, materially, all citizens might agree upon (Rorty, 1999, Chap. 2). However harsh it might seem, the reaction to the fateful events surrounding the attack on the Twin Towers exemplified this retreat from the public. Of course such a retreat is perfectly proper for those whose lives have been so utterly devastated, and the individual stories of victims are a difficult thing outside the "transforming realm of poetry" (Arendt, 1963b & 1992, p. 229). It is not proper for everyone else, and politicians, who have made deliberating on our behalf an occupation rather than an obligation, are wont to assist us in our willingness to turn away. Arendt's concern with this reduction or, indeed inversion, of the public and private realms in our collective lives is an enduring theme with a timeless resonance.

Second, we are forced to ask the most rudimentary of questions: "In what does such happiness consist?" For Arendt, as for Baudrillard (2001, Chap. 2), modern humanity, isolated in its mass, seeks to find itself in the consumption of product. Modern economies are not, as in a Marxist analysis, producer driven but consumer led. In the aftermath of the attack on the Twin Towers, a central plank of government response was the exhortation by the president of the United States, that Americans act patriotically and go out and spend money, offers a kind of testimony to this reality. But spend money on what? And to what end? To lift spirits? Possibly. To keep an ailing economy afloat? Undoubtedly. To maintain the dream of happiness as the manifest ability to purchase? Assuredly. This dream has wrapped itself in the "cotton wool" of consumption, turning the public spaces into centers for the regulation of such consumption. But for Arendt, the relationship between public appearances and consumption was no longer simply a matter of the one providing a sort of venue for the other. Rather consumption had become so deeply enmeshed in the social fabric that it might be proposed that it now constituted that very fabric. This is seen in the manner in which, for Bush, consumption is not simply articulated as an activity of defiance but as a value. Arendt recognized that this had become the case, initially because of the inversion of the *polis* and the *oikos* and the concomitant obliteration of the distinction between labor and work in modern society. For her, everything that was now transacted in the public spaces had become a commodity with a particular attached value.

> Historically, the last public realm . . . is the exchange market on which his [homo faber] products are displayed. The commercial society, characteristic of the earlier stages of the modern age . . . sprang from this "conspicuous production" with its concomitant hunger for universal possibilities of truck and barter, and its end came with the rise of labor and the labor society which replaced "conspicuous production and its pride with conspicuous consumption" and its vanity. (Arendt, 1958, p. 162; see also Meade, 1996, pp. 115ff)

However compromised it might have been in respect of action, production, the creation of some artifact or device, could bear something akin to a legitimate pride (sense of satisfaction) in one's achievement. Consumption, on the other hand, carries only the empty state of vanity. This was indeed a far cry from the categories that defined the public spaces in ancient Greece. Drawing on Aristotle's *Politics,* Cartledge observes that "Thebes had once had a law banning from office those who had participated in commercial exchange *(agora)* within the past decade" and that access to *politeuma*[25] "was granted only to those [manual workers] who had not laboured at their menial occupation for a stated period" (2000, p. 404). If labor and making one's living was deemed a distraction from the business of being an actor in the public world of appearances, what are we to say of consumption?

In modern societies the dream is not particularly ambitious, but it is false. It serves only to obscure the truth of the human condition—that to be born is to act. And that action takes place in the public places. It confuses the public and the private, conflating them in a socially determined supermarket. In doing so it has replaced action with behavior and freedom with a kind of enslavement—an enslavement that has, in its turn, precipitated a withdrawal from public life. The power to consume has replaced the power to act. An Arendtian interpretation of the Twin Towers attack enables us to comprehend it as an attack on a way of life but one whose inherent flaws are likely to be obscured by the adoption of a Manichean theology that merely serves to reinforce the moral rightness of an enmassed, apolitical consumer society. Modernity's attachment to the "empty set" of private happiness is as much anathema to Arendt's thought as was the wickedness of the Third Reich. In fact, they both have the same roots—the absence of political action. As Margaret Canovan puts it, "Arendt is as uncompromising as her republican predecessors in insisting on the duties of citizenship, for the catastrophes of her own time seemed to her to be at least partly traceable to lack of public spirit. Citizens of a republic ought to be conscious of their obligation to look after and pass on the public world that they inherit, and when necessary to place its interests above those they have as private persons" (1963b & 1992, pp. 224ff).

Conclusion

In one short essay it is impossible to come close to doing justice to the thought of one of the most original and comprehensive thinkers of modernity. Rather than attempt a sweep of her thought I have sought to demonstrate how reading Arendt offers original and important ways of configuring the political and public life of late modernity when it might appear as if things were indeed falling apart. Like Yeats, Arendt recognized that, where the best have no "passionate intensity," the detritus of human existence fills the space. Consequently she is truly the philosopher of the public space. It would be easy to see Arendt as unremittingly pessimistic about the human condition, but this would be to underplay the many important ways in which she offers hope. Throughout her work Arendt regards action as offering humanity the possibility of redemption. To act into the world as it appears to us is in itself a political act. Action is of course irrevocable—once committed an act cannot be undone. If it can't be undone, does this necessarily imply that there is no way forward? Ancient civilizations recognized that there had to be some way of redressing the balance in the public space; it was for this reason that Judaism evolved the *talion* laws.[26] Recognizing that "without being forgiven, released from the consequences of what we have done, our capacity to act, would, as it were be confined to one single deed from which we could never recover; we would remain the victims of its consequences for ever" (Arendt, 1958, p. 237). Thus forgiveness (deeply embedded in the Judeo-Christian tradition) becomes itself an act of hope. Equally, promising offers hope for the future: The performative act of promising offers us the possibility of continuity of both our personal identity and that of the public spaces. Even where behavior has routinized the self and consumption has undermined the discharge of our obligations as citizens, Arendt offers the hope for something more and better. The attack of September 11 may in an unforeseen way, because it must perforce challenge our understanding of what it means to be a citizen in a liberal democracy rather than a consumer in a behavior-driven globalized society, open up new possibilities for the morally acting person.

Arendt's own work reflected the widening gyre of modernity but it also embodied a forensic archaeological quality, which impelled her to go down to the roots not to relive history but to use it to shed light on our own conditions. In his poem about his farmer father, entitled "Digging," the Irish poet Seamus Heaney compares himself to his father in a way that might apply similarly to Hannah Arendt. Heaney writes of hearing his father digging in the gravely ground beneath his window with a spade. His father handled a spade with the same skill his grandfather—who, in his time, could cut more turf during a day's work than any of the others working on Toner's bog. Heaney describes his father "nicking and slicing neatly" at the turf, and heaving the sods he had cut over his shoulder as he went "down and down" to get "the good turf." His father was Digging. But Heaney confesses that he has no spade with which to follow "men like them." Rather, a "squat pen" rests between his finger and his thumb, and Heaney resolves: "I'll dig with it."

Surely Hannah Arendt may be counted a "digger," in Heaney's poetic sense.

Notes

1. This should be distinguished from the Rhennish model of capitalism that had been dominant in European political economy from the end of the Second World War until the 1990s.
2. "American" is used here in preference to European or liberal or democratic only because (a) that's where Miller's play is located and (b) the American dream is one to which the masses in liberal democracies aspire.
3. Miller's literary output and Arendt's thought find a further valence in Miller's play *The Crucible*, which details Miller's view that even in putative democracies the individual, and indeed the *polis*, remain radically unfree if they fail to assert their political being.
4. Address of The Right Honourable Tony Blair PM to the British Trades Union Congress on 8 September 1997, where he "warned" the TUC to modernize so as to be partakers in the global economy.
5. A phrase that I have borrowed from the nineteenth-century Jesuit poet Gerard Manley Hopkins.
6. Jaspers was her doctoral supervisor and teacher when she moved to Marburg after her affair with Heidegger. The "affair" is now detailed in Ettinger (1995).
7. The italics within the quotation marks are mine and the quotation itself comes from (pp. 40ff) Merleau-Ponty, M. (1968). *The Visible and the Invisible* (NewYork, Evanston).
8. It is worth noting that, like Nietzsche, Kierkegaard's thought, most especially in the *Concluding Unscientific Postscript*, was deeply aphoristic, a style lending itself more easily to the deeply narratival quality of Arendt's work.
9. Kierkegaard represents something of an ambivalent figure for Arendt insofar as she recognized that it was he who was responsible for the demise of modern religion because he had introduced radical Cartesian doubt into its very heart through the pseudonymous Johannes Climacus (Kierkegaard, 1936 & 1962).
10. It is certainly true, as Kristeva (2001, pp. 14–16) points out, that the passion and pain of their relationship influenced Arendt. It might be suggested that this sense of unrequited love was the first experience to give rise to the deeply personal engagement with the political. Alienation is never simply a singular thing
11. This was an acceptance speech on being conferred with the Lessing Prize of the Free

City of Hamburg. While Lessing is not a twentieth-century figure, Arendt treats him as such because of the need in "Dark Times" to have men of principle.
12. It might be argued that the suicide bombers of New York and Washington have no such notion of natality, being governed not by action in this life so much as "happiness" in the next.
13. It is because of this perception that the life, the person that was Adolf Eichmann, becomes the means by which evil is to be conceptualized. No account of evil could simply be reified into the person of the evil genius (which had it been would indeed have followed the script of the Great Men theory) without regard to the embodied banalities of those who internalized the ideology together with its clichés.
14. In any event Arendt regarded contemplation since Plato as derivative of the experiences of *homo faber*, who only had to "let his arms drop" so that he could behold what he had been trying in any event to capture in his creations (see *The Human Condition*, pp. 303ff).
15. Arendt makes much of the Greek distinction between the *oikos* and the *polis*, where the *oikos* or household concerned itself with the material needs of its members and the business of which had no place in the public domain—the *polis*, which was the space where men deliberated on what might constitute appropriate living of, say, the "good life" and how they might organize themselves to so live it.
16. Dietz's interpretation of the Arendtian distinction between labor and work is interesting in that she argues that the two concepts have no settled meaning in Arendt's work as she attributes so many elements to each that have intimations of the other. Dietz then proceeds to list the multifarious elements of each and suggests that "the features Arendt assigned to labor and work can be viewed as points along a single continuum that shade from the human condition 'under which life on earth has been given to man' into a condition in extremis under which life on earth has been taken away." Near the end of the continuum, labor manifests itself *in extremis* in the form of dehumanizing automatic processes and compulsive repetitions that displace human death; work manifests itself in extremis in the form of dehumanizing fabricating processes.
17. Not Arendt's but Buber's word.
18. Of course Arendt doesn't wish to suggest that this change has suddenly taken place in late capitalist society. Rather she believes that it has been the result of the gradual processes of history and has its roots in the Platonic division between the *archein* and the *praktein*.
19. There are some interesting parallels with Martin Buber's I and Thou (*Ich und Du*) where Buber's now famous distinction between the word pairs "I-It" and "I-Thou" parallel Arendt's distinction between making and acting. The one ("I-It") is always concerned to appropriate and use whereas the other ("I-Thou") is focused on the singularity of the encounter itself.
20. For a fuller discussion and most interesting account of this see Dunne (1997), Ch. 3.
21. Arendt held that the social was what had emerged from the obliteration of the distinction between public and private.
22. Arendt's account of Eichmann's banal embodiment of evil was received badly in some sections of the Jewish press on account of the deeply held desire to see the perpetrators of the Final Solution as unspeakably wicked and therefore not like us. Even her friend Mary McCarthy wanted her to see Eichmann in these rather more "elevated" terms so that at least a due measure of anger and blame might be heaped upon him. For interesting insights into this controversy see Brightman (1995), pp. 144–149 and 151–155.

23. Arendt herself recognized the uniqueness of Totalitarianism as a twentieth-century phenomenon and that the combination of strategies to make people superfluous were unique, having "never [been] used before in the varied forms of political dominance" (1973, p. 474). There are plenty of critics who challenge the clarity of all Arendt's claims in "The Origins of Totalitarianism" as well as her sense of history (Crick, 1990, pp. 50–51) but, given the scope of her reflections and the complexity of her subject, this is hardly surprising.
24. In this discussion I am not unaware of the nature of the regimes that harbor and support the kind of attack carried out in New York and Washington. Indeed it is precisely the kind of philosophy embodied in the totalitarian structures of the Taliban government of Afghanistan that was the target of Arendt's devastating analysis and critique. Theirs is indeed a doctrine of the superfluity of the person, where the political has been utterly evacuated of any notion of plurality. But the obvious totalitarianism of such regimes must not be permitted to blind us to the serious implications of Arendt's analysis for modern liberal democracies.
25. The collective noun for all those who had full status as citizens.
26. *Talion* laws were instituted to ensure balance in the community and are colloquially expressed in the formula of "an eye for an eye."

MARX, WITTGENSTEIN, AND THE PROBLEM OF CONSCIOUSNESS

> *Language is as old as consciousness, language is practical consciousness, as it exists for other men, and for that reason is really beginning to exist for me personally as well; for language like consciousness arises only from the need, the necessity of intercourse with other men.*
>
> —Marx & Engels (1845/1939, p. 51)

The Cartesian View and Its Fatal Flaw

Marx's view that language and consciousness are closely related and that both take shape in human praxis can seem to be ideologically rather than logically motivated to those of us with Western individualist conceptions of mind and thought. For many in the philosophical tradition a form of "Cartesianism," according to which consciousness is a typical mental state internal to the mind of the subject, frames all discussion of the mind. It follows from this that the first person subject has privileged and direct access to the states and events comprising her own conscious life, but others only have indirect access to them. Allied to this thesis is the idea that language is merely a vehicle of expression for thought and has no intrinsic role in the structure or contents of consciousness. Thus it has seemed obvious to many thinkers about education that a child must have certain ideas before those ideas can be "clothed in language" and that the structures of the mind have their own inner workings, which may differ from person to person. These Cartesian ideas are, however, suspect in purely philosophical (rather than ideological) terms. What is more, I think we can locate Marx's view within a philosophical tradition that emphasizes the active and engaged role of the subject, the material nature of the objects of experience, and the practical functions of thought and language. That at least is the bill of fare.

Problems with Cartesianism

Let us begin with the Cartesian premise that my thoughts are in my head and essentially private to me, and yours are similarly internal and private to you. Let us also acknowledge that I can communicate my thoughts to you by using language. For many this is not only philosophical orthodoxy but common sense. Frege, the theorist who dominated philosophy of language and thought in Wittgenstein's era, held that a subject's "inner thought" gives meaning to his words and that these meanings were captured, more or less perspicuously, by language (Frege, 1977, p. 5). On this account my inner thought gives meaning to what I am writing and your inner thought is the basis of your understanding of what I have written. But how is it that you know what you take from my words? I cannot see what thoughts accompany your reading of my words and therefore I do not know what they mean to you. I cannot assume that your understanding bears anything more than a fortuitous relationship to my meaning because there is no essential relationship between my thoughts and yours. What is more, this disturbing realization undermines the very possibility of my educating you or anybody educating anybody. How do I know what is happening in your thoughts when I try to inform you of this or that and how do you know what I am trying to inform you about? In the Cartesian view we have no way of detecting the meanings that lie behind our words and therefore no way of knowing what to make of what another person says.

Frege found this a particularly disturbing conclusion because it implies that we have no justified expectation of achieving a shared conception of truth. To be justified in jointly settling the truth or falsity of a given thought we would need to have some reason to believe that you and I mean the same thing, or express the same thought, when something is said. Consider, for example, a remark such as "That cat is black." In the Cartesian view, what this remark actually means is given by the thoughts it expresses. Thus, for all you know, I might have the thoughts that go with your words "The dog is white" when I say, "The cat is black." This implies that what I say or think could be true while what you say (or think), using the same words, is false. Frege argues that this is an intolerable conclusion because scientific knowledge is built on the presumption that what is true is true for anyone who thinks it and that the truth can be communicated and understood by different thinkers. If, however, what I think when I report a scientific result or write an essay like this is quite possibly opaque to you and vice versa because neither of us can ascertain the connection between words and their accompanying inner states, then a universal foundation for scientific inquiry is undermined. For this reason Frege claims that the communication of thoughts and therefore the determination of truth cannot depend on what he calls "men's varying states of consciousness"

(1977, p. 17). His objection seems to be not only cogent but in fact devastating if we conceive of our words as conveying some thought in virtue of states of consciousness according to the Cartesian (individualistic "inner state") conception. The package of ideas that form the essence of that conception condemns us to the view that the truths conveyed in discourse depend on inner states and that our apparent store of objective knowledge about the world could be based on nothing more than guesswork about the thoughts behind the words of others. Surprising as it may seem, some people do, in fact, believe this strange idea.

This view cannot, of course, be taken seriously; it is as absurd as it is unavoidable in the Cartesian model, which informs our common conceptions of consciousness and its mysteries. We therefore need a slightly better conception of consciousness and the mind and such is, I believe, to be found in the work of Marx and Wittgenstein.

Language and Consciousness: Marx

Marx, in his discussion of consciousness in "The German Ideology," echoes an idea that might be gleaned from the etymology of the word *conscious* or, alternatively, be derived from Hegel's view of experience and knowledge.

The etymology is suggestive of a link with our social being in that the word *conscious* is plausibly made up of parts associated with the stems *con*—with—and *scio*—I know. It remains to be seen whether this etymological clue leads to any fruitful reflections, but it is the kind of thing much beloved by continental philosophers of the late nineteenth and early twentieth centuries.

Hegel makes explicit the link between consciousness, shared concepts, and our dealings with objects in some deep and difficult passages at the beginning of *Phenomenology of Spirit*. He argues, in accordance with the thoughts of his own teacher Kant, that the perception of any object is an active process whereby the human being encounters a thing that is primarily itself and self-contained and then likens it to other things by using universal concepts that articulate or specify properties conceivable as distinct from the object itself and combined in the object. Kant clearly enunciated the fact that the thing as presented to us was not an idea or mental object but something that existed apart from the knower and was merely "clothed in conceptual form" by the mind of the knower. Hegel repeatedly points out the difference between the object as it exists (for itself and in itself) and the concepts, determinations, or abstractions that we use to frame thinkable truths about it. Kant was clear that this latter is a discursive activity but did not explicitly invoke language in that. However, language hovers in the background of Hegel's account. In particular Hegel announces the structuralist thesis that all determinations or conceptualizations involve distinctions and contrasts whereby one concept obscures or sets itself against another while the object remains the same (1977, pp. 77–78). Hegel also famously discusses the lord and the bondsman or the master and the slave, according to which actual work or interaction with actual material things (by the slave) is the fount of real knowledge about them rather than the abstract or second order knowledge (of the master), which derives from conceptualizing things according to categories related immediately to consciousness rather than the existence or "thinghood" of the objects themselves (1977, pp. 115ff).

The discussion of conscious experience of the world in terms of universal concepts (like red, square, and newt) and the objects to which they are applied suggests an important link between language and thought in understanding the contents of conscious mental acts. This link becomes explicit in the development of Hegel's view by Marx toward the thesis with which this chapter begins. Language is the medium in which concepts are articulated and through which we impart their use to our cognitive apprentices (Gillett, 1992). Through language we articulate our thoughts and train other thinkers (as Vygotsky, following Marx, clearly saw). Our concepts are our ways of identifying and marking those aspects of things that make them amenable to the kinds of things we do to the world. This is deeply congenial to Marx's view of consciousness, whereby our patterns of thought are socially produced and guide us in developing an awareness of what is around us and what we might call "the nature of things." It is not difficult to see the way that language forms the connection between consciousness, the material conditions of our existence, and society, but it remains to spell out how those connections work. In exploring these links we should elucidate the extent to which the social basis of language, and therefore thought, works against, on the one hand, a conception of individuality and consciousness and, on the other, the objectivity of certain features of human consciousness as manifestations of the kind of creatures we are. We might wonder whether it is possible to think or act relatively independently of the society in which one lives.

The Cartesian view, as extended by contemporary analytic philosophy, tends to focus on objects that might be identified as such relatively independently of language. Things whose nature is elaborated by causal processes in which we have little part (trees, rivers, birds, and other critters). But much of the domain we inhabit as human beings is not like that. We live in the midst of a profusion of our own artifacts and even the "natural" parts of the world often bear our imprint (rivers are channeled, forests are grown and tended, animal husbandry changes the species with whom we share the ecosphere, and so on). Thus the productive effects of language and social being are evident all around us. What is more, language provides many of the concepts and conceptualizations necessary for a wide range of human thoughts. Think, for instance, of trying to entertain thoughts about the fact that the president of the United States should not allow himself to be ruled by his biological urges if one had no words to denote the conceptions and concepts constituting that thought. Consequently, language and its social or communal determinants have a profound effect on the contents of human consciousness and action in that language allows one to be aware, *inter alia:*

(i) that there is a certain type of situation to be engaged with (a marriage, for instance);

(ii) that there is a specifiable action that could be performed (e.g., objecting to it); and
(iii) that the action concerned has a certain significance in human affairs or dealings with the environment.

Some situations—the president's incontinence, the objectionable marriage—depend on a complex social order, but others do not. We might wonder whether language is so important in these more natural cases. It is plausible that it is. For instance, if I see that a heavy rock is delicately poised on a ledge over a point that a herd of buffalo will pass on their way to drink and I am equipped with stories about using pieces of wood as levers, I might conceive a plan to roll that rock down on the buffalo as they pass and secure a meal for the tribe. Cooperative effort and communication may then allow us to become aware of some means of repeating the trick by getting yet another heavy stone into the strategic position that we previously exploited. If we do that it will be because language has entered into the development and understanding of how to perform the action concerned. Language and social cooperation, we might say with Marx, jointly create possibilities for different ways of knowing and behaving. Our language is, however, an artifact or cultural production of the particular time and place in which we live. Thus there is an important connection between our thoughts and a given sociohistorical context.

Vygotsky pursued this thought and realized that children make use of speech to structure their practical activity and extend their cognitive skills in the world.

[T]he most significant moment in the course of intellectual development, which gives birth to the purely human forms of practical and abstract intelligence, occurs when speech and practical activity, two previously independent lines of development, converge. (1978, p. 24)

In discussing perception and attention he remarks, "[t]he system of signs restructures the whole psychological process" (1978, p. 35). Action and identity can also, on this basis, be seen in part reflecting a radical role for culture in the construction of mind in that when one comes to behave in a certain way, X, one adopts a possible way of being (for instance, being a successful student), devised in a cultural setting (such as the education system), which may be adopted by other human beings who are active in that setting. An accumulation of such hexes or habits of thought and action then forms the mind of those human beings and influences their consciousness of the world.

It is often thought that this Marxist strand of sociohistorical theory about mind and consciousness makes us prone to a radical form of relativism or idealism whereby even the possibility of individuality and critical knowledge is rendered incoherent. But that is an exaggeration of the emerging view, as a foray into Marx very soon reveals.

Language and Social Constructivism

Social constructionism is, as I have noted, often associated with damaging forms of epistemic relativism and a denial of the possibility not only of reasonable objectivity but also of creativity and free thinking by dissidents or other critical voices. That creativity and free thinking still occur is sometimes taken to refute the theoretical orientation I am developing but the lines of the argument are not so simply drawn. However, a defensible form of social constructionism must limit itself to the domains in which it is a plausible explanation of what we think and do. In so doing such a thesis should pay some attention to the fact that our epistemic virtues rest on cognitive equipment that has a venerable history, with biological influences having shaped certain features of it. These are all theses mooted by Marx and Engels as they develop some of the Hegelian themes we have already encountered.

> The production of ideas, of conceptions, of consciousness is at first directly interwoven with the material activity and the material intercourse of men, the language of real life. (Marx & Engels, 1845/1939, p. 47)

This passage links consciousness, and the discursive or conceptual tools by which it is given form and content, to practical activity in a way that is immediately congenial to a world-involving view of perception, thought, and action. Intentionality in this sense is object-directedness, where the objects are material things in the public domain. The strand of continental philosophy that emphasizes the link between consciousness and intentionality sometimes neglects this fact. Marx and Engels do not; they keep squarely in view the dual realization that consciousness concerns actual things in a material world with which human beings are engaged and that it is a social product designed to meet the challenges of that world.

> Men are the producers of their conceptions ideas etc.—real active men as they are conditioned by a definite development of their productive forces and of the intercourse corresponding to these, up to its furthest forms. Consciousness can never be anything else than conscious existence, and the existence of men is their actual life processes. (ibid., p. 47)

Consciousness is therefore (according to Marx and Engels) essentially a social product and remains so as long as men exist as living interacting beings who notice what is around them and intervene in their environment. They emphasize the role of social production even while tying consciousness to actual life processes that are constitutive of the material or bodily engagement between human beings and their environment. This is meat and drink to the view of intentionality that we will come to see is championed by Wittgenstein. It is an important entailment of this view that the contents of consciousness are constrained by the bodily engagement of individuals in the world and cannot float free of the actual world in any quasi-idealistic way.

The identity of nature and man appears in such a way that the restricted relation of men to nature determines their restricted relation to one another, and their restricted relation to one another determines men's restricted relation to nature, just because nature is hardly modified historically: and on the other hand, man's consciousness of the necessity of associating with the individuals around him is the beginning of the consciousness of society at all. This beginning is as animal as social life itself at this stage. It is mere herd consciousness. (Marx & Engels, 1845/1939, p. 51)

Notice that the restrictions or constraints that are here applied to thought and consciousness arise jointly from the relations between human beings in their shared environment and their relation to nature. At this point Marx and Engels introduce an absolutely crucial point in the discussion of human thought by setting in place foundations in the natural and cultural worlds that are nowise separable from one another. The environment in which we live is not natural in any sense that can be given by natural science alone in that it is being transformed by human activity into a context for thought that contains agriculture, buildings, artifacts of all kinds, and complex social arrangements. But to think that a culture could be unconstrained rather than adjusting its practices to the exigencies of the ecological environment it inhabits is also unrealistic. (Which is compatible with the view that a cultural more might become so powerful as to have maladaptive effects.) Thus the contents of the mind must engage not only with nature and the presence of others but with its own physical and abstract products. What is more, we should not move from the acknowledgment that consciousness and its products are shaped by a process of social production to the conclusion that the consciousness of any individual is no more than an artifact that deterministically reflects social norms: "[T]hese three moments, the forces of production, the state of society, and consciousness, can and must come into contradiction with one another (Marx & Engels, 1845/1939, p. 52).

Here consciousness is set against the forces of production on the one hand and the state of society on the other so that it takes on a life of its own in any individual. The possibility of a distinct moment among the forces of social change arising from individual consciousness may not be a universal feature of all varieties of Marxism but it clearly has a place in the views of Marx and Engels. In fact, it seems inescapable.

Consider the fact that any individual is exposed to a variety of discursive influences that affect that person's subjectivity or, if you prefer, multiple subjectivities. A moment's reflection reveals that any individual's particular trajectory through the experiences that configure them is likely to be unique (if examined in sufficient detail) even though certain general features might emerge as a result of their sociohistorical situation (Harre & Gillett, 1994, p. 133). Therefore, if we do take seriously the effect on consciousness of the cumulative experiences undergone by an individual, we are committed to the conclusion that each individual person's conscious life is potentially different in content from that of any other person. It follows that there is a potential tension between a set of social norms for self-configuration and the lived experience of the individual. This is constrained by the sociohistorical context of the person but also by his or her biology (or life processes) in ways that allow for broad psychological generalizations, but it is not determined by anything approaching the status of laws of nature. This is because the discourse that provides our concepts supplies us merely with the tools of thought, and what one does with those tools is a matter of individual determination. The exact analogy drawn by Wittgenstein is with chess as a rule-governed system of moves; despite the fact that every chess player conforms to the rules, the actual moves that a player makes are original. In a similar way patterns of thought can be as original as moves in a game of chess (and they can even, by use of metaphor and innovative departure from conventional usage, creatively violate the rules).

What is more, even if the meaning of a term or element in thought can be considered a social construct, this does not mean there is not a real thing to which that term refers in the world and a unique relation between the people engaging with the thing and the thing itself. The fact that each of us has a unique trajectory in the world and that the many discourses that each of us inhabit are forced together by their co-occurrence in one lived bodily subjectivity gives us an *a priori* argument for the singularity of conscious experience as lived by each individual human being.

Thus it seems that two of the most damaging theses developed from the social constructivist position, namely, that there is no thing as the individual conscious subject and that thought and meaning are related only to language and not to the world in which that language is developed, are both untenable. The first is refuted within the theory by the uniqueness of the sociohistorical location of each human being and the individual path he or she follows in reaching adulthood. The second is refuted by the fact that words are aids to practical adaptation and thus they only have meaning as they are interwoven with the activity of human beings. The two together imply that the meanings that inform consciousness are both world-involving and allow for considerable individual difference in the ways that they configure the conscious experience of any individual.

At this point we can usefully summon Wittgenstein to the conversation as his perspective on consciousness supports many of the points that emerge from Marx's analysis.

Wittgenstein

> Consciousness is as clear in his face and behaviour, as in myself. (Wittgenstein, 1967, #221)

This is a startling claim to one who has been bewitched by the Cartesian tradition of other minds' skepticism and has come to believe that consciousness is inner and privately known through introspection by its subject but not accessible to others.

However, I have already cast aspersions on Cartesianism in virtue of its inability to give a coherent account of linguistic meaning. We therefore need, not only as a matter of interest to critical theory but also as a philosophical puzzle in itself, to develop further an understanding of consciousness that might explain the fact that we can communicate, without systematic ambiguity, about contentful conscious experience. Marx has asserted, on the basis of a sound Hegelian tradition, that consciousness is practical and world-involving in a way that links it closely to language, and his thesis is strengthened when we take the trouble to visit (albeit briefly) the intellectual bloodbath surrounding the private language argument.

The Private Language Argument

In the section referred to as the private language argument, Wittgenstein draws together strands from the early parts of the *Philosophical Investigations* (PI).[1] These strands concern the argument that meaning is use, the idea of rule following, and the central importance of "agreement in judgements" (PI #241) in any theory of meaning and truth. What Wittgenstein seeks to establish is that it is not plausible to believe that a person can speak, reason, and have thoughts about objects that are only ever experienced in their own private conscious world. But if mental contents are not private in this sense, then there is an essential and typical link between consciousness and the public sphere.

Meaning Is Use

Wittgenstein's first major claim in PI is that understanding what a word means is a matter of correct use. He remarks: "For a large class of cases—though not for all—in which we employ the word 'meaning' it can be defined thus: the meaning of a word is its use in the language (PI #43).

Thus, if someone were to say, "Get me the book!" and I got the newspaper, there would be some doubt about my understanding of the term book. If the person asking me wanted to check up on my understanding of the term book, then she might ask, "Do you know what a book is?" or ask me to say whether or not certain things she showed me were books. If I failed to demonstrate any familiarity with the use of book in real-life situations such as these, then she would be entitled to conclude, from my failure to use the term properly, that I did not understand it. Thus, we could say, with Wittgenstein, that the criterion of understanding is correct use and that in the general run of things that is a public fact, which is evident through the way I relate to things around me.

In fact, when you try to give any other definition of understanding it fails. For instance, an obvious candidate is the Cartesian inner idea or image associated with the word (which I have already criticized on Fregean grounds). Consider the following scenario. The person whose understanding is in question says, "I am trying to understand what you mean by 'book' but I can't concentrate because this image of a thing with two covers and pages inside it keeps coming up in my mind and distracting me." Obviously the person has an appropriate image in his mind and, *ex hypothesi*, the image comes to mind when the term book is mentioned but he does not know how to use whatever is going on inside him and therefore he cannot be said to understand the meaning of book. By contrast, he would be said to understand if, in the relevant circumstances, he responded in the right kind of way or exhibited an ability to make correct use of the term book even if no image occurred to him at all.

Rules

When we reflect on what is required to latch on to the meaning of a word or phrase and to use it in the right way it becomes clear that there is a set of informal and perhaps inchoate rules that must be obeyed. The word "aardvark," for instance, has a role to play in discourse only when certain conditions apply (one wants to induce thoughts about hairy anteaters or some such). The rules, *inter alia*, determine what kinds of things the word should be applied to and what linguistic links fill in its meaning. Obeying a rule, I would argue—with Wittgenstein—is a matter of mastering a practice or technique (PI #202) and the conditions in which it is properly exhibited. Such mastery is gained by using the relevant term (overtly or covertly) to structure one's activity. Initially one must do this in such a way that one's mistakes and successes are manifest and can be corrected, usually through communicative interaction with others (Gillett, 1995). After one is clear what, for instance, an aardvark is, there is no problem in that term being used in relation to perception and action even though what is afoot may be covert or even secret. Some have objected to this on the basis of remarks such as the following.

> Hence it is not possible to obey a rule "privately": otherwise thinking one was obeying a rule would be the same thing as obeying it. (PI #202)

This has been taken to impose a very strong sociality condition on any conscious activity, but it should not be interpreted that way. The important claim is that any individual has to have some sufficiency of correct application and discursive knowledge to count as understanding a given concept, even if the understanding that is present is not manifest on a particular occasion when it figures in conscious experience.

It follows from the consideration of rules, correction, and mastery of the skills or techniques involved in the use of words (and therefore the concepts they mark) that the cognitive or discursive grasp of any rule is predicated on the actual use that one is able to make of it in practice. This is important because it reinforces the idea that a key aspect of thinking—understanding the meanings of words—is something that is tied to the public domain and to things we do. The public nature of meaning brings us to our third point in setting up the private language argument.

Agreement in Judgments

A person counts as having mastered the rule-governed ability to make use of a term when s/he has achieved a sufficient level of agreement in judgments with others who have mastered the relevant ability or practice (as we have noted in the case of book). For instance, I would count as a person who grasped the concept <square> when I was able reliably to judge <that figure is square>, <this is not square>, <a square is a four-sided plane figure>, and so on. Such an ability, evident in my use of propositions containing the term "square," would both constitute, in part, and exhibit a grasp of the concept <square>. Thus my understanding—or grasp of a concept—goes hand in hand with exchanges in which my judgments are manifest to others and corrected by them so that they can correct me when I am wrong. The result of this process is that I gradually converge with the judgments of those who already understand the concept I am trying to learn. Note again that, analogously to the shared agreement about the rules of chess, this does not mean that I will always form the same opinions as others.

These reflections serve to tie understanding and meaning to rules and thereby to communicability and corrigibility and have important implications both for our view of what it is to have contentful conscious experience and for our use of mental terms such as "anger," "seeing something red," "being in pain" and "conscious." First, they imply that conscious experience and the categorization or conceptualization of its contents are tied to my participation in a public milieu where I have learnt rules governing the use of concepts. As a corollary of this, it emerges that my use of concepts to make sense of the experiences I have is built upon my being with other minds and their interactions with me.

Wittgenstein on Consciousness

Wittgenstein had some very instructive things to say about consciousness and the mind. These things make plausible his "startling claim" and give us a basis on which we can say something about language, practice, social relationships, and consciousness. One or two preliminaries are in order.

First, one can be conscious *simpliciter* or conscious of this or that thing. An act of being conscious of something necessarily takes an object; that may be an external object, a state of affairs in the world, or one's own state of mind. It is therefore intentional (in the phenomenological sense that I have alluded to above). If, as Marx surely did, we follow the Hegelian path here, we will accept that consciousness as intentionality engages us with other things and people. As a result of that engagement, consciousness is interwoven with the use of language (which subtly pervades all we do as we communicate about the things we encounter and benefit from the diverse knowledges elaborated by each of us).

What is more, the corrigibility of our concept use and the communicability of what our concepts reveal about the things with which we interact imply that our language about our own mental attributes, such as consciousness, shares an important feature with all other meaningful words.

I have already discussed the fact that words must relate to what is public and manifest and not to ideas in a Cartesian realm, and turning the spotlight on the mental life of a human being is just an extension of the same argument. I have noted that, in general, the meaning of any word depends on more than one person knowing if it is being used correctly on a sufficient number of occasions so that the requisite "agreement in judgments" (PI #241) to establish rule-governed use is achieved. This in turn implies that one cannot learn the meaningful use of a term like "conscious" unless there is some way that correct use of that term can be established intersubjectively. Thus my saying of you that you are conscious (and therefore, if you are learning the concept, your use of "conscious" to describe yourself) must be based on something that can be agreed on by both of us and not merely on my guess about hidden goings on in your mind or head. This in turn implies, among other things, that consciousness is a property of beings about which we can make judgments and not a feature of internal processes and states about which we can only conjecture. Wittgenstein emphasizes this point when he remarks,

> Look into someone else's face, and see the consciousness in it, and a particular shade of consciousness. You see on it, in it, joy, indifference, interest, excitement, torpor and so on. (Z #220)

Of course, we may not always be sure about whether a given individual is conscious but we must, in principle, be able to agree on what would count as being in that state for the word "conscious" to have a determinable meaning. Thus an adequate account of consciousness should be able to say how, in general, we are quite competent in judging whether self or others are conscious. What is more, this must go for any concept that we apply to the life of the mind. Formulating such an account brings together the best of the ideas enunciated by both Marx and Wittgenstein.

Convergences

Both Marx and Wittgenstein are, for their own reasons, allergic to the Cartesian idea that the mental life of a person is primarily a succession of inner states and events. Marx, following Hegel, embraces the idea of the mind's engagement with real objects as a material encounter between the organism and the world. To this he adds the further (Kantian and Hegelian) point that the concepts we apply to things to reveal the characteristics of those things are contributed by us. These concepts must be applied to actual material things to have any use in experience but they are generated by us as we search for regularities and recurrences in the way things strike us and we deal with them. Kant and Hegel both saw that this involved a discursive ability on the part of human thinkers, and Marx enunciated the view that language and consciousness were coeval, arising in our dealings with the world around us.

To this increasingly cogent view of thought and experience we bring Wittgenstein's insight that we conceptualize what we are doing by using the terms that mark and link certain conditions in the world to structure our activity (both cooperative and individual). Society provides us with the toolbox of language and we use the tools it gives us to make our world tractable for experience and intervention.

Our consciousness of the world around us is therefore articulated and given practical form by our use of language. Through the resources that language gives us we achieve a kind of power over the ecosphere that our fellow creatures cannot even begin to comprehend. Through the use of language we also ensure that our good tricks are passed on directly to our offspring without the cumbersome need to use the genetic route. When we learn to chop off our tails (or mutilate any other parts of our anatomy), as Lamarck did to his mice, we pass the tendency on to the next generation even though the trait has not been coded in any sequence of DNA nucleotides (Gillett, 1999).

Marx noticed that we as thinking subjects were in many ways artifacts of our own creation or social productions and that language was the means by which we made minds in the image we wanted them to be. Wittgenstein also noticed that we are formed by our forms of life and that language is an essential part of the medium through which that happens.

Note

1. I shall use the initials PI throughout to refer to *Philosophical Investigations* and #nn to refer to paragraph numbers within that work, and Z #nn in a parallel way for *Zettel*.

7   *Robert Young*

HABERMAS'S POSTMODERNISM

If the honorific (?) postmodern is eclectic enough to embrace both Foucault and Derrida, it is a mere trifle to extend it to include Habermas. After all, Habermas shares both some of Derrida's distrust of language and some of Foucault's distrust of knowledge claims. Habermas is a pragmatist—a transactional realist—so he sees meaning as an ever shifting negotiation which, like all negotiations, can be shaped by power, and knowledge as a part of a cluster of intertwined claims of power, morality, and truth. But it is precisely because of Habermas's realism that there is a role for politics in his theory, and one in which the political is internal to the processes that make power and meaning.

Gramsci (1967) was not the first exemplary political intellectual to argue for a kind of "organic" engagement between intellectuals and the class that they championed. But Gramsci's organicism was also one in which there was an internal connection between the illuminative power of intellection and political partisanship. When this connection is severed, the distinction between the engagement *of* intellectuals and engagement *qua* intellectual gains more than merely analytical force, that is, when the internal connection is severed intellectuals as intellectuals can negate ("criticize") the existing order but only arbitrarily, and as a matter of faith, rather than theory, adopt a politics to go beyond it. An organic or internal connection between theory and politics requires some account of the role the intellectual life plays or can play in politics. This may be glossed as "the political significance of theory," but, equally, it may be glossed as the connection between critique and praxis. Insofar as any theory of education contains an account of the development of the intellectual life of learners, which also involves the development of balanced powers of critique (viz., not just negation), education is also *implicated* in the political significance of theorizing. The current debate between "postmodern" and "critical" intellectuals about the contribution of "postmodern" ideas to educational thought is also a debate about the political significance of these ideas, and of ideas in general. Parsed another way, it is a debate about the nature of critique and its relation to action. Political relevance provides a touchstone in this debate, since both postmodern and critical intellectuals find common ground in the notion that educative action in society should be political. Where the two groups may part company is in the character of their understanding of the political and of the possible contribution of theory and theorizing to it.

However, I contend that despite their apparent differences, some versions of critical theory have become infected by postmodernism and share with it the same flawed architecture of praxis. Whatever the specific faults of Habermas's theory, its architecture is not flawed in this way. Habermas's theory of critique is one among a number of theories of critique. The present argument applies as much to the requirements for any theory of critique as it does to Habermas's specific theory.

The problems of many existing theories of critique are problems of praxis, and they stem from a shared absolutism. They may possess a historical absolutism, of the kind found in some versions of historical materialism, or in Foucault's absolute regimes/dispositifs of power/knowledge, which have no margins to play in. Or they may possess an absolute semiological skepticism, which is also a cultural skepticism, as found in some of Derrida's writing, but even more so in his English-speaking reception (as Derrida himself complains [1984]). Sometimes this absolutism is overtly revealed in talk of "nothing but," "never," and "always" (What never? Hardly ever?). Often it is covert, identified by the absence of qualification and connection with the risky pragmatic business of real political action.

The appropriate method for critique of this absolutism is not yet another absolutism used as a standpoint for external critique, but an immanent critique that confronts theory with the failure of its own claims. Comparative immanent critique goes beyond monistic immanent critique in that it operates in a field of critique where more than one theory is present. Monistic immanent critique explores the contradictions inherent in an object of criticism by identifying its values and its telos and showing how these are denied realization. If all theory is imperfect, such critique can readily become covertly absolutist or utopian, essentially complaining that theory is not perfect; however, comparative immanent critique identifies values common to two or more objects of critique and compares the relative success of the rival theories in the realization of their values, thus avoiding the importation of a covert absolute standard.

Monistic immanent critique on its own can contribute to the reform or reconstruction of a theoretical tradition, but not to the selection of one. Comparative critique can also be immanent, because it proceeds from touchstone, which is immanent to the theories being compared by definition. Thus it can provide some reason for preferring one theory over another, while avoiding the employment of merely external critique that involves preferring the values of one theory over another, or expecting theories to be perfect against some abstract standard of coherence, completeness, or evidentiality. Postmodern thinkers rightly complain when the very points that are at issue are employed in critique of their views. This has been called "enlightenment blackmail." Rorty (1992) makes just this point in his rejection of evaluations of Derrida that judge him as a deficient system-builder. Thus, Rorty sees accusations of "internal incoherence" as being irrelevantly "logocentric" and finds "little use, in reading or discussing [Derrida], for the notion of 'rigorous argumentation.'" (1992, p. 9). But Derrida does claim political relevance for his work, as does Foucault, arguably the two most influential "postmodern" theorists. In fact, it is not an exaggeration to say that both writers, although differing profoundly in almost every other respect, agree in desiring that their work be seen to have great political significance. This would appear true of their English-speaking appropriators, too, if the flood of books and articles with titles that include the word "political" is any guide. It is equally true of their educational appropriators. But what kind of politics is involved in these claims and what roles for theory, theorizing, and intellectuals? As will be shown below, the kind of political relevance that is claimed is in some ways, and at first sight, quite traditional. But although post-Marxist theories of critique differ in many ways from postmodern ones, they sometimes share a common absolutist architecture, via a covert historicism, the absence of a historical addressee, or the absence of any theory of the posthistorical.

The Postmodern Political

It has sometimes been argued that postmodern thought points to an entirely new conception of politics, but a closer examination reveals a more ambiguous picture. It is more accurate to say that we are presented with a juxtaposition of conventional and unconventional political claims. On the one hand there are conventional references or allusions to relevance at the level of the politics of macroscopic political systems, such as "regimes" of power/knowledge and "oppressed groups," and on the other hand, there is a new kind of talk about specific and contingent forms of "resistance," "action," "going beyond limits," uncovering metaphysical commitments, "cultural politics," and the like.

Some accounts of the relevance of postmodern thought speak of a kind of politics of "the margin." Foucault talks about the political role of "specific" intellectuals and "local politics." Lyotard (1984) too recommends the development of "smallish, localized narratives" in which "grand narratives" are subverted, implying a political activity that can take place only where grand narratives do not dominate discourse. But, as Fraser and Nicholson (1988) have pointed out, Lyotard himself is dissatisfied with a merely local politics, and calls for more. Fraser and Nicholson argue that large narratives are necessary if the political needs of large oppressed classes, such as women, are to be met:

> [E]ffective criticism . . . requires at a minimum large narratives about changes in social organizations and ideology, empirical and social-theoretical aspects of macrostructures and institutions. (1988, p. 362)

Quite apart from the adequacy of the reasoning that led to this conclusion, the essence of the Fraser-Nicholson case is that the political needs of feminist intellectuals cannot be met without a macroscopic critique and a macroscopic politics, that is, that an effective politics demands more than merely local politics. There would appear to be some common ground here, insofar as it is implicit in condemnations of "totalizing" social regimes, that large-scale systems need to be changed in some way. But even if this were so, the question of the basis on which macroscopic critique was developed would still be at issue. If macroscopic political positions and strategies were simply *enunciated,* their politics would be arbitrary and vulnerable to the charge that they represented mere posturing rather than a reasoned basis for effective action. If their overcoming is made to depend on some osmotic process in which millions of specific and local initiatives seep out into macroscopic history, there is a burden of demonstration of how the accumulation of critique could attain the necessary weight or direction.

Foucault, echoing Adorno, speaks of a "permanent critique" of our historical era. But notoriously, his rhetorical style is such that he constantly holds out the promise of critique while simultaneously withdrawing it. As Taylor points out, Foucault's style is to make an implicit claim, and then deny it explicitly. For instance, in *Discipline and Punish,* torture and the infliction of bodily pain are shown to have given way (in France) to a penal system based on "modern humanitarian" notions of rehabilitation, but Foucault refuses to prefer the latter, because it is seen to constitute part of a more effective system of control. This would seem to valorize some notion of the opposites of control—freedom perhaps. But in his critique of normalization, Foucault goes on to reject the possibility of valid evaluation of this kind. Nevertheless, elsewhere Foucault characterizes his work as seeking to give new impetus, as far and wide as possible, to the undefined work of freedom (see Taylor, 1984).

Fraser is another who draws our attention to the rhetorical devices whereby Foucault shows his negative attitude to modern forms of power, while arguing that it is necessary to bracket questions of normative validity.

Defenders of Foucault have pointed out that reading Foucault in this fashion is to miss the point. They draw attention to the disruptive intention of his way of speaking, the use of hyperbole, and the Heideggerian way in which he sees permanent critique as a necessary protection against the permanent "dangers" of each new totalizing arrangement of society, and as a necessary prerequisite of the possibility of recognizing opportunities to make oneself in a new way. However, when Foucault speaks of the "ethics" of this possibility, he retreats from the social to talk of ethics as the morality of one's relationship with oneself as one's life is made "a work of art" (Foucault, 1988a, p. 49, and Foucault 1990, Conclusion).

Derrida's writing is very different from Foucault's. His political claims are more integrally woven into the constant disruption of every form of fixity and the undermining of every form of hidden violence in the denial of the otherness of others and of their right to it. But Derrida also speaks of "taking a position" and of "intervening" politically. His primary mode of critique is the critique of texts in a view of life in which its "textuality" is emphasized, but he also speaks of the "real conditions . . . (economic, ideological, political)" under which the struggle of the women's movement progresses, and of deconstructing the metaphysical assumptions of these social conditions "at a practical level" (Derrida, in Kamuf, 1991, p. 455). Consequently, Derrida has also struggled with the fact that there is a gap between his intentions and the actuality. So much of the deconstruction of texts his work has inspired has had conservative consequences. No less a figure than Said has pointed to a complicity between much recent deconstructive literary critique and neo-conservativism. This is particularly galling for Derrida because he himself has argued that connections of this kind cannot be "entirely fortuitous" (ibid.). All texts, and particularly what Derrida calls "metaphysical" texts, take an ethical-political position, including Derrida's own. Indeed, identifying the semiotic apparatus whereby this is encoded is much of the point of deconstruction. But Derrida makes little more than oblique references to the basis whereby we may chose among alternative deconstructions—that is, among implicit alternative ethical-political positions. It is this methodological failure that opens Derrida's form of postmodern or postmetaphysical thinking to conservative political appropriation and allows us to suggest that at the least, despite Derrida's perhaps impeccable intentions, his theory is radically incomplete as a guide to "intervention" in real struggles.

Foucault and Derrida, in their very different ways, offer us the fruits of skepticism. These are considerable, and to the intellectual sweet, since they allow a clear vision of the complicity of history in the flaws we always find at the core of every noble intention. But the fruit of skepticism comes at a price. As Charles Taylor (1984) tells us, we must also deny, with Foucault (1984), the possibility of seeking to identify "good *and* bad elements . . . in the enlightenment and, with Derrida, seek to make *every* arché tremble" (p. 156, emphasis added).

Habermas's theory of critique has sought to tread a fine line between skepticism and some notion of a standard of critique. We will examine its relative success or lack of it below, but first, it is necessary to look at the political logic of a kind of critical thought that both postmodernists and Habermas would accuse of complicity in forms of "left authoritarianism."

Essential to the analysis of that logic is the recognition that issues of agency, reference, and praxis are involved and it is just those long unexamined notions of the autonomous liberal agent, drawing on expert knowledge of a professional knowledge "base," effectively combining technical action and values to bring about "progress," that postmodern thought throws into question. At the same time, the problems of agency, theory, and praxis remain. For any theory of schooling the motivational/developmental issues of character, love of justice, respect for difference, and the like make it clear that some theory of agency cannot be dispensed with. Issues of curriculum choice, different cultures, and the acquisition of real empowering capabilities in literacy, numeracy, articulateness, and so on make it clear that some theory of an at least pragmatic, fallible, and nonfoundational conception of "truth" is essential. And issues of resistance, struggle, and the need for students from oppressed groups to achieve political effectiveness implicate schooling in some conception of theory/practice relationships.

But some readings of poststructuralist thought claim political relevance while denying the cognitive prerequisites of a possible politics—a possible connection between political/social theory and effective strategy. This amounts to denying in words what is being claimed by the speaking position adopted. The epistemological radicalism (or skepticism) of the philosophical stance undercuts the possibility of an *effective* political radicalism by denying theoretical guidance to its politics.

Indeed, it is no less a writer than Derrida (1984) who accuses Foucault of using the form of argument while denying its force. That is, of claiming to tell a story of the inevitable absence of critique while encouraging it rhetorically, to tell a story that unveils the absolute historical power of cultural/historical regimes from a government-endowed chair at one of the leading research institutes in France.

Such writing is apocalyptic. I call writing and theorizing apocalyptic if it manifests a desire for radical change and exhorts us to radical or subversive/transgressive thought and action and, at the same time, is virtually or even relatively silent about how we might act effectively, or exactly how and why such general advice as "act subversively" through "acts of dissonance and structured refusals" or "repudiate bureaucratic imperatives, embrace the literary enterprise and organize for free textual plurality" (Parker 1997) should be followed.

As Beyer and Liston (1992) have shown, some readings of Derrida would reduce politics to silence or a form of play. It was not only unsympathetic Marx–influenced critics who identified the political cul-de-sac of the undermining of the theory of reference implicit in Derrida's critique of the metaphysics of presence, but also Foucault, who argued that this led Derrida to abstract from the particularity of real, historical contexts, and so misunderstand the conditions of the production of texts. It was to be expected that Foucault, who absolutized historical/cultural processes, would see Derrida's work in this way. Equally, it is no surprise to find that Derrida's critique of Foucault identifies an equivocation on the meaning of argument in his speaking position. Any relatively absolute (if I can coin an oxymoron) anti-metaphysics undercuts the possibility of the reasoned emergence of new forms of social life over time, or at least, of any theoretical account of this, let alone any theoretically perspicuous politics.

It is clear that poststructuralist analysis is heavily parasitical on the linguistic and interpretive "turns" in social theory and in every way hostile to the realist elements of Marxist critique. How then is poststructuralism going to offer us some guidance in replacing the failing apparatus of past realist political theory?

The Politics of the "Old Left"

One of the ways those intellectuals who seek to be identified as profound critics of existing society label themselves is as "radicals." But the word radical has always had two semiotic dimensions: one that derives from its etymology and refers to a going to the roots of a problem or situation (radix = root), and another that derives from its connotations of being dangerous or extreme. The two meanings could be seen as one because most radicals were once possessed of *both* an analysis of modern (capitalist) society that systematically theorized its character from basic premises provided by materialism, historicism, and political economic analysis of its institutions of private property, commodity, and value, *and* a revolutionary political program *based on this analysis* and aimed at the very heart of that society. Today, left-leaning theorists have all too often abandoned the old mechanism of theory/practice unity without replacing it, while at the same time clinging to the term "radical," not recognizing that they are now radical only in their minds. The two meanings of radical have become separated. The first meaning—going to the root of things—has been replaced by an analysis of society that sees it as a totalizing[1] process of power/knowledge, in which protest and political action are pushed to the margins,[2] with, as we have seen, no strong theoretical grounds for seeing their action there as anything but arbitrary.

The absence of a replacement for the "grand narrative" of Marxist critique casts doubt on the otherwise impressive achievement of postmodern educational intellectuals at the level of ideology critique of schooling. There, the problem of power/knowledge in the teacher/student relationship is manifestly crucial for any analysis of teachers *qua* critical teachers. When educational radicals speak of oppression and oppressed groups, they are, of course, speaking of "power over." But the separation of "power over" from class interests via an alternative critique of race and culture depends on the possibility of group-transcending criteria of an ethical or epistemic kind, that is, universals. The reduction of the concept of power to systemic power denies us this move. While aspects of the oppression of classes may be theorized in terms of "pastoral power" or "governmentalization," the relations of classes cannot.[3] As Fraser argues, there is a need for an analysis that distinguishes in some way between bad and less bad forms of power. Foucault (1988b), in his last interview, also acknowledged this point.

Marxist "grand theory" took an undifferentiated and functional view of power, denying the possibility of a perspicuous role for intellectuals and for theory as a source of effective historical agency:

> As the *economists* are the scientific representatives of the bourgeois class, so the *socialists* and *communists* are the theoreticians of the proletarian class. So long as the proletariat is not sufficiently developed to constitute itself as a class, consequently so long as the struggle itself between proletariat and bourgeois does not yet have a political character, so long as the productive forces are not yet sufficiently developed in the bosom of the bourgeoisie itself to permit a glimpse of the material conditions necessary for the emancipation of the proletariat and the formation of a new society—so long are these theoreticians merely utopians who improvise systems and pursue a regenerative science to meet the needs of the poorest classes. But as history develops and within it the struggle of the proletariat becomes clearly defined, they no longer need to seek science in their minds. They have only to give an account of what is happening before their eyes and give voice to it. (Marx, 1967, p. 494)

Marx's intellectuals are placed in an invidious position. They appear as mere spectators. Their theory and their critique is marginal to the historical process. It is notorious that this impotence was extended by some Marxist intellectuals to the process of education, which was depicted as an ideological apparatus of the state, or a tool of capitalism, rather than a potential agent in the class struggle. In this view, theory and theorists provided cognitive insight but no agency. Only the material power of the historical dialectic had agency. How strange to see that same agency now also denied by postmodern thinkers, not by refraining from grand claims about the political validity of theory and the capacity for real political action of intellectuals but by simultaneously denying or failing to describe the way in which that action could be *historical* (i.e., progressive).

In contrast, Habermasian critical theory views critique as historically immanent political process, fallibly moving riskily beyond existing meanings and organizations of culture, via discursive/political movements epitomized by the environmental and women's movements.

It has been proposed by several commentators, some claiming postmodern, or at least anti-enlightenment credentials, that we accept that the term "critical" also involves in some sense the notion that it is "the self-clarification of the struggles and wishes of the age" (Holt & Margonis, 1992, p. 231).[4] But this definition, so often quoted with approval, involves the rankest historicism. It sits quite easily with the quotation from Marx's *The Poverty of Philosophy* discussed above, and implies the same theory of the role of the proletariat and change in the forces of production. Any intellectuals who adopt it as a definition are under a burden to demonstrate that they are organic to the "spirit of the age." In Marx's view this would have meant "organic to the proletariat," since it was the proletariat that embodied the wishes of the age. If postmodern or critical intellectuals still cling to this notion of the intellectual's role, while endorsing the skeptical strategies of Foucault and Derrida, they raise the specter of a *macroscopic* politics without theory. And this is the specter of a politics of vanguardism, of dictatorships "on behalf of" the masses similar to that which Marxism has been at such great pains to abandon.

The articulation of theory with politics in earlier versions of Marxism is instructive. For Marx, the interests of the proletariat were potentially universal, not simply because they constituted the overwhelming majority of the population of the societies he studied, but because their interest in equity was the only group or class interest that was *in principle* universalizable. To this extent, we find in Marx, via Hegel, an echo of Kant's ethics. In the absence of such a proletariat or its replacement by some other addressee or addressees this particular path to a universalizability of interest dissolves. But one of the reasons that the notion of universalization of interest was important for Marx was because it was only through the historical realization of universal interests that social contradiction of a fundamental, dialectical kind could be overcome and the class-based phase of history, indeed history in general, in the sense of fundamental progress of human political institutions, brought to a close. Theory was politically significant because it was historically immanent in the agency of those whose interests it expressed. It was also *strategically* important, because the idea of an end to contradiction, oppression, and strife was a great source of motivation to those who took up the cause. Who would risk as much as so many socialists risked (and sacrificed) were it not for the ideal of peace and true community that they yearned toward, based on the conviction that what they fought for was in the objective interests of all? Today, with a hindsight informed by watching the Soviet Union break up into a swirl of warring ethnic groups, we may take leave to be wiser than Marx. In the absence of an adequate theory of the possibility of the universalization of interest, the liberal view of society would begin to look more cogent—a balance among a plurality of incommensurate interests, even individual interest, maintained via the exchange of all values through a market mechanism. This is a view increasingly embraced now by many former eastern bloc "left" intellectuals (i.e., former dissidents; see, for example, Nowak, 1990). It may also be the practical residue of a radicalism characterized only by local and specific critique where there is no larger narrative to guide a multiplicity of local initiatives. That is why it puzzles me when so-called critical theorists reject Habermas's theory of communicative action *because* of the universality of its postulate of an interest in "understanding," or object to systematic theory of the *methodology* of critique (note: not critique itself) because it is said to be a "grand narrative," "idealist," or merely "deductive."[5] To do this is simply to accept that the analyses of Derrida and others are so decisive as to bring philosophy to an end.[6] I would like to see some recognition of the role universal ideas once played in underpinning a coherent politics and perhaps a greater optimism about the possibility of devising some at least minimal replacement. It is difficult to see how a perspective could in any sense retain the label "critical" while insisting that all *theory* of critique must be local, particular, and concrete. If we resolutely eschew a more universal moment in the analysis, how are we to distinguish local, particular and concrete dogmatism from local and particular manifestations of critique? While absolute universalism may be abandoned, there is a middle ground of quasi-universals (e.g., of speech and communication) that all practical accounts of critique must draw on.

A brief examination of Rorty's discussion of the women's movement may serve to illustrate this point as well as the price we have to pay for the abandonment of all narratives beyond the local and specific. Rorty's recommendation to the women's movement is to "speak with the universalist vulgar" while thinking "with the pragmatists" (Rorty, 1989, p. 5). By this he means that while it may be politically useful when speaking publicly to characterize women's struggle for a share of power in terms of universalist notions like "equality," it is inappropriate for feminists themselves to think of their struggle in any other terms than group interest.

One can see that the argument in terms of *individual* self-interest might have a kind of biological base in the self-interest of each organism, but the abandonment of the notion of equality between the sexes may well carry with it the abandonment of the notion of equality among women. If our common humanity is insufficient basis for the universalist argument to equality, why should common sex be any better? When the appeal for equality was an appeal for equality among men (as it still tends to be in much of the world), its main obstacle was the possibility of smaller and smaller sectional interests, ethnicity, religion, locality, and finally family and self. Why should an appeal for the solidarity of women as an interest group be any less vulnerable to these sectional alternatives?

Rorty would have us abandon the possibility of strategy, too. For Rorty, there is no method or procedure to be followed in ethical/political action, except "courageous and imaginative experimentation" (1989, p. 7). He reads Dewey's account of pragmatic experimentation in a way that runs against the grain of Dewey's constant insistence that such experimentation should be "intelligent" (almost Dewey's favorite word). Rorty's women's movement appears in history as a blind process akin to random mutations and natural selection, entirely lacking in "immanent teleology" (ibid., p. 5). But intelligent social theory, albeit made up only of Dewey's "warranted assertions," is immanent, since it is the best (lousy) theory of a community of inquiry at any given time. In any case, how is the *agency* of experimentation to be determined? Each group of women going their own way? Each woman going her own way? Or can there be dialogue, sharing, and solidarity among them on the basis of something *other than* mere safety in numbers? Rorty endorses solidarity, but gives us only weak reasons for indulging in it.

The question we must address begins to define itself as the political necessity of some mediating level of analysis between the particular/local and the universal. In situations where the plurality of forms of exploitation and constraint, of uneven distribution of power, and of privileging of one culture over another are attested, Marx's idea of a single political organization and a single category of intellectuals corresponding to all of the oppressed groups and categories appears less than plausible. That means several things for us. First, it means we must continue to struggle with the possibility of a discourse that goes *behind* interests, to a dimension in which conflicting group or class interests can be reconciled. That means some form of universalism even if only procedural quasiuniversalism of the kind Habermas employs more as a counterfactual premise of human solidarity than anything else. Second, it means we must have a thicker conception of justice than that which typically inhabits much educational critique. In a situation where the members of an oppressed class *can* be themselves, in another context, members of an oppressor class (and vice versa), can we rely any longer on the implicit universalism of appeals to "justice" and "equity," or implicitly carry over the assumed universality of the interest of a single oppressed class to the present plurality of overlapping classes? Surely a procedural understanding of universality is a useful halfway house between the substantive (essential) universals of strong historicism and political relativism?

One candidate for such a halfway house was the notion of "the Party." In less historicist versions of Marxism (e.g., Rosa Luxembourg's) the role of the party was an active rather than a historically passive one. The party was the organizational form of the politics of the enlightenment of the working class. The task of the Party was politics, and politics was not defined in terms of the ascendency of one class over another but in terms of the concrete universalization of power.

The reasons for abandoning this understanding of the appropriate form of a politics of emancipation are many, not the least of which are the cluster of problems Habermas identified under the label "the organization of enlightenment." The fundamental problem of the Party was that political necessity dictated solidarity, while moral injunction pointed to the Party's role being guided by the *voluntary* participation in dialogue of its members and potential members. "Correct" theory was required, but so was an open dialogue (Habermas, 1974).

In more recent work, Habermas seeks to rehabilitate the idea of the democratic institutions of the rule of law in such a way that a critical apparatus may be applied to the evolution of the processes of democracy. In this view, the role of the party would be taken over by the institutionalization of critical processes in a form of organizational or institutional learning. It is too early to say how successful this analytical project will be.

Foucault himself points us toward a possible replacement for the idea of the Party and at the same time toward a kind of normativity that is less implicated in power than other kinds, when he responds to a question about Hannah Arendt's conception of the positive power of a consensual group in the following way:

> [I]t is a critical idea to maintain at all times: to ask oneself what proportion of non-consensuality is implied in . . . a power relation . . . one must be against nonconsensuality. (Foucault, 1984, p. 379)

Here, Foucault comes very close to a meeting of minds with Habermas. In this view, agency and universals are not to be taken for granted but are to be contested, explored, and formed through processes of care for self and other, yet they *are* to be explored.

Derrida's particular form of play, with serious intent, makes it a little more difficult to surprise him in admissions of the kind that are so easy to find in Foucault's work. Rather, a more holistic analysis, tracing the traces of the game, is the necessary approach to Derrida. Richard Bernstein (1991) does this and draws out of his analysis of Derrida the view that Derrida always seeks to problematize what we lose whenever we reach a consensus and form an intersubjective understanding, the "what might have been," especially the lost possibilities of the less powerful or articulate party to the production of a text. It is this that Derrida seeks to "affirm" in his renaming of deconstruction as "affirmative interpretation."

However, it is sometimes difficult to know to whom Foucault and Derrida are addressing themselves. Foucault (1988b) appears to believe that

> criticism consists in driving . . . thought out of hiding and trying to change it: showing [who? R.Y.] that things are not as obvious as we [who? R.Y.] might believe, doing it in such a way that what we might accept as going without saying no longer goes without saying. (34)

But this is a limited, reflective, dare I say idealist, conception of critique.

In his turn, Derrida claims that his work makes a political difference, that it "intervenes," but that it does not intervene by providing any theoretical basis for praxis, because ethical/political questions are "undecideable" and "incommensurate with my intellectual project."[7] How, then, does this "work," presumably in the form of publishing texts, intervene? Who reads it? To whom is it addressed?

The Addressee of Critique and the Structuration of Discourse

In Marxist theory, the addressee of critique was the proletariat and its allies (including the intelligentsia). The proletariat, by understanding its class situation (a class *in* itself), would sooner or later become a class *for* itself,[8] and act decisively to sweep away the system that oppressed it. Clearly the message and the audience were well matched, except for one thing. Most of the members of the proletariat prior to 1883 (the year Karl Marx died) were functionally illiterate and effectively unable to understand Marx's theory. The group that did listen were certain disaffected intellectuals—who constituted themselves as a vanguard *for* the proletariat. We all know the fate of Marxist ideas. They were never able to reach the class whose interests they addressed. The intellectuals who took them up, in most cases, were not "organic" to the working class, but articulated their own interests more forcefully than those of the class whose fate they theorized. Instead of a proletarian revolution, they gave us a *nomenklatura*, a bureaucratic/intellectual ruling class.

For this class, education was indoctrination. The content of the curriculum was crucial, and the form of pedagogy was determined by the need for political correctness. Educational critique had a place before the revolution, but after it the role of socialist education was the formation of the subjectivity required by the socialist state. Thus, educational critique became largely critique of technical details of means, and was addressed to educators as technical questions or advice.

To whom then is educational critique addressed today? The ostensible addressee of much of it has been teachers, although the *de facto* audience seems to be other educational intellectuals and perhaps teachers in training. However, in making recommendations for teachers, even if they are read mainly by teachers in their role as coursework students, radical educators often fail to do justice to the full professional function of teachers, and little guidance is offered as to just how teachers are to reconcile conflicting interests and demands. Those attempting to incorporate the insights of postmodern thinkers into hitherto critical-theoretic frameworks are, like the present writer, struggling with this issue.

The notion of justice that supports a great deal of radical writing is too thin to be of much use to real teachers in their particular contexts. It is not that some critical educators are unaware of these issues. Giroux (1981a), for instance, writes of a sphere in which there can be a balancing of competing voices. Apple, among others, explores cases of real teachers coping with real but limited opportunities.[9]

Nor is it the case that there is an absence of insight into the ideological character of schooling and its micropolitics. What is at issue is whether or not we have seen emerge a clear and concordant politics, with organizational and macroscopic rather than simply individualistic, local, or pluralistic implications. The burden of this essay is not to suggest that the author has found an answer that others, such as Giroux, have failed to find, but to make the quite pragmatic point that an adequate theory must address this issue quite directly.

However, we can agree with Giroux, Apple (and Foucault and Habermas), and with Derrida to honor the "other," by arguing that the content of the curriculum can never be univocal. Of course, this does not mean that we should impose on learners the task of discursively redeeming every claim or of recapitulating the whole history of philosophies and cultures. It does mean that the conversation of humankind should be drawn into the classroom so that those in the classroom, partly via their own experience inside and outside it, should be drawn into that conversation. And it does imply recognition that that conversation is not simply a European or a male one. Pedagogically, Dewey has already given us a great deal of guidance for the way in which the problem situations of students can become the starting points for entry to that conversation and the touchstone for ensuring that the conversation of the classroom not only gets beyond mere "bull sessions" but also is disciplined by the specificity of its contextual ties. But the conversation must also be critical if it is to have any value, and the discursive standard of critique has already been enunciated by Foucault (above). However, it is a standard that cuts two ways. It must permit some form of expression of cultures, metaphysics, subjectivities with which any given student or teacher might profoundly disagree. In this sense, there is common ground with some liberal/libertarian conceptions of schooling, and it is reasonable to ask how this view escapes from accusations of falling back into mere modern privileging of instrumental reason or the dominant values of any society.

Dewey, too, saw educators and other professionals as the main agents of historical change, and addressed his critique to them. But what about most of the oppressed themselves? The masses of functionally illiterate poor people? Women? People of color? Indigenous peoples? Etc.? Surely these groups come closest to fulfilling Marx's requirements for revolutionary motivation? But the contemporary problem remains. If critical intellectuals wrote for these groups, what they wrote would be written in several different languages.

In these circumstances, the task that faces critical intellectuals is essentially the task of effective intercultural communication and the promotion of intercultural learning. The problem postmodern critics face is not just that their abandonment of historicism means that they are shouting from the bleachers and are thus too far away to be heard; it is also that they are, more often than not, speaking the wrong language. In the presence of a plurality of categories or classes of "oppressed" people, including, but by no means confined to, the old working class, critical intellectuals must answer two questions, not one: How to get closer to those they would address and what language to speak to them when they get there.

These questions may be answered in two ways. First, intellectuals could abandon the attempt to stand in the liminal zone between cultures, and cease to seek to pursue a strategy of unification and coalition of groups concerned with oppression. This is what a strong rejection of universalism would entail for them *qua* intellectuals. If in the postmodern manner they have abandoned any pretence to universal dimensions of theory they have already abandoned this strategy. They have also effectively denied themselves any political strategy. Alternatively, they could have opted for a new, ambiguous positioning, informed by the postmodern questioning of modernity, but not wholly given over to it. But to stand there also implies a commitment to a minimal universalism, to intercultural communication and learning (rather than simple or absolute pluralism), and to a willingness to adopt a historically and culturally decentered understanding of their own position—as critical intellectuals. Habermas's position on these questions points to a process of intercultural learning in which difference is not absolutized or critique monoculturally constrained (Young, 1996a). This also implies a less absolute, less self-indulgent or avant-garde position vis-à-vis other less "oppositionary" or "radical" groups in society—and not merely as a cooptatory tactic. And this communication must approximate politically symmetrical communication, if for no other reason than necessity, since the minimal universalism of which I just spoke requires it, and, in any case, inconsistency here would undermine coalition building.

But if educational intellectuals must now stand in a liminal zone, with only limited allegiance to any tradition, who will they address? No longer organic to any clearly defined community of interest, where will they bestow their allegiance—each to his and especially her own faction? Or is there still some basis for a universalism that will somehow take in all the oppressed—that is, all those denied justice? To answer the last question, we would have to ask ourselves questions concerning the conception of human flourishing[10] or the good, which lie in the background of our concerns for those denied access to this or that specific good, and most particularly, we would have to define the good that education mediates, if we are to sustain a concern about the injustice of its denial to certain groups. Absent an idea of this good, there seems little role for "intellectuals" as such, other than that which is parasitic on the existing social order—that is, intellectuals or "experts" just happen to be in an influential position, due to a mistake about the nature of social knowledge, and they should use this happy advantage to influence the society culturally through the instrument of the schools, while they still can.

If we reject this bleak perspective, perhaps there is still a role for the kind of utopian thinking that Foucault (Foucault, 1988b, p. 18) and others have criticized. Critical educators could still see themselves as organic, but as organic to the *future* unity of interest of *presently* diverse oppressed groups. This is a prophetic role concerned with the "end in view," as Dewey called it, of educational politics in a democracy.

While modern conceptions of the educative possibilities of schooling may now be suspect, it may be necessary to repudiate the apparent need of postmodern educators to distance themselves from the possibility of an enlightening function for schools, a truth function for curriculum, or a truthfulness function for pedagogy.[11]

A final contrast between Habermas and Rorty should make the differences, which I have only just begun to outline, a little clearer:

> Radicals think that there is a basic mistake being made... deep down at the roots.... Utopians however... abandon the contrast between superficial appearance and deep reality in favor of the contrast between a painful present and a possibly less painful, dimly-seen, future. Pragmatists cannot be radicals, in this sense.... Philosophy's function is... to clear the road for prophets and poets [and intellectuals R.Y.]... who have visions of life in new communities. (Rorty, 1989, p. 6)

But Habermas is neither Utopian nor radical, and it is in everyday communication that the moment of vision comes as much or more than in the communication of intellectuals, since the seeds of critique and change are present in every human communicative act. In this sense, the gap between theory and practice is closed; indeed, it never existed. The only gap is between theorists and everyday life. For Habermas, the fundamental problems of knowing and communicating are the same. There are *aporiae* in all of our best theories, but these are the same *aporiae* of communication and understanding that we all face. *Aporiae* of differentiation, desire, and dialectic (Young, 1996b) are reflections of the human condition. We are always different, no matter how much we pretend to sameness, we have conflicting desires, because of our difference and our separateness, and we can only resolve this human situation to the extent that it becomes livable or even joyful through dialectic. Whatever the inadequacies of our theories, we must recognize the concrete immanence of

> an ideal tension... imported into social reality itself, which comes to conscious awareness in participating subjects as a force that explodes the limits of the given context and transcends all merely provincial standards. (Habermas, 1993, p. 165)

Notes

1. It is necessary to distinguish between a totalizing process, in which the structure, culture, or assemblage of "dispositifs" leaves little room for agency or action, and a holistic analysis, in which there is seen to be a dialectical tension between structure and agency, mediated by the level of large-scale human organization. There are many examples of holistic analyses, some better than others. Giddens's flawed but still useful theory of structuration is one such, Habermas's analysis of the tension between system and lifeworld is another.
2. Thus Foucault (1978, p. 85), but at the same time as embracing the power/knowledge identity, the absolutist radical wants to generate a relevant and nonmarginal politics.
3. See Ian Hunter (1990) for an examination of related questions in which, whatever its other merits, Hunter entirely fails to recognize that governmentalization might have to come to grips with societal diversity and group or class structures of various kinds.
4. This is Holt and Margonis quoting Nancy Fraser quoting Marx.
5. While this essay is not a belated reply to the Holt and Margonis essay review of one of my books (Young 1990), I do think that essay displays some misunderstandings about

the theorist's relation to practice and practitioners. Theory is always ideational, but is not rendered idealist thereby. Ideas are a part of the real, emergent process of life. It is their relation to practice that is crucial. The work of the theorist cannot substitute for the contextually located *practical* choices of political actors, but the theorist can explicate the situations and general competencies of classes of actors. Such reconstructions remain "testable" in terms of their empirical usefulness. The method of reconstruction involves *inter alia* hypotheses and inferences or deductions to and from conduct, as is the case in linguistic discovery methods. In this way it is possible to reconstruct a generic model of communicative *teaching* action, which is a special case of the more general model of universal pragmatic assumptions of all speaking subjects. Such a model implies nothing specific for actual teachers, unless other premises, including some derived from teachers' local knowledge, are also provided, and some model of practical reasoning is also adopted.

And, yes, its construction does involve deductions at certain points. See L. Holt and F. Margonis (1992).
6. Which even Derrida himself vigorously repudiates: Jacques Derrida (1984).
7. I discuss this sense Derrida has of the strategic relevance of his work in Young (1995).
8. In the absence of a universal interest, how is it possible that an oppressed group could be "for itself" and at the same time be for others, except as a temporary alliance of convenience?
9. See almost any work by M. Apple, since *Ideology and Curriculum* (1979).
10. In using this term I offer qualified support to the notion of ethical realism of a transactional kind. For a discussion see P. L. Ternasky (1992).
11. As contrasted with Holt and Margonis's doubts about Freire's faith in the "enlightenment" function of education (op cit., p. 241), I see no reason why Dewey's faith in dialogue and pedagogy as instruments of rational critique cannot be coupled with the kind of organizational and political means for change that he did not theorize as fully. Indeed, such coupling is necessary for both valid politics and valid inquiry.

Deborah P. Britzman and Don Dippo

ADMITTING "A PERHAPS": MAXINE GREENE AND THE PROJECT OF CRITICAL THEORY

One

Why discuss the work of Maxine Greene in relation to the historical contributions of the Frankfurt School of Critical Theory and in relation to what we can imagine of the future for education? After all, Greene (1986) herself spoke of her distance from their concerns in her essay, "In Search of Critical Pedagogy," even as she acknowledged her debt to and affinity for European thought and its arts and literature. In this chapter, we will suggest, through the lens of education and with illustrations from literature, the different preoccupations, tensions, and methods for thinking that Greene offers to critical theory and to the imagination. What Greene offers to both fields of thought are questions of commitment, affinity, affection, trauma, and destruction, all relations that summarize the inchoate yearning of imagination. And, in centering questions of why and how imagination mediates our encounters in the world, the ideas we can make, and our capacity to make from these encounters and these ideas creative relations with others, we highlight three indiscrete moments—the time of education, the time of being and becoming, and the time of the arts and imagination—that draw upon the immediacy of the present, but in ways that place in tension historical memory and "that which is not yet." For now, listen to how Maxine Greene characterizes the difference collective history makes to social memory:

> But it also seems necessary to hold in mind the fact that European memories are not our memories. The sources of European critical theory are to be found in responses to the destruction of the Workers' Councils after the First World War, the decline of the Weimar Republic, the rise of Stalinism, the spread of fascism, the Holocaust, the

corruptions of social democracy. As climatic as any contemporary insight was the realization that reason (viewed as universal in an Enlightenment sense) could be used to justify the application of technical expertise in torture and exterminations. Europeans saw a connection between this and the rationalization of society by means of bureaucracy, and in the separating off of moral considerations long viewed as intrinsic to civilized life. The intimations of all this could be seen in European literature for many years: in Dostoevsky's and Kafka's renderings of human beings as insects; in Musil's anticipations of the collapse of European orders, in Camus's pestilence, in Sartre's nausea, in the Dionysian and bestial shapes haunting the structure of the arts. We have had a tragic literature, a critical literature, in the United States. . . . But it has been a literature rendered tragic by a consciousness of a dream betrayed, of a New World corrupted by exploitation and materialism and greed. In background memory, there are images of Jeffersonian agrarianism, of public spheres, of democratic and free-swinging communities. We do not find these in European literature, nor in the writings of the critical theorists. (437)

We heard these words spoken by Maxine Greene at the First Working Conference on Critical Pedagogy in 1986. It was a heady time, when teachers and students were inventing new identities as critics and transformers of their world and when even the name "Critical Pedagogy" sounded transgressive, oppositional, and intellectually challenging in its political claims. Many of us drawn to the conference were engaged in efforts to link continental philosophy with Latin American revolutionary politics and, in so doing, tried to rethink educational politics in North America. It was a time when questions of education were inexorably linked with problems of social transformation. Indeed, looking back, the name "Critical Pedagogy" held open the promise of praxis, when thinking and doing were in dialogic relation, when concerns for being and becoming were brought to problems of how people understood and confronted their own conditions, and when potential for self and social transformation were a part of our theories of learning. At this conference, critical theory and the writings of the late Paulo Freire dominated discussion. But these ideas also vied for the commitment of conference goers with feminist pedagogy, African-American Studies, the thinking of Miles Horton and the Highlander Folk School for activists, and Maxine Greene's insistence on the relevance of works of imagination and the arts. She asked us to think about our own existential dilemmas of having no choice but still having to choose vistas of interpretations and impositions that urge responsibility. This responsibility will always be fragile because it will rest upon what Greene (1998) calls "the haunting problem of 'multiple realities'" (11) and because there is a sense that education cannot separate itself from the question of interference. Throughout the conference people argued passionately about education and ideology, critical teaching and student alienation, gender and education, capitalist oppression and its reproduction in schooling, and teachers as intellectuals in spite of the press to be technicians.

Greene's conference address stood out for a great many reasons; whereas some people at the conference assumed that there was already an existing critical pedagogy that could be implemented if only people could be divested of their illusions, Greene situated critical pedagogy as a problem of the future experienced in the present. Critical pedagogy, she insisted, has yet to be made, but it will not culminate in our finding its proper object, but through developing our capacity to search. Perhaps Greene cast her lot with Sartre's (1968) *Search for a Method,* where he, too, wonders about questions of freedom and argues for a way of thinking that could hold in tension individual existence and the large events of history. Sartre, as well, makes the point that while there is no truth to be found, truth "becomes"; it emerges from human projects. Method, it turns out, is neither given in advance nor applied with proper instructions. Rather, if the search is also to be a search for freedom, Greene suggests these places to begin: in uncertainty, in multiple perspectives, and in landscapes of meaning. For Greene, these places are fraught with contingency and conflict. Yet they also represent both potential and inhibition.

Years later, Greene's search for a critical pedagogy and her insistence on the arts as offering the conditions for new modes of thought, new identifications, new relevancies, and new questions for education continue to call for our attention. We believe that the arts can also open preoccupations with three identifiable yet indiscrete moments of time that affect the topology of imagination: the time of education, the time of the arts, and the time of being and becoming. Each moment offers a thought of the future, but perhaps not in ways we typically expect. The sense of time we will try to convey is also a confusion of time: hopes for things that are not yet, enlargements of certain memories of loss and mourning. Rather than a nostalgic return to the past, the confusion of time we are trying to convey begins with a question: What of the past is worth keeping? "We have reached a point," Greene (1986) writes in that essay, "when that past must be reinterpreted and reincarnated in light of what we have learned" (440).

Occasionally, thinkers identified with the Frankfurt School address the question of education, but only from the ruins of past destruction and the hope that education can make a future. They do so through the temporality of crisis. Arendt (1954/1993) writes of "the crisis of education" and wonders how the public would come to defend not just its right to exist, but to transform the ways we think of education as possibility and as limit, as tradition and as change. Whereas Arendt's audience was postwar North America, Adorno's (1998) discussion of education addressed postwar Germany and asked how a nation that ostensibly valued education consented to destroy its own citizens. "Education after Auschwitz" begins: "The premiere demand upon all education is that Auschwitz not happen again" (191). In "Taboos on the Teaching Vocation," Adorno laments the ways teachers are disparaged and the ways some teachers choose to implement a cruelty in their pedagogy, qualities not unrelated to "barbarism . . . delusional prejudice, oppression, genocide, and torture" (190) and those things that must not happen again.

Adorno's preoccupation with whether it is possible for education to work against fascism as opposed to being put in its service, also turns from the problem of barbarism to the question of banality. After returning to Germany from his exile in the United States, his chief means of employment was at a teachers' college. He was assigned the charge of examining secondary teachers on the topic of philosophy (Hohendahl, 1995). Adorno (1998) noticed that, whereas most candidates could give adequate answers, they also admitted that philosophy meant nothing to them. They passed the exam by offering clichéd accounts and platitudes. The point of the test was missed because, for Adorno:

> This test should . . . permit us to see whether those candidates, who as teachers in secondary schools are burdened with a heavy responsibility for the spiritual and material development of Germany, are intellectuals, or as Ibsen said more than eighty years ago, merely specialized technicians (21).

Greene (1978a) would also address problems of meaning and significance in the lives of teachers, speaking not of barbarism, ferreting out the evil in people's hearts, nor of vigilance, lest fascism return under the guise of technical knowledge. For Greene, the problem is one of somnambulism, of sleepwalking and not noticing, of good people who cannot entertain the possibility that their actions may do harm and cannot recognize their own tendency toward "malefic generosity." These, Greene insists, are not problems of consciousness-raising but awakening:

> I want to concentrate on the confrontations and insights required of the teacher who chooses himself and or herself to be a convert to the critical cause. I say that rather than following Freire on the matter of conversion because it seems to me that the significant conversion, in the North American context, is to a mode of negative thinking with respect to taken-for-granted values and needs and with respect to certain lawlike statements used to explain and legitimate what happens in the socio-economic world. To move from a so-called "oppressor class" to the side of the oppressed—the disinherited, the minorities, the submerged working class—is not necessarily to experience a shift in consciousness. (101)

For Greene, there must be a shock: a crisis made from a combination of negative critique and questioning one's own existence in relation to the existence of others. In the struggle to make an everyday life, people are understandably disinclined to open their world to disruption. Part of the problem, and here is where Greene leaves the world of consciousness-raising, is the difficulty of noticing that one is submerged, numbed by routine and thoughtlessness in everyday life. Another difficulty has to do with the ways the concept of "critical" in North America has been disparaged, rendered as a pathological response, and viewed as destructive and not constructive or helpful. Criticism, in this commonsense view, can only mean to criticize a judgment that punctuates the end of a process. But critique can signify a moment in a process rather than a culminating of judgment. In North American education, the relentless insistence on "the positive," whether that be found in discourses of self-esteem and cooperation or in the power of positive thinking and happy face stickers, means that the negative has been relegated to the realm of hostile and unwelcome thought. Even if these barriers of language and thought can be broken, and one can accept the work of negative critique, not accept the way things are, and not be satisfied with one's own sedimentations, there is still the problem of righteous self-assurance.

Confidence in the unassailability of one's assumptions, for Adorno (1998), is characteristic of a certain immaturity of intellect. There is an inaugural tension in the education of teachers, where two sorts of anxiety meet, one having to do with the present, the other with the future; one having to do with teachers having to learn, the other with teachers trying to teach. And this tension, Adorno goes on to argue, structures the work of professors who teach teachers, who offer goodwill but may sustain a certain intellectual immaturity:

> But we wish to be humane not only toward the candidates, whose anxiety we can well understand, but also toward those who will one day sit before them, whom we do not see, and who are threatened with greater injustice at the hands of an immature and uneducated intellect than anyone who might be threatened by our intellectual demands. One does not need what Nietzsche called the "love of strangers" for this: a little imagination is quite sufficient. (20)

But what makes imagination sufficient? Greene (1995b) writes, "of all our cognitive capacities, imagination is the one that permits us to give credence to alternative realities. It allows us to break with the taken for granted, to set aside familiar distinctions and definitions" (3). This is where, we think, Maxine Greene departs from critical theory, even as she draws upon its grand themes: mystification, deception, alienation, instrumental rationality, cultural malaise. Her understanding of what it is teachers face when they face the curriculum, students, parents, communities, and their own sense of project making, is quite different from that of Adorno, both in the historical contexts from which arguments are made and in the restless search for resources for imagination. If one does not need the love of strangers, what makes "a little imagination" sufficient?

Two

If we have signaled some of the educational concerns of those intellectuals most closely associated with the Frankfurt School (Horkheimer, Adorno, Benjamin, Marcuse, Arendt, Habermas), we also must note that they wrote only occasionally about education and even less frequently about teaching and learning. For most of her life, Maxine Greene has written for and about teaching and teachers. We read this address as posing a notion of the future that conjugates the past and present with the uncertainties of becoming, with the future, not as a completion of all that has occurred, but rather as where imagination will be. "I cannot," writes Greene (1995a), "divorce the idea of shaping the future from the practice of teaching; nor can I abandon the notion of context, the many facets of life to which we respond"

(65). Part of what distinguishes her work from much of the professional and academic literature in education is the profundity of the context of her work and the eloquence and beauty of her writing. She does not offer helpful tips for harried classroom practitioners. Nor does she offer expert advice and answers to frequently asked questions. Indeed, it is precisely the frequency, the numbing routine of education, the utter dismissal of the imagination, the censorship of ideas that disturb, that concerns Greene. So she invites teachers, as fellow travelers, to think with her about what Arendt (1954/1993) calls, "the human condition," and what Greene sees as fundamental concerns related to the existential problem of being and becoming, of having to choose something more than bad faith, passivity, or cynicism. To think about these negative themes, Greene (1978) surrounds herself with those thinkers who tried to use their thoughts as a way to transform what we can imagine for ourselves and others. And yet, this work of imagination also supposes a kernel of negativity, and hence responsibility for the destruction of illusions, "for *praxis*, for self-fulfillment, for awareness, and a degree of happiness" (54).

Because we are in the context of education, it is not enough merely to ally oneself with the great critiques, as if it is this knowledge that will somehow put our problems to rest, raise our consciousness, end interpretative work, and then allow our actions to be adequate to all that is wrong. To write for and about teaching means offering crucial questions to students and then turning these questions back upon ourselves. Greene (1986) writes:

> How are we to justify our concern for their awakening? Where are the sources of questioning, of restlessness? How are we to move the young to break with the given, the taken-for granted—to move toward what might be, what is not yet? (427)

In another essay, Greene (1995b) seems to offer a tentative reply, a model of education that is not bound by what teachers "do" to students, but by enjoining a search when the destination is still in the making:

> All depends upon a breaking free, a leap, and then a question. I would like to claim that this is how learning happens and that the educative task is to create situations in which the young are moved to begin to ask, in all the tones of voice there are, "Why?" (6)

Why indeed. For Greene, throwing off sleep and awakening critical sensibilities in ourselves and in our students, while necessary, is not sufficient for making an educative project. Even when she lists all the theoretical insights we have made in education, about ideology, about cultural reproduction, about technical rationality, the poverty of affluence, mass deception and the manufacturing of consent, about meta-narratives, about hegemony, about structural inequalities, about textbook wars, about race and gender inequalities, meritocracy and the culture industry, Greene turns her attention to questions of becoming. Invoking a restorative hermeneutics, Greene challenges us to reinvent ourselves, to recreate our social practices and institutions, to envision our future together. Greene turns to Hannah Arendt (1954/1993) and the choices she saw for education, for the bonds education might create:

> Education is the point at which we decide whether we love the world enough to assume responsibility for it and by the same token save it from that ruin which, except for renewal, except for the coming of the new and young, would be inevitable. And education, too, is where we decide whether we love our children enough not to expel them from our world and leave them to their own devices, nor to strike from their hands their chance of undertaking something new, something unforeseen by us, but to prepare them in advance for the task of renewing a common world. (196)

Education, it seems, must waver between hope for the future—that one's efforts in education can matter to the quality of lives lived—and despair toward the present, who one is becoming as one initiates and responds to the expectations, demands, and pressures of history, generation, and renewal. There is the generous impulse to hope that people matter and there is the persistent anxiety that raises the awful question: What is the matter with people? As we have tried to suggest, critical pedagogy bears the weight of these questions. But from whatever side, many have already raised important ethical questions at the heart of education: "What is it to live a life in education?" (Greene, 1978b); "How does it feel to be a social problem?" (DuBois, 1969); "With whom do I cast my lot?" (Felman, 1993); and "What is it to notice the difficulties of knowledge?" (Britzman, 1998). These questions raise themes of affiliation, commitment, trauma, destruction, and community. They are, we believe, the grand themes of our present education because they point to the vulnerabilities made in knowledge and in action. To trace these restless movements, we now turn to where such themes are elegantly staged, and where Maxine Greene searches for the resources of imagination: literature and the arts. There, perhaps, we can witness the complexity of lived experience in order to do something more with our own. Samir Dayal (2000) offers, in his introduction to Kristeva's *The Crisis of the European Subject*, a way to bring the reflexivity of art into the creation of public life: "If narrative is an art as well as praxis, it is art that can provide the best witness to human experience and action, and the creation of a truly free public space would itself be a work of art" (12).

Three

Encounters with literature, the arts, and works of the imagination provide the opportunity to engage experiences that may not be our own, but might be. We can contemplate commitments that are not ours, but might be, consider affiliations not made, but might be, witness crises that are not ours, but might be, ponder destructions we have not lived, but may, and conceive of solitaries not yet made. If literature is a witness to the choices narrative can make, surely when encountering literature we might witness our own narratives differently. This is certainly the case for dialogue, a relation that Maxine Greene suggests inaugurates our search. We offer two different examples of that search drawn from contemporary literature: one from the vantage of a writer, who finds himself rethinking the very nature of his own imagination, the other of two people conversing on a topic that threatens to overwhelm them. Our selection is influenced by Maxine Greene's view that ideology critique is not the only path to clarity and insight; that the study of lived experience, the shock of awareness, and the qualities of thinking needed for the time of that which is not yet can be observed in the workings of imagination.

All of the characters in Philip Roth's (2000) novel *The Human Stain* grapple with the question, "Who knows what?" The first long chapter is titled, "Everybody knows" and if that phrasing is familiar, it is because it is a childhood chant of humiliation, of a secret that cannot be kept, of a lie that cannot be protected, of reputations ruined, and, perhaps, of the force of gossip to spread wildly and to resist correction. It is not until the middle of the novel that our narrator, Nathan Zuckerman, a writer whose work is to know, suddenly comes to the idea that maybe he really doesn't know. Zuckerman is sitting in a concert and he sees a friend he thought he knew. Zuckerman is observing this friend and his lover whispering to one another. And Zuckerman cannot hear what they are actually saying. All he has is his imagination, but he suddenly thinks, even that is insufficient. And then, Zuckerman, the writer, whose work it is to try and know something about someone else, thinks to himself:

> Because we don't know, do we? . . . How what happens the way it does? What underlies the anarchy of the train of events, the uncertainties, the mishaps, the disunity, the shocking irregularities that define human affairs? Nobody knows. "Everybody knows" is the invocation of the cliche and the beginning of the banalization of experience, and it's the solemnity and the sense of authority that people have in voicing the cliche that's so insufferable. What we know is that, in an uncliched way, nobody knows anything. You can't know anything. The things you know you don't know. Intention? Motive? Consequence? Meaning? All that we don't know is astonishing. Even more astonishing is what passes for knowing. (208–209)

What should Nathan Zuckerman know? And how does Nathan Zuckerman know? He knows about the ways imagination works: the ways we wish to see others, project our fears onto other people, hope others will see ourselves as good, forget things we do not wish to think about, and continually reinvent selves through plotting our narratives. All these things Zuckerman knows. But this knowledge is, after all, also about the limitations of imagination. And experiencing this limitation, the place where imagination cannot enter, offers Zuckerman the thought of his own limits, his own unreliability.

Rohinton Mistry's (1995) epic novel of city and country life in India, *A Fine Balance*, takes place in 1975, the year Indira Gandhi declared a national emergency and suspended civil rights. Much of the novel is organized by characters describing their lives to one another. Rather than present discrete stories and a competition of suffering, Mistry arranges both the storyteller's offerings and the listener's reflections on them in alternate paragraphs. This is a sense of time closest to the conversation—the meeting of events and their transformation by thoughts. Near the end of the novel, Dina, who has been served with a notice of eviction, goes to the courthouse to find a lawyer. Discouraged by the crowds, she walks away to the side of the building and finds, on a broken bench, sitting in front of his cardboard sign, Mr. Valmik, a lawyer, who apologizes for the court's chaos. Dina recounts her troubles to him. And the lawyer responds with his own philosophical thoughts.

> "After all, our lives are but a sequence of accidents—a clanking chain of chance events. A string of choices, casual or deliberate, which add up to that one big calamity we call life."
>
> Here he goes again, she thought. But the words did ring true. She tested them against her own experience. . . .
>
> The rasping noises from his throat were so distorted that Dina was having trouble understanding him. But her ears became attuned to the rare timbres and bizarre frequencies. She realized that although Mr. Valmik depicted life as a sequence of accidents, there was nothing accidental about his expert narration. His sentences poured out like perfect seams, holding the garment of his story together without calling attention to the stitches. Was he aware of ordering the events for her? Perhaps not—perhaps the very act of telling created a natural design. Perhaps it was a knack that humans had, for cleaning up their untidy existences—a hidden survival weapon, like antibodies in the bloodstream. (653–654)

Despite the unwieldiness of events experienced and recounted, Mr. Valmik's narrative provokes Dina's thinking about her own views, about his, and about the very construction of narration—its distance from the event and how the narration's fine balance depends not just on the story as artifice but on what the listener does with its offerings. This mode of thought does not repeat the emergencies, but rather attempts to notice, even at its most seamless, life's seams. The thought that holds Dina back—"here he goes again"—is frayed by her own test. Then her immediate attempt to make Mr Valmik into a caricature of her own worries and dismiss his views as insignificant to her own is ruined by admitting *a perhaps*.

To think with Maxine Greene is to admit "a perhaps" into considerations of how we live our lives. This is a sense of time not yet lived but that animates the imagination. For Greene, imagination does not come out of nowhere. Nor does it signify a special creativity that is situated in artistic genius or extraordinary talent. For imagination to turn toward the world, away from wishful thinking that serves as a substitute for risking the knowledge we already have, or even the knowledge we wish we could have without effort, imagination must encounter new ideas, discussions one could not have alone, and confrontations with arguments and controversies that are not so easily settled. Our search for critical pedagogy should take us into all sorts of settings: novels, art, theory, philosophy, and yes, even ordinary classrooms that can do extraordinary things. If, as we have been arguing, a great deal of education can put us to sleep, we can, "with a little imagination" and with choosing to think, become wide awake, passionate, and make from the our narratives, to return to Samir Dayal's hope, a free education that itself would become a work of art.

PART 2
Critical Theory: Projects and Movements

9   Henry A. Giroux

PEDAGOGY OF THE DEPRESSED: BEYOND THE NEW POLITICS OF CYNICISM

> *The trouble with our civilization is that it has stopped questioning itself. No society which forgets the art of asking questions or allows this art to fall into disuse can count on finding answers to the problems that beset it — certainly not before it is too late and the answers, however correct, have become irrelevant.*
> —Cornelius Castoriadis (in Bauman, 1999, p. 7)

Politics, Pedagogy, and the Culture of Cynicism

At the present moment in American history, there appears to be a growing hostility, if not cynicism, toward addressing the basic problems of society.[1] The absence of a widespread public debate or even substantive resistance over issues such as racial injustice, the dismantling of social welfare programs, the alarming incarceration rates among youth of color in the inner cities, the full-scale attack on the public schools, the widening gap between the rich and the poor, along with the refusal on the part of many individuals, especially young people, to participate meaningfully in political elections, indicates a widespread public cynicism and indifference to the world of public politics.[2] As freedom is defined increasingly through the logic of consumerism, the dynamics of self-interest, an e-commerce investment culture, and all things private, there appears to be a growing indifference on the part of the general population to those noncommercial values such as empathy, compassion, love, and solidarity that bridge the private and the public and give substance to the meaning of citizenship, democracy, and public life.[3] As the state is increasingly stripped of its public services, it is defined less through its efforts to invest in the public good than to exercise its police and surveillance functions in order to contain those groups deemed as a threat to social order. As the obligations of citizenship are narrowly defined through the imperatives of consumption and the dynamics of the marketplace, commercial space replaces noncommodified public spheres, and the first casualty is a language of social responsibility capable of defending those vital public spheres that provide education, health care, housing, and other services that are crucial to a healthy democracy.[4] Instead of celebrating the historical struggle to advance public life, the media now largely celebrate financial markets. Models of leadership are no longer drawn from the ranks of those heroic individuals in connection with social movements who have struggled to expand civil rights, individual liberties, and relations of democracy. On the contrary, political leadership has now given way to celebrity, representatives of which are drawn from Hollywood film studios and the ranks of corporate culture. Narcissistic behavior now generates media attention like never before, while admiration for private success turns people like Bill Gates into cultural icons. Collapsing intellectual ambition and social vision are matched by a growing disdain toward matters of equality, justice, and politics.

The upshot is a growing indifference toward those aspects of education that foster critical consciousness and a respect for public goods, and affirm the need to energize democratic public life and reinvigorate the imperatives of social citizenship. Evidence of the privatization of public life and the pervasive culture of cynicism is most obvious in the debates over educational reform and the speed at which public schools and colleges have become training grounds for corporate agendas. As Jeffrey Williams rightly argues, "universities have become licensed storefront[s] for name brand corporations . . . reconfigured according to corporate management, labor, and consumer models and delivering a name brand product. . . . The traditional idea of the university as a not-for-profit institution that offers a liberal education and enfranchises citizens of the republic, not to mention the more radical view that the university should foster a socially critical if not revolutionary class, has been evacuated without much of a fight" (Williams, 1999, p. 744).

In what follows, I want to analyze various ways in which the institution of education and the discourse of pedagogy have been largely removed from discussions of politics, power, and democratic transformation. In doing so, I will provide examples that extend from high-profile conservatives and progressives to some radical views on critical pedagogy. These positions share a willingness either to depoliticize pedagogy or to render its critical attributes a reinscription of particular forms of oppression. In many respects there is a cynical refusal on the part of all of these positions to engage schools as critical sites of cultural and political struggle and pedagogy as a crucial element in waging such battles. All of these discourses remove forms of personal and social development from any association with power, struggle, and social transformation, and in doing so provide a regular confirmation of the retreat from pedagogical and political engagement. Politics in these views is considered either a corrupting force or it is relegated to other spheres and practices largely removed from public and higher education. I want to explore and challenge such criticisms as they emerge across the ideological spectrum and conclude with a brief commentary on the importance of situating pedagogy as a political and ethical practice grounded in a notion of hope in an effort to highlight the tension between the possibilities of schooling and the promise of democracy itself. Throughout this essay, I use pedagogy as a referent for analyzing how knowledge, values, desire, and social relations are constructed, taken up, and implicated in relations of power in the interaction among cultural texts, institutional forms, authorities, and audiences. At stake here is acknowledging the productive, political, and ethical character of pedagogy as a deliberate attempt to influence how and what knowledge, experiences, and identities are produced within particular social formations and relations. Viewed as a performative practice that must be understood, in part, as the outcome of numerous struggles, I attempt to provide an alternative commentary that redefines the implications of a critical pedagogy as part of a broader ethical and political project wedded to furthering social and economic justice and making multicultural democracy operational.

Disavowing Pedagogy as a Political Practice

> Individuals cannot be free unless they are free to institute a society which promotes and guards their freedom; unless they institute together an agency capable of achieving just that. . . . This is not going to be an easy job, considering the present [perilous] state of the private/public sphere. . . . To make the *agora* [public space] fit for autonomous individuals and autonomous society, one needs to arrest, simultaneously, its privatization and depoliticization. One needs to re-establish the translation of the private into the public. One needs to restart (in the agora, not just in philosophy seminars) the interrupted discourse of the common good—which renders individual autonomy both feasible and worth struggling for.
> —Zygmunt Bauman (1989, p. 107)

In the above quote, the eminent sociologist Zygmunt Bauman foregrounds one of the growing dangers faced by democratic societies in an age dominated increasingly by the forces of neoliberalism, thus commenting implicitly on an important challenge that educators must address as engaged intellectuals. For Bauman, democratic life is now under siege by those commercial and market-driven pressures that exalt an utterly privatized notion of citizenship that not only undermines a commitment to valuing and investing in public goods, but also devalues forms of critical citizenship that encourage people to organize collectively to engage and resolve pressing social issues. As the state's "police functions tend to overpower and mediate its diminishing social functions," those social agencies aimed at providing opportunities for debate, deliberation, and solidarity are eliminated and there is less and less room within the dominant society to develop forms of citizenship based on a respect for both individual rights and public goods (Aronowitz, 2000, p. 61). Moreover, as market-driven policies eliminate noncommodified space, critical inquiry fashioned in the spirit of social justice, the common good, and the promise of democracy appears either irrelevant or threatening to the cultural warriors and managers of neoliberalism. For Bauman, one of the central obligations of education in the current era is to provide forms of pedagogy that foster a respect for public life and provide the conditions for translating private issues into public considerations. Additionally, Bauman rightly argues that critique and dissent are central to any viable notion of democracy but are increasingly under siege as a growing number of public spheres are commodified, making it all the more difficult for educators and others to provide the conditions for students to learn how to be critical agents willing to task risks, think oppositionally, and participate in shaping public life.

Central to the rise of a depoliticized citizenry marked by apathy and cynicism is the emergence of a view of education in which schools are defined as a private rather than a public good. This emergent view of education is clearly complicitous with the mounting vocationalization of public and higher education. In addition, it makes a strong claim for pedagogical practices that venerate political disinterestedness while fostering modes of aesthetic analysis that celebrate a retreat into private experience at the expense of critical inquiry and an active social engagement with public life. Perhaps unsurprising in a climate of growing cynicism, the move toward a depoliticized pedagogy that strips students of any sense of critical and social agency cuts across the ideological spectrum. Before focusing on those progressive and radical theorists who align themselves with this view of pedagogy, I want to address briefly how high-profile conservatives such as Harold Bloom legitimate such a position.

In *How to Read and Why,* Bloom argues that the function of reading is neither self- nor social improvement but to alleviate loneliness. The pleasures of reading are in short, "selfish rather than social."[5] Bloom wants to separate reading as an act of pleasure from reading as a form of self-production and agency that connects the reader to a wider public conversation and involvement in public life. He argues that good reading demands clearing one's mind of "academic cant" in order to reject the assumption that reading might have a social function, particularly improving "your neighborhood by what or how you read." According to Bloom, "self-improvement is a large enough project for your mind and spirit: There are no ethics of reading. The mind should be kept at home until its primal ignorance has been purged; premature excursions into activism have their charm, but are time-consuming, and for reading there will never be enough time." Clearly, for Bloom, time is predominantly a burden because it infringes on reading; as such, it appears to be an important precondition only for the act of privatized reading and problematic only if it takes the reader outside of "home." Bloom's elitist attitude toward temporality, his reduction of reading to an act of pleasure, and his exclusively bourgeois focus on the unproblematic comforts of "home" collapses reading as a public pedagogy into the aesthetics of privatized pleasure. Moreover, Bloom depoliticizes pedagogy by defining it exclusively as an instrument of self-improvement and a form of high-minded diversion, thereby eliminating it as a practice for critical engagement and social transformation. There is no sense in Bloom's notion of reading that the act of pedagogy is dependent on a number of political circumstances and conditions. For instance, teaching always takes place within an arena of diverse political and social relations organized around particular relations of power. As Paul Smith points out, the "universities, colleges, and schools we inhabit are crucial for the production and reproduction of social relations of power," but "in all cases, the production and transmission of what we call (in shorthand) 'knowledge' always comports a relation to the *polis* and to the *oikos*—in our contexts, a relation to the political economy of an apparently ever-expanding capitalist entity, to which our knowledge is always related, in which it is always implicated, and which defines and is defined by it" (Smith, 1990, p. 81). Bloom is indifferent to the cultural capital that defines both his notion of authority and the pedagogical categories he uses to give meaning to his definition of correct reading, legitimate knowledge, cultural sanctioned texts, acceptable values, and the admissible uses of literature by his students within the broader industrial circuits of neoliberal society. To teach students how to read, to teach in general, under these conditions is already to engage in an irrefutable political act.

Politics in Bloom's view is an unwarranted if not barbaric intrusion into the sphere of higher education—a degrading affirmation of forms of dissent and inquiry that emerged out of the upheavals of the 1960s and that are antithetical to the world of contemplation and civility. According to this logic, critical pedagogy and critical learning as preconditions for social change have no place in the university and simply represent "speech overflowing with pious platitudes, the peculiar vocabulary of a sect or coven."[6] And, Bloom adds, in case the sexist implication is missed, that "a university culture where the appreciation of Victorian women's underwear now replaces the appreciation of Charles Dickens and Robert Browning sounds like the outrageousness of a new Nathanael West, but is merely the norm" (Bloom, 2000, pp. 102–103). For Bloom, the covens not only gather together in haunted domiciles but have now gone public on university campuses, empowered through struggles waged in the name of multiculturalism, gender, and sexuality, all of which he abruptly dismisses as "a mask for mediocrity for the thought-control academic police, the Gestapo of our campuses" (ibid.). Bloom wants to situate knowledge, literacy, and pedagogy exclusively within the sphere of aesthetic transcendence, unhampered and uncorrupted by theoretical considerations, the struggle over public goods, or what it might mean for students to become social agents capable of influencing those political, economic, and cultural conditions that shape their lives (Bloom, 1998, p. 27). Politics for Bloom is a form of pathology, but it is exclusively a left-wing disease. Though a facile attack even in terms of his own standards, it allows him to ignore the corporate assault on public and higher education, the brutal tearing apart of all forms of solidarities that do not mirror the logic of the market, or those forces in American life that increasingly transform citizenship into an act of consumption. For Bloom, those pedagogical practices that prompt critical engagement—that provide students with the conditions necessary for them to reconceptualize themselves as active citizens capable of altering the terms of debate and structures of power that bear down on their lives—represent one aspect of the excesses of democracy and should be avoided by educators at all costs. Bloom believes that the political irrelevance of the intellectual is a mark of distinction rather than an embarrassment and consequently becomes an apologist for the status quo. But in the end, he does more than shower contempt on those academics who would bridge the world of higher education and public life.[7] More important, Bloom represents a new breed of public relations intellectual, what Pierre Bourdieu (1996, p. 35) calls "fast thinkers—specialists in throw-away thinking," whose willingness to heap contempt on any individual or group that critically engages public life ensures them high-visibility coverage in all of the dominant media outlets.

Erasing the Politics of Pedagogy

> It ultimately comes down to individuals; the students, the parents, and the teachers. Students don't care about their own futures let alone about anyone else's (as the "kids having babies" phenomenon shows), and the teachers don't want to give a real education. It's much easier, after all, to "affirm students' personal lives and experiences" than to write a rigorous lecture on A Portrait of the Artist as a Young Man.
> —Daniel Kaufman (1996, pp. 47–48)

Traditional theories of education generally begin with the premise that knowledge is the fulfillment of (Western) tradition, and pedagogy is a technical practice primarily concerned with the process of transmission. Although it seems reasonable to assume that there is a relationship between what we know and how we act, it does not follow (although it often does in conservative educational discourse and theory) that what we learn and how we learn can be measured solely by the content of an established discipline. This is a fatally flawed argument with respect to its refusal to engage the particular discursive and institutional conditions under which learning takes place. And yet, against the onslaught of an educational reform movement that emphasizes standards and excellence while ignoring issues of equity, this position is increasingly being taken up by a number of progressives who seem unaware of the long-standing criticisms it has received among many critical educators over the last thirty years.[8]

Many liberal and leftist educators emulate their conservative counterparts by either refusing to engage pedagogy as an immanently political and ethical practice or by simply dismissing critical pedagogy as an authoritarian, if not oppressive, practice. Missing from much of this work is a concern with the role that schools play in either extending or closing down the possibilities for students to participate within a wider democratic culture. Nor is there interest in exploring how power works through particular texts, social practices, and institutional structures to produce differences organized around complex forms of subordination and empowerment. Given these omissions, it is not surprising that little is said about how the dominant culture of schooling legitimates as well as excludes, under vastly different conditions of learning, different forms of cultural capital, or what ideological and institutional conditions are necessary to provide teachers with the opportunities they need to function as critical, public intellectuals. Among both groups, there is little sense of what it means to "turn pedagogy into an exploration of its own limits" (Bhabha, 1994, p. 181). While progressives make a claim to the discourse of educational reform, they simultaneously undermine such possibilities by generally ignoring the discourses of power and politics. While clearly sensitive to the politics of education, many radical educators can theorize politics only within notions of domination that reify the complexities of power, authority, and teacher resistance. Distancing themselves from the discourse of social change, a number of these critics appear utterly cynical, if not paralyzed, in exploring the connection between pedagogy and the possibilities of moral and civic agency. As such, they have little to say about the ways in which educators might develop strategies to unsettle and disrupt ongoing attempts by the right-wing ideologues and other conservative forces to deskill teachers, corporatize higher education, and dismantle public education as part of a broader attack on democratic public life. The most egregious examples deal largely in polemical diatribes against other progressives, while a less cynical version attempts to address some of the problems facing public and higher education but do so in ways that abstract such issues from broader political considerations.[9]

In both discourses, there is a theoretical indifference to what it might mean to seize upon the paradox of appropriating authority vested in dominant institutions in order to push against the grain and subvert the very ideological and institutional foundations on which such authority rests. At the very least, turning authority against itself might suggest making visible and challenging how dominant intellectuals and institutions function to incapacitate the intersection of critical thought, political agency, and collective struggle. Taking seriously the relationship among power, politics, agency, and pedagogy might also enable critical educators to connect meaning and pleasure with commitment and passion, as part of a concerted effort to open up pedagogy's discursive and performative possibilities as part of a broader strategy of self and social formation. Refusing to treat pedagogy as a moral and political practice does more than undermine the opportunity for educators to explore its transformative possibilities; it also means that they often have no language for recognizing the abuses often exercised under the rubric of teaching. For instance, how would an educator who defines pedagogy as either irrelevant or as simply a mechanism for transmitting knowledge as a technical function unpack the pedagogical terrorism implicit in the following pronouncement by a conservative educator?

> It's not fashionable to blame the students for anything, but there are plenty of fools among them too. What is most shocking is the fact that many of them seem not to have even a clue as to what's good for them. When we were studying Saint Anselm's proof for the existence of God, one girl was noticeably impatient; finally, I called on

her. She wanted to know why she needed to learn "this stuff," of what use it would be to her. My answer was short: "Because it is better to be smart than stupid. Because there is dignity in being educated and cultivated." Her face was a mask of utter puzzlement.... And so she simply stopped coming to class. (Kaufman, 1996, pp. 47–48)

The above scenario is reflective of the ideologically driven assumptions at work in dominant notions of knowledge as fixed and indisputable; it also points to the ways in which pedagogy can be used to silence and humiliate students. Within this approach to pedagogy, the ideological nature of knowledge production, legitimation, and circulation is often subsumed by appeals for excellence and standards. At the same time, the productive character of pedagogy as a moral and political practice is routinely dismissed as the imposition of bias, derided as a utopian fantasy, renounced as an obstacle to learning, or relegated to a grab bag of depoliticized methods that define pedagogy exclusively in technical and instrumental terms. The latter two positions (obstacle and depoliticization) are not limited to conservative educators. They can be found in the work of Leon Botstein (1999), the outspoken president of Bard College, and in the recent foray with the pedagogical undertaken by Elaine Showalter (1999a), the former president of the Modern Language Association. While it might be argued that neither of these individuals provides a sustained scholarly argument, I focus on them because they not only command large popular followings as well-known public intellectuals, but also because their positions—unlike those of many academics such as E. D. Hirsch, Jr. (1996) and Nat Gage (1978), who develop these positions in much greater detail—get enormous public exposure through extensive distribution in the mainstream media. Though occupying seemingly divergent positions on the role of education and the value of pedagogy, both theorists represent examples of so-called progressive educational reforms that deny the political nature of education and the transformative possibilities of pedagogy itself.

In a recent editorial in the *New York Times*, Botstein suggests that the root cause of the failure of education in the United States is largely due to the inadequate preparation of teachers. Taking aim at education programs in universities nationally, Botstein argues that prospective teachers are taught pedagogy at the expense of formal training in their subject matter and, consequently, are inadequately prepared to teach students even the fundamentals of the basic subject disciplines, contributing both to the lowering of academic standards and the failure of students to learn.[10] The solution, according to Botstein, is to "disband the education schools and integrate teacher education into the core of the university" (1999, p. A19). In short, Botstein argues that schools of education do prospective teachers a great disservice by focusing on the social, historical, and philosophical trajectories of education's own disciplinary traditions at the expense of learning subject matter taught by professionals in the liberal arts.

For Botstein, the key to educational reform lies in raising academic standards, particularly through the mastering of discipline-based subject matter. Missing from Botstein's short-sighted and simplistic appeal is any attempt to engage broader questions of what public schools or higher education should accomplish in a substantive democracy, and why they sometimes fail (see also Botstein, 1997). His facile appeal to academic content cannot engage the relationship between schools and democracy because it has been depoliticized within the discourse of disciplinary purity. Botstein does not have anything to say about how knowledge is related to the power of self-definition and self-determination. Rather, pedagogy is generally assumed to be about processing received knowledge rather than actually transforming it in the interest of the public good. Botstein is utterly indifferent to questions regarding the purpose and meaning of schooling, which actually set the context for understanding the relationship between knowledge and power, as well as to the fact that the real crisis in schools is not simply about whether students are learning subject matter but whether students are capable of meeting traditional educational goals, that is, learning to think critically about the knowledge they gain, engaging larger social issues, and developing a sense of social responsibility. Botstein's appeal to standards ignores what it means to educate prospective teachers about the roles they might play as public intellectuals informed about how power works both within and outside of the classroom. What the role of education should be in a democratic society, how the conditions of teaching affect how students learn, what it might mean to educate students to discern between academic norms and critical intellectual work, or what it might mean to educate students to use knowledge critically in the service of shaping democratic identities and institutional arrangements, are left unanswered in Botstein's analysis. Knowledge for Botstein is an end in itself as opposed to an ongoing process of struggle and negotiation, and the conditions of its production or the limits it embodies in its institutionalized and disciplinary forms appear irrelevant to him.

Botstein's inclusive emphasis on teaching disciplinary knowledge in opposition to any serious engagement with pedagogical issues reveals a fundamental incapacity to address what it might mean to create the conditions to make knowledge meaningful in order to become either critical or transformative. Botstein aside, knowledge doesn't speak for itself. Unless the pedagogical conditions exist to connect forms of knowledge to the lived experiences, histories, and cultures of the students we engage, such knowledge is reified or "deposited" in the Freirian sense, through transmission models that ignore the context in which knowledge is produced and simultaneously function to often silence as much as deaden student interest. Moreover, the emphasis on teaching as knowledge production has little to say about teaching as self-production. In this discourse, it becomes almost impossible to use pedagogy as a way of making teachers attentive to their own biases, values, and ideologies as they work through and shape what and how they teach. In other words, Botstein's exclusive emphasis on disciplinary knowledge offers no theoretical language for helping prospective educators register and interrogate their own personal and social complicities in what, how, and why they teach and learn within particular institutional and cultural formations. This may explain why educators such as Botstein, while opposed to standardized testing, decline to address the plight of students in rundown urban schools, whose performance is largely framed with a vicious cycle of poverty, inadequate school resources, and endless turnover of poorly trained teachers.[11] Nor do such educators offer any concrete challenge to the ways in which such standardized tests function to deskill teachers, remove knowledge from the context and experience in which students negotiate everyday life, or address the pedagogical implications of state-mandated forms of testing, for example, how the latter do not just standardize knowledge but make a mockery of educating students to be critical citizens.[12] At most, Botstein can only suggest new ways to redesign testing procedures while having nothing to say about the necessity to change the very conditions for the production of knowledge, the distribution of power in schools, or the dissemination of resources. Lost here is the possibility of addressing educational reforms that deny the centrality of providing teachers with more control over their academic labor, the necessity of linking equity and excellence by closing the resource gap between rich and poor schools, and the primacy of developing pedagogical practices that both respect students' differences and empower them as critical and active citizens.

Botstein's emphasis on the virtues of disciplinary knowledge as a way of discrediting both pedagogy and colleges of education ignores the crucial importance of pedagogy for raising a number of serious questions. Moreover, it denies the obvious fact that education has its own disciplinary body of knowledge worthy of investigation, ironically reinforcing the necessity of schools of education. There is a long tradition, for instance, of educational knowledge, extending from Thomas Jefferson and John Dewey to Lawrence Cremin and Maxine Greene, that examines the relationships between democracy and schooling, theory and practice, formal and hidden curricula as well as analyzing the ethical, social, political, and historical foundations of schooling. Such knowledge is crucial for contextualizing and engaging the ways in which academic knowledge has been mobilized to define the race, gender, and class-specific purposes of public and higher education. Similarly, the history of education provides a rich and expansive literature for analyzing pedagogy as a moral and political practice through which knowledge, values, and social relations are deployed within unequal relations of power in order to produce particular forms of citizenship and national identity. Botstein depoliticizes knowledge and pedagogy in his analysis and in doing so renders mute the need to understand how they mutually inform each other and what their complicated interaction suggests for addressing both the teaching of prospective educators and teaching itself as a deeply ethical and political issue. For Botstein, education is about the management of knowledge divorced from questions of power, place, ideology, self-management, and politics. In this context, Botstein provides a model of education that is unaware of its own pedagogical assumptions and deeply indebted to a theory of learning that is indifferent to either how power works in education or how teachers and students alike might employ education in the service of democratic struggles.

In contrast to Botstein, Elaine Showalter, in a recent commentary in *The Chronicle of Higher Education,* recognizes the importance of sound pedagogical practice, particularly the responsibility of faculty in preparing their graduate students to teach undergraduate courses. Showalter rejects the popular attitude among her professional colleagues that any "interest in pedagogy [be seen] as the last refuge of a scoundrel" (Showalter, 1999b, p. B4). For Showalter, such derision is unfounded and simply perpetuates the general complaint that teaching assistants don't know how to teach and that faculty are unwilling to do anything about it.

Born out of a general impatience with the lack of will and effort to address the problem of pedagogy, Showalter brought together in 1998 a number of graduate students in a noncredit course on teaching in order to take up the problem. The first challenge for Showalter was to locate materials on teaching in order to "find out what other people are doing behind their closed classroom doors" (ibid.) Conducting an intensive search on the Internet, Showalter surprised herself and her students by how many books she was able to find on teaching. For Showalter, texts on university education fall into four general categories: personal memoirs, spiritual and ethical reflections, practical guidebooks, and reports on education research. Unfortunately, her search left her and her students unaware of a long tradition of critical theoretical work on pedagogy, schooling, and society. The result is that both she and her graduate students came away with a conception of teaching as simply a matter of methods, exclusively and reductively concerned with practical and technical issues. Hence, their enthusiasm for books that "provide lots of pointers on subjects as varied as choosing textbooks and getting feedback from students and colleagues" or books that help "instructors make the most effective use of the lecture/discussion mode" (ibid., p. B5). Even those books that Showalter claims deal with ethical and spiritual issues become significant to the degree that they "can offer both inspiration and some surprisingly concrete advice" (ibid.). In the end, Showalter recommends a number of books such as Wilbert J. McKeachie's *McKeachie's Teaching Tips* and Joseph Lowman's *Mastering the Techniques of Teaching* because they "offer practical, concrete advice about learning to ask students good questions and encouraging them to participate" (ibid., p. B6).

The upshot is that Showalter and her students ignore an entire generation of scholarship in critical pedagogy that addresses teaching as a moral and political practice, as a deliberate attempt to influence how and what knowledge and identities are produced within very particular contexts and relations of power.[13] In her zest for "concreteness," she abstracts pedagogical practices from the ethico-political visions that inform them, and has little to say about how pedagogy relates the self to public life, social responsibility, or the demands of critical citizenship. Showalter has no pedagogical language for dealing with student voice and experience, nor the social, racial, and class inequalities that animate them. Nor does she offer her students guidance on matters of justice, equality, liberty, and fairness that should be at the core of pedagogical practices designed to enable students to recognize social problems and injustices in a society founded on deep inequalities. Even basic pedagogical issues regarding how teacher authority can manifest itself without being inimical to the practice of freedom are ignored in Showalter's discourse. By defining pedagogy as an a priori discourse that simply needs to be uncovered and deployed, Showalter has nothing to say about pedagogy as the outcome of specific struggles between diverse groups to name history, experience, knowledge, and the meaning of everyday life in one's own terms. Unfortunately, Showalter offers up a depoliticized pedagogy of "tips" that is effectively silent on matters of how knowledge, values, desire, and social relations are always implicated in power and broader institutional practices. Showalter's stripped-down version of pedagogy is not surprising given her conservative views on the increasing corporatization of the university and the ongoing proletarianization of faculty as adjunct workers (Showalter, 1999b). What is surprising is her silence on the role that her own version of pedagogy plays in preparing students in the "new corporate university" for forms of citizenship that define them exclusively as consumers and forms of knowledge whose only value appears to be in helping them put together attractive job résumés. What Showalter conveniently refuses to engage is the role pedagogy might play in educating students to take risks, engage in learning how to exercise power, and extend the boundaries of economic and social justice.

If Botstein depoliticizes and instrumentalizes questions concerning the production of knowledge and reduces pedagogy to the logic of transmission, Showalter similarly reifies pedagogy by stripping it of its political and ethical referents and transforming it into a grab bag of practical methods and techniques. Neither scholar can theorize the productive character of pedagogy as a political and moral discourse. Hence both are silent about the institutional conditions that bear down on the ability of teachers to link conception with execution, and what it means to develop a better understanding of pedagogy as a struggle over the shaping of particular identities. Nor can they raise questions about education as a form of political intervention that cannot elude its role in creating potentially empowering or disempowering spaces for students, critically interrogate the role of teacher authority, or engage the limits of established academic subjects in sustaining critical dialogues about educational aims and practices. These questions barely scratch the surface of issues that are often excluded when education is linked solely to the teaching of content and pedagogy is instrumentalized to the point of irrelevance.

A number of radical educational and cultural theorists have also argued against the relevance and importance of critical pedagogy. Advocates of this position include Ian Hunter (1994), Elizabeth Ellsworth (1994), and Tony Bennett (1996, 1998).[14] All of these theorists dismiss critical pedagogy by claiming it is simply another instrument for reconciling the self with the dominant social order; moreover, they reject the importance of pedagogical practices that call critical attention to the ways in which authority might be used to challenge the ideologies and practices that characterize much of public and higher education—tracking, cutbacks in student loans, aggressive advertising in schools, corporate-friendly curricula, "zero tolerance" policies aimed mostly at minorities of race and color, use of noncertified teachers, and downsizing of full-time faculty by increasing adjunct positions.

Reducing critical pedagogy to the imposition of dominant authority, Hunter, for instance, can only imagine teacher authority working in the interest of moral regulation and social control. Self-reflexive dialogue drops out of his argument, as does the possibility of teachers and students becoming critical of the very institutional forms, academic relations, and disciplinary knowledges and regulations that constitute the complex and varied spaces of schooling. Within this narrow understanding of the relationship between culture and politics, there is no possibility for imagining schools as a place to resist hegemonic authority, unsettle strategies of domination, or re-elaborate institutional authority from a position of engaged self-criticism and as a critical object of classroom analysis. That the legacy of such cultural and moral regulation can be challenged, pedagogically turned in on itself, or used as a resource to refigure the basis of teaching as a deliberative practice in the service of a progressive cultural politics seems impossible within this discourse.[15]

Critical pedagogy in this approach is not only reduced to a form of oppression, it is also commodified and turned into an inert theory to be enacted irrespective of the historical realities and material circumstances that shape the context in which it is enacted. Treated merely as a commodity, if not a caricature, critical pedagogy is transformed into a fixed body of knowledge and reified as a taken-for-granted and totalizing theory. Under such circumstances, critical pedagogy is no longer shaped, in part, by the contexts it attempts to address. Nor are its aims mediated and modified with respect to the questions posed by different circumstances, enabling it to be used differently by educators as a resource to produce new social relations, spaces of opposition, or forms of critical agency. Lost here is the important recognition that critical pedagogy is not an a priori discourse that imposes itself on teachers and students alike with the arrogance of theoretical certainty. On the contrary, any viable notion of critical pedagogy has to recognize its own indeterminate and partial character, particularly since it is constantly being shaped by the particular contexts in which it is taken up. Given that its usefulness rests on its ability to respond to the problems posed within particular contexts marked by changing configurations of students, cultural resources, community histories, and relations of power, critical pedagogy can neither be defined as a static theory nor can it be required to provide theoretical and political guarantees.

In an article that has been and continues to be cited as a seminal argument against critical pedagogy, Elizabeth Ellsworth contends that when she attempted to put into practice the basic principles of critical pedagogy in a class she taught at the University of Wisconsin–Madison in 1988, "the results were not only unhelpful, but actually exacerbated the very conditions we were trying to work against, including Eurocentrism, racism, sexism, classism, and 'banking education'" (Ellsworth, 1994, p. 301).[16] According to Ellsworth, the failure of critical pedagogy lies in its claims to enforce the "rules of reason in the classroom" (ibid., p. 305),[17] which not only reproduce violence against all those "others" traditionally excluded within its purview, but prevents those critical pedagogues who make a claim to authority in the service of a political project from making their own ideologies and practices problematic. Authority in this context is always on the side of domination, and its attempts to forge a connection between critical learning and social change is doomed to reproduce a master narrative of domination.

Theorists such as Ellsworth ignore the radically contextual nature of critical pedagogy and not surprisingly condemn it for being dogmatic and oppressive rather than open, contextually strategic, and potentially liberatory. Commenting on how pedagogy becomes commodified in Ellsworth's work, particularly as it relates to a course she taught, Bruce Horner rightly critiques her propensity to treat power, authority, and domination as if they were identical. Horner also argues that the failure of Ellsworth's class was inevitable given the way in which she reduces critical pedagogy to a commodity isolated from the material circumstances in which it was enacted. Rather than recognizing that it was *her* reification of critical pedagogy that guaranteed its failure, Ellsworth blames it for functioning as a commodity unable to address the particular issues and problems that emerged within the context-specific conditions of her own teaching. Horner is worth quoting at length on this issue.

> That she expected critical pedagogy to operate as a commodity is apparent in the ways in which she was asked by her students what she meant by "critical" in her syllabi descriptions of critical pedagogy, she simply "referred them to answers provided in the literature," as if such a pedagogy were monolithic and fixed in meaning and effect. . . . [Ellsworth] was shocked to discover that the actual historical realities of the students, herself as professor, and C71607 failed to match the ideal to which critical pedagogy aims. But rather than concluding with a recognition of the need for both students and teacher to rework the meaning and substance of critical pedagogy anew in each historical instance of its practice, as one might expect, Ellsworth uses the inevitable gap between the aims of critical pedagogy and the lived experience of the C71607 course to condemn the pedagogy for its failure, by itself, to close that gap. Like an angry consumer, she rejects critical pedagogy as repressive rather than liberatory, as a commodity that does not "work" as advertised. (Horner, 2000, p. 130)[18]

Under such circumstances, power is almost exclusively associated with domination and teacher authority simply becomes another register of authoritarianism. This is not to suggest that critical educators should overlook either the kind of pedagogical abuses that can take place in the name of authority that makes a claim to critical pedagogy or ignore the long history in which pedagogy has been complicitous with constructing the state's version of citizenship and national identity. Nor should critical educators be indifferent to the fact that institutional practices forged within dominant economic, cultural, and political conditions exercise an enormous influence in shaping the very conditions under which pedagogy takes place. But to acknowledge the latter, as Alan O'Shea (1998) has recently pointed out, does not legitimate the presupposition that power is entirely on the side of domination within schools, or that teachers and students can only be complicitous with hegemonic power, however they challenge its structures, ideologies, and practices.[19] Such criticism rests on more than passé functionalist accounts of society and its social forms, it also legitimates a totalizing model of power and authority that marks a retreat from making the political more pedagogical as it simultaneously celebrates the marginalized role of the detached, objective educator. This notion of power and education rooted in a Foucauldian notion of governmentality signals a form of theoretical paralysis (not simply anti-utopianism) that undermines the more crucial problem of how schooling as a terrain of struggle functions to shape the possibilities of political agency and critical engagement against dominant cultural and institutional formations. Missing in this approach is any understanding of the importance of teachers and students analyzing how authority is used in public and higher education to give particular forms of knowledge, culture, and social relations political and ethical valence. Nor is there any attempt to construct and analyze pedagogical authority as a tool for social critique. Instead, authority and the rule of reason come to symbolize a form of violence, offset by the wonders of indeterminacy and endless excursions into autocritique. Social critique tends to drop out of this formulation while politics is reduced to the level of formalistic critique. Under such circumstances, authority itself becomes antithetical to transformative politics, and any determinate form of political engagement exercised in its name becomes synonymous with all that is dogmatic. This is a politics that seems made for the academy because it threatens no one, for it is against nothing that would challenge material relations of power.

Such versions of authority, pedagogy, and politics preclude engaging pedagogy as the outgrowth of specific struggles that take place within varied contexts marked by unequal relations of power, differentiated opportunities, and varied resources for social change. In some cases, theorists such as Tony Bennett actually replicate older models of social and cultural reproduction that were prevalent among radical educational theorists in the United States in the 1970s and early 1980s (Aronowitz & Giroux, 1994). According to Bennett, radical classroom interventions are caught within the paralyzing grip of governmental institutions that normalize all pedagogical practices. Similarly, Bennett argues that radical educators overemphasize agency at the expense of institutional pressures, embracing what he calls "all agency and no structure" (Bennett, 1998, pp. 223). This criticism, however, does little to explore or highlight the complicated, contradictory, and determining ways in which the institutional pressures of schools and the social capacities of educators are mediated within unequal relations of power. Instead, Bennett simply reverses the formula and buttresses his own notion of governmentality as a theory of structures without agents. Ultimately, Bennett's pessimism collapses into something worse than the liberalism he accuses radical educators of emulating.

Beyond Pedagogies of Despair and the Politics of Cynicism

> The irreducible distance, the always [irresolvable tension] between the "idea of democracy" and that which presents itself in its name remains forever ambiguous. That idea is not altogether a "Kantian idea," at the same time regulating and infinitely expanded. It commands the most concrete urgency, here and now. If I keep its old

name of "democracy" nevertheless, and often speak of a "democracy to come," it is because that is the only name for a political regime which declares its historicity and its perfectibility, in that it carries in its concept the dimension of inadequation and of that which is to come. Democracy allows us in all liberty to invoke these two openings publicly in order to criticize the current state of all so-called democracy.

—Jacques Derrida (2000, p. 9)

In opposition to these increasingly dominant views of education and cultural politics, I want to argue for a transformative pedagogy—rooted in the project of resurgent democracy—that relentlessly questions the kinds of labor, practices, and forms of production that are enacted in public and higher education. Such an analysis should be both relational and contextual, as well as self-reflective and theoretically rigorous. By relational, I mean that the current crisis of schooling must be understood in relation to the broader assault that is being waged against all aspects of democratic public life. As Jeffrey Williams has recently pointed out, "the current restructuring of higher education is only one facet of the restructuring of civic life in the U.S. whereby previously assured public entitlements such as healthcare, welfare, and social security have evaporated or been 'privatized,' so no solution can be separated from a larger vision of what it means to enfranchise citizens of our republic" (Williams, 1999, p. 749). But as important as such articulations are in understanding the challenges that public and higher education face in the current historical conjuncture, they do not go far enough. Any critical comprehension of those wider forces that shape public and higher education must also be supplemented by an attentiveness to the conditional nature of pedagogy itself. This suggests that pedagogy can never be treated as a fixed set of principles and practices that can be applied indiscriminately across a variety of pedagogical sites. Pedagogy must always be contextually defined, allowing it to respond specifically to the conditions, formations, and problems that arise in various sites in which education takes place. Rather than treating pedagogy as commodity, progressive educators need to engage their teaching as a theoretical resource that is both shaped by and responds to the very problems that arise in the in-between space/places/contexts that connect classrooms with the experiences of everyday life. Under such circumstances, educators can address the meaning and purpose that schools might play in their relationship to the demands of the broader society while simultaneously being sensitive to the distinctive nature of the issues educators address within the shifting contexts in which they interact with a diverse body of students, texts, and institutional formations.

Critical pedagogy locates discursive practices in a broader set of interrelations, but it analyzes and gives meaning to such relations by defining them within particular contexts constructed through the operations of power as articulated through the interaction among texts, teachers, and students. Questions of articulation and contexts need to be foregrounded as matters of both ethics and politics. Ethically, critical pedagogy requires an ongoing indictment "of those forms of truth-seeking which imagined themselves to be eternally and placelessly valid"

(Gilroy, 2000, p. 69). Simply put, educators need to cast a critical eye on those forms of knowledge and social relations that define themselves through a conceptual purity and political innocence that clouds not only how they come into being but also ignores that the alleged neutrality on which they stand is already grounded in ethico-political choices. Thomas Keenan rightly argues that ethics on the pedagogical front demands an openness to the other, a willingness to engage a "politics of possibility" through a continual critical engagement with texts, images, events, and other registers of meaning as they are transformed into public pedagogies.[20] One consequence of linking pedagogy to the specificity of place is that it extends the possibility of making the pedagogical more political. Not only does it foreground the need for educators to rethink the cultural and political baggage they bring to each educational encounter, it highlights the necessity of making educators ethically and politically accountable for the stories they produce, the claims they make upon public memory, and the images of the future they deem legitimate. Pedagogy is never innocent, and if it is to be understood and problematized as a form of academic labor, educators must not only critically question and register their own subjective involvement in how and what they teach, they must also resist all calls to depoliticize pedagogy through appeals to either scientific objectivity or ideological dogmatism. Far from being disinterested or ideologically frozen, critical pedagogy is concerned about the articulation of knowledge to social effects and succeeds to the degree in which educators encourage critical reflection and moral and civic agency rather than simply mold it. Crucial to the latter position is the necessity for critical educators to be attentive to the ethical dimensions of their own practice.

But as an act of intervention, critical pedagogy needs to be grounded in a project that not only problematizes its own location, mechanisms of transmission, and effects, but also functions as part of a larger project to contest various forms of domination and to help students think more critically about how existing social, political, and economic arrangements might be better suited to address the promise of a radical democracy as an anticipatory rather than messianic goal. Jacques Derrida has recently suggested that the social function of intellectuals as well as any viable notion of education should be grounded in a vibrant politics that makes the promise of democracy a matter of concrete urgency. For Derrida, making visible a "democracy" that is to come as opposed to that which presents itself in its name provides a referent for both criticizing everywhere what parades as democracy—"the current state of all so-called democracy"—and for critically assessing the conditions and possibilities for democratic transformation (Derrida, 2000, p. 9). Derrida sees the promise of democracy as the proper articulation of a political ethics and by implication suggests that when higher education is engaged and articulated through the project of democratic social transformation it can function as a vital public sphere for critical learning, ethical deliberation, and civic engagement. Moreover, the utopian dimension of pedagogy articulated through the project of radical democracy offers the possibility of resistance to the increasing depoliticization of the citizenry, provides a language to challenge the politics of accommodation that connects education to the logic of privatization, refuses to define the citizen as simply a consuming subject, and actively opposes the view of teaching as market-driven practice and learning as a form of training. Utopian in this sense is not an antidote to politics, a nostalgic yearning for a better time or for some "inconceivably alternative future." But, by contrast, it is an "attempt to find a bridge between the present and future in those forces within the present which are potentially able to transform it" (Eagleton, 2000, p. 22).

In opposition to dominant forms of education and pedagogy that simply reinvent the future in the interest of a present in which ethical principles are scorned and the essence of democracy is reduced to the imperatives of the bottom line, critical pedagogy must address the challenge of providing students with the competencies they need to cultivate the capacity for critical judgment, thoughtfully connect politics to social responsibility, and expand their own sense of agency in order to curb the excesses of dominant power, revitalize a sense of public commitment, and expand democratic relations. Animated by a sense of critique and possibility, critical pedagogy at its best attempts to provoke students to deliberate, resist, and cultivate a range of capacities that enable them to move beyond the world they already know without insisting on a fixed set of meanings.

Against the current onslaught to privatize public schools and vocationalize higher education, progressives need to defend public and higher education as a resource vital to the democratic and civic life of the nation. Central to such a task is the challenge of academics, cultural workers, and labor organizers to find ways to join together in broad-based social movements and oppose the transformation of the public schools and higher education into commercial spheres, to resist what Bill Readings (1994, p. 11, 14) has called a consumer-oriented corporation more concerned about accounting than accountability. The crisis of public schooling and higher education—while having different registers—needs to be analyzed in terms of wider configurations of economic, political, and social forces that exacerbate tensions between those who value such institutions as public goods and those advocates of neoliberalism who see market culture as a master design for all human affairs. The threat corporate power poses can be seen in the ongoing attempts by neoliberals and other hyper capitalists to subject all forms of public life, including public and higher education, to the dictates of the market while simultaneously working to empty democracy itself of any vestige of ethical, political, and social considerations. What progressives must challenge is the attempt on the part of neoliberals to either define democracy exclusively as a liability or to enervate its substantive ideals by reducing it to the imperatives and freedoms of the marketplace. This requires that educators consider the political and pedagogical importance of struggling over the meaning and definition of democracy and situate such a debate within an expansive notion of human rights, social provisions, civil liberties, equity, and economic justice. What must be challenged at all costs is the increasingly dominant view propagated by neoliberal gurus such as Milton Friedman that profit making is the essence of democracy and accumulating material goods the essence of the good life.

Defending public and higher education as vital democratic spheres is necessary to develop and nourish the proper balance between public values and commercial power, between identities founded on democratic principles and identities steeped in forms of competitive, self-interested individualism that celebrate selfishness, profit making, and greed. Progressives also must reconsider the critical roles educators might take up within public and higher education so as to enable them to oppose those approaches to schooling that corporatize and bureaucratize the teaching process. A critical pedagogy should, in part, be premised on the assumption that educators vigorously resist any attempt on the part of liberals and conservatives to reduce their role in schools to that of either technicians or corporate pawns. Instead, progressive educators might redefine their roles as engaged public intellectuals capable of teaching students the language of critique and possibility as a precondition for social agency. Such a redefinition of purpose, meaning, and politics suggests that educators critically interrogate the fundamental link between knowledge and power, pedagogical practices and social consequences, and authority and civic responsibility.

By redefining the purpose and meaning of schooling as part of a broader attempt to struggle for a radical democratic social order, progressive educators can begin to vigorously challenge a number of dominant assumptions and policies currently structuring public and higher education, including but not limited to: ongoing attempts by corporate culture to define educators as multinational operatives; escalating efforts by colleges and universities to deny students the loans, resources, and public support they need to have access to a quality education; the mounting influence of corporate interests in pressuring universities to reward forms of scholarship that generate corporate profits; increasing attempts to deny women and students of color access to higher education through the reversal of affirmative action policies; and a growing emphasis on the production of knowledge and modes of teaching designed to creating marketable products and active consumers. Rather than providing students with an opportunity to learn how to shape and govern public life, education is increasingly being vocationalized, reduced to a commodity that provides privileges for a few students and industrial training for the service sector for the rest, especially those who are marginalized by reason of their class and race.

Increasingly, the corporatization of education functions so as to cancel out the democratic values, impulses, and practices of a civil society by either devaluing or absorbing them within the logic of the market. Educators need a critical language to address these challenges to public and higher education. But they also need to join with other groups outside of the spheres of public and higher education in order to create a national movement that links the defense of noncommodified education with a broader struggle to deepen the imperatives of democratic public life. The quality of educational reform can, in part, be gauged by the caliber of public discourse concerning the role that education plays in furthering, not the market-driven agenda of corporate interests, but the imperatives of critical agency, social justice, and an operational democracy. In this capacity, educators need to develop a language of possibility for raising critical questions about the aim of schooling and the purpose and meaning of what and how educators teach. In doing so, pedagogy draws attention to engaging classroom practice as moral and political consideration animated by a fierce sense of commitment to expanding the range of individual capacities that enable students to become critical agents capable of linking knowledge, responsibility, and democratic social transformation.

Approaching pedagogy as a critical and political practice suggests that educators refuse all attempts to reduce classroom teaching exclusively to matters of technique and method. In opposition to such approaches, progressives can highlight the performative character of education as an act of intervention in the world—focusing on the work that pedagogy does as a deliberate attempt to influence how and what knowledge and experiences are produced within particular sets of classroom relations. Within this perspective, critical pedagogy foregrounds the diverse conditions under which authority, knowledge, values, and subject positions are produced and interact within unequal relations of power; it also problematizes the ideologically laden and often contradictory roles and social functions that educators assume within the classroom. Pedagogy in this view can also be reclaimed as a form of academic labor that bridges the gap between individual considerations and public concerns, affirms bonds of sociality and reciprocity, and interrogates the relationship between individual freedom and privatized notions of the good life and the social obligations and collective structures necessary to support a vibrant democracy.

The question of what educators teach is inseparable from what it means to locate oneself in public discourses and invest in public commitments. Implicit in this argument is the assumption that the responsibility of critical educators cannot be separated from the consequences of the subject positions they have been assigned, the knowledge they produce, the social relations they legitimate, and the ideologies they disseminate to students. Educational work at its best represents a response to questions and issues posed by the tensions and contradictions of the broader society; it is an attempt to understand and intervene in specific problems that emanate from those sites that people concretely inhabit and actually live out their lives and everyday existence. Teaching in this sense becomes performative and contextual, and it highlights considerations of power, politics, and ethics fundamental to any form of teacher-student-text interaction. As I mentioned previously, this suggests the importance of addressing education in political and ethical terms. By drawing attention to pedagogy's productive character, critical educators can highlight pedagogy as the outcome of specific deliberations and struggles that need to be addressed in terms of the "material and historical specificities of (its) enactments" (Horner, 2000, p. 141), and in doing so reject the conservative notion that pedagogy can be theorized as either an a priori set of prescriptions or as a commodity to be applied in any context.

It is crucial to reiterate that any pedagogy that is alive to its own democratic implications is always cautious of its need for closure; it self-consciously resists totalizing certainties and answers. Refusing the pull of dogmatism and imperious authority, progressive educators must at the same time grasp the complexity and contradictions that inform the conditions under which they produce and disseminate knowledge. Recognizing that pedagogy is the outgrowth of struggles that are historically specific, as are the problems that govern the questions and issues that guide what and how we teach, should not suggest that educators renounce their authority. On the contrary, it is precisely by recognizing that teaching is always an act of intervention inextricably mediated through particular forms of authority that teachers *can* offer students—for whatever use they wish to make of them—a variety of analytic tools, diverse historical traditions, and a wide-ranging knowledge of dominant and subaltern cultures and how they influence each other. This is a far cry from suggesting that critical pedagogy define itself within the grip of a self-righteous mode of authority or completely remove itself from any sense of commitment whatsoever. On the contrary, at stake here is the need to insist on modes of authority that are directive but not imperious, linking knowledge to power in the service of self-production, and encouraging students to go beyond the world they already know to expand their range of human possibilities. Robert Miklitsch rightly argues that teacher authority and institutional positioning are pivotal considerations for analyzing the politics of teaching and the ethical responsibilities that define both the project and the articulation of pedagogy to particular effects. He writes:

> I want to argue . . . that teachers must begin from the pedagogic subject-position to which they have been assigned. If the latter position is not necessarily one of mastery (in either sense of the word), it nonetheless remains one of authority. In other words, to attempt absolutely to renounce the pedagogic subject-positon—from whatever motivation, liberal or otherwise—is not only to accede to a "bad" egalitarian logic, it is to evade our responsibility as teachers. And that responsibility—which needless to say, is an implicitly political one—involves recognizing those structures (social, cultural, economic, and so forth) that both enable and constrain our activities. (Miklitsch, 1990, p. 93)

Academics must deliberate, make decisions, take positions, and in doing so recognize that authority "is the very condition for intellectual work" and pedagogical interventions (Michael, 2000, p. 2). Miklitsch suggests above that teacher authority cannot be merely renounced as an act of domination, but should be addressed dialectically and deployed strategically so as to enable students to become witnesses to the material and cultural relations of power that often prevent them and others from speaking and acting in particular ways. Authority in this perspective in not simply on the side of oppression, but is used to intervene and shape the space of teaching and learning to provide students with a range of possibilities for challenging a society's commonsense assumptions, and for analyzing the interface between their own everyday lives and those broader social formations that bear down on them. Authority, at best, becomes both a referent for legitimating a commitment to a particular vision of pedagogy and a critical referent for a kind of autocritique. It demands consideration of how authority functions within specific relations of power regarding its own promise to provide students with a public space where they can learn, debate, and engage critical traditions in order to imagine otherwise and develop discourses that are crucial for defending vital social institutions as a public good.

Progressive educators need to rethink the tension between the pedagogical and the performative by asking how the performative functions pedagogically. While pedagogy can be understood performatively as an event where many things can happen in the service of learning, it is crucial to stress the importance of democratic classroom relations that encourage dialogue, deliberation, and the power of students to raise questions. Moreover, such relations don't signal a retreat from teacher authority as much as they suggest using authority reflexively to provide the conditions for students to exercise intellectual rigor, theoretical competence, and informed judgments. Thus students can think critically about the knowledge they gain and what it means to act on such knowledge in order to expand their sense of agency as part of a broader project of increasing both "the scope of their freedoms" and "the operations of democracy" (West, 1991, p. 35). What students learn and how they learn should amplify what it means to experience democracy from a position of possibility, affirmation, and critical engagement. In part, this suggests that progressive educators develop pedagogical practices that open up the terrain of the political while simultaneously encouraging students to "think better about how arrangements might be otherwise" (Dean, 2000, p. 3).

To be at its best, critical pedagogy must be interdisciplinary, radically contextual, engage the complex relationships between power and knowledge, critically address the institutional constraints under which teaching takes place, and focus on how students can engage the imperatives of critical social citizenship. At the same time, critical pedagogy must be self-reflexive about its aims and practices, conscious of its ongoing project of democratic transformation, but openly committed to a politics that does not offer any guarantees. But refusing dogmatism does not suggest that educators descend into a laissez-faire pluralism or an appeal to methodologies designed to "teach the conflicts." On the contrary, it suggests that in order to make the pedagogical more political, educators afford students with diverse opportunities to understand and experience how politics, power, commitment, and responsibility work on and through them both within and outside of schools. This, in turn, enables students to locate themselves within an interrelated confluence of ideological and material forces as critical agents who can both influence such forces and simultaneously be held responsible for their own views and actions. Within this perspective, relations between institutional forms and pedagogical practices are acknowledged as complex, open, and contradictory—though always situated within unequal relations of power (O'Shea, 1988).

I also want to stress the importance of addressing in any viable theory of critical pedagogy the role that affect and emotion play in the formation of individual identities and social collectivities. Engaging education as a productive and performative force suggests taking seriously those maps of meaning, affective investments, and sedimented desires that enable students to connect their own lives and everyday experiences to what they learn. Pedagogy in this sense becomes more than a mere transfer of received knowledge, an inscription of a unified and static identity, or a rigid methodology; it presupposes that students are moved by their passions and motivated, in part, by the affective investments they bring to the learning process. This suggests, as Paulo Freire points out, the need for a theory of pedagogy willing to develop a "critical comprehension of the value of sentiments, emotions, and desire as part of the learning process" (Freire, 1998, p. 48). Not only do students need to understand the ideological, economic, and political interests that shape the nature of their educational experiences, they must also address the strong emotional investments they may bring to such beliefs. For Shoshana Felman, this suggests that educators take seriously the role of desire in both ignorance and learning. "Teaching," she explains, "has to deal not so much with lack of knowledge as with resistances to knowledge. Ignorance, suggests Jacques Lacan, is a 'passion.' Inasmuch as traditional pedagogy postulated a desire for knowledge, an analytically informed pedagogy has to reckon with the passion for ignorance" (Felman, 1987, p. 79). Felman elaborates further on the productive nature of ignorance, arguing, "Ignorance is nothing other than a desire to ignore: its nature is less cognitive than performative . . . it is not a simple lack of information but the incapacity—or the refusal—to acknowledge one's own implication in the information" (ibid.). If students are to move beyond the issue of understanding to an engagement with the deeper affective investments that make them complicitous with oppressive ideologies, they must be positioned to address and formulate strategies of transformation through which their individualized beliefs and affective investments can be articulated with broader public discourses that extend the imperatives of democratic public life. An unsettling pedagogy in this instance would engage student identities and resistances from unexpected vantage points and articulate how they connect to existing material relations of power. At stake here is not only a pedagogical practice that recalls how knowledge, identifications, and subject positions are produced, unfolded, and remembered but also how they become part of an ongoing process, more strategic so to speak, of mediating and challenging existing relations of power.

Conclusion

The current cynicism and despair that informs the discourses of many social and educational theorists points to one of the more startling acts of forgetting that has taken place since the 1980s. Increasingly, theorists across the ideological spectrum have either dismissed or ignored the central role that pedagogy has played in foregrounding the connection among teaching and politics, knowledge and power, and learning and social change. Their social amnesia is all the more troubling since pedagogy has a long and critical tradition of defending schooling as a vital public good while promoting the goal of educating students to become socially concerned citizens "who could help determine, through vision and wisdom, the nation's political course" (Becker, 1995, p. 388). Theorists as different as Frederick Douglass, W. E. B. DuBois, Paulo Freire, and Cornel West have all stressed the crucial link between education and democracy, on the one hand, and pedagogy and the production of critical agents and citizen activists on the other. As a moral and political practice, pedagogy has often been addressed by such theorists as one of the principal means through which to provide students with the knowledge, skills, and experiences that would enable them to understand, engage, and shape the symbolic and institutional conditions that influenced their lives. Within this progressive legacy, education constitutes the ongoing task of being more than a mechanism for social and cultural reproduction. Rather, it is indispensable for understanding public agency and the necessity for creating democratic identities, values, and relations that provide the conditions for students and others to influence and participate in ongoing conversations about important political and social issues that shape the common good and expand and energize democratic life. In light of the current assault on education and all other aspects of public life by reactionary cultural warriors, heavily financed conservative think tanks, and corporate power, progressives need to rethink the legacy of education as a force for democratic social transformation and pedagogy as a crucial practice for both understanding and engaging culture as the primary educational force through which agency is shaped, identities are produced, and resistance in constructed. Within this context, pedagogy becomes synonymous with a form of cultural politics that provides an opportunity to expand the sites in which critical pedagogical work takes place (what Raymond Williams called the sites of permanent education) and offers new hope for challenging and transforming the politics of despair and cynicism through strategic interventions that offer opportunities for educators to redefine and transform the connections among language, desire, meaning, everyday life, and material relations of power as part of a broader social movement to reclaim the promise and possibilities of a substantive democracy.

Notes

1. This theme is taken up in Jeffrey C. Goldfarb (1991), Joseph N. Capella and Kathleen Hall Jamieson (1997), Russell Jacoby (1999), William Chaloupka (1999), Bauman (1999), Boggs (2000).
2. *New York Times* columnist Frank Rich recently captured the mood of such cynicism in his claim that "more Americans care about who is going to be voted off the island on *Survivor* or will succeed Kathie Lee Gifford on the Regis morning ticket than who will be the next vice president." See Frank Rich (2000), Zygmunt Bauman (1999), Henry A. Giroux (2000).
3. For an insightful analysis of the breakdown of civic life as a condition for such cynicism, see Robert D. Putnam (2000). For an analysis of the relationship between work and the corrosion community and social values, see Richard Sennett (1998) and Paulina Borsook (2000).

4. For systemic and critical accounts of the hollowing out of the state and its impact on social services, see Noam Chomsky (1999), Frances Fox Piven and Richard A. Cloward (1997), Deborah R. Connolly (2000).
5. Excerpt from *How to Read and Why*, cited in Harold Bloom (2000: 102).
6. I have addressed the political nature of education and pedagogy in a number of books. See, for example, Henry A. Giroux (1998 and 2000).
7. In this sense, Bloom echoes right-wing ideologues such as Stephen H. Balch, the president of the National Association of Scholars. Balch argues that any attempt to critically engage, or for that matter even question, what he calls the civilizing mission of academe, amounts to an "embrace of radical relativism." Rather than recognizing such forms of inquiry as an attempt to think through the responsibility, rights, and claims made in the name of authority, knowledge, and pedagogy, Balch simply dismisses such inquiry as an affront to academic standards and cultural values. Balch appears totally indifferent to the pedagogical and political implications of suggesting to students that they have no ethical or political right (foundation) to critique the regimes of meaning they are asked to learn and act on as a basis for developing a sense of individual and political agency. What kind of agency is being put into place under these circumstances? For Bloom and Balch, knowledge is sacred, leaving little if no room for critical inquiry, and hence pedagogy is rendered to a methodology of transmission, a process that refuses questions and takes no risks. See Stephen H. Balch (2000).
8. I summarize and extend many of these arguments in Henry A. Giroux (1997).
9. For a classic example of a polemical educational discourse that substitutes cynicism and critical pragmatism for passionate principle, and in doing so banishes hope, if not possibility itself, from the very realm of politics, see Ilan Gur-Ze'ev (1998). In fact, the entire issue of *Educational Theory* in which Gur-Ze'ev's piece appears is filled with the work of a number of theorists who represent this position. The equally depoliticized but less cynical work I am referring to can be seen a recent issue of *The Nation*, organized by Herbert Kohl. Kohl appears to have become a broker for an educational discourse that is utterly hostile to radical versions of critical educational theory and practice. See the special issue of *The Nation*, June 5, 2000. If we were to believe these critics, with few exceptions, schools have little to do with the assault on the welfare state, corporate power, the rise of the right in America, or any other broader political issue. For a representative view of Kohl's acrimonious views toward radical pedagogy, see his interview, "Herb Kohl Interview, NYC—June 2, 1997," at *http://www.zmag.org/sep/kohlint.htm* Also see Stan Karp, "Lesson Plans: The Politics of Education: An Interview with Herbert Kohl," *http://zena.secureforum. com/znet/ZMag/ articles/April94 Krp.htm*.
10. Needless to say, this debate has been central to the history of a number of educational reform groups arguing for the professionalization of the teaching field. For a brilliant analysis of this history, see David F. Labaree (1997).
11. A typical example of such conditions and how they affect the quality of education for students in such schools can be found in Lynette Holloway (2000).
12. Leon Botstein (2000). For an excellent recent critique of standardized testing, see Peter Sacks (1999). Also David Owen with Marilyn Doerr (2000).
13. To be fair to Showalter, she is not alone among humanities scholars in refusing to step outside of her discipline in order to gain some theoretical purchase on important work done in critical pedagogy. Another example can be found in Biddy Martin (1997).
14. This section draws heavily from Henry A. Giroux (2000).

15. A particularly telling and theoretically sloppy example of this position can also be found in Maria Koundoura (1998, pp. 69–87). Most of these critics appear to have little or no knowledge of the long history of debates within educational circles in the United States over issues of reproduction, resistance, and the politics of schooling. Koundoura is especially uninformed on this issue, citing one article to defend her attack on "border pedagogy." An interesting critique of the limits of governmentality can be found in Toby Miller (1998), and in Alan O' Shea (1998).
16. Originally published in the *Harvard Educational Review* 59 (1989), pp. 297–324.
17. In her most recent book, *Teaching Positions,* Ellsworth has modified her position on authority by embracing what she calls "a pedagogy of manipulation," further defined or defended as a "a paradox that doesn't make sense." Indeed! Elizabeth Ellsworth (1997, p. 150). What is often surprising about the way in which her work is addressed both by critics and supporters is their refusal to examine her representations of the texts she often attacks. I would argue that many of her representations border on pure caricature, a position that Nicholas Burbules reiterates in talking about her treatment of his work. See Nicholas C. Burbules (2000, p. 266).
18. The initial part of the long quote is worth repeating so as not to lose the point. Horner writes: "This account is troubling because the 'failure' of [her] course seems simultaneously inevitable and therefore indisputable and yet beside the point because that failure arises from her treatment of critical pedagogy as a commodity. Having reduced critical pedagogy to a commodity isolated from the material circumstances of its specific enactments, she then critiques it for its failure, as a commodity, to address just such circumstances."
19. Another challenge to the governmentality model can be found in the brilliant article on pedagogy and cultural studies by Richard Johnson (1997).
20. For a brilliant discussion of the ethics and politics of deconstruction, see Thomas Keenan (1997, p. 2)

KNOWLEDGE, DIALOGUE, AND HUMANIZATION: EXPLORING FREIRE'S PHILOSOPHY

This chapter explores elements of Paulo Freire's ontology, epistemology, and ethic, with a view to elucidating some of the distinctive features of his philosophy. In developing his philosophical and pedagogical ideas, Freire drew on a wide range of intellectual traditions, including liberalism, Marxism, existentialism, radical Catholicism, phenomenology, and aspects of postmodern and poststructuralist thought (Elias, 1994; Mackie, 1980; Mayo, 1997, 1999; Peters, 1999). While the programs he developed in working with illiterate adults in Brazil and Chile in the 1960s constitute perhaps the most memorable aspect of his work, Freire's practical activities need to be understood in the light of his views on the nature of reality, his conception of what it means to be human, his theory of knowledge, and his ideas on oppression and liberation. These dimensions of Freire's work lie at the heart of this chapter.

Freire on the Nature of Reality

In his written work Freire adopts a dialectical approach toward understanding the world. This statement has a dual meaning. In one sense, Freire conceives of reality as dialectical; in another sense, he is (or strives to be) dialectical in his style of social analysis. In other words, Freire attempts to think dialectically about a reality that is dialectical. Drawing on ideas from Hegel and Marx, among others, Freire posits a dynamic relation between consciousness and the world (Freire, 1998b, p. 19; Torres, 1994). He explicitly rejects two positions that ignore the dialectical nature of this relationship: mechanistic objectivism and solipsistic idealism. The former reduces consciousness to a mere "copy" of objective reality; the latter sees consciousness as the creator of (all) reality (Freire, 1972b, p. 53). Objectivist views negate human agency since all human actions become merely a product of material or environmental influences. Mechanistic behaviorism, for example, sees human practice as analogous to the operation of a machine. Human beings exist as material bodies (with sense organs) who respond to stimuli. For the mechanistic behaviorist, no human event could be other than it is. A human being could not act other than he or she does in any particular situation, given the combination of stimuli—past and present—to which he or she has been subject. For the extreme idealist, on the other hand, there is no world at all: material reality is simply an illusion, a construction of consciousness. Both stances deny the possibility of reality being transformed through conscious human activity.

According to Freire, all aspects of objective reality are in motion. Objective reality encompasses both the world of nature and socially created material objects, institutions, practices, and phenomena. The world, for Freire, is necessarily unfinished and ever-evolving: "the more I approach critically the object of my observation, the more I am able to perceive that the object of my observation *is not yet because it is becoming*" (Freire & Shor, 1987, p. 82). As reality changes, ideas, conceptions, attitudes, values, beliefs, etc.—in short, all the products of consciousness—shift also. This is not a sequential, lockstep, "cause and effect" relationship, but a complex process of constant, multilayered interaction between human beings and the world. From Freire's point of view, neither "consciousness" nor "world," is comprehensible without the other. Consciousnesses are constituted by the world, but without someone to say "this is a world" there *is* no world (cf. Freire, 1997a, p. 32).

Freire, like Marx (1976) and Mao (1968), places particular emphasis on contradictions in the social world. The most important of these in Freire's ethical and political theory is the contradiction between oppressors and the oppressed. Oppressors can only exist *as* oppressors in the presence of their opposite, the oppressed. The two groups stand in an inherently contradictory relationship, irrespective of how either group perceives itself. The possibility of oppression being negated through an act of (liberating) revolution is always latent if not made manifest.

Thinking dialectically involves seeking out contradictions in social reality; it implies a penetration beyond and beneath surface appearances. A dialectical approach demands that social phenomena and problems be understood not in abstract isolation but as part of a totality, and theorized in global terms. A true dialectician is always striving to relate one aspect of world to another, and is always seeking to more deeply explain the object of study by contrasting it with that which it *is not*. This is a form of "epistemological encircling": a means of moving closer by gaining a certain kind of distance (Freire, 1997a, p. 92). Thinking dialectically is, for Freire, equivalent to thinking critically: it means being constantly open to further questions, and to the possibility—indeed, probability—of current assumptions being revised, repudiated, or overturned. There are obvious similarities here with Giroux's (1981, p. 114) view of the dialectic as "a critical mode of reasoning and behavior, one that represents both a part as well as a critique of conflicts and solutions that define the nature of human existence." In an interview with Carlos Alberto Torres, whom Freire describes as "a man who thinks dialectically and doesn't merely talk of dialectics," Freire gives an example of this orientation toward engaging social problems:

> Today I live the enormous joy of perceiving with every passing day that the strength of education resides precisely in its limitations. The efficiency of education resides in the impossibility of doing everything. The limits of education would bring a naive man or woman to desperation. A dialectical man or woman discovers in the limits of education the raison d'être for his or her efficiency. It is in this way that I feel that today I am an efficient Secretary of Education because I am limited. (Torres & Freire, 1994, p. 106)

Freire's Epistemology

Freire's epistemology can be seen as an extension of his ideas on the dialectical nature of reality. We come to *know* through our interaction with an ever-changing world (Freire, 1976, p. 107). Knowing, for Freire, necessarily implies transformation: It is the task of human subjects encountering a world dynamically in the making. Knowledge arises not from abstract thinking or theorizing, but from human practice. The ordering of moments in the process of knowing is important in understanding Freire's philosophy. Freire is adamant that theory never precedes practice: "First of all I have to act. First of all I have to transform. Secondly I can theorize my actions—but not before" (Freire, 1971a, p. 2). Freire (1972a, p. 50) talks of thinking becoming authenticated only when it is "concerned with reality," "generated by action upon the world," and carried out through communication with others. Authentic thinking constitutes an act of knowing. Freire's position here is consistent with the fundamental tenets of dialectical materialism, one of which is that "the production of ideas, of conceptions, of consciousness is at first directly interwoven with the material activity and the material intercourse of men" (Marx & Engels, 1976, p. 42).

Given that all aspects of reality exist in a constant state of change, it follows that we can never know absolutely: we can, at best, come closer to knowing the "*raison d'être* which explains the object [of study]" (Freire & Shor, 1987, p. 82). Knowing involves searching for the reason for (or behind) the existence of an object or fact (Freire and Macedo, 1987, p. 78). Knowledge, in the Freirean view, is necessarily incomplete:

> [K]nowledge always is becoming. That is, if the act of knowing has historicity, then today's knowledge about something is not necessarily the same tomorrow. Knowledge is changed to the extent that reality also moves and changes. (Horton & Freire, 1990, p. 101)

Knowing for Freire is a permanent process of discovery—of searching, investigating, inquiring, and probing (cf. Davis, 1980, p. 66; Freire, 1985, pp. 1–4). To know is not to have reached a predetermined destination; rather, it is a manner of "traveling"—a way of being in, and interacting with, the world (through dialogue with others). It is precisely through recognizing that they know little that people strive to know more. Freire speaks of knowing as a *praxis,* implying both a reflective and an active component. Knowing demands a curious, attentive, restless attitude toward, and interaction with, social reality. This cannot be reduced to rational processes alone. In Freire's words: "I know with my entire body, with feelings, with passion, and also with reason" (1997a, p. 30). From Freire's point of view, there can be no "final" act of knowing. Knowledge has historocity: It is always in the process of being. If absolute knowledge could be attained, the possibility of knowing would disappear for there would no longer be any questions to ask or theoretical problems to address. All statements about "knowledge" and its opposite, "ignorance," must be qualified: these terms only make sense when defined in relation to something specific. In the Freirean view, neither knowledge nor ignorance is complete: "No one can know everything, just as no one can be ignorant of everything" (Freire, 1976, p. 117). This insight provides the ground, by implication, for a redefinition of conventional constructs of "the intellectual." As Giroux points out, Freire regards all men and women as intellectuals in the sense that every person constantly interprets and gives meaning to the world (Giroux, 1985, p. xxiii; cf. Gramsci, 1971, pp. 5–23; Lankshear, 1988).

The distinctiveness of Freire's view can be elucidated through a comparison with the Platonic conception of knowledge. Plato (1974) distinguishes true knowledge from mere opinion. Opinion pertains to the visible (physical, practical, material) world; knowledge is confined to the supersensible, intelligible realm (§507. Editors' Note: *The Republic* is written in sections numbered using the symbol §). At its lowest level, opinion takes the form of "illusion," by which Plato means simple impressions of the world, or perceptions of objects as they appear in their material form. Given their focus on images and outward appearances, such impressions provide an inherently distorted view of reality (§§509d, 510a). A higher level of opinion is "belief," which is manifest in "commonsense" ideas about "matters both moral and physical, which are a fair practical guide to life but [which] have not been fully thought out" (translator's note, p. 311). Neither illusion nor belief can provide genuine understanding of the nature of reality, since both remain tied to that which can be perceived by the senses. The sensible world deals with particulars, is always changing, and as such is never truly knowable. The world of ideas or forms, by contrast, is unchanging: It is the realm of universals from which the particulars we observe derive. Mathematical (deductive) reason participates in this higher intelligible realm. The pinnacle of pure intelligence, however, is dialectical reason, which Plato describes as follows:

> [I]t treats assumptions not as principles, but as assumptions in the true sense, that is, as starting points and steps in the ascent to something which involves no assumption

and is the first principle of everything; when it has grasped that principle it can again descend, by keeping to the consequences that follow from it, to a conclusion. The whole procedure involves nothing in the sensible world, but moves solely through forms to forms, and finishes with forms. (§511b)

The highest level of knowledge, Plato argues, is knowledge of the form of the good (§505a). The good is "the end of all endeavor, the object on which every heart is set" (§505d). The form of the good "gives the objects of knowledge their truth and the knower's mind the power of knowing" (§508e). Attaining knowledge, for Plato, is a matter of "remembering" or "recovering" that which existed in the soul before its incarnation in a body. Knowledge has a divine origin; the capacity for pursuing it—that is, recalling what is already there—is "innate in each man's mind" (§518d), though few progress beyond mere opinion to the higher forms of intelligence.

Freire's position is precisely the opposite. "True" or "authentic" knowledge arises not in some realm beyond the sphere of objective reality; to the contrary, knowing is thoroughly grounded in the material world. The origins of knowledge lie not in some form of celestial divination but in the day-to-day transforming moments of human activity. As Freire sees it, knowledge is not recollected through philosophical thought but created through reflective action in a social world. Freire, like Plato, wants to go beyond a mere apprehension of appearances, but speaks of searching beneath the surface of the object of study as an intensely practical endeavor. The path to knowledge is not to be found in some form of abstract, inner, individual activity, but in active, communicative relationships with others. Knowing through dialogue does not transcend, but rather is mediated by, the (material) world. For Freire, there is no world of "forms" to be known. Dialectical thinking is elevated above other modes of understanding for Freire, as it is for Plato, but the modes of knowing implied by each theorist's conception of the dialectic are quite distinct. From Plato's perspective, dialectical reason is distinguished by its complete separation from worldly particulars; for Freire, dialectical thinking is defined by its focus on interrelationships between concrete particulars within a social totality. Goodness and knowledge are closely connected for Freire, as they are for Plato. But where Plato speaks of the good as the supreme form from which all particular acts of goodness in the world derive, these acts (i.e., those that are praxical), from Freire's point of view, are the supreme good and it is through them that knowing occurs.

Freire is not an epistemological relativist. As McLaren and Silva (1993) point out, he does not believe all ideas are of equal merit. In the Freirean view, some ways of thinking, some theories, some appraisals of the nature of reality are better than others. As we shall see shortly, this line of argument applies to Freire's ethic as well: certain ways of living one's life, of acting toward others, of being in the world, are, according to Freire, superior—that is, morally preferable—to others. On the other hand, Freire's theory of knowledge is not absolutist in the Platonic sense: There are no static, unchanging truths that transcend time and space. Instead, Freire argues that ideas "must be understood contextually as historically and culturally informed discourses that are subject to the mediation of the forces of material and symbolic production" (McLaren and Silva, 1993, p. 55). In Freire's view, knowledge is constructed rather than derived or bequeathed: It is forged within particular social relations, is reflective of (and partially constitutive of) given ideological and political formations, and is always grounded—whether directly or indirectly—in human practice. Certain constructions of reality, though, are better than others: A dialogical and critical reading of the world, for Freire, affords a deeper understanding of the object under investigation than antidialogical or passive stances allow (Roberts, 1996a).

As humans, we have the capacity to reflect on the very process of knowing itself, on (our) consciousness and its relationship with the world. We can not only know, but know that we know (Davis, 1980, pp. 58–59). For Freire, the essence of human consciousness is intentionality toward the world. Humans can "stand back" from the immediate reality of their material existence and reflect on it. Freire speaks of this as a crucial moment in human evolution: what Teilhard de Chardin (1959) calls "homonization"—the shift from instinct to thought. Humans have the ability to problematize not only the object of attention but the process through which this problematization takes place. This, then, is a form of "meta-awareness"—an awareness of our conscious efforts to understand ourselves, others, and the world.

Humanization: Freire's Ethical Ideal

Just as Freire sees knowledge as necessarily incomplete—as always evolving—so he sees human beings as always in a state of "becoming." The human ideal Freire espouses is one of humanization, or "becoming more fully human." One can never, on the Freirean view, become fully human—one can, at best, become *more* fully human. Freire sees this calling to "be more" as an expression of human nature making itself in history (1994, pp. 98–99; 1997a, p. 32; 1998b, p. 18). Humans are necessarily imperfect, unfinished, incomplete beings, who exist in and with an ever-changing world (Freire, 1972a, p. 57). To be human, from Freire's point of view, is to be engaged in a permanent process of searching (Freire, 1999, p. 21). Humanization, which Freire sees as both an ontological and an historical vocation of human beings, is opposed by dehumanization, which, although a historical reality, is not an ontological inevitability. Humans pursue their vocation of becoming more fully human when they engage in authentic praxis, through dialogue with others, in a critically conscious way.

The Freirean concept of an ontological vocation can be explained through reference to the ancient Greek notion of human beings having a "function" (cf. Lankshear, 1993, pp. 108–109). Plato (1974) suggests that the "function" of a thing is "that which only it can do or that which it does best . . . everything which has a function [has] its own particular excellence" (§§353a–353b). For every distinctive excellence there is a corresponding defect. Hence, if the function of the eyes is to see, the eyes perform this function well when X has perfect vision but perform their function poorly if X suffers from blindness (§353b). Plato's intent in this line of inquiry is to establish grounds for arguing that a just society is one in which each person performs his or her proper role in accordance with his or her particular function. Different individuals in Plato's ideal society have different functions: philosophers have one function, military experts another, shoemakers yet another, and so on. Aristotle (1976), however, wants to know whether there is a function all human beings have simply through being human: "Just as we can see that eye and hand and foot and every one of our members has some function, should we not assume that in like manner a human being has a function over and above these particular functions?" (§1097b). Aristotle's concern is to discover that which is uniquely human. It cannot be the "life" generated by nutrition and manifested in growth, for plants share this with us; nor is it our "sentient" life, for animals possess this quality too. It must, Aristotle concludes, be our capacity for practical reason which sets us apart from all other beings or things. The function of humankind, thus, is "an activity of the soul in accordance with, or implying, a rational principle" (§1098). Whether one reasons well or poorly, the function remains generically the same: All human beings are distinguished (from other beings) by their reason. A function is "performed well when performed in accordance with its proper excellence" (§1098). For Aristotle, happiness—the "best, the finest, the most pleasurable thing of all" (§1099)—is the ultimate end to which human actions are directed (§1097). A good, truly happy, ideal human life is one lived (properly and well) in accordance with the highest human virtue, namely, reason.

Freire's notion of an ontological vocation can be understood in a similar light. According to Freire, what makes us distinctly human is our ability to engage in praxis. Praxis is "reflection and action upon the world in order to transform it" (Freire, 1972a, p. 28). Only human beings can engage in praxis. While animals alter aspects of the material world in the process of adapting to it, their modification of objective reality is purely instinctive. Human beings, however, have the ability to consciously and intentionally transform the world. Humans are the only beings to treat not merely their actions but themselves as the object of reflection (p. 70). Animals are submerged in reality: they cannot stand back from the world and consider themselves in relation to it. Humans, by contrast, have the capacity to reflect on the world and to transform it in accordance with this reflection. Only human beings *work* in the sense of engaging in *purposeful* activity: consciously directed action on and interaction with the world (Freire, 1974, p. 141). Animals, for the most part, merely react to stimuli from the environment; humans, by contrast, perceive and respond to challenges in the world. These ideas resonate strongly with Marx's often cited example of the differences between the activities, respectively, of architects and bees:

> [A] bee would put many a human architect to shame by the construction of its honeycomb cells. But what distinguishes the worst architect from the best of bees is that the architect builds the cell in his mind before he constructs it in wax (Marx, 1976, p. 284).

Animals are creatures of contacts; they simply adapt to the world. Humans, on the other hand, can become both adapted to the world and integrated with it. Animals are merely *in* the world. Humans are both *in* the world and *with* the world. Animals have no conception of time; they live in a permanent "today." They cannot "confront life," give meaning to it, or become committed to it (Freire, 1969, p. 3). Humans, though, are historical beings, aware of a past and able to conceive of a future. As responsible beings, humans have an awareness of their own unfinishedness (Freire, 1999, p. 56). Humans, unlike animals, *make* history (and in so doing confirm their temporality) in consciously transforming the world around them (Freire, 1972a, pp. 70–73; 1976, pp. 3–5).

For human activity to be praxical there must be a synthesis of reflection and action. Action that is not accompanied by reflection amounts to nothing more than activism; reflection without concomitant action is mere verbalism (Freire, 1972a, p. 60). Action that is praxical "envelopes the whole being of the actors—their emotions, their feelings, their 'language-thought-reflection'" (Freire, 1970a, p. 1). This does not mean that reflection ought to always be followed by action: sometimes, Freire notes, action is not "feasible." Critical reflection is also a form of action (Makins, 1972). The "feasibility" of action—including educational intervention—in any given situation can only be determined by reflection through communication with others (Roberts, 1996b).

To live well, in the Freirean view, is to transform the world through reflective, critical, dialogical action. The vocation of all human beings is to realize this capacity—to live as "social, historical, thinking, communicating, transformative, creative persons" (Freire, 1999, p. 45)—in the fullest way possible. The pursuit of humanization is a quest to become more profoundly what we already are as humans: that is, beings *of* praxis (Freire, 1970b, p. 16). Not all forms of praxis, though, are humanizing. Freire distinguishes, for instance, between "revolutionary praxis" and "the praxis of the dominant elites," the former being humanizing and the latter dehumanizing (1972a, p. 97). The crucial element fundamental to the first form of praxis but absent in the second is *dialogue*.

Dialogue and Social Transformation

The pursuit of humanization can never, in Freire's view, be an isolated, individualistic activity (Freire & Shor, 1987, p. 109; Horton & Freire, 1990, p. 111). Humans, as communicative beings, enter into relationships with one another, and create a *social* world. "Our being," Freire says in *Pedagogy of Freedom* (1999, p. 58) "is a *being with.*" In participating in this process, humans simultaneously re-create themselves (cf. Marx, 1970, p. 21; Marx & Engels, 1976, p. 42; Freire, 1972b, pp. 29–30, 51–57). Just as it makes no sense (in Freirean terms) to talk of pursuing one's humanization in isolation from others, so too is it nonsensical to think of having (sole) responsibility for one's dehumanization. We humanize ourselves through dialogue with others. This goes to the heart of what it means to be human for Freire.

Where Descartes (1931, p. 101) theorized self-identity in his famous dictum "I think, therefore I am," for Freire an "I think" is comprehensible only in the presence of a co-existing "We think" (Roberts, 1996c). Freire does not deny that individual human beings are unique—that they understand and respond to the world and to others in distinct ways—but argues that it is only through intersubjectivity that individual existence makes sense. The existence of an "I" is only possible because of the concomitant existence of a "not-I," where "not-I" implies both others and world. For Freire, the "we exist" explains the "I exist": "I cannot be," he observes, "if you are not" (Fonseca, 1973, p. 96). The "I exist" does not precede the "we exist" but is fulfilled by it (Freire, 1985, p. 129). Knowing, on the Freirean view, cannot be a purely individual process but is only possible through dialogue—through a relationship with others, whether this is direct (face-to-face) or indirect (e.g., via texts), mediated by the objective world (cf. Buber, 1958, 1961).

In Freire's moral philosophy, praxis and dialogue are closely related: Genuine dialogue represents a form of humanizing praxis. Dialogue is "the encounter between men, mediated by the world, in order to name the world" (Freire, 1972a, p. 61). "Naming the world" is the process of change itself; the human quest to understand and transform the world, through communication with others. This naming is a continuous process of creating and recreating: The world, once named, always presents itself afresh as a problem demanding a new naming. Freire claims that humans have a *primordial right* to "speak their word." It is in speaking a "true word" that human beings name the world and thereby transform it. A "true" word is an authentic, dialogical synthesis of reflection and action. Ultimately, "no one can say a true word alone" (p. 61). To "speak a true word" is to enter the historical process as a Subject, changing (objective and subjective) reality through consciously directed action, informed by critical discussion with others.

If it is to be humanizing, dialogical communication must involve a "love" of the world and of other human beings. This in turn demands a certain sense of humility. Faith in the ability of others to "name the world," together with trust between participants, and a hope that dehumanization can be overcome, are necessary. Finally, Freire stipulates that critical thinking is vital if dialogue is to become a humanizing praxis (1972a, pp. 62–65). When these conditions are satisfied, and where two or more people communicate with one another in seeking to understand a common object of study, there is, Freire argues, a true dialogue and an authentic, humanizing praxis.

The Politics of Liberation

While humanization through critical, dialogical praxis represents the ethical *ideal* as far as Freire is concerned, the pursuit of humanization by some groups and individuals is frequently impeded by the actions of others. Where this occurs the situation becomes one of oppression. To prevent someone from engaging in praxis—either through limiting the range of possible actions open to that person, or through inhibiting his or her ability to think critically—is to dehumanize that person. Hence oppression, as Freire sees it, is dehumanizing. This is what makes us *ethical* beings: Our capacity "to intervene, to compare, to judge, to decide, to choose, to desist makes . . . [us] capable of acts of greatness, of dignity, and, at the same time, of the unthinkable in terms of indignity" (Freire, 1999, p. 53). Fighting against discrimination is an ethical imperative (Freire, 1997a, p. 87). In dehumanizing another, one also—albeit in a different way, and with different implications and consequences—dehumanizes oneself (Freire, 1972a, p. 24; 1996, p. 180). To deny someone else's humanization is also to deny one's own, since for Freire, humanization is a *dialogical* process. Those who dehumanize others practice a profound form of anti-dialogue, and thus cannot be engaged in the task of becoming more fully human.

Humanization and dehumanization are both concrete possibilities for human beings, but only humanization is an ontological and a historical vocation. The vocation of becoming more fully human is what defines us as human beings; it is the *essence* of being human. Humanization is a historical, as well as an ontological, vocation because it calls us to act (on the basis of critical reflection) in the objective world of lived social relations. Dehumanization represents a distortion of this vocation. Freire stresses that dehumanization arises from specific (oppressive) *social* practices: It does not, therefore, constitute a given destiny. If human beings have *created* social structures, living conditions, and modes of thinking and acting that are oppressive, it follows that humans can also change these circumstances.

The task of those who are oppressed is *liberation*. For Freire, liberation is not a psychological process, something that occurs (purely) as a shift in consciousness or as some form of inner transformation (Brandes, 1971, pp. 6–7). Rather, liberation takes place in the transformative action of human beings on the world, under specific historical and social circumstances. Freire is thoroughly Marxist in his stance here. As Marx and Engels state in *The German Ideology*,

> [I]t is possible to achieve real liberation only in the real world and by real means . . . people cannot be liberated as long as they are unable to obtain food and drink, housing and clothing in adequate quality and quantity. "Liberation" is a historical and not a mental act. (Marx & Engels, 1845/1976, p. 44)

For Freire, liberation is a form of critical, dialogical praxis directed toward overcoming oppression. In earlier works he makes the claim that the oppressed cannot be liberated by their oppressors, but must liberate both themselves and those who oppress them. Paradoxically, only the "weakness" of the oppressed is strong enough to liberate the oppressor (Freire, 1975, p. 17; 1972c, p. 2). Freire believes that faced with a situation in which their pursuit of humanization is impeded, sooner or later the oppressed will begin to resist (Freire, 1972a, p. 21). Conflict between dialectically opposed groups is always possible, even if temporary "settlements" and periods of apparent calm may be reached at certain moments in history. Indeed, conflict can be seen as a fundamental part of social life (Freire, 1998a,

p. 45). Freire argues, however, that the oppressed have often been so dominated by their oppressors that they take on the oppressors' view of the world—they see oppression as inevitable. Freire acknowledges that the direct experience of discrimination or exploitation can provide a distinctive understanding of oppression, but he also stresses that submersion in an oppressive reality can impair one's perception of oneself and one's relation to others (1972a, p. 22).

Where a distorted perception of reality prevails, there is a danger that the oppressed, in fighting against their oppression, will themselves become oppressors. The model of humanity presented to the oppressed by the oppressors portrays a vision of the oppressor individual as the ideal. Under these circumstances, "to be" (human) is to be like the oppressor (Freire, 1975, p. 16). The psyche of the oppressed person becomes haunted by the "invasive shadow" of the oppressor (Freire, 1999, p. 78). Yet the oppressed are never entirely engulfed by, or reduced to, the reality of the oppressor. There is an "almost tenuous trace of themselves that makes their creation, their language, and their culture something more than just a copy, makes it a kind of muffled cry of resistance, of the rebel in them" (Freire, 1996, p. 118).

The problem of confronting the ideology of the oppressors is compounded by what Freire, drawing on the work of Fromm (1984), calls the "fear of freedom." The oppressed "are afraid to embrace freedom . . . [whereas] the oppressors are afraid of losing the 'freedom' to oppress" (Freire, 1972a, p. 23). Freire regards freedom as an "indispensable condition for the quest for human completion": Liberation *requires* freedom if it is to be authentic (p. 24). Freedom implies autonomy and responsibility, and must be won by the oppressed: it cannot be given to them. Freedom, as Freire understands it, is not unfettered liberty: it takes place within the bounds of human action, intervention, and struggle and is always subject to certain constraints (cf. Freire, 1999, p. 96). Freire speaks of revolutionary action by the oppressed against the conditions that oppress them—and this may include violent struggle—as an act of "love." The violence of the oppressed, though, is "not really violence at all, but a legitimate reaction [to an oppressive situation]" (Freire, 1972c, p. 3). Hunger, racism, sexism, and economic domination within and between countries represent forms of *hidden* or disguised violence (Freire, 1996, p. 185). Sometimes conditions are so intolerably dehumanizing for the oppressed that the violence of revolutionary struggle is justified where it is the only means for overcoming the greater violence of oppression (cf. Fanon, 1967). In later works, however, Freire makes it clear that there are limits to this:

> My point of view is that of the "wretched of the earth," of the excluded. I do not accept, however, under any circumstances, acts of terrorism in support of this point of view. Such acts result in the death of the innocent and the spread of insecurity that affects everyone. Terrorism is the negation of what I call a universal human ethic. I am on the side of the Arabs in their struggle for their rights, but I cannot accept the acts of terrorism perpetuated in Munich and elsewhere in favor of those rights. (1999, p. 22)

Freire warns that the oppressed, having internalized the view of the oppressors, may have little consciousness of themselves as a class. This works against the possibility of effective revolutionary action and serves as a prop for continuing oppression. Freire is socialist to the core in the stress he places on unity, solidarity, and a shared sense of commitment among the oppressed to a better social world. Unity among diverse oppressed groups is essential if their struggles are to be effective; without it, domination via "divide and rule" policies can prevail (Freire, 1996, pp. 180–181; 1997a, p. 86). Solidarity, for Freire, is a reflection of our need, as humans, to be *with* others (Freire, 1999, p. 72). Echoing the immortal (but now, in postmodern times, somewhat unfashionable) call by Marx and Engels at the end of the *Manifesto of the Communist Party* for working people of all countries to unite (Marx & Engels, 1848/1967, p. 121), Freire argues: "[t]he universal solidarity of the working class is far from being achieved, but it is essential and we must struggle for it" (Freire & Faundez, 1989, p. 59). Unity is, he insists, all the more important in our current "perverse era of neoliberal philosophy" (Freire, 1999, p. 115). While highly critical of the authoritarianism in some socialist regimes, Freire is adamant that capitalism is an inherently unjust mode of production. For him, the work of those committed to liberation lies in bringing the ideals of socialism and democracy together (see Freire, 1996, p. 188).

Liberation, Freire (1972a, p. 25) concludes, is "a childbirth, and a painful one." The struggle for liberation must be ongoing—a permanent process of reflection and action—as social reality changes and new forms of oppression unfold. While liberation cannot be reduced to merely a process of class transformation, thus denying the individual altogether (Freire, 1996, pp. 159–160), neither can its essentially social character be denied:

> I don't believe in self-liberation. Liberation is a social act. . . . Even when you individually feel yourself *most* free, if this feeling is not a *social* feeling, if you are not able to use your *recent* freedom to help others to be free by transforming the totality of society, then you are exercising only an individualist attitude towards empowerment or freedom. (Freire & Shor, 1987, p. 109)

In any given historical epoch in a given society there will be a complex array of (often-conflicting) ideas, values, hopes, and challenges that, in their concrete representations, constitute the *themes* of that epoch (Freire, 1976, p. 5). Critical examination of these themes reveals a set of *tasks* to be carried out. Freire terms impediments to critical thought and transforming action "limit-situations." The tasks implied by limit-situations require "limit-acts" (Freire, 1972a, p. 73). Freire speaks, for example, of the economic dependence of Third World countries on the First World as a limit-situation: Those countries subject to this relationship become "beings for others." In order to become "beings for themselves" (cf. Sartre, 1969), such societies require limit-acts directed toward revolutionary independence and political sovereignty (cf. Freire, 1970c; 1971b, p. 115).

Freire (1993, p. 84) maintains that liberation is "the most fundamental task . . . we have at the end of this century." Overcoming domination or oppression (Freire uses these terms synonymously) entails negating those aspects of an oppressive reality that limit the oppressed. Hence, within a single society where the dominant theme is oppression, there will be a whole range of limit-situations that characterize that oppression. In the Third World countries in which Freire worked, these might have ranged from the poor living conditions endured by peasants, to the payment of low wages to workers, to the broader limit-situation of national economic dependency. While the ultimate task of the oppressed in such situations is liberation, the pursuit of this task calls for the negation of each of the limit-situations that (together) form an oppressive reality. Freire notes: "[E]pochs are fulfilled to the degree that their themes are grasped and their tasks solved; and they are superseded when their themes and tasks no longer correspond to newly emerging concerns" (1976, p. 5).

In times of transition, as in Brazil during the 1950s and 1960s, "[c]ontradictions increase between the ways of being, understanding, behaving, and valuing which belong to yesterday and other ways of perceiving and valuing which announce the future" (Freire, 1976, p. 7). In the Brazilian case, the movement was from a "closed" society to one in the process of opening. With this shift, themes such as democracy, popular participation, freedom, property, authority, and education were invested with new meaning. The transition from one epoch to another is a dynamic mix of "flux and reflux, advances and retreats," filled with confusion and uncertainty, but also the hope and anticipation of impending change (p. 9).

Moral Principles in Freire's Philosophy

Freire's moral philosophy cannot be understood apart from his metaphysic, ontology, and epistemology. Ultimately, the significance of a Freirean ethical position can only be appreciated via an examination of the educational and literacy programs with which Freire has had major involvement (see Brown, 1974; Freire, 1972b, 1976, 1978, 1993; Freire & Macedo, 1987; Lloyd, 1972; Sanders, 1972; Taylor, 1993). These practical initiatives provide both an exemplification of key principles in Freire's moral philosophy and the source for many of his educational ideas (cf. Aronowitz, 1993; Freire, 1972a, 1997b; Freire & Macedo, 1995; Shor, 1980, 1993). Given space constraints, however, it is not possible to examine either Freire's educational theory or his approach to adult literacy education here. I have addressed these dimensions of his work, and the arguments of some of his strongest critics (e.g., Berger, 1974; Bowers, 1983; Walker, 1980), at length elsewhere (e.g., Roberts, 1994, 1996a, 1996b, 1996c, 1996d, 1998, 2000).

In extracting key moral principles from Freire's philosophy, three points from the preceding discussion bear repeating:

(i) All aspects of reality are constantly changing. This idea, which reflects Freire's dialectical approach toward understanding the world, permeates every dimension of his philosophy. From its starting point in his metaphysic (where Freire speaks of change within and between the objective and subjective dimensions of reality), to his epistemology (where it is assumed that knowledge is never fixed nor absolute), to his ontology and ethic (where he argues that human beings are necessarily incomplete and always in a process of becoming), the principle remains the same: Our world—in its myriad material, social, and personal spheres—is a world of change, of interaction, of incompleteness.

(ii) Freire assumes a certain essence to the human condition. Humans, unlike animals, are conscious, temporal, historical beings. Most important, for Freire, all human beings, simply through being human, have an ontological vocation of humanization. In this sense, while he acknowledges the educational significance of differences across class, race, and gender lines, there is nevertheless an implicit assertion in his work that there is something about being human that transcends these differences (cf. Freire, 1999; Freire & Macedo, 1993; Weiler, 1991).

(iii) Humans interact with objective reality (altering it and modifying themselves in turn) and enter into relationships with others. We live in a *social* world, and any attempt to consider how the world ought to be must take this observation into account. It makes little sense to talk of Freirean ethics purely in terms of certain ideal qualities in, or modes of conduct for, the *individual:* Liberation is a dialogical, collective process of struggle.

What, then, can we say about Freire's moral philosophy? In keeping with point (iii) above, two related facets of his ethical position must be addressed:

(a) At one level, Freire upholds the notion of human beings becoming critical, praxical Subjects, in control—as far as this is possible—of their own destinies as creators of history and culture (and thus of themselves).

(b) At another level, Freire's theory points toward a vision of a social world characterized by relations of liberation rather than oppression—that is, a world where all people have the opportunity to engage in humanizing praxis, through dialogue with others.

Given this dual focus (at least) four key principles in Freire's moral philosophy can be identified:

(i) People ought to pursue their ontological vocation of becoming more fully human (through engaging in critical, dialogical praxis).

(ii) No person or group of people ought to knowingly constrain or prevent another person or group of people from pursuing the ontological vocation; that is, no person ought to oppress another.

(iii) We ought (collectively and dialogically) to consider what kind of world—what social structures, processes, relationships, etc.—would be necessary to enable (all) people in a given social setting to pursue their humanization.

(iv) All people ought to act to transform existing structures where critical reflection reveals that these structures serve as an impediment to the pursuit of humanization (by any groups within a society). This is the task of liberation.

For those concerned with issues of pedagogy (broadly conceived), a further principle can be added:

(v) Educators and others who assume positions of responsibility in the social sphere ought to side with the oppressed in seeking to promote a better (more fully human) world through their activities.

These moral principles are necessarily intertwined in Freirean philosophy, for the pursuit of the ontological vocation by one person inevitably depends on the affording of an opportunity for this pursuit by others (and by the structures, institutions, attitudes, practices, etc., of the world in which one lives). In all cases, the processes involved in pursuing or adhering to Freirean moral principles are continuous and necessarily incomplete: We can, it will be recalled from earlier discussion, only ever become *more* fully human, never *fully* human; similarly, the task of creating a better social world must be renewed each time that world takes on a new face (with a new set of themes and tasks to be confronted).

Summary

The moral philosophy of Paulo Freire is built on a dialectical conception of reality and an epistemology in which theory and practice are dynamically related. The ontological and historical vocation of all human beings is humanization, or becoming more fully human. We pursue this ideal when we engage in critical, dialogical praxis. Constraints imposed by one group to the quest for humanization by another group indicate a situation of oppression. An oppressive reality is dehumanizing for both the oppressed and the oppressors. Oppressive social conditions are negated by a praxis of liberation. Given an ever-changing world, humanization is a continuous, unfinished process, with new problems to be addressed as each epoch unfolds.

CRITICAL RACE THEORY IN EDUCATION: POSSIBILITIES AND PROBLEMS

Narrative story personal reflection #1 (late September 2000):

I kept watching the Olympics, thinking that the U.S. television stations would devote more extensive coverage of the Aborigines' plight and press for an apology from the Australian government over the overt racial warfare inflicted on them. But aside from the glory stories of Cathy Freeman, nothing.

Narrative #2, told to me by my advisee, a Latino graduate student (Fall 1999):

I started teaching at the middle school this September, and one of the major issues that came up at the sessions was how inclusive I was going to be on multicultural education, race, and student empowerment issues. But all that came to a head in one class, early on when a student in my Spanish class challenged me and said, "Hey, you better not fail me or I'll call immigration and get your ass deported back to Mexico." At that point I said to him, "Here is a critical race theory teachable moment for me and you!" I proceeded to sit him down and explicitly tell him that I was a Latino and born and raised in the United States and that his prejudice is what is going to get him sent to the principal's office. To me, it is attitudes like this kid's that are the root causes of problems today with the United States and other countries in terms of U.S. white ethnocentrism and domination over others through globalized racial and capitalist colonialism.

Narrative #3. Session at a Philadelphia high school (March 28, 1995):

I was having a discussion at a session on race and school achievement with some of the teachers. We had just seen part of a documentary film on racial desegregation at a high school. Most teachers commented on the ways in which the teachers (in the video) conducted class; racial separation caused by tracking; and how to deal with African-American students who spurned the achievement ideology. For instance, one African-American teacher with twenty-two years of experience said, "My goal is to find ways to help motivate the African-American students to succeed at school." Another African-American teacher said she wanted to "give her students the tools to succeed." But these statements were countered by the comments of the college access counselor at this high school, who said that he wanted to help students "not to fit into the system but to take their anger and power to challenge the system."

The purpose of these opening narratives is to illustrate the importance of critical race theory in education with respect to naming racism and its connection to the larger social context and ideological forces of domination, and to show how critical race theory, linked to educational praxis, can be potentially useful for the empowerment of communities of color. Critical race theory has garnered increasing attention from various academic circles and disciplines as an emerging perspective in jurisprudence scholarship addressing race (Crenshaw, Gotanda, Peller, & Thomas, 1995; Delgado, 1995; Delgado & Stefancic, 2000; Symposium, 1994). Critical race theory does not adhere to a strict definition or interpretation. For example, it can be argued that the theory's roots are located in the plethora of postmodern critiques of the law as the source of objective truth and legal doctrine on race (Hayman, 1995). Another position is that critical race theory is marginally related to postmodernism and is much more grounded in a specific race-based criticism of the law and legal scholarship (Astin, 1989; 1992). However, critical race theorists share some common undergirding points that challenge the legal pragmatist and constitutional traditionalist interpretations of race and the law.

One shared point of critique is that racism should not be viewed as acts of individual prejudice that can simply be eradicated. Rather, it is an endemic part of everyday life, deeply ingrained through historical conscious and ideological choices about race, which in turn have directly shaped the U.S. legal system and the ways people think about the law, racial categories, and privilege (Harris, 1993; Lopez, 1996). Another common position argued by critical race theorists is a reinterpretation of U.S. civil rights law regarding its ineffectiveness in addressing racial injustices, particularly institutional racism and structural socioeconomic racism in the political economy (Guinier, 1991; 1994). In addition, critical race theory seeks to decloak the objective nature of the law and legal doctrine. Concepts such as color-blind interpretations of the law or meritocracy are "unmasked" by critical race theorists to be precursors for white European American hegemonic control of the social and structural arrangements in U.S. society. Responding to this conservative view of the law and race, the critical race theorists have developed a body of legal scholarship and alternative and intersecting paradigms based on the perspectives of "outsider groups" that experience racism and sexism. This scholarship evolved not only through alternative interpretations of traditional legal doctrine (Harris, 1994), but also through the legitimating of narrative, "story-telling," and legal testimony, which present a different interpretation of how the law has been used to justify an ideology of racism against persons of color (Delgado, 1989).

In this chapter, I wish to briefly explicate critical race theory and raise some questions for dialogue and conversation with respect to its future direction in education. What could be the specific areas of intersection and difference with feminist theory, postmodern theory, social class-based criticism, queer theory, and the like? Or is critical race theory just another form of identity politics with not much new to offer in terms of radically different methodologies in qualitative or quantitative inquiry? Can critical race theory push educational policy and research in the direction of acknowledging a "social justice validity" (Deyhle & Swisher, 1997) that values researcher-connected involvement with students, parents, and communities in an ongoing truly mutual participation in the research effort with the underlying goal of striving for positive change for the community of interest against discrimination (Tuhiwai Smith, 1999)? Or will the color-blind perspective of the law, which is also gaining increasing political popularity, muzzle the voices and actions of persons of color who bring these research frameworks into the academy (Stanfield, 1993)?

There is a need to raise these and other crucial questions for conversation and dialogue with others who share a concern about issues related to race, research, and education because the debate between critical race theorists and the color-blind advocates of the law is a reflection of what is taking place in the larger societal arena, as well as the academy. For example, just as more members of groups previously shut out of the academy (e.g., gays, lesbians, feminists, African-Americans, Latinos-Chicanos, Asian Americans, tribal nation indigenous populations) are making inroads in the student body and faculty positions, and more race-based research and social activist critiques are being leveled at the traditional canons of knowledge, the conservative reaction has been to call for the end of affirmative action, or question the merits of research that falls outside of the traditional academic boundaries (Kennedy, 1989; Parker & Lynn 2002). Furthermore, Scheurich and Young (1997, 1998) and Ladson-Billings (2000) have pointed out the inherent racial bias in educational research that unquestioningly accepts a white European American epistemological framework over more race-based paradigms. These trends, coupled with an increasingly hostile campus atmosphere for African-Americans (Feagin, Vera, & Imani, 1996) and other minority groups in predominantly white higher education institutions, are at the root of my concern about the larger controversy over race and other areas of difference in the academy.

Given these positions, this chapter will review critical race theory as it relates to qualitative inquiry in education. The first section of the chapter will provide readers with an overview of critical race theory, and counterpoints of view based on more traditional legal doctrine. Critical race theory will be explained as more than just racial identity politics; it is a race-based epistemology that also partially relies on other interpretive frameworks such as feminism, critical theory, and postmodernism. In this way, critical race theory seeks to analyze and speak to the ways in which race and racial discrimination fundamentally operate in the larger society through the law, as well as how race sometimes intersects and connects with gender, social class, culture, language, and other areas of difference (Delgado & Stefancic, 2000). The second section will provide examples of how critical race theory research has emerged through the use of fictional narratives that have served as explanatory frameworks for critically analyzing race, legal testimonies from narrative interviews in racial desegregation higher education discrimination cases. The final sections of the chapter will review some key work done in the particular area of education and LatCrit as an example of critical race theory's impact on education and what education has had to offer critical race theory. In educational research, critical race theory does not necessarily provide a new set of methodological tools (e.g., interviews, document analysis, observations) for the qualitative researcher. However, the theory does provide one with a race-based epistemological and interpretive data framework based on social justice that has generally been absent from mainstream research and can be connected to educational policy (Ladson-Billings, 2000; Tate, 1997). In addition, critical race theory can move into critical race praxis through the use of qualitative inquiry in education.

Color-Blindness and Critical Race Theory

Race has played a major part in shaping the modern and postmodern world (McCarthy & Crichlow, 1993). Even though race is a mythology that has been socially constructed for purposes of control and power and economic exploitation, racialism (i.e., attitudes, actions of stereotyping, discriminatory policies, unequal distribution of resources) is fundamental to everyday life, shaping moral character, the forming and implementation of law, policy, and overall social context (Stanfield, 1999). Critical race theory (and its connecting parts, e.g., LatCrit, Asian-American poststructural critical legal positions, critical race feminism) argues that race is central in the making of our world. Race has played a fundamental role in (1) the making of nation-empire, which evolves into a system of conquest and enslavement; (2) the creation of capital; and (3) the shaping of culture and identity, especially in the creation of subordinate racialized groups (Winant, 1999). Modern white racism evolved ideologically and philosophically in Europe and North America as a system of human classification based on physical characteristics that were considered fixed (Goldberg, 1995; Smedley, 1999). White Europeans and European Americans rank-order was hierarchically placed on other racial groups; this order was used to justify discrimination as well as the imposition of the colonialist culture of the most powerful dominant group, in the name of assimilation based on inequality between races (Flecha, 1999). Postmodern racialized discourse in the United States has taken on the ideology of color-blind interpretations of law and political, social, and economic relations. Edsall and Edsall (1991) and Omi and

Winant (1994) have commented on how race has increased in political significance as elected leaders manipulate the ideology of race neutrality in U.S. elections. The core of these racialized arguments posits that there are no fundamental differences between the races based on inequality. Overt discriminatory laws have been repealed and there is more popular acceptance of different racial groups (Bollick, 1996; Reynolds, 1986). Therefore, equal treatment of all groups under the law should be mandated, regardless of race. Furthermore, no special treatment of racial groups should be justified due to past discrimination.

Antidiscrimination law was designed to eliminate individual injustice against minority group members. However, when that injustice was found, the competing interests of white European Americans must balance it. The supporters of this position, known as the color-blind theory of law, reject state acceptance of affirmative action for African-Americans, or land reparations and compensation for Indigenous tribal nation groups under the U.S. Constitution. They contend that such actions cannot be justified, since there is no factual basis for tracing the injustices to individuals, and no evidence linking past wrongs against a racial group with their present claims. The color-blind position has steadfastly maintained that race should be viewed as an arbitrary factor because it tells us nothing about an individual's capabilities. Flecha (1999) noted how postmodern racism in Europe has also rejected previous notions of racial/ethnic assumptions of superiority or inferiority. Rather, there are cultural differences among racial groups in European countries. However, because of these differences, there is very little possibility for dialogue or discussion, and laws and policies should be directed at restricting immigration and segregation of minority groups (pp. 155–159). This has also manifested itself in the form of discrimination against Afro-Caribbean youth in the United Kingdom, as some British scholars (Gilborn, 1990; Sewell, 1997) have reported in their research on racism in British schools. Some of the trends in this research document how teachers and administrators speak to how they believe in color-blindness regarding curriculum, instruction, and discipline policy.

However, in reality, their actions showed increasing racialized tension between the youth and the white school personnel. Overt discipline measures were taken against Afro-Caribbean males, who were racially profiled not only for punishment but low academic expectations as well. The teachers, being so disconnected from the lives and culture of these males and the racism they faced in their everyday lives, held stereotypes about the youths. In Australia, Rizvi (1993) examined how racism was popularized in four schools. The study of the organization of instructional practices showed that popular forms of racism were sanctioned by the schools to privilege Anglo-Celtic culture over the positions of Asians and Aborigines, yet the language of the teachers and administrators was couched in the rhetoric of color-blindness and fairness to all in a multicultural curriculum.

Critical race theory seeks to expose these proposals for color-blind initiatives and the accompanying political discourse as pretexts for racial discrimination. The critical race legal position challenges the dominant racial ideology through law and seeks to use the power of the courts to "further the goal of eradicating the effects of racial oppression" (Crenshaw, 1988, p. 134). The critical race legal position argues that "white European American" as a racial classification has enjoyed a tremendous legal advantage over persons of color (Bell, 1988; Lopez, 1996). Such power has been effectively wielded in U.S. society because it has been legitimized through law, as "whiteness" has been legally protected and equated with property rights over African and Indigenous tribal nations (Harris, 1993).

To be sure, people of color have made significant strides in using the law and federal courts to dismantle symbolic racism during the civil rights era of the 1950s and 1960s. However, the color-blind view of race has a "powerful strategic appeal" (Aleinikoff, 1991) for sweeping away racial classifications but leaving intact political majorities that use the power of racism to undermine minority interest (Guinier, 1991). This is not so much done now through legalized measures of overt discrimination; rather, it is through more general everyday racism, where racism and prejudice is embedded in the simple psychological decision-making rules that we use to make inferences and draw conclusions about groups (Essed, 1991; McMorris, 1996). Therefore, according to Gotanda (1991), critical race legal theory offers a vision that would attack less overt forms of racial subordination, while counteracting the devaluation of minority cultural and racial institutions in a color-blind society. Essentially, the color-blind perspective of race calls for assimilation, while critical race theory calls for the awareness of the ideology of race as a determining factor in how the law has been used against racialized minority groups.

One of the ways to promote this social awareness of race has been through the telling of true stories of discrimination. Matsuda (1987) argued for the legitimization of stories about discrimination from the perspective of people of color because too often the law has not currently "looked to the needs of the bottom which recognizes economic as well as racial injustice and views reparations awards as a step forward in the long journey toward substantive equality" (p. 397). Matsuda used the example of Japanese-American internment camps and reparations for World War II confinement: Those who argued against reparations for groups such as Japanese Americans asserted that legal facts can not be specifically traced to victims of groups, and their voices lacked sufficient connection between past wrong and present assertions of discrimination (p. 376). However, Matsuda argued that the stories of victims were useful under critical race legal theory because these experiences were real, and connections from the past have to be understood in order to see how the hierarchical relationships of power protect the legal interests of white European Americans over persons of color.

Brown (1992) discussed the fallacy of reverse discrimination and the color-blind interpretation because it attempts to ignore the contextual analysis of history and the political realities of race:

> Critical race scholars have convincingly critiqued the tendency of courts to disengage law from the political and cultural realities of our multicultural society and create the illusion either that racial discrimination against blacks and other racial minorities no longer exists, or that it is no longer influenced by state conduct. (p. 80)

The role of critical race theory is important because it serves as a way for members of the majority race to enrich their own reality (Delgado, 1989). The "storytelling" constitutes an integral and invaluable part of historical and current legal evidence gathering and findings of fact in the higher education desegregation cases. The federal courts and the white European American majority should be interested in these "stories" because, as Delgado asserts, it is only through listening that the conviction of seeing the world only one way can be challenged, and "one can acquire the ability to see the world through others' eyes" (Delgado, 1989, p. 2439). Critical race theory exposes the flaws in the color-blind position by documenting how, for example, African-American students have to compromise their race and culture in order to fit into the white European American majority campus experience.

Critical Race Theory: Examples from U.S. Higher Education

In the 1995 *Ayers* v. *Fordice* higher education desegregation decision, the federal district court noted the high percentage of African-American students graduating from the majority white institutions since the 1960s. Therefore, it was surmised that these institutions must be successful. However, the federal district judge failed to consider the converse; that is, how many African-American students have to tolerate a hostile racial climate to survive at the majority white institutions as evidenced from the personal testimonies of African-American students who submitted briefs in the previous *Fordice* cases. Throughout the final *Fordice* opinions at each level, evidence presented addressing racial harassment of African-American students at the majority white institutions in Mississippi was given scant attention. The personal testimonies of former black students (amicus curiae brief) who attended the University of Mississippi illustrated the depth of racial prejudice they were subjected to as they tried to exercise their "freedom of choice" to attend the flagship majority white institution. Furthermore, despite the appearance of fairness and equality, these students were held to higher and more negative standards. In one instance, Linda Campbell, who attended Ole Miss between 1975 and 1979, testified about a professor she encountered who consistently gave less favorable clinical assignments and the more difficult parts of joint reports. At one point she said that the professor counseled black students to choose another major or encouraged them to enroll in therapy because "black people could not talk, and therefore if we were going to work as speech language pathologists we needed to receive therapy ourselves" (Motion of former black students, 1990, p. 9). Others who attended the University of Mississippi in the early to mid-1980s testified about incidents of racial harassment such as when one of the black students was "slapped in the face with a confederate flag in the middle of the university, while whites were driving by yelling racial slurs but the university police did nothing to stop it" (p. 10).

In the amicus brief filed by these students, they argued that habits of speech, conduct, and attitudes should have been considered along with equal access to the race-neutral system of higher education. These students tried to argue that despite the assertions of race neutrality at the majority white institutions, the campus culture held African-American students to a higher set of discriminatory standards and actions. Yet the court did not see this as a legitimate vestige of segregation.[1] A critical race theory perspective illustrates how much these students have had to adapt to a brutal bargain to survive and graduate from the majority white colleges, which is not necessarily the case for white students (Feagin, 1992; Johnson, 1993).

The critical race theory interpretation of these legal narratives of racism and racial discrimination should play a role in challenging the prevailing notion of legal neutrality and race. The thick descriptions and interviews, characteristic of case study research, not only serve illuminative purposes, but can also be used to document institutional racism as well as stories of overt racism. The interviewing process pulls together to create narratives that can be used to build a case against racially biased officials or discriminatory practices.

Other Emerging Trends in CRT Scholarship

Critical race theorists have also called for a reexamination of the concept of race, recognizing that it is not a fixed term. Rather, "race" has fluid, decentered social meanings that are continually shaped by political pressures (Calmore, 1992).[2] Some critical race theorists, like Patricia Williams (1991) in her book *The Alchemy of Race and Rights,* have expressed the possibility of racial justice by exposing white European Americans to racism through her personal narratives, and they believe that perceptions about race and the law can be transformed by these narratives to truly achieve justice. Other critical race theorists, such as Derrick Bell (1992), have little hope in white European American society and the law being used to the progressive betterment of race and racism. Bell has written a series of fictional accounts about this issue in the book *Faces at the Bottom of the Well.* In one story, entitled "Space Traders," aliens come down to earth from outer space and promise to solve all U.S. resource problems if Americans in return give the aliens all of the African-Americans. After much debate, the best decision for the greater good of the nation is made and the expendable blacks are sent off to the alien planet. These aforementioned opposing views on social justice and race are common within critical race theory discussions, and indeed some have pointed to the strength of the theory in that it allows for these divergent points of view (Calmore, 1992; Hayman, 1995).

Hayman (1995, p. 70) has also posited that critical race theory has postmodern threads in that both reject traditional legal realist and conceptualist epistemologies, and rely instead on the importance of perspective and context in assessing truth claims. He saw similarities in that both the postmodernists and critical race theorists reject the assertion that established doctrine and texts have objective truth and universal meanings. Instead, race goes through "relentless deconstruction and reconstruction" (p. 70), and, like other aspects of identity, it is indeed a sociopolitical construction. However, critical race theory deviates from postmodern legal critique in the "insistence that justice can not be merely theoretical. Furthermore, it must be informed by and realized in lived experiences, and while the struggle for racial justice may offer no prospects for immediate or ultimate success, the struggle has to be continuous" (Hayman, 1995, p. 70). In continuing with this struggle, Jinks (1997) argued that CRT has had noble intentions in terms of its social justice goal and combating racism. But a postmodern-Foucault critique of CRT was important because of the theory's grounding in essentialized versions of antiracism, oppositionalist stances from the academy toward the conditions of poor minority racial groups, and liberal views for the claim for social justice.

Some critical race theorists also seek to go beyond the black-white paradigm. Harris (1993), for example, looked at the role of law in shaping "whiteness" or the notion of white as a race being associated with property and power, and examined how Native Americans have had the law used against them to take their property (i.e., land) from them and relegate them to reservations and subordinate tribal nations status to the U.S. government.[3] In another example of critical race theory's expansion, a special issue of the *California Law Review* (Symposium, 1994) was devoted to Asian American legal scholarship that has sought to examine the "honorary white" status of Asian Americans at various points in U.S. legal history, juxtaposed against massive discrimination at other times such as during World War II and the Japanese intern camps. Chang (1993) criticized the inadequacy of the traditional civil rights law with respect to nativistic racism faced by Asian Americans, and the impact of the Asian-American model minority myth, which has shaped an image of Asian Americans having no need for legal protection against racism. Chang (1993) and Hune (1995) argued that the "black-white" race paradigm that has determineded the way we view race in the United States is inappropriate for examining how the law and public policy have affected Asian Americans. Chang called for critical race theory to not just be inclusive, but to fundamentally alter the lens used to analyze Asian-American race issues. The theory must account for their different racial status and how it is constructed by the larger society, and it must take into account other factors such as immigration and U.S. foreign policy in analyzing differences within the Asian-American population. These considerations and challenges have also had an impact on shaping LatCrit, as Latino legal scholars have borrowed from the basic tenets of CRT to develop a Latina/Latino-specific critique of the law as it relates to various Latino populations in the areas of immigration, international relations, language, and sexual orientation (Delgado Bernal 1998; Iglesias & Valdes, 1998; Soloranzo, 1997; 1998; Soloranzo & Villalpando, 1998; UCLA Law Review Symposium, 2000; Valdes, 2000).

Still, a third emerging expansion of critical race theory is in the area of key intersections of other areas of difference such as feminism. Crenshaw, Gotanda, Peller, and Thomas (1995) have sought to combine feminist legal theory with critical race theory to uncover the patterns of disempowerment on gender and racial lines in the areas of law as well as popular discourse.

Crenshaw's work specifically seeks to: (1) expose the concept of whiteness to critique in law and explore its association with unspoken acceptance of power and authority in U.S. society; (2) bring issues that affect women, such as domestic violence, gender role-socialization, child care, and so on into the public discourse to expose how these issues are excluded from public debate because they are seen as private issues or family issues; and (3) address the marginalization of African-American women in public discourse and the law, and eventually seek ways in which connections can be made with other women on common issues of intersection. In her lecture at the University of Utah, she discussed how narrow identity politics exemplified by the "Million Man March" couldn't really be supported because it isolated African-American women and served to ossify already strong well-defined gender roles and male/female expectations.[4] Rather, work should be done by African-American women and other women of color to create intersections not only on race, but in terms of common interest with community groups, filmmakers, and artists, in the hope of creating a different public intellectual, one who intersects and is in conjunction with race and other areas of difference, in order to build a feminist discourse space for women. Still, the use of personal narratives about racial discrimination is not without obstacles. For example, narratives and personal storytelling about race and homosexuality have been problematic for gays and lesbians because their stories have been used against them by homophobic political, religious, and educational leaders (Capper, 1999; Sears & Williams, 1997).

In addition, as critical race theory becomes more widely discussed, it has come under attack from the color-blind conservative position in the legal arena. The critics of critical race theory (Farber & Sherry, 1993; 1994; Tushnet, 1992) argue that experimental forms of argumentation in law lack normative content. Another complaint about the research in critical race theory has been that the data is unreliable and unverifiable; the stories might portray atypical data, or the stories lack integrity and are just "my story" related to racial identity politics and not to the broader issues of legal doctrine, standards, evidence, or analysis. The critics also maintain that the narrative style of presenting evidence serves to stifle discussion rather than encourage it because it promotes defensiveness among white European Americans who are not guilty of discrimination and prejudice. It elevates the rhetoric about race to argumentative levels, and it confuses narrative with scholarship.

In sum, critical race theory has emerged from the legal arena to uncover the deep patterns of exclusion and what is taken for granted with respect to race and privilege. As illustrated, there are many emerging strands that critical race theory borrows from in order to expand to include other critical epistemologies, and to seek intersections and conjunctions with other areas of difference to push a social justice agenda into the legal and public discourse on race and gender. The critical race theorists seek to break the dominance of storytelling about success of merit, equality, the market, and objectivity that are so deeply entrenched and accepted unquestioningly by larger society, through the legitimating of legal narratives of racial discrimination and the power of the law used against persons of color. The importance of narrative for the purpose of social justice, and the implications of intersections and conjunctions related to difference, are just a few of the various aspects of critical race theory that have important implications for education.

Examples of Critical Race Theory in Education Research

Given that critical race theory utilizes narrative and storytelling in terms of documenting discrimination, parallels can also be drawn between the use of the narrative and qualitative research. Pizzaro (1998), as well as that of other Latina/Latino and Chicana/Chicano scholars such as Villenas (1996), Soloranzo (1998), Delgado Bernal (1998, 2002), and Villalpando (2000), provide a useful bridge in terms of linking research methods to the use of the narrative in critical race theory, LatCrit, and feminism by undermining traditional notions of identity, empowerment, and social justice.

To be sure, critiques can be made of qualitative research that has attempted to engage in praxis with regard to research methods and those involved in the research (e.g., Fine, 1994; Gitlin, 1994). Yet those researchers employing critical race theory, LatCrit, and Chicana feminist epistemology have argued that even though the intent is valid, for the most part educational research has rarely produced research that is truly participatory or emancipatory for Latina/Latino or Chicano/Chicana students. For the most part, the studies still emerge from the researcher and are interpreted and "written up" by the researcher. There are few attempts at dialogical praxis-oriented research.

The common thread among these aforementioned researchers is that they are working with groups of Chicano/Chicana middle school, high school, and college students in the southern California area to dialogue with them to get insights into their views about discrimination, racial identity politics, assimilation, language, gender, school and postsecondary education success, and the importance of being a Chicano or Chicana in majority white American institutions. In their individual critical race theory-praxis research projects, each of these researchers, in varying degrees, is attempting to engage in an ongoing dialogue with the Chicano/Chicana and Latino/Latina students and have them participate in establishing the research agenda(s). Furthermore, this work is trying to move away from one-dimensional racial identity politics by examining how these students negotiate racially shifting contextual environments that range from racially mixed settings, to predominantly Chicano-Latino schools, to predominantly white European American colleges. In this way, their educational research and continuous involvement with Chicano/Chicana students, and other Chicano/Chicana-Latino/Latina scholars can be seen as moving the use of critical race theory into the area of critical race praxis as called for by Yamamoto (1997). Their work also adds to a growing body of work that has pushed for a "fundamental epistemological shift in the academy to demolish the distinction between the researcher and the researched, and where student voices and critiques are seen as objects and demands constant questioning of power and authority in research" (Pizarro, 1998, p. 21). Furthermore, the critical race theory framework could undergird Diaspora research across various Chicano-Latino groups, and what intersecting and/or conflicting roles these researchers play within these communities and the white Eurocentric academy (Villenas, 1996).

The use of narrative in critical race theory adds a different dimension to the purpose of educational research. Previously, Stanfield (1993, 1994, 1999) and Foster (1994) noted how qualitative research was used to describe various aspects of black life and the African-American community. Yet this description was fraught with problems of subject exploitation by white European American researchers; it also neglected various discourse styles and failed to deal with a plethora of power struggles between the researchers and the "subjects" of color. However, the use of narrative stories takes on a different potential dimension when it is an integral part of legal testimony.

Embedded in critical race theory, particularly with regard to its legal implications, is a notion of "social justice validity." This was called for by Deyhle and Swisher (1997) and Tuhiwai Smith (1999) in their respective analyses of the impact of exploitative research on Native American tribal nations and education in the United States and on the Maori in New Zealand. They argued for a research validity connected to methodologies and methods that was seriously grounded in social justice and commitment to tribal nations on their terms, and long-term involvement in challenging white supremacy over Native American and Maori affairs. Similarly, ethical questions in postcolonial contexts are crucial for educational researchers to address. Based on her research and involvement in the Workers' School in South Africa, McKeever (2000) argued for consideration of the specifics of the ravages and legacies of colonialism and how it varies from country to country, depending on the historical context, and how it has had an impact on different sectors of the society. It would also be crucial to see and document the resistance to colonialism and how it manifests itself in the current postcolonialist context of specific countries.

In the academy, the study of Indigenous tribal nations (in the United States and other countries), Americans, African-Americans, Asian/Pacific Island Americans, Latino/Latina Americans, Chicano/Chicana Americans, and other multiracial groups has historically followed and mirrored the norms of studying white European Americans, even though the groups are not the same. Most of the research conducted on persons of color is undergirded by a white Eurocentric epistemological framework (Scheurich & Young, 1997; Torres, Miron, & Inda, 1999). Therefore, a CRT research methodology perspective argues for race and racism to be fundamental in explaining the particular and distinct experiences that have shaped the experiences of racial groups (Parker & Lynn 2002). There are some salient assumptions that undergird a critical race methodology. These are: (1) the experiences of the racial groups are worthy of intellectual pursuit; (2) the historical and contemporary experiences of people of color can prove instructive about human relations; (3) that cultural, historical, and contemporary experiences of persons of color are unique, and (4) one of the most significant tasks of a scholar who plans to utilize CRT as a methodological lens is to develop tools that help generate knowledge designed to describe, analyze, and empower people of color and to help change negative social forces into positive social forces as they impact on everyday life. Before a researcher goes to do research with groups of color, it would be essential to know the history of the race and race relations, as well as the connection of race to a community of interest with regard to the group's struggle for power and self-determination. Part of CRT methodology would entail linking qualitative methods to general practical knowledge about the forces that impact on life according to the subjects' understandings. This type of methodology would also question the Eurocentric theories that are used to explain racial behavior. This is not to say that the basic quantitative (e.g., surveys, statistical studies) or qualitative research tools of interviewing, observation, document review, etc., would be completely discarded. Rather, the CRT researcher in education would reshape them (use some and not others in racially/culturally specific ways) to engage in activist work with these communities and their complexities, and not explain "behavior" from a distance. The CRT researcher also grounds the interpretation of the data in a race-centered epistemological framework that is connected to practice. For the CRT scholar, practice always informs theory.

The same issue of exploitation of the "researched" can occur if educational researchers use the minority students and communities for personal gain and academic career exploitation. For example, the adversarial nature of the academic educational research process can heighten the tension around the relationship between Indigenous tribal nations and university researchers; the tribes have had to establish guidelines and protocol for research because of continual abuse of community trust that has been violated "off the backs" of minority students and parents (Hermes, 1998; Lomawaima, 2000). A second criticism asks: will the critical race theory narratives be heard? As the general society and its key legal, cultural, and educational institutions continue to uphold the norm of a color-blind perspective of the law and society, we can expect those in education to mirror this pattern as well (Young & Laible, 2000). An example of this was found by Schick in her study of white Canadian preservice teachers as they professed antiracist attitudes, yet engaged in unknowing racist actions that demonstrated the power of dominant groups to resist change and their possessive investment in white power and privilege (Lipsitz, 1998). The future of critical race theory and its place in education will partially depend on the efforts made by researchers and scholars to explore its connections to life in schools and communities of color. For example, the emerging broader theoretical framework related to race and widening the lens of race to take into account other perspectives besides the black-white paradigm would be very useful in terms of developing a more "layered" research discussion about life in racially diverse schools with different populations of students. Connections can be made in educational research through the use of narrative in critical race theory, which has already been a part of African-American literature and commentary on racism, and various forms of feminist research from scholars of color that utilize narrative methods in connection to women's lives and activist scholarship (Hill Collins, 1998).

Conclusion

What is the role of race in educational research, particularly in terms of methodological issues? Critical race theory can ideally provide some help as we grapple with this question. This chapter has introduced the concept of critical race theory and its problematic and potential for providing us with ways to theorize and take point to actions that can be done in the area of race-based epistemology and methodology for educational research. Furthermore, critical race theory holds possibilities of intersection and conjunction with other areas of difference in educational research. To be sure, the legal debate surrounding the legitimacy of the theory in relation to the color-blind approach to the law will become even more prominent in education and the social science research circles as well. Yet I feel that the future of critical race theory is part of a larger ongoing power struggle pertaining to the dominant ideological racial context, and it is one that will engage concerned researchers, teachers, and activists within the academy, the schools, and the larger community. As we continue to hold epistemological and methodological debates in educational research and practice, critical race theory will potentially add to the research methods debate about narrative and discrimination, as well as discussions in education regarding how we conceptualize and think about research on race and the cause(s) of social justice.

Notes

1. I asked Kimberlie Crenshaw (law professor at UCLA and Columbia University and one of the leading scholars in the field of critical race theory) the question of how critical race theory can be taken seriously by judges when it seems as if the federal judiciary has recently ignored the legal claims and testimonies of discrimination voiced by persons of color. She asserted that one of the ways in which it can start to be taken seriously is if a growing body of scholarship can be developed to challenge the canon of the color-blind perspective (personal communication at the Tanner Lecture Series—University of Utah, May 9, 1996).
2. For a more extensive definition of social construction of areas of difference (e.g., gender, race) identity, and the law, see Minow (1990). Also, some African-American legal scholars have taken issue with the more postmodernist slant of the fluidity of race. Rather, they see the consistency of white European American supremacy and its impact on African-Americans, particularly in urban areas (Austin, 1992).
3. The discussion of whiteness as property has led to an explosion of literature on this topic, ranging from historical tracings of white as a race and its connection to power, to essays and cultural studies analyses of whiteness and privilege (see, e.g., Frankenberg, 1997; Ignatiev, 1995; Lipsitz, 1998; Roediger, 1998; Sleeter, 1996). This has also given rise

to works in education that seek to problematize whiteness such as those of Fine, Weis, Powell, and Wong (1997), as well as studies in teacher education on whiteness (McIntyre, 1997). However, as Thompson (1999) and Sheets (2000) have noted, the extensive discussion of whiteness and white views on race may serve to privilege it over the perspectives of other racial groups and serve to ignore the hard issues that a critique of whiteness seeks to ask about race and racism.

4. Personal communication, Tanner Lecture Series, University of Utah, May 9, 1996.

CRITICAL MULTICULTURALISM

Some thirty to forty years after the genesis of the multiculturalist movement, even its critics are now being forced to acknowledge its increasingly significant impact on public policy, particularly within education. Nathan Glazer (1998), a longtime skeptic of multiculturalism, does just that when he concedes "we are all multiculturalists now." Multiculturalism, at least in his view, has finally "won" because the issue of greater public representation for minority groups is increasingly commonplace in discussions of democracy and representation in modern western nation-states (see, e.g., Goldberg, 1994; Joppke & Lukes, 1999; Kymlicka, 1995a; Kymlicka & Norman, 1999; Taylor, 1994).

But things are never quite what they seem. As a proponent of multiculturalism, I obviously do not share Glazer's sense of wearied resignation. But neither do I share his sense of inevitability, for it seems to me that while multiculturalism has accomplished much since its origins in the 1960s, it has many obstacles yet to overcome. As Carlos Torres notes, for example:

> [T]he multitude of tasks confronting multiculturalism is overwhelming. They include the attempt to develop a sensible, theoretically refined, and defensible new metatheoretical and theoretical territory that would create the foundations for multiculturalism as a paradigm; the attempt to establish its epistemological and logical premise around notions of experience, narrative, voice, agency and identity; the attempt to pursue empirical research linking culture/ power/ knowledge with equality/ inequality/discrimination; and the need to defend multiculturalism from the conservative Right that has demonized multiculturalism as an unpatriotic movement. (1998: 446)

Taken in reverse order, the challenges Torres highlights can be usefully paraphrased as:

- the ongoing critique of multiculturalism from the Right

- the tendency of multiculturalism to concentrate on culture at the expense of structural concerns such as racism and socioeconomic inequality
- the challenges that postmodernist understandings of identity present for multiculturalism
- the urgent need to develop a multiculturalist paradigm that effectively addresses—and, where necessary, redresses—all of the above.

I have already discussed and critiqued at length elsewhere the often vitriolic and largely misconceived responses of the Right to multiculturalism (see especially May, 1999a, 2001, 2002) and will not revisit these here. However, I do wish to review here the second and third challenges to multiculturalism—what might be termed the "culturalist" and "postmodernist" critiques respectively—since these bear directly on the subsequent development of critical multiculturalism, my principal concern in what follows. In so doing, I will highlight key aspects of critical multiculturalism, and the implications attendant upon it, and suggest that it is a paradigm that is sufficiently "sensible, theoretically refined, and defensible" as to lead multiculturalism successfully into this new century.

The Problem of Culture

For much of its history, multiculturalism has been plagued by an idealistic, naive preoccupation with culture at the expense of broader material and structural concerns. If only cultural differences could be recognized, so the story went, the prospects of a harmonious multiethnic society could then (more easily) be achieved. This strain of multiculturalism is most evident in the rhetoric of early forms of multicultural education, developed throughout the 1970s and 1980s (see Modood & May, 2001). It is encapsulated, usefully, by Richard Hatcher's observation that while "culture is the central concept around which [this] multiculturalism is constructed, the concept is given only a taken-for-granted common sense meaning, impoverished both theoretically and in terms of concrete lived experience. It is a concept of culture innocent of class" (1987, p. 188).

Hatcher's acerbic assessment formed part of a sustained assault by "antiracist" theorists on what they perceived to be the endemic utopianism and naivete associated with the multicultural education movement (and its municipal variants) of that era—a movement that has since come to be described as "benevolent multiculturalism" (see May, 1994; Troyna, 1993). Such critics, notably the late Barry Troyna (1987, 1993), argued that benevolent multiculturalism constituted an irredeemably "deracialized" discourse, an approach that reified culture and cultural difference, and that failed to address adequately, if at all, *material* issues of racism and disadvantage, and related forms of discrimination and inequality. While this broad antiracist position has been dominated by British commentators—a result of its origins there as a neo-Marxist critique of multiculturalism—it has also been articulated forcefully in the United States (see, e.g., Alcoff, 1996; McCarthy & Crichlow, 1993; McLaren & Torres, 1999).

Similar criticisms have been leveled at this approach from within the multiculturalist paradigm itself. Thus, Kalantzis and Cope can observe:

> Whilst mouthing good intentions about pluralism . . . this sort of multiculturalism can end up doing nothing either to change the mainstream or to improve the access of those historically denied its power and privileges. It need not change the identity of the dominant culture in such a way that there can be genuine negotiation with "minorities" about matters social or symbolic or economic. It need not change education in such a way that issues of diversity are on the agenda for all students. It need not change education so that diversity might become a positive resource for access rather than a cultural deficit to be remedied by affirmation of difference alone. (1999, p. 255)

Multiculturalists have responded to this critique from both within and without by acknowledging more directly the role of unequal power relations and the inequalities and differential effects that ensue from them (see Kanpol & McLaren, 1995; Kincheloe & Steinberg, 1997; May, 1999a; McLaren, 1995, 1997). This more critical response—a central feature of "critical multiculturalism," as it has come to be known—acknowledges that the logic of much previous multiculturalist rhetoric failed "to see the power-grounded relationships among identity construction, cultural representations and struggles over resources." Rather, it engaged "in its celebration of difference when the most important issues to those who fall outside the white, male and middle class norm often involve powerlessness, violence and poverty" (Kincheloe & Steinberg, 1997, p. 17). In contrast, a more critical conception of multiculturalism:

> takes as its starting point a notion of culture as a terrain of conflict and struggle over representation—conflict for which resolution may not be immediate and struggle that may not cease until there is a change in the social conditions that provoke it. Rather than present culture as the site where different members . . . coexist peacefully, it has to develop strategies to explore and understand this conflict and to encourage creative resolutions and contingent alliances that move [away] from interpreting cultures to intervening in political processes. (Mohan, 1995, p. 385)

However, in developing this broadly critical response, multiculturalists have also more recently come to face another, perhaps more intractable problem—a problem brought on to some extent by this very process of accommodation with antiracist theory. For example, the privileging of racism over other forms of discrimination in early conceptions of antiracism resulted in an increasing preoccupation with "color racism" and the black-white dichotomy (Modood & May, 2001). This, in turn, led to a "grand theory" approach that, in attributing racism as the primary modality in intercultural relations, came to be seen as both reductive and essentialist (see Donald & Rattansi, 1992; MacDonald, Bhavnani, Khan, & John, 1989: Modood, 1992, 1998a, 1998b). Such an approach subsumes other factors such as class, religion, and gender, and fails to address adequately postmodernist accounts of identity as multiple, contingent, and subject to rapid change. These emphases in antiracist theory also considerably understate both the multiplicity of racisms and their complex interconnections with other forms of inequality (Gilroy, 1992; Modood, 1998a, 1998b; Rattansi, 1992, 1999). As McLaren and Torres observe of this: "[the] conflation of racialized relations into solely a black-white paradigm has prevented scholars from engaging more fully the specificities of particular groups and from exploring more deeply comparative ethnic histories of racism and how these are linked to changing class relations in late capitalism" (1999, pp. 45–46).

But this is not all, since antiracist theory, up until recently at least (see Gillborn, 1995), also consistently failed to conceptualize and address adequately the increasing articulation of new "cultural racisms," where "race" as a signifier is transmuted into the seemingly more acceptable discourse of "cultural differences" (cf. Rattansi, 1992, 1999; Short & Carrington, 1999). Thus, essentialist racialized discourses are "disguised" by describing group differences principally in cultural and/or historical terms—ethnic terms, in effect—without specifically mentioning "race" or overtly racial criteria (Barker, 1981; Small, 1994; Wetherell & Potter, 1992). New racisms, in this sense, can be described as a form of *ethnicism*, which, as Avtar Brah describes it,

> defines the experience of racialized groups primarily in "culturalist" terms: that is, it posits "ethnic difference" as the primary modality around which social life is constituted and experienced. . . . This means that a group identified as culturally different is assumed to be internally homogeneous. . . . ethnicist discourses seek to impose stereotypic notions of common cultural need upon heterogeneous groups with diverse social aspirations and interests. (1992, p. 129)

Avoiding Essentialism

And this brings us to another key challenge for multiculturalism, since the problems of cultural essentialism and the reification of group-based identities highlighted by Brah, and mobilized so effectively by new racist proponents, also continue ironically to haunt much multicultural theory and practice. This is particularly evident within multicultural education, for example, where the regular invocation of "cultural difference" often presents culture as sui generis (Hoffman, 1996). In the process, ethnicity is elided with culture and both come to be treated as "bounded cultural objects," to borrow a phrase from Richard Handler (1988), which are seen to attach unproblematically to particular individuals and/or groups.

This naive, static, and undifferentiated conception of cultural identity, and the allied notion of the incommensurability of cultures, end up being not that dissimilar from the new racisms of the Right. Both appear to abandon universalist notions of individual choice, rights, and responsibility in order to revalorize closed cultures, roots, and traditions (Lloyd, 1994; Werbner, 1997a).

It is perhaps not surprising then that criticism of multiculturalism with respect to this issue comes predominantly from what one might term the "postmodernist/left" (see Phillips, 1997). The challenge posed by postmodernist/left critics is this: How can multiculturalism, based as it is on a notion of group-based rights, avoid lapsing into reification and essentialism? In effect, how can it codify without solidifying corporate identities, thus accounting for postmodernist understandings of voice, agency, and the malleable and multiple aspects of identity formation? Not easily, is the short answer.

The principal problem for multiculturalism here is that any notion of group-based rights stands in direct contrast to much postmodernist theorizing on identities which—with its related concepts of hybridity, syncretism, creolization, and new ethnicities—highlights the "undecidability" and fluidity of much identity formation. Indeed, it is now almost de rigueur in this postmodernist age to dismiss *any* articulation of group-based identity as essentialist[1]—a totalizing discourse that excludes and silences as much as it includes and empowers (see, e.g., Anthias & Yuval-Davis, 1992; Bhabha, 1994; Gilroy, 1993, 2000; Hall, 1992; Yuval-Davis, 1997a). Viewed in this way, multiculturalism's advocacy of group-based identities appears irredeemably passé.

Left/postmodernist critics are particularly exercised by, and skeptical of, any claims to the validity of distinct (ethnic) group identities, especially if such identities link cultural difference and identity ineluctably to a historical past of supposed cultural authenticity. Such critics argue that this form of "left-essentialist multiculturalism" (Kincheloe & Steinberg, 1997; McLaren, 1995), of which Afrocentrism is often seen as an exemplar (see Howe, 1998), may well be motivated by a principal concern to acknowledge positively cultural difference, to address historical and current patterns of disadvantage, racism, and marginalization, and, from that, to effect the greater pluralization of the public sphere. However, it does so at the cost of overstating the importance of ethnicity and culture, and understating the fluid and dialogic nature of inter- and intragroup relations. In effect, communitarian conceptions of multiculturalism are charged with operating a model of group membership that is at odds with the complexities of identity in the modern world (Burtonwood, 1996). As Edward Said argues, "no one today is purely one thing. Labels like Indian, or woman, or Muslim, or American are no more than starting points" (1994, p. 407).

This broad critique of "left-essentialist multiculturalism" is illustrated by two allied, although theoretically quite distinct conceptions—cultural hybridity and the cosmopolitan alternative. Both celebrate the notion of cultural mixture and, concomitantly, disavow the validity of so called "rooted" identities like ethnicity.

Cultural Hybridity: The Postmodernist Critique

The articulation of cultural hybridity—and related concepts such as mestizaje and creolization—is a prominent feature of the work of British theorists Stuart Hall, Homi Bhabha, and Paul Gilroy, among others. Hall's (1992) discussion of "new ethnicities," Bhabha's (1994) celebration of creolization and subaltern voices from the margin, and Gilroy's (1993, 2000) discussions of a Black Atlantic—a hybridized, diasporic black counterculture—all foreground the transgressive potential of cultural hybridity. Hybridity is viewed as being able to subvert categorical oppositions and essentialist ideological movements—particularly ethnicity and nationalism—and to provide, in so doing, a basis for cultural reflexivity and change (Werbner, 1997a).

Within the discourses of hybridity, and of postmodernism more broadly, the new social agents are plural—multiple agents forged and engaged in a variety of struggles and social movements (Giroux, 1997). Conversely, hybridity theory is entirely opposed to universalism, traditionalism, and any idea of ethnic or cultural rootedness. In line with postmodernism's rejection of totalizing meta-narratives, exponents of hybridity emphasize the contingent, the complex, and the contested aspects of identity formation. Multiple, shifting and, at times, nonsynchronous identities are the norm for individuals. This position highlights the social and historical constructedness of culture and its associated fluidity and malleability. It also posits contingent, local narratives—what Lyotard (1984) has described as *petits récits*—in opposition to the totalizing narratives of ethnicity and nationalism. The rejection of totality and foundationalism in hybridity theory, and its replacement by a plethora of local identities, thus lends itself at one level to a politics of difference that is commensurable with multiculturalism. Hybridity theorists, like multiculturalists, are fundamentally opposed to a static, closed sense of national identity where majoritarian (usually white) ethnicities come to be elided/equated with national ones, a position articulated most trenchantly by conservative opponents of multiculturalism (cf. Frost, 1997; Schlesinger, 1992). Instead, and again like multiculturalists, they argue for a *differentiated* politics of representation in the public sphere.

However, where hybridity theorists differ from multiculturalists is in sharing with conservative commentators a view of ethnicity and nationalism as misconceived "rooted" identities. Similarly, these identities are almost always ascribed with the negative characteristics of essentialism, closure, and conflict. Postmodernists, like multiculturalists, may thus argue for the pluralization of the public sphere via a differentiated local politics, but they do so via a *rejection,* not a defense, of singular ethnic and cultural identities. Rather, as Homi Bhabha (1994) argues, it is the "inter" and "in-between," the liminal "third space" of translation, which carries the burden of the meaning(s) of culture in this postmodern, postcolonial world. Others have described this process as one of "border crossing" (see Anzaldúa, 1987; di Leonardo, 1994; Giroux, 1992; Rosaldo, 1989).

Hybridity theory, as part of the wider postmodern critique, appears to offer us, among other things, a more contingent, situational account of identity and culture—a process that involves "decentring" the subject (Rattansi, 1999) and contesting essentialism wherever it is found. But there are also limits to hybridity. First, in arguing for the inter- and in-between, hybridity is still predicated on the notion of (previous) cultures as complex wholes (Friedman, 1997; Wicker, 1997). In juxtaposing the merits of the heterogeneous hybrid against the homogeneous ethnicist or nationalist, hybridity assumes that the liminal "third space" is replacing the bounded, closed ones that preceded it. Border crossing, in effect, assumes that (closed) borders were there to begin with. However, as Jonathan Friedman (1997) points out, this simply perpetuates an essentialist conception of culture rather than subverting it since, as Lévi Strauss (1994) has argued, all cultures are heterogeneous, arising out of cultural mixture. The juxtaposition of purity/hybridity, authenticity/mixture—so central to hybridity theory—is thus fundamentally misconceived. In the end, hybridity is meaningless as a description of "culture" because it museumizes culture as "a thing" (Werbner, 1997a; see also Caglar, 1997; Modood, 1998a).

Second, an advocacy of hybridity carries with it the imputation that all group-based identities are essentialist. This is most clearly demonstrated in the frequent conflation of ethnicity and nationalism with racism, which, as so-called "rooted" identities, are all treated with equal disparagement (see Anthias & Yuval-Davis, 1992; Chambers, 1994; Gilroy, 1987). This is simply wrong. There are many examples of ethnic and national categorization that do involve the imputation of essentialized notions of racial and/or cultural difference, leading in turn to social and/or political closure, hierarchization, exclusion, and/or violence. The cultural racism of the New Right is an obvious example here. But while ethnic and national categories may be essentialized in the same way as "race" categories have been historically, they need not always be. Nor are ethnic relations necessarily hierarchical, exploitative, and conflictual in the same way that "race relations" invariably are (Jenkins 1994, 1997; Rex, 1973). Indeed, it has often been the case that the global impact of racism has overridden previously nonhierarchized ethnic categories (Balibar, 1991; Fenton, 1999). In a similar vein, Werbner (1997b) has argued that the politics of ethnicity, which objectifies communities situationally and pragmatically with regard to questions of redistributive justice in the public sphere, can be clearly distinguished from the violent essentializing of racism.

The failure to make these crucial distinctions points to a third weakness of hybridity theory—the considerable disparity between the intellectual celebration of hybridity and the reality of the postmodern world. This world *is* increasingly one of fractured, and fracturing, identities. But these identities are generally not hybrid; just the opposite, in fact. Nation-states, as conservatives will be the first to tell you, are facing a plethora of ethnic, regional, and other social and cultural minority demands, many of which are couched in singular, collectivist terms. The tendencies to rootedness and to boundary maintenance thus militate against ecumenism, and these tendencies, in turn, are generated and reinforced by the real fragmentation occurring within and between nation-states in a global era (Friedman, 1997).

Given this, as Friedman argues, the valorization of hybridization is largely self-referential and self-congratulatory:

> hybrids, and hybridization theorists are products of a group that self-identifies and/or identifies the world in such terms, not as a result of ethnographic understanding, but as an act of self-definition—indeed, of self-essentializing—which becomes definition for others via the forces of socialization inherent in the structures of power that such groups occupy: intellectuals close to the media; the media intelligentsia itself; in a sense, all those [and, one might add, only those] who can afford a cosmopolitan identity. (1997, p. 81)

Ahmad (1995), in a similarly scathing critique, argues that articulations of hybridity fail to address adequately the social and political continuities and transformations that underpin individual and collective action in the real world. In that world, he argues, political agency is "constituted not in flux or displacement but in given historical locations." Moreover, it is sustained by a coherent "sense of place, of belonging, of some stable commitment to one's class or gender or nation" (1995, pp. 16, 14).

Friedman and Ahmad's critiques of hybridity accord here with two wider criticisms often leveled at postmodernist discourses. First, postmodernism is criticized for an overemphasis on aesthetics at the expense of politics—a preoccupation that as Berman (1992, see also 1983) acerbically observes, has seen postmodernism appropriate the modernist language of radical breakthrough, wrench it out of its moral and political context, and transform it into a purely aesthetic language game. Second, and relatedly, postmodernism is attributed both with failing to describe accurately and with retreating from the (post)modern world as it actually is, thus offering little, if any, real hope of accomplishing any kind of radical, emancipatory democratic change (Habermas, 1979).

The Cosmopolitan Alternative

These arguments and counterarguments with regard to hybridity theory are strongly echoed in debates within liberal political theory around the closely allied notion of the "cosmopolitan alternative" (Waldron, 1993, 1995; see also Hannerz, 1992). Jeremy Waldron, in a trenchant critique of group-based rights (aka multiculturalism), objects to the idea that our choices and self-identity are defined by our ethnicity and asserts, instead, the need for a "cosmopolitan alternative." As he dismissively observes, "though we may drape ourselves in the distinctive costumes of our ethnic heritage and immure ourselves in an environment designed to minimize our sense of relation with the outside world, no honest account of our being will be complete without an account of our dependence on larger social and political structures that goes far beyond the particular community with which we pretend to identify" (1995, p. 104). In this view, people can pick and choose "cultural fragments" from various ethnocultural sources, without feeling an allegiance to any one in particular. Thus, Waldron argues, an Irish American who eats Chinese food, reads *Grimm's Fairy Tales* to her child, and listens to Italian opera actually lives in a "a kaleidoscope of cultures." While Waldron concedes that we need cultural meanings of some kind, he argues that we do not need *specific* cultural frameworks: "we need to understand our choices in the contexts in which they make sense, but we do not need any single context to structure our choices. To put it crudely, we need culture, but we do not need cultural integrity" (1995, p. 108).

Like hybridity theory, Waldron proceeds on this basis to argue that any advocacy of group-based identities, and specific (multicultural) rights that may be seen to attach to these, necessarily assumes a homogeneous conception of ethnic groups (see Waldron, 1995, pp. 103–105). Likewise, he is particularly critical of notions of cultural "purity" and "authenticity" which, he asserts, are regularly employed by ethnic minority groups in support of differential treatment in the public sphere. These attempts at cultural delineation are manifestly artificial in his view and can only result in cultural stasis and isolationism.

However, as Will Kymlicka (1995a) has countered, also from within liberal theory, the assertion of minority recognition and difference, and particular rights associated with them, is most often *not* based on some simplistic desire for cultural "purity." Advocates of multiculturalism are rarely seeking to preserve their "authentic" culture if that means returning to cultural practices long past. If it did have such a meaning, it would soon meet widespread opposition from individual members. Rather, multiculturalism is the right "to maintain one's membership in a distinct culture, and to continue developing that culture in the same (impure) way that the members of majority cultures are able to develop theirs" (1995a, p. 105). Cultural change, adaptation, and interaction are entirely consistent with such a position. As Kymlicka argues elsewhere (1995b, pp. 8–9), minority cultures wish both to be cosmopolitan and to embrace the cultural interchange that Waldron emphasizes. However, this does not necessarily entail Waldron's own "cosmopolitan alternative," which denies that people have any deep bond to their own historical, cultural, and linguistic communities.

In a similar vein, Kymlicka asserts that minority rights "help to ensure that the members of minority cultures have access to a secure cultural structure *from which to make choices for themselves,* and thereby promote liberal equality" (1989, p. 192; my emphasis). In this view, minorities continue to exercise their individual (citizenship) rights within their particular cultural (and linguistic) milieux and, of course, contextually, in relation to other cultural groups within a given nation-state. The crucial element, however, is that members of the minority are themselves able to retain a significant degree of control over the process—something that until now has largely been the preserve of majority group members. The key issue thus becomes one of cultural autonomy rather than one of retrenchment, isolationism, or stasis.

In a related critique of Waldron's position, Margalit and Raz (1995) argue that people today may well adopt (and adapt) a varied range of cultural and social practices but that this does not necessarily diminish their allegiance to an "encompassing group" with which they most closely identify (see also Taylor, 1994). Moreover, "if members of dominant ethnic groups typically value their own cultural membership, it is clearly unfair to prevent minority groups from continuing to value theirs." As Kymlicka again observes, "leaving one's culture, while possible, is best seen as renouncing something to which one is reasonably entitled" (1995a, p. 90). Relatedly, he argues:

> The freedom which liberals demand for individuals is not primarily the freedom to go beyond one's language and history, but rather the freedom to move within one's societal culture, to distance oneself from particular cultural roles, to choose which features of the culture are most worth developing, and which are without value. (1995a, pp. 90–91)

Developing a Critical Multicultural Paradigm

Which brings us to the final challenge currently facing multiculturalism that I want to discuss here: What components are essential for multiculturalism to develop into a sensible, theoretically refined, and defensible paradigm, fit for the twenty-first century? In light of the above discussion, I want to suggest that the following key components of what has come to be known as "critical multiculturalism" constitute just such a paradigm.

Theorizing Ethnicity

There is an obvious and ongoing tension that needs to be more adequately addressed in multicultural theory and practice between, on the one hand, recognizing the significance of ethnicity and culture for (some) individuals and group identities, while, on the other hand, avoiding essentializing them. Critical multiculturalism attempts this difficult task. Indeed, unlike all the critiques of multiculturalism discussed in this chapter, critical multiculturalism aims to provide an adequate understanding and theorization of the ongoing collective purchase of ethnicity and the social and cultural practices that may be associated with it in the modern world. We may well demonstrate, as individuals, a considerable degree of latitude in our attachment to, and choice of, particular social and political identities. As such, ethnic choices and identifications may vary in their salience—both in themselves and in relation to other social identities—at any given time and place. Yet, at the same time, we need to acknowledge and explain why "at the collective as opposed to the individual level, ethnicity remains a powerful, explosive and durable force" (Smith, 1995, p. 34).

One way we can manage this apparent tension is via Pierre Bourdieu's notion of habitus (see Bourdieu, 1984, 1990a, 1990b; Bourdieu & Passeron, 1990; Bourdieu & Wacquant, 1992). The application of habitus to ethnicity and ethnic identity formation has been discussed at length elsewhere (see Bentley, 1987; Smaje, 1997; Wicker, 1997). However, for my purposes, it is enough to say that the four key dimensions of habitus highlighted in Bourdieu's work—embodiment, agency, the interplay between past and present, and the interrelationship between collective and individual trajectories—provide us with a useful means by which the continuing purchase and malleability of ethnicity, in its particular contexts, can be critically examined (see May, 1999b, 2001 for an extended discussion).

Another basis for theoretical analysis might be via a more Foucauldian approach to representation, discourse, and identity, of which hybridity theory is an obviously prominent component. If the limits to such an approach are acknowledged (see above), ethnicity can be usefully examined here in relation to other discursive constructions of identity—in terms of both their complex interconnections and, crucially, their ongoing distinctions. The intersection of knowledge and power—that is, discourse as both a technique of power and the terrain on which identity and meaning are contested—is also usefully highlighted by such analysis (see, e.g., Fiske, 1996; Giroux, 1997; Hall, 1997; Shohat & Stam, 1994).

These examples are, of course, not meant to be taken as comprehensive—indeed, theoretical eclecticism is a prominent and welcome feature of critical multiculturalism (McLaren 2001)—but they do point to the urgent need to theorize ethnicity, and its consequences, more adequately than we have hitherto. In so doing, the durability and malleability of ethnicity, its varied forms of cultural expression, and its complex interconnections with other forms of identity can be critically examined.

Acknowledging (Unequal) Power Relations

In addition, a sensible and defensible theory of multiculturalism requires a central recognition of unequal power relations—a feature at the heart of critical multiculturalism. Such recognition allows one to avoid the mistake made by many hybridity theorists (as well as liberal advocates of the cosmopolitan alternative) of "flattening out" differences, making them appear equal (Alcoff, 1996). This is both inadequate as theory and unreflective of practice, since it is clear that when it comes to ethnicity—or any other identity for that matter—some have more choices than others. In this respect, individual and collective choices are circumscribed by the ethnic categories available at any given time and place. These categories are, in turn, socially and politically defined and have varying degrees of advantage or stigma attached to them (Nagel, 1994). Moreover, the range of choices available to particular individuals and groups varies widely. A white American may have a wide range of ethnic options from which to choose, both hyphenated and/or hybrid. An African American, in contrast, is confronted with essentially one ethnic choice—black; irrespective of any preferred ethnic (or other) alternatives he or she might wish to employ.

The preceding example highlights the different ethnic choices available to majority and minority group members. In short, identities are not—indeed, *cannot*—be freely chosen and to suggest otherwise is to adopt an ahistorical approach that reduces life to the level of "a market, or cafeteria" (Worsley, 1984, p. 246). Rather, identity choices are structured by class, ethnic and gender stratification, objective constraints, and historical determinations (Hicks, 1991; McLaren, 1997). Put another way, individuals and groups are inevitably located, and often *differentially* constrained, by wider structural forces such as capitalism, racism, colonialism, and sexism. Both hybridity theory and the cosmopolitan alternative—as well as conservative critiques of multiculturalism—fail to recognize the often fundamental inequalities that ensue from this selective, differentiated, albeit articulatory process.

Critiquing Constructions of Culture

Relatedly, culture has to be understood as part of the discourse of power and inequality. In particular, attention needs to be paid here to the processes by which alternative cultural knowledges come to be *subjugated,* principally through the hegemonies and misrepresentations—what Bourdieu (1991) has termed, for instance, "méconnaissance" or "misrecognition"—that invariably accompany such comparisons (see Corson, 1993, 1998; Kincheloe & Steinberg, 1997; May, 1999b, 2001). When this is grasped, alternatives become possible. For example, previously subjugated cultural knowledges can be *re*valued and simultaneously employed as counterhegemonic critiques of dominant forms of knowledge, along with the wider social, cultural, and material processes of domination to which the latter contribute (Kincheloe & Steinberg, 1997).

But even this may not be enough, since the recognition and incorporation of ethnic and cultural differences, even when allied to a critique of wider power relations, does not necessarily resolve or redress the problem of essentialism. Indeed, the problem may be compounded, since an emphasis on distinctive ethnic and/or cultural boundaries may lead in turn to a further (unhelpful) implication of ethnic and/or cultural *boundedness*. Certainly, in much of the actual educational practice of multiculturalism, including some of its more critical variants, minority ethnic groups have often come to be represented as being *contained* within their culture(s) and the discursive practices associated with them (Hoffman, 1996, 1997).

Maintaining Critical Reflexivity

Thus, the final, and perhaps key, tenet of critical multiculturalism is the need to maintain at all times a reflexive critique of specific ethnic and cultural practices—one that avoids the vacuity of cultural relativism and allows for criticism (both internal and external to the group), transformation, and change (see Phillips, 1997). This reflexive position on culture and ethnicity is encapsulated by a distinction drawn by Homi Bhabha (1994) between cultural *diversity* and cultural *difference*. The former, he argues, treats culture as an *object* of empirical knowledge—as static, totalized, and historically bounded, as something to be valued but not necessarily *lived*. The latter is the process of the *enunciation* of culture as "knowledg-

able," as adequate to the construction of systems of cultural identification. This involves a dynamic conception of culture—one that recognizes and incorporates the ongoing fluidity and constant change that attends its articulation in the modern world. Likewise, Stuart Hall has argued that a positive conception of ethnicity must begin with "a recognition that all speak from a particular place, out of a particular history, out of a particular experience, a particular culture, *without being contained by that position*" (1992, p. 258; my emphasis). In other words, the recognition of our cultural and historical situatedness should not set the limits of ethnicity and culture, nor act to undermine the legitimacy of other, equally valid forms of identity.

In the end then, this kind of critical, reflexive multiculturalism must foster, above all, people who can engage critically with all ethnic and cultural backgrounds, including (and especially) their own. Such an approach would allow all participants in the multicultural debate, however they may be situated, to recognize and explore the complex interconnections, gaps, and dissonances that occur between their own and other ethnic and cultural identities, as well as other forms of social identity.[2] At the same time, how ethnic and cultural identities differ in salience among individuals and across given historical and social contexts, and how these identities are situated in the wider framework of power relations, along with the value, or lack of value, that attends them, can also be highlighted. This dual approach can involve for members of minority groups the retention of their ethnic and cultural identities, not by a retreat into traditionalism or cultural essentialism but by a more *autonomous* construction of group identity and political deliberation (Kymlicka, 1995a; May, 2001). For members of particular majority groups, this can involve a critical interrogation of the normalization and universalization of majoritarian forms of identity—most notably whiteness—and their subsequent "invisibility" in many discussions of multiculturalism and multicultural education (McLaren & Torres, 1999). In either instance, critical multiculturalism must engage with the present and the future as well as the past, and remain open to competing conceptualizations, diverse identities, and a rich public discourse about controversial issues (Calhoun, 1993).

Conclusion

These four components, in combination, constitute what has come to be known as "critical multiculturalism." Despite its detractors (see, e.g., McLennan, 2001), critical multiculturalism offers, I believe, the most useful way forward in the contested arena that is multiculturalism. Critical multiculturalism combines both structural and culturalist concerns—linking culture to power, and multiculturalism to anti-racism—in its advocacy of a greater politics of recognition and representation in the public sphere. Critical multiculturalism engages actively with postmodernist conceptions and analyses of the contingent nature of identity, while still holding onto the possibility of an emancipatory, group-based politics. In so doing, it manages to avoid the great limitation of postmodernism, which, in Habermas's (1979) memorable riposte, is its tendency toward a politics of exhaustion. And, perhaps most important, critical multiculturalism provides a defensible, credible, and critical multiculturalist paradigm that can act as a template for a more plural, inclusive, and democratic approach to nation-state organization in this new century. Glazer, as much as he might not have wished it, may actually be proved right after all—it looks like (critical) multiculturalism, and its social and political consequences are here to stay, and long may it continue.

Notes

1. Essentialism is taken to mean here the process by which particular groups come to be described in terms of fundamental, immutable characteristics. In so doing, the relational and fluid aspects of identity formation are ignored and the group itself comes to be valorized as subject, as autonomous and separate, impervious to context and to processes of internal as well as external differentiation (Werbner, 1997b).
2. In a parallel argument drawn from feminist discourse, Nira Yuval-Davis describes this process as one of "transversal politics" in which "perceived unity and omogeneity are replaced by dialogues that give recognition to the specific positionings of those who participate in them, as well as to the 'unfinished knowledge' . . . that each such situated positioning can offer" (1997b, p. 204).

THE GROTESQUE BODY AS A FEMINIST AESTHETIC?

It is one thing to draw attention to women's bodies—artists and advertisers do it all the time. It is quite another to insist that the ugly, comic bodies of women can be mobilized as a feminist politics. I want to explore this "ugly turn" in feminist knowledge production in the 1990s—and its legacy—because of the inescapable ironies that accompany it. It is certainly an ironic twist in the context of a long struggle against the hegemony of male spectatorship in Western cultural genres. After so much work has been done by feminists to counter the objectification of women's bodies, surely it could not be in the interests of women to direct attention to their "illness[es], aging, reproduction, nonreproduction, secretions, lumps, bloating, wigs, scars, make-up, and prostheses" (Russo 1994, 14). What could be in it for women? Why would any feminist take the risk?

I want to explore these questions by means of three tasks. The first is to understand how the body has become increasingly important to critical theory as both a material and a discursive node for mobilizing relations of power. The second is to consider the case Mary Russo makes in *The Female Grotesque* (1994) for foregrounding the vulgar and unaesthetic in the cause of women. The third is to ask about the trouble this disruptive turn might make for feminism itself.

Carry That Weight

In moving to enact the first task, I make no attempt to construct a definitive genealogy of "body" discourse in feminist politics. Rather, I want to acknowledge the growing importance of the body—material, discursive, and symbolic—in informing feminist thinking over the last two decades.

In 1981, Betty Friedan wrote of a necessary second stage of feminist politics, one that was emerging in the light of the many conflicts and contradictions felt by those trying to live in terms of first stage feminism and the emergence of full-scale backlash with and after the 1980 Reagan election (Friedan, 1981, p. 4). This second stage, she argued, should take up some of the thornier problems of the enactment of a reactive politics in order to push beyond critique and refusal of the "feminine mystique," the title of her foundational feminist work published in 1963. She was not signaling an end to reactivity as ongoing political work, but drawing attention to the importance of understanding feminism's reactions as half-truths (p. 31), with their own limited view of personhood and thus of possibility. This more reflective and reflexive tone in the politics of resistance was, among other more noble things, a product of fatigue—the fatigue of the women campaigners themselves and the fatigue of a first stage politics of liberation as a system of language use. In the case of the women's movement, the truncating of women's liberation to women's lib, and the designation of women as "libbers," signaled not simply the trivializing of feminist agendas by commercial media, but the exhaustion of a vocabulary of resistance that had served well the reactive politics of the 1960s and 1970s.

By the mid-1980s, there was an increasing discomfort among a number of feminist writers with the self-congratulatory and evangelical tone that had come to characterize radical writing in general. In particular they noted a number of gaps and silences in the very writing that purported to be advocating social justice and equity. In 1988, Madeleine Grumet devoted the introduction of her book *Bitter Milk: Women and Teaching* to the fact that "women constitute the majority of all public school instructional personnel; nevertheless, our experience of this work is hidden" (p. xi), not simply by the legacy of patriarchy, but—importantly—by radical critiques of "reproductive schooling." Grumet argued that the Marxist "collapse" of the schooling system into the economic system produced a profound silence about "experiences of family life, of bearing, delivering and nurturing children"—silence about "the language of the body, the world we carry on weight-bearing joints, the world we hear in sudden hums and giggles" (p. xv). For Grumet, issues of intimacy, of nurturance, of family—all such "women's" issues—seemed inevitably to "slide down under the discourse, weighted down by centuries of talk about education dominated by the history and preoccupation of male experience" (p. xix). Radical thought, in her view, left the *matter* of bodies—and thus what matters to women—completely unattended.

As Sherry Shapiro (1994) and others have since pointed out, silence about "the language of the body" is historically constituted out of Western epistemological traditions (radical or not) that understand human being through the binary formulation of "body *as distinct from* mind." Whether scholars blame Descartes or Rousseau for the prevalence of a mind/body dualisms in Western scholarship, the fact remains that, in the history of Western thought, a mind/body dichotomy has privileged the mind as that which defines human "being," while the body has been interrogated as the excess baggage of human agency.

It is not that the human body as a physical essence has been ignored. It has certainly been stressed in relation to the education and training of young people. The idea of "a healthy mind in a healthy body," of a necessary relation between physical well-being and cognitive performance, has been at the heart of childhood education, physical education programs, and popular physical culture, for over a century. However, the body's importance has been perceived, in the main, in terms of the necessity of its careful management in order to enhance, or to avoid distracting from, "mental effort." As Susan Stinson (1995, p. 45) notes, the secondary status accorded to "physicality" is certainly a theme in the shaping of young lives, whether it is through the notion of encouraging children to burn off excess energy before getting down to "serious work," to be still when studying, or to rein in adolescent sexual experimentation.

This standpoint about the human body in social institutions is an effect of understanding the body as a "fixed system of muscle, bone, nerves and organs," which transcends history and culture and thus is "amenable to scientific examination . . . a site of established fact" (Kirk, 1993, p. 3). Until relatively recently, such an understanding went unchallenged as biomedical and academic orthodoxy. For more than a decade, however, the theoretical project of recovering the importance of the body as a field of political and cultural activity did not reject the body as the biomedical *korper* out of hand, but distinguished it from the idea of the body as *leib,* or "lived body." And once *corporeality* or *embodiment* was understood as a generative principle (Leder, 1990, p. 5), the lived body became available as a subject of discourse as well as an object of external gaze.

Of all the theoretical issues this new work was to generate, the nature of the body/language relationship was a crucial one for critical theory in the 1990s. Tension remained for feminists and queer theorists around the notion of the body as a (purely) discursively constituted social and cultural product. Judith Butler (1993), for example, responded to the question, "Are bodies purely discursive?" by arguing that language cannot be opposed to materiality but neither can materiality be collapsed into an identity with language (p. 68). She noted that there is a kind of materiality that is associated with the body's physicality as well as its location (including social and political locatedness) and a materiality that characterizes language (p. 69). Drawing on the psychoanalytic work of Jacques Lacan and Julia Kristeva, she examined the relation between the materiality of bodies and that of language as a "morphological imaginary," with the body sustaining itself as a visual production only through submitting to language and to a marking by sexual difference (p. 72).

Elizabeth Grosz (1994) likewise looked to psychoanalysis as part of a theoretical terrain "somewhere between traditional philosophy and postmodern feminism" (p. xiv) on which she struggled to generate nonessentialist feminist approaches to the body. In *Volatile Bodies: Towards a Corporeal Feminism,* Grosz argued that psychoanalysis is useful inasmuch as it makes a radical presumption about the relation between forms of the body and forms of the mind or *psyche,* which allows exploration of "how the body functions . . . as a psychical, lived relation," with particular emphasis on the psyche "as a projection of the body's form" (p. 27). She listed six criteria for a *feminist* corporeality: avoiding mind/body dichotomies; avoiding the association of body with one sex or race such that they must bear the burden of corporeality; refusing singular or normative models of the body; rejecting any essentialist ontology of the body; including psychical representation of the subject's lived body; and lastly, problematizing binary pairs such as private/public, nature/culture, psychical/social, instinct/learning, genetic/environmentally determined (pp. 21–24).

As Colleen Keane (1994) noted in her review of *Volatile Bodies*, this sort of theorizing was a departure from the notion that bodies, in particular women's bodies, are mere passive ground upon which male conceptual transcendence is enacted (p. 16). Keane also saw this work as straining the problematic relations between what she called "academic or theoretical feminism" and "more socially oriented feminisms" (p. 16). Grosz had preempted this concern in her own acknowledgment of the "delicate negotiations" necessary for her to do the new theoretical work, indicating that she was aware of "alarming some feminists" because of "the perilous closeness" of her material to "those facets of patriarchal that have in the past served to oppress women" (Grosz, 1994, p. xiv).

Body, Desire, Pleasure

Whatever the ongoing tensions between feminists as "theorists" *or* "activists," the recovery of the body and the emergence of a psychoanalytic feminism was to draw attention to the absence of a discourse of *desire* from rational discourses (including critical theory), an absence that had had the effect of reducing the subject to "delibidimised actor" (Lash 1991, p. 260). Desire was to be restored to feminist discourse not only through applications of the psychoanalytic concept of *oedipality* (desire as a lack, barred or repressed from articulation) but also through the "anti-oedipal" work of Gilles Deleuze and Felix Guattari (1984), who posited desire as a material *presence,* a productive force. In re-membering the desiring body, by whatever theoretical means, new feminist theorizing of corporeality began to recover notions of pleasure, sexuality, and eroticism in ways that disturbed the more unified stance of feminists in the 1980s.

I am aware that this narrative about "feminism-recovers-the body" may be too easily read as a unified march away from modernist essentialist tyrannies toward poststructuralist diaspora. It is important therefore to reiterate that feminist attempts to ground knowledge in the body were not all of a piece in taking on board the above-mentioned theoretical turns, nor was it simply a case of taking our poststructuralisms neat. However, new conceptualizations of the body did provide critical theorists with a means to reflect on the way in which subjectivities and identities get produced out of the body's location in culture. Far from understanding the body as a fixed biological system and/or excluded from and dematerialized by Reason, a number of feminist scholars argued the value of reconceiving the body as a location of human capability, either as a surface of biological and sociosexual inscription (Liz Grosz), or as a crossroads for desire enacting the consumerite dream of production and consumption (Pasi Falk), or even as a site of technological transmutation for new communicative games (Donna Haraway and Zoe Soufoulis).

By the mid-1990s a number of feminist writers (e.g., Gamman & Marshment, 1994; Grant, 1993) were revisiting erotic possibilities for women by challenging the idea of an aesthetic erotic as *inevitably* pornographic, the property of men as the objects of male gaze (e.g., Dworkin 1981). They insisted that the task now for women was to find a way out of a feminist-inspired "sex-negative cul-de-sac... in which Eros was confined to the nether hells of rape, pornography, prostitution, incest and child abuse" (Grant, 1993, p. 9). Instead, such feminists began to speak of a heterosexuality that insisted on bodily pleasure while still acknowledging the symbolic power of penetration. No longer could it be assumed, according to Stevi Jackson, that all women who took pleasure in heterosexual sex were "simply wallowing in a masochistic eroticisation of their own subordination" (Jackson, 1995, p. 133).

It would now be possible for a new generation of feminist writers to explore both the means by which women can remain trapped by an aesthetic of appearance *and at the same time* explore the possibilities of a feminist aesthetic of embodied *pleasure*. In foregrounding pleasure, it would be possible to avoid the medical and naturalistic connotations inherent in the notion of desire-as-lack. This move expands possibilities for considering any range of pleasures, including those that might have been previously thought perverse or degraded. Foucault elaborates:

> Tell me what your desire is and I will tell you who you are, whether you are normal or not, and then I can qualify or disqualify your desire. [O]n the other hand, [pleasure] is... almost devoid of meaning. There is no pathology of pleasure; no abnormal pleasure. It is an event "outside of the subject," within something that is neither body nor soul, which is neither outside nor inside, in short a notion which is neither ascribed nor ascribable. (Foucault, cited in Macey, 1994, p. 363)

A key theme of feminist writing was—and still is—the extent to which the dominant culture fears and distorts women's desire. If pleasure, as Foucault argued, is less amenable to the recuperative and distorting effects of the dominant culture, then pleasure has, at least in theory, much to offer women as site/sight of knowledge (counter)production.

Grotesque Pleasures

In the mid-1990s, Camille Paglia expressed the view that Western feminism had come to mirror the general tendency in Western modes of thought to privilege tragedy over comedy, to follow the seductions of a call to seriousness rather than attribute any value to the obscene, the comic, or the burlesque. In *Sex and Violence, or Nature and Art* (1995), she argued:

> Modern criticism has projected a Victorian and, I feel, Protestant high seriousness upon pagan culture that still blankets teaching. . . . Paradoxically, assent to savage chthonian realities leads not to gloom but to humor. Hence Sade's strange laughter, his wit amid the most fantastic cruelties. For life is not a tragedy but a comedy. . . . Nature is always pulling the rug out from under our pompous ideals. (p. 9)

Paglia's insistence that "[e]very road from Rousseau leads to Sade" (p. 20) was risky indeed! It meant refusing the modernist logic of an enlightened movement of identity, insisting instead that "we go full circle" as libidinal beings (p. 20)—that intellectual control over identity and meaning is no more than a "comforting illusion" (p. 25). In evoking "Sade's strange laughter," Paglia called forth a murky and subversive tradition of pleasure-as-unreasonableness that cuts across the classical renderings of the body, the stuff of which modernist accounts are made.

Mary Russo's *The Female Grotesque* appeared in 1994 to occupy the space that was opening up for engagement in theoretical and applied work that was neither oppositional nor reactive. As Russo argues it, the feminist imperative was now to "a redeployment or counterproduction of culture, knowledge, and pleasure" (p. 62), one that allowed feminists to reconfigure the classical body politic as "an uncanny connection characteristic of the discourses of the grotesque" rather than "as the basis of a new universalism" (p. 14). Her feminist imagining of the space of a freakish pedagogy is one in which the material body is not the classical body of modernity, "transcendent and monumental, closed, static, self-contained, symmetrical and sleek" (p. 8), but the grotesque body of carnival—"open, protruding, irregular, secreting, multiple, and changing" (p. 8).

Grotesque bodies, according to Russo, are "only recognizable in relation to a norm," which they exceed in a way that makes for "serious risk" (p. 10). Russo acknowledges the importance of Foucault's *Discipline and Punish* (1979) in demonstrating the power of normalization as an instrument of modernity. The body of every modern citizen has been normalized—measured, catalogued, segmented, and examined—through disciplinary discourses. Such practices work to eliminate risk inasmuch as risk means the real possibility of mistake, error, failure. This is not simply failure to complete a particular task to an acceptable standard, but failure to produce oneself as a reasoning, reasonable being, and it is this possibility that makes risk-taking so serious in terms of the production of a social self.

Drawing on Foucault, Russo argues the importance of a discourse of risk for resisting the normalizing process:

> Unlike the models of progress, rationality and liberation which disassociate themselves from their "mistakes"—noise, dissonance or monstrosity—this "room for chance" emerges within the very constrained spaces of normalization. It is not, in other words, that limitless, incommensurable, and transcendent space associated with the Kantian sublime. (p. 12)

In privileging chance over certainty, discourses of risk protrude to unsettle and disorder, "telling flesh" (Kirby 1997)[1] as asymmetrical, comic, vulgar, and ugly. Russo re-members the historical figure of woman as hysteric, hag, witch, and whore—that is, as a body marked as deviant and thus subjected historically to pathological attention. She does so by reiterating Natalie Davis's argument that "disorderly women" have always "undermined as well as reinforced" power hierarchies and social order (p. 58).

The significance of grotesque female bodies, then, is their capacity to incite deviance and, at the same time, be the means for bringing it under control. For Russo, they function as *carnivalesque,* a disruptive materiality in the social world, one that is at the same time transformative and counterproductive, hovering as it does around the threshold of chaos and order. As was true of the space of the carnival, they connote a temporal and social space where genuflecting to hierarchies gives way to disguise and masquerade, parody and excess, where distinctions like performer and spectator are blurred, where new categories are generated and people take risks and live more dangerously.[2]

As embodiments of the carnivalesque, grotesque bodies have a "'degrading' significance" (Ferguson, 1990, p. 109), pitted as they are against enlightened aspirations to transcend the material world. They drag us down from spirituality and intellect into a Rabelaisian world of mockery, ribaldry, foolishness, and excess. The possibilities that the grotesque female body opens up for generating new social categories between and beyond performer and spectator are particularly important to enactments of feminism because they allow women to imagine new pleasures in performing the feminine and in female spectatorship, while at the same time drawing attention to the fact that the meaning and performance of the pleasure of gender and sexuality can and will continue to change (Fradenburg & Freccero, 1996: viii).

To consider more closely the nature of the work that such bodies can do, one must inevitably grapple with the apparently oxymoronic idea of an *aesthetic* of the grotesque. Antonio Strati's *Organization and Aesthetics* (1999) is helpful here. She names the categories "ugly" and "comic" as a discordant duo among eight mobilizing social categories within a modernist order of organizational life. For Strati, the comic and ugly are similar categories in that both have "a desecratory thrust" (p.187), but can be differentiated inasmuch as the comic does not bring with it the negative connotations for organizational life that the ugly has for the desanctification process. Comic encompasses "the grotesque in organizational life: the irony that it provokes, the laughter that penalises it, the sarcasm that dismisses it, the sense of humour that attaches labels to it" (p. 187). The ugly, on the other hand, is not deliberately chosen in organizational life, having an "active, dangerous and aggressive" character in that it foregrounds "whatever is shocking, monstrous, dull, impure, horrid, eccentric, disgusting, lascivious and repugnant" (p. 186).

Anything Goes?

What enables also constrains. As carnivalesque, the grotesque female body opens up possible spaces of resistance but in doing so it must, by definition, close down possibilities for an essential politics of political emancipation. As carnival, it cannot, by definition, offer itself as an *alternative* to officialdom and orthodoxy. It cannot be finally outside orthodoxy, just as pleasure is never finally outside reason. Carnival in the feudal order of things was a temporal space in which it became possible to indulge the appetites and at the same time parody the practices of officialdom. It was not an alternative to officialdom. Individuals were not freed from orthodoxy by carnival; they were simply permitted to indulge themselves, to experience that "unrestrained sensuousness" (Strati, 1999, p. 109) that in all other times and places is *verboten*. No final moment of liberation is intended or likely. There is merely a time and space of perverse pleasure. In its substitution of fart for faith, the grotesque body does not ask "whose faith?" Feminism is as vulnerable as Father in the space and time of the female grotesque.

The idea of a grotesque that is temporally and spatially "contained" by carnival also belies the productive power of the grotesque to be harnessed to other potentially more sinister modes of desanctification. Paul Jay's (1994) reading of Cindy Sherman's photographic work is illustrative of this point. To Jay, the "steady demise towards the grotesque" (p. 198) evident in Sherman's self-portraits is complicit with "the slide toward dispersal and obliteration" (p. 198) in her self-depiction as "literally exploded," a series of body parts strewn across a landscape. Here the freakish gives way to the macabre in a "double gesture of renunciation" of both an authentic and an objectified self. Self becomes a semiotic maze, an assemblage, a cultural death. As a "spectre of the death of the subject" (p. 195), her work must renounce any "authentic" identity. Any concept of a sexed and gendered self is rendered illusory. All is simulacrum. The individual "explodes . . . amidst a pile of rubble" (p. 197), and with it any prospect of personhood as a more authentic existence.

So what women make of the grotesque body is dangerous, given what it can make of women. As a space of feminist possibility, it can "unmask" much that is oppressive and objectifying for women. In combination with the monstrous and macabre, it can "unmake" any identity politics, including the very feminist work that insisted on bringing it forward for scrutiny. As Victor Turner (cited in Russo, 1994) puts it:

> The danger here is not simply that of female "unruliness." This unruliness itself is the mark of the ultraliminal, of the perilous realm of possibility that "anything *may* go" which threatens any social order and seems the more threatening the more that order seems rigorous and secure. (p. 197)

Teasing and leering, fascinating and repulsive, the female grotesque draws us to the edge of identity and the collapse of meaning—to a place that, as feminists, we would not go.

Notes

1. *Telling Flesh* is the title of Vicki Kirby's (1997) interrogation of critical theoretical developments in the study of corporeality.
2. It is useful to be reminded here that carnival was more historically than a fleeting moment involving a few individuals. As Harvie Ferguson (1990) describes it, carnival in early modern Europe could occupy up to a quarter of the calendar year, and involved not just the downtrodden but the privileged (p. 109). The "ceremonials, feasts, theatrical shows and public spectacles" that marked it included more than one "feast of fools," and similar "grotesque degradations of various church rituals and symbols" (p. 109). Moreover, it was strongly sanctioned by the very officials and hierarchies it parodied.

CRITICAL THEORY AND BRITISH CULTURAL STUDIES

Introduction

This chapter considers the relationship between the Critical Theory of the Frankfurt School and British Cultural Studies (BCS) in the light of two recent arguments about cross-cultural influence. The first is that of Pierre Bourdieu, who suggests that, out of their domestic context, translations of leading theory may not properly reflect their original meanings or make sense within the host culture. The second is that of Douglas Kellner, who makes an interesting, though ultimately flawed, case for the missed articulation of Frankfurt Critical Theory and British Cultural Studies. I conclude by trying to sketch in a prehistory of BCS that locates its genealogy within two conflicting traditions. The first is the high cultural literary critique that originated in the public sphere opened up by the Scottish Enlightenment but, drawing increasingly on German Romantic skepticism, became select and withdrawn. Second, the tradition of plebeian activism that originated with the pamphleteering and political program of the Levellers and through various reformers and agitators such as Wilkes, Spence, and Cobbett led to the political institutions of cooperation and labor. I want to suggest that critical theory (lowercase) has always informed BCS but that with the postmodern turn the activist, reforming element has become subordinated to a debilitating academic quietism.

In his contribution to a recent critical reader of his work, Pierre Bourdieu suggested that we need a scientific knowledge of national fields of production in order to illuminate the "national cultural unconscious" (Bourdieu, 1999, p. 226). Bourdieu offered this suggestion in the context of a discussion of the way bodies of thought and argument were taken from one national context and used within another. He felt that ripped from the context in which these bodies were formed it was possible for substantial misreadings to be made and fictitious oppositions to be constructed between writers who in many respects agreed. He illustrated this argument with the way that Habermas and Foucault had been juxtaposed in academic debate. Rather than see the positions adopted by these deeply influential figures as absolutely opposed, Bourdieu makes that case that you could see grounds for reconciliation. Thus, he suggests Foucault's use of Nietzsche's genealogical method was a critical response to the Sartrian subjective, spiritual existentialism then dominant in postwar French intellectual culture. In this sense Foucault could be interpreted as rehabilitating a kind of Durkheimian positivism or even, to use Bourdieu's preferred term, "scientism." Whereas Habermas, who regarded any use of Nietzsche and Heidegger as courting a dangerous irrationalism in the German context, missed its rationalist potentiality in the French.

Whatever the merits of this particular suggestion, the national cultural context for adopting a body of thought generated in a different national context should be thoroughly explored. The emergence and influence of British cultural studies is a case in point. I've tried at length to reconstruct the British adult educational context in which the seminal texts of the earliest phase of British cultural studies were produced (Steele, 1997), and Dworkin has made a fine analysis of the Marxist intellectual and political scene of the same period (Dworkin, 1997). From these and other studies it is possible to see the particularity of this intellectual endeavor and why it happened "here and nowhere else."

What such studies reveal is a "national" culture thoroughly porous to some external bodies of thought while wholly resistant to others *at specific times*. It may be argued, for example, that modern British culture has consistently borrowed from and added to both French and German intellectual cultures since the end of the eighteenth century. As a case in point, take the way scientific and positivist thought has shuttled across the channel between Britain and France and has been received back in a variety of guises—from Bacon, Hobbes, and Locke to the French Enlightenment philosophes and from the Scottish Enlightenment philosophers Smith, Ferguson, and Hutchinson to Saint-Simon and Comte. The return track of Comteian positivism through John Stuart Mill and Bentham gave rise to Utilitarian thought, which subsequently became the dominant strand in British Fabianism. At the same time the skeptical anti-Enlightenment thought of Herder and Goethe in Germany galvanized Coleridge and Carlyle into generating the conservative oppositional tendency that informed the dominant strand of English cultural criticism. Significantly, it was this broad critical strand, which also included Arnold, Ruskin, and Morris, that Raymond Williams in *Culture and Society,* a founding text of British cultural studies, then began to interpellate as the Romantic critique of capitalism.

In his seminal critique of British culture, "Components of the National Culture," Perry Anderson (of Irish patrician descent) denied outright any intellectual weight to indigenous British intellectual life. Implicitly, he relegated the achievement of two of the founders of *New Left Review,* Raymond Williams and Edward

Thompson, to the intellectual backwaters of European thought (Anderson, 1968). Arguing that there was an absent center to British culture, in which the mediocre attempts to see the culture whole were left to the conservative literary criticism that had mutated by way of T. S. Eliot and F. R. Leavis from the Romantic critique, Anderson demanded instead a totalizing Marxist sociology on European lines.

Both the idea of "Europe" and European thought had already illuminated the postwar British left keen to throw off the burden of colonialism with one hand and fend off American populism with the other. Williams and Thompson were among the many who had welcomed the channels of European Marxism, existentialism, and structuralism being opened up. But intellectually, the Britain Anderson described was a wasteland, indeed Eliot's "Wasteland," in which the Fisher King of social regeneration was being allowed to die of his wounds. The cure was Faustian enough. Anderson proposed a major program of translations of European Marxism and allied structuralist thought through the journal he now edited, and largely financed, *New Left Review* and its press, New Left Books (NLB).

In the following decade the resulting change in the intellectual atmosphere in Britain was truly electrifying; but it was a revolution that lacked its soviets. The extraordinary list of titles that flowed from New Left Books and then Verso changed the reading habits of an entire generation of younger left intellectuals and induced an intellectually docile British academic publishing industry to rise to the new demand for European thought. Marxism, so long the burden of a very orthodox Communist Party of Great Britain, over the course of a generation became for the first time in Britain a vital intellectual force (Dworkin, 1997, p. 136). Other publishing houses followed suit and a plethora of radical journals began to appear. It was, however, a largely academic revolution that failed to connect with the broader movement of organized labor or create any resonance among the working class itself.

Was this a case of bodies of thought lost in translation, or alternatively, that Anderson's view of the national culture failed to recognize signs of domestic intellectual vitality not immediately visible from the windows of London W1? Thompson's *Making of the English Working Class,* for example, was hardly a sign of intellectual inertia and spoke directly to a body of younger activists, whom it released from thraldom to the economic determinacy of Soviet Marxist thought and the positivism of conventional economic history. It significantly boosted the development of British *social* history as a field of study and spawned the History Workshop movement. Inspired by the "left Leavisism" of L. C. Knights and others in the *Scrutiny* group, books like Williams's *Culture and Society* and Hoggart's *The Uses of Literacy* were also focusing literary criticism on the study of social context and the popular media. In the social sciences, John Rex and others were attempting to develop Mannheim's vision of a "science of society," ethnicity, and race. Much of this unacknowledged intellectual effort was absorbed into the early BCS movement, where it acted as a catalyst for the study of popular culture and attempted to maintain a reciprocal contact with working-class politics.

British Cultural Studies and the Frankfurt School

Recently Douglas Kellner has suggested that, despite the heroic program of translations initiated by Anderson and NLB, BCS might have missed an important conjunctural meeting with the Frankfurt School (FS) (Kellner, nd). This, he argues, might have enabled BCS to avoid the charge of cultural populism alleged by Jim McGuigan and suggested important connections with oppositional forms associated with the avant-garde (McGuigan, 1992). Kellner suggests that BCS should return to its older interest in the political economy of culture with its stress on production and consumption.

Kellner argues convincingly that BCS and the Frankfurt School share a great deal in common. Frankfurt indeed initiated an early form of cultural studies in the interwar period with its studies of mass communication. It investigated the "cultural industries" in a political context as a form of working-class integration into capitalist consumer society by means of mass manipulation. Such a viewpoint was indeed not far removed in tone from the critiques of mass communications by the Leavises and those of Richard Hoggart. For the Frankfurt School, mass consumer society depended on the manipulation of taste by the culture industries, rendering both working-class politics and the Germanic sense of deep *Kultur* inoperative. While BCS was always highly political in orientation (although never simply Marxist), with the exception of Williams, it rarely engaged with modernist and avant-garde movements and remained, at base, populist in approach. But also, more significant, except for some historians, it did not engage with Marxist political economy in the sophisticated Frankfurt manner.

However, it should be emphasised that BCS itself became multifaceted as it expanded from its base in Birmingham into the polytechnics and universities. Indeed, in many of the other sites of BCS, high theory of the Frankfurt kind had a significant profile, particularly where there was an orientation toward feminist theory. In the Leeds Centre for Cultural Studies, where I (and Jim McGuigan) taught for a while during the 1990s, for example, there was always an engagement with avant-garde art, film, and postcolonial theory, through the work of Adorno and Benjamin especially. It may be argued, however, that these facets of BCS never connected enough to become a "school" in the Frankfurt sense and certainly no connection was made with traditional labor organizations. Neither, however, was political economy entirely neglected, although it frequently took a back seat to theory and semiotics.

Interdisciplinary study and boundary transgressing are also common to BCS and the Frankfurt School (although it could be argued that Cultural Studies is in danger of becoming a new discipline itself). But for Kellner cultural studies no longer maintains the critical edge that characterized its formative stage, largely because of the postmodern turn it has taken. Thus, against Stuart Hall's celebration of postmodern pluralization, Kellner maintains that Frankfurt would characterize this as merely a cultural concomitant of the expansion of global capitalism:

For Hall therefore, the global postmodern involves pluralizing of culture, opening to the margins, to difference, to voices excluded from the narratives of Western culture. But one could argue in opposition to this interpretation in the spirit of the Frankfurt School that the global postmodern simply represents an expansion of global capitalism on the terrain of new media and technologies, and that the explosion of information and entertainment in media culture represents powerful new sources of capital realization and social control. (Kellner, nd, p. 7)

This squares with Bourdieu's case that the pluralization of culture, like the international circulation of ideas, always depends on interests at once political, academic, and commercial. Cultural analysts of a more sociological frame of mind will be concerned with how publishing and marketing decisions are taken, who are the gatekeepers, and what filters are placed on both the production and reception of culture and ideas. It is not that BCS is wholly unconcerned with all this but that other analytical interests predominate. Increasingly, as cultural studies has found a more secure seat in the academy and professorial chairs multiply, this globalization or international circulation of ideas has become an important source of symbolic capital. As Bourdieu notes, introducing and editing a collection of translated papers by a respected foreign philosopher in a publication by an influential publishing house attracts academic kudos. You don't need to read a David Lodge campus novel to appreciate just how important the international conference circuit is to the academic prospects of a rising star.

Kellner, in my view rightly, insists that Frankfurt School perspectives on the commodification of culture would indeed add critical edge to what in much postmodern discussion appears to be a lazy pluralism. Although Hall, whose work is distinguished by its principled political stance, can never be implicated in this, much fashionable talk does not distinguish between a proper tolerance of cultural difference and an uncomplaining acceptance of injustice, exploitation, and inequality, particularly as it affects women. The inverse point, though, is how to separate a necessary critical stance toward a rapaciously exploitative commodity system that has now successfully globalized itself, from an intellectual and cultural intolerance of different ways of life.

Would the articulation between BCS and FS advocated by Kellner have made a difference or would it too have suffered from the mistranslation Bourdieu notes affecting bodies of ideas removed from their national context? It is worth looking at the directions taken by BCS before the mass program of translations took effect.

Prehistories of BCS

As I have argued elsewhere, the emergence of BCS cannot be separated from the political and educational intentions of its early protagonists, many of whom were engaged in adult education rather than mainstream university teaching (Steele, 1997). Williams quite unequivocally located the initial project of cultural studies in the broader world of adult education in the immediate post–Second World War period, when he, E. P. Thompson, Richard Hoggart and many others found in adult education a radical political vocation. It was, for him, a renewal of that attempt at "a majority democratic education" that had been present in the early days of English literary studies and then in Leavisism but that had got sidetracked into minority and elitist attitudes. Williams's own short-lived journal, *Politics and Letters,* and a companion volume called *The Critic,* were an attempt to engage politically with that world that Williams increasingly saw as the "decisive" world for his political work:

> Virtually every WEA tutor was a Socialist of one colour or another. We were all doing adult education ourselves. So we saw the journals as linked to this very hopeful formation with a national network of connection to the working-class movement. If there was a group to which *Politics and Letters* referred, it was the adult education tutors and their students. (Williams, 1979, p. 69)

Adult education was the primary vehicle for developing what was not then called Cultural Studies, which then was not separate from this broader political task of socialist renewal in Britain. The practice of interdisciplinary work was already well developed within British adult education. This was identified with a complex of related features such as dialogic democratic practice, mature and experienced students, political commitment and class-consciousness, links with the organized labor movement, the ethic of "social purpose," resistance to academic compartmentalizing of knowledge, and other noninstitutional aspects. Crucially, it took education to be student-based rather than discipline-orientated, starting with the problems a group of socially aware and politically committed adults might want to study in their own time.

The problem was, as Thompson put it, that the academic world was so saturated with class responses that the intelligent working-class adult who went in search of enlightenment might come away only with perplexity and deracination.

> For a century and more, most middle class educationalists could not distinguish the work of education from that of social control: and this entailed too often, a repression of or a denial of the validity of the life experience of their pupils as expressed in uncouth dialect or in traditional cultural forms. Hence education and received experience were at odds with each other. And those working men who by their own efforts broke into the educated culture found themselves at once in the same place of tension, in which education brought with it the danger of the rejection of their fellows and self-distrust. The tension of course continues still. (Thompson, 1968, p. 16)

One source of tension was that the division of knowledge into discrete disciplines often concealed the very connections to their lives that adults wished to make. Another was that university lecturers without connection to the labor movement assumed that adult education was a "deficit" education, that they had nothing to learn from working people. There was inevitable conflict between academics and self-educated workers. The fiercest debates in fact took place during the 1930s over the role and status of the "literary" and the "sociological" in adult liberal studies, when often it was the student groups themselves that insisted on relevance and cross disciplinarity. Further, the study of "popular culture" in adult classes dates from the early 1930s, in particular the studies of the *Scrutiny* group of mass communication and George Orwell's journalism. Workers also believed that they had much to learn from "culture," but they were travelers in a strange country.

Thus while one form of class struggle raged over interdisciplinarity, the increasing importance of a totalizing and theorized sociology dates from the activity of Karl Mannheim, Karl Polanyi, and other European émigrés who were involved in adult education from the late 1930s. Mannheim, in particular, insisted that sociology should get away from its dry LSE empiricism to become a true "Science of Society." His concern for what was then called the sociology of consciousness fed into the work of socialist and communist historians in the creation of a social history freed from mechanical determinisms. This kind of social history, of which the Communist Party Historians Group and the work of R. H. Tawney and G.D.H. Cole were of central importance, was more open to "cultural" effects. Adult education was supported by cheap popular editions and pamphlets published by the WEA and Plebs League, Dent's "Everyman Library," and Allan Lane's press, Penguin Books. Later, Lane himself alertly responded to Richard Hoggart's appeal to fund the Birmingham Centre for Contemporary Cultural Studies in 1965 and published the classical texts of BCS.

The Communist Party too, in the wake of 1930s popular frontism, postwar reconstruction, and subsequently the Chinese Revolution in 1948 began to rethink its political strategy in terms of a cultural struggle. Its decision to foreground the *British* Road to Socialism was supported by a number of conferences on what was distinct in the "national culture" to which a number of left intellectuals contributed, including E. P. Thompson and George Thomson, the classical scholar. (It was significant that three decades later the most ambitious attempt to bring the insights of cultural studies into a post-New-Left politics was also led by a Communist journal, *Marxism Today*.)

From this innovative pedagogic climate there came a preoccupation with the term "culture," which ultimately led to the foundation of the Birmingham Centre for Contemporary Cultural Studies and subsequently the widespread flowering of cultural studies within polytechnics and Open University. The strategic relevance of the work of Hoggart, Thompson, Williams, and their colleagues in adult education in Oxford, Leeds, and elsewhere to the formation of the New Left was organically related to their educational project. There was then in the opening flourish of BCS a determined connection with a wider politics of postwar democratic renewal by practitioners who were not for the most part engaged in mainstream university departments. Adult education was often the only arena for developing this way of thinking.

Marxism and Revisionism

British intellectual culture was not entirely insular. Anderson notes the émigré intellectuals, often refugees from Nazism, who made significant impact in a variety of disciplines such as Namier in history, Gombrich in art history, Popper in sociology, and Wittgenstein in philosophy (Anderson, 1968). But he argues that intellectually important as these contributions were they also served to contest "Marxist" approaches in the humanities and social sciences. Marxism itself, that other "foreign" intellectual tradition, had anyway made little headway in the universities and was very much a minority pursuit of intellectuals clustered around the CPGB and even smaller Trotskyist factions. Despite the overwhelming orthodoxy of British Marxist writing, occasional heretics like Christopher Caudwell did suggest a critical vitality in Marxism. His *Illusion and Reality* (1937) was important both to Williams and Thompson and many others working in adult education who wanted to transcend the unfruitful "base and superstructure" dichotomy. Moreover, in the Communist Party Historians group a new wave of Marxist historical writing was maturing in the works of Donna Torr, A. L. Morton, Christopher Hill, Eric Hobsbawm, and Rodney Hilton. Without this background it is difficult to imagine Thompson completing *The Making of the English Working Class* or Williams writing *The Long Revolution*.

It was, however, the pronounced émigré presence that opened up Britain to European thought. For example, the Routledge series of International Library of Philosophy and Scientific Method, edited by Karl Mannheim, introduced a wide range of European writers on philosophy and social science. Mannheim's own book on the Sociology of Culture (Mannheim, 1956) may also have lain claim to be among the founding texts of BCS, but was, curiously, largely neglected. Although Mannheim had been a member of Lukacs's cultural circle meetings in Budapest and was working in the University at Frankfurt at the same time as Horkheimer and Adorno, he was never closely identified with Critical Theory or the Frankfurt School. He was more closely associated with Lukacs, from whose *History and Class Consciousness* he derived his own sociology of knowledge (Watnick, 1962, p. 154). His *Ideology and Utopia* (1949) was very influential, and he adapted the English edition for the climate he found in Britain. Mannheim was also responsible for the publication of Arnold Hauser's classic *Social History of Art* (1951), which was also written by Hauser as a recent émigré in Britain (although he was not employed in a university until it had been completed). Hauser's book virtually established in Britain the academic study of the Social History of Art. Mannheim became involved with a semisecret Christian Socialist group attached to A. D. Lindsay, Master of Balliol, which advanced a kind of Third Way politics during the opening of the Cold War. This arguably made the shift toward a cultural politics in Britain more possible or, as Williams put it, "politics by other means."

Mannheim's views on the commitment and autonomy of the intellectual, the need for a "science of society," and the centrality of culture in creating social consciousness were of inestimable importance in shaping the debates to come.

Similarly, Karl Polanyi's insistence on realigning the academic curriculum to reflect the needs of the political working class and supersede "bourgeois" divisions of knowledge was extremely suggestive of new subjects of knowledge. Polanyi's still widely influential *The Great Transformation* (1944) was developed in the course of his lectures for the WEA and the Oxford Extramural Delegacy.

The Soviet invasion of Hungary in 1956 and Khrushchev's official recognition of the crimes of the Stalinist period led to mass desertion from the CPGB and increased critical distance from orthodox Marxism. In this climate other "revisionist" influences took root in the 1960s, especially those of Sartre, Lukacs, Goldman, and Gramsci. Subsequently, the translation of Marx's *Grundrisse* and a program of translations of Marx and Engels by Lawrence and Wishart and Penguin opened up the possibilities of materialist cultural analysis as never before. Raymond Williams noted that:

> It was in this situation that I felt the excitement of contact with more new Marxist work: the later work of Lukacs, the later work of Sartre, the developing work of Goldmann and of Althusser, the variable and developing syntheses of Marxism and some forms of structuralism. (Williams, 1977, p. 4)

As Dworkin notes, Williams discovered his own intellectual homologies with continental thought, finding affinities in Goldman's "genetic structuralism" with his own "structures of feeling" (Dworkin, 1997, p. 150). Lukacs's *History and Class-Consciousness,* translated and published in 1971 by Merlin Press, was similarly read as a "humanist" text in line with the socialist humanism of Williams and Thompson.

Also published in 1971, another widely influential translation of European Marxism was *Selections from the "Prison Notebooks"* by Antonio Gramsci, which also valued human agency in the political struggle while suggesting that more structural forces were at work in the way that agency was channelled. Significantly, Gramsci's work was translated and introduced largely through the press most linked to the CPGB, Lawrence and Wishart. (I remember buying my copy of the *Modern Prince* from the bookstall in the Communist Party offices in Leeds in 1969 because it was the only place in town you could get it.) Selections from his political and cultural writings followed after longish periods. His theory of hegemony was widely interpreted as demonstrating that the working classes actually consented to their subordination by taking on board many of the dominant ideas of the middle class. The idea that the cultural domination of the middle class can be resisted in various subcultural or countercultural ways has penetrated deeply into cultural study in Britain.

Gramsci's discussion of the role of intellectuals suddenly made space to see education as a fundamental part of the struggle. His distinction between organic and traditional intellectuals and his insistence on seeing all kinds of work as having an intellectual content and not just that of the class of intellectuals gave new impetus to those working in adult education. More problematic, however, was the role of the "collective intellectual," which Gramsci had envisaged as the revolutionary party. In Britain, the discredited and already fragmenting CPGB was clearly not in the running, while the fissiparous Troskyist "groupuscules" were little more than student and youth organizations that, unlike the CPGB, had no base in the organized working class.

Structuralism and After

For a younger, more impatient generation, the translation of Althusser's work appeared to give British cultural studies the "scientific" and structural base it needed to establish a secure intellectual foundation. His attack on the socialist humanism that had been the political ideology from which BCS had sprung, although routed intellectually by Thompson's conservative defense of history in his *Poverty of Theory* (1978), took root among a younger generation of scholars. Something about the arcane, almost theological tone of his writing, the elevation of "Theory" to mystical status, and the Olympian tone of his pronouncements suddenly equipped the militant postgrad in the humanities with a very powerful instrument of polemic.

Hall and his colleagues at BCCCS (Birmingham Centre for Contemporary Cultural Studies) struggled bravely to see how they could use Althusser by, for example, applying his "ideological state apparatuses" to Gramsci's concept of hegemony, but as Hall subsequently confessed:

> I remember wrestling with Althusser. I remember looking at his idea of "theoretical practice" in *Reading Capital* and thinking, "I've gone as far in this as it is proper to go." I felt I will not give an inch to this profound misreading, this super-structuralist mistranslation, of classical marxism, unless he beats me down, unless he defeats me in spirit. (Hall, 1996, p. 266)

What became increasingly clear was that the resurgence of Marxist and structuralist cultural analysis was indeed altering the intellectual landscape of academia while appealing to a radical generation of younger scholars. However, this same generation had less and less to say to the members of the organized working class. Unlike the generation of the old New Left, for whom workers' education was central, many among the younger generation were openly hostile to what they saw as the labor movement's endemic racism and sexism.

One area where Althusserianism did make progress was among a section of women intellectuals for whom Althusser, and by extension Lacan, did offer a way of thinking about the specificity of women's subordination. Juliet Mitchell, for example, in a seminal rejoinder to *New Left Review* in 1966, "Women: the Longest Revolution," had already criticized the way traditional (male) narratives of power always subordinated the family to industrialism and were never analyzed structurally (Swindells & Jardine, 1990, p. 71). Indeed, the origins of Women's Studies can be dated from the growth at this time of women's liberation through consciousness-raising groups and militant activity.

Within the BCCCS the Women's Studies Group took over the eleventh issue of the *Working Papers* to take issue with sexist practices at the Centre, subsequently published as *Women Take Issue*. Dworkin argues that feminism's impact on the center was significant in that it "called into question its exclusively 'public' and 'class' conception of power, and problematized its way of conceiving subjectivity and subject position" (Dworkin, 1997, p. 177). Feminism subsequently radically altered the profile of BCS, which could never again innocently ignore gendering and patriarchy.

This historical detour into BCS has tried to demonstrate that although it clearly has a distinctively British identity, it has grown in the context of a high level of contact and engagement with European thought. Was there, as Kellner argues, a missed articulation with the Frankfurt School or was it that the sheer complexity of external influence and contact over the last half century has meant that no single body of thought could dominate any other? Can we say that Critical Theory has been neglected, that it has not been a presence in BCS? In an interesting consideration of Hall's "Cultural Studies and the Centre" (1980), Steve Baron argues that critical theory (lowercase) had always been a part of the BCS. This was largely through the centrality it placed on the concept of ideology, which he believed was "essential for any social science to aspiring to be critical" (Baron, 1985, p. 84). BCCCS, particularly, treated "the immediate concepts of common sense with systematic doubt" (Baron, 1985, p. 84). Critical theory, if not Critical Theory, then, has been implicit in BCS.

The Cultural Specificity of BCS

Beyond the immediate intellectual context of the formation of BCS lies a distinct national history of cultural struggle and tradition. As Williams notes, the notion of a tradition always implies a selection from what is historically available as sources of identity and inspiration. In Britain it is possible to discern at least two historical strands that have contributed to the specific conjuncture inhabited by the early BCS. Williams himself identified, even one might say interpellated, the Romantic critique of capitalism inscribed in the poets, novelists, and essayists of the nineteenth century. Likewise Thompson, Hobsbawm, Hill, and other historians have described a tradition of plebeian resistance and revolt that preceded working-class formation and reached back to the Diggers and Levellers of the Commonwealth period.

In a recent highly suggestive doctoral thesis, Benchimol has utilized Habermas's theory of the bourgeois public sphere to identify at least two contrasting spheres of cultural activity. These are themselves located in social class: the elite bourgeois spheres of the Whig Scottish Enlightenment and its journal the *Edinburgh Review,* and the tradition of political activism from the Levellers through Wilkes, Paine, and Spence to Wooller's *Black Dwarf* and Cobbett's political journalism (Benchimol, 2001). Both traditions were acutely critical of the rapacious entrepreneurialism of the emergent capitalist economy that cared neither for Art nor for the welfare of its servants, but they adopted opposing stances toward it.

Benchimol contrasts the liberal bourgeois sphere created during the Scottish Enlightenment in the mid- to late eighteenth century that was centered in Edinburgh, with the artisan and laboring "plebeian" sphere of radical polemic and social action that developed in London and the northern industrializing cities in the late eighteenth and early nineteenth centuries. The main contention of the thesis is that while the bourgeois sphere aestheticized culture and accommodated itself to mass industrialism and commercialism by retreating into literary forms, the plebeian sphere aimed at transforming the power relations by social action. Using Williams's methodology of emergent, residual, and dominant cultures, Benchimol suggests that while the bourgeois public sphere sought an elite ethical and intellectual separation from the economy (which was allowed to remain laissez faire), the plebeian sphere initiated a "popular" rallying court of appeal pursuing radical alternatives. The dynamism of the original Edinburgh public becomes transformed into a quietistic receptive journalistic culture later and in London. Unlike the plebeian public sphere, the bourgeois sphere becomes characterized by a literary elite of writers like Carlyle, while the public is forced to take on an essentially interpretative role. The activism of the plebeian sphere, on the other hand, becomes inscribed in a theorized political practice that ultimately becomes "socialism," a term invented by Robert Owen. This political practice is further refined by the emergent industrial working class into trade unionism and cooperation, ultimately bringing into being the party of Labour itself.

Benchimol discusses the formative discourses of the major publications and their effect in establishing identities and dominant meanings within the sphere. He also documents the shifts in emphasis, for example, from heroic first principles to "commonsense" philosophy in the Scottish context and the relocation of this style to Whig circles in London. By contrast, he attempts to display continuity in the Radical Cultural Tradition he identifies from the Levellers in the seventeenth century to Cobbett's *Rural Rides* and beyond which gravitates from spontaneous acts of revolt to radical programs of reform.

Here we can see two public spheres opening up at roughly the same time but characterized by two contrasting class compositions and styles. While the Scottish Whig sphere is informed by measured debates from first principles conducted by professional men through their journals and clubs, the plebeian sphere is altogether different. This is often characterized by a rowdy activism conducted through pamphleteering and agitation in public houses and coffeehouses developing a discourse of rights and liberties. However, another distinct formation within this public sphere is that of the intellectual earnestness and moral purpose of the Corresponding and Constitutional Societies of artisans. Although this group never eschews activism, it focuses on the serious business of collective self-education in "really useful knowledge" to inform its political campaigns of national rights and social justice, taking as its canonical text Paine's *Rights of Man*.

This activist element was in my view an important feature of the project of BCS, which as we have seen identified itself with social regeneration through cultural activity. While Williams saw in this tradition a "whole way of life," culturally distinct from that of the British middle class, in his review of *The Long Revolution,* Thompson critically reminded Williams that this was not so much a way of *life* as a way of *struggle,* which only served to increase its identity with working-class activism.

However, the strand of Whig cultural criticism that begins with the *Edinburgh Review* also informs BCS and to an extent stands in a complex relation to that other. From its dynamic origins in Edinburgh, this tradition becomes increasingly an elite practice conducted through prestigious reviews with the public now engaged only in a secondary way. Through the critical activity of Coleridge and Carlyle, especially, it informs the new practice of literary criticism with a Germanic sense of *kultur,* or the deeply rooted needs of men for "organic" ways of life and belief, radically in opposition to those offered by industrial "civilization" and "mechanism." Although this is in Williams's terms a conservative residual formation, it contributes a powerful discourse of opposition to laissez-faire capitalist economy that guild socialists like Morris and the Christian Socialist tradition would utilize to imagine a different way of life. At the other extreme, however, it generated a catastrophist religious ideology of withdrawal as imaged in Eliot's *Waste Land* that could turn into haughty dismissal of popular democratic activism.

A history of British cultural thought and institutions would therefore reveal among other relationships a complex interaction and disruption of the two distinct European traditions identified by Bourdieu, the Germanic deep regard for *kultur* and the French post-Enlightenment sense of "civilization." I think both of these can be found with varying emphases within BCS.

Raymond Williams and Cultural Materialism

Another way of coming at the national specificity of British cultural studies is through the historical etymological approach of Raymond Williams, which analyzes the changing meanings of key English words associated with discourses of society. The strength of this approach is that the meanings of words in social usage are located historically and can be seen to change within major shifts in the economy and society. Three words that Williams returns to constantly are "society," "economy," and "culture." He notes that the meanings of all three words altered substantially over the last two centuries. "Culture," for example, meant something similar to "civilization" in the early nineteenth century, but by the end of the century had become an opposed term. While "civilization" now came to signify a settled achieved state, as opposed to "barbarism," culture increasingly signified the deeper sphere of religion, myth, and tradition. Similarly, both "society" and "economy" move from domestic and local signification toward denoting larger more complex groupings associated with national and even international formations. This patient historicism and scientistic side of Williams's work offers affinities with

Bourdieu, which Williams himself recognized latterly. He sees language as a materialist production where meanings are not fixed for all time but change according to usage within limits and possibilities of actual productive activity, a view not dissimilar to Habermas's communicative action theory.

Williams is at once the foremost British cultural theorist, yet curiously the most neglected. Famously relegated to the historical sidelines by Anderson and attacked by Eagleton during the 1980s for his attachment to a socialist humanism (later recanted), Williams nevertheless persisted with a series of works like *The Country and the City* (1973), *Television, Technology and Cultural Form* (1974), and *Problems in Materialism and Culture* (1980) to work across the boundaries of literary criticism, history, sociology, and political economy. His reconciliation with Marxism in the 1970s produced his only sustained theoretical text, *Marxism and Literature* (1977). The strand of BCS associated with this work became known as Cultural Materialism because of its insistence on a grounded analysis of culture in sociology, history, and political economy.

Although Williams's work lacked the glamour associated with the latest translations of the Parisian West Bank, it has been influential in, for example, Edward Said's postcolonial theory and in Schools of English in Britain and North America. As Williams makes clear in *Marxism and Literature,* his own socialist humanism learned from structuralist approaches but was never shaken by them. Hence his attachment to Lucien Goldman's "genetic structuralism," which attempts to embed social structures in historical change rather than estrange them from change. Williams developed the categories of "emergent," "residual," and "dominant" cultures to describe this historical flux, adding to them the categories of "oppositional" and "alternative." In subsequent books his analysis of the Godwin Circle, the Pre-Raphaelites, and the Bloomsbury Group show clearly how specific intellectual and cultural production can be located historically.

Williams, it seems to me, also made creative uses of the tension Bourdieu points to between the traditions of German *kultur* and the French Enlightenment belief in civilization as a virtue. Williams takes the argument one step back and locates what he notes as "probably the effective origin of the general sense of culture" in Vico's book *The New Science* (1725). For Williams "the most important intellectual advance in all modern thought" was Vico's insistence that "man makes his own history" (Williams, 1977, p. 19). This formulation overcomes the false dichotomy of society and nature and also discloses the constitutive relations between society and economy. But while celebrating the humanist turn in cultural thought, Williams is also keenly aware of the counter-enlightenment stream epitomized in Herder's *Ideas on the Philosophy of the History of Mankind* (1784–91), which is deeply critical of the "external universalism" of the Enlightenment (Williams, 1977, p. 17).

It was significant that Williams should note in Herder the anti-enlightenment themes that were subsequently picked up in much postmodernist writing. Although Herder accepted the emphasis on the historical self-development of humanity, he could not allow its reduction to the evolution of a single principle such as abstract reason. Similarly, historical change was much too variable to be reduced to a progressive unilinear development culminating in "European civilization." It was necessary to talk about plural cultures rather than Culture as a singularity, which added strength to Williams's emphasis on comparative ways of life and structures of feeling.

Williams then reads the "new" Marxism of the 1970s in a way that locates it within a stream of progressive European thought dating back to the Enlightenment but which is critical of the historical forms of life actually generated by capitalism. He sees Marxism as an intervention that has two critical consequences. Firstly, instead of the general term "civilization," Marx develops the Hegelian term "civil society," which he sees, concretely, as bourgeois society created by the capitalist mode of production. In his critical analysis of civil society, Marx can therefore avoid what he sees as the false dichotomy, posed by many earlier socialists, of civilization as against a "natural" human order. Second, Marx rejects the "idealist historiography" of the Enlightenment, which saw history as a process of overcoming ignorance and superstition by knowledge and reason. Instead, while generally celebrating the growth of scientific method, he reveals the real consequences of historical "progress" in terms of the exploitation of labor and industry. Hence Marx's famous revision of the "man makes his own history" principle by adding "but in circumstances not of his own choosing."

The National Critical

In conclusion we can return to Bourdieu's original problems of how national cultures adopt and adapt systems of ideas from other national cultures with some thoughts on Critical Theory and BCS. Kellner's thesis on the missed articulation of BCS with the Frankfurt School of Critical Theory is highly suggestive at a time when cultural studies seems to have drifted away from its original radical purposes. However, I think it clear from this brief historical overview that critical theory (lowercase) has always energized elements of BCS. The engagement with Enlightenment thought, Marxism, and socialism has run through BCS as a continuing though disrupted relationship. It is equally clear, however, that an anti-enlightenment "culturalist" strain has also been active that has drawn attention to the genuine attrition of certain ways of life engendered by "progress" but that has also cultivated deep antiprogressive myths. These myths have contributed to another sort of idealist historiography, which denies that any intervention into human affairs can contribute to greater equality and social justice. With Kellner and McGuigan, I believe that some of this conservatism and elitism has drifted into BCS, particularly where it is most estranged from social movements.

It seems to me that Williams's appropriation of Marxism in the 1970s is an attempt to recreate it in the British context as "Critical Theory" in the cultural sphere as opposed to the earlier British reception of Soviet Marxism as a political/economic theory. It was possible for Williams (and others, including especially

Eagleton) to make this step because of both the programs of translations undertaken by New Left Books and others and the program of translation of the complete works of Marx and Engels that revealed many hidden treasures. Was this a crude importation of foreign theory unsuited to the domestic climate? I don't think so for a number of reasons. The sheer doggedness of Williams and others in treating texts, institutions, and events as material productions with histories has tethered theory to concrete analysis. But also, far from being a foreign import, the greater bulk of Marx's *Capital* is of course a deep historical analysis of *British* capitalism. The health of the continued engagement of BCS with Critical Theory and critical theory will depend on sustaining these material connections.

CRITICAL THEORY AND THE ENVIRONMENT

This chapter reconsiders what an environmentally grounded critical theory might stand for in the twenty-first century. It works toward this end by reviewing how environmental concerns fit into the project of critical social theorizing, while, at the same time, indicating why any effective critique of capitalist exchange today must involve itself with environmental concerns. There is much that Marxism and the Frankfurt School can contribute to an environmental critical theory today, but other traditions of criticism, ranging from postmodernism to populism, also have much to add to this evolving political discourse. Ultimately, an environmental political theory, as Horkheimer (1972, pp. 232–233) claims, must become another "transformative activity associated with critical theory," which works from within the present society toward a future one in which "mankind will for the first time be a conscious subject and actively determine its own way of life."

The critical theorists of the Frankfurt School sought to account for the failure of the socialist revolution that Marx confidently anticipated would occur in advanced capitalist economies. Working amid the rise of fascism in Germany, they identified the state and culture as the dual deterrents that forestalled a successful working-class revolt. On the one hand, state repression could effectively crush many workers' uprisings, as they witnessed in Austria-Hungary, Germany, and Italy from 1918 into the 1920s. And, on the other hand, state intervention in the economy increasingly maintained low rates of unemployment, acceptable levels of pay, and modest measures of social welfare benefits, which kept most workers fairly mollified under the existing regime. At the same time, the rising culture industry also provided the soothing reified goods of a very comfortable alienation whose domination over independent thinking has made active resistance against capitalism even more difficult (Kellner, 1995). This industrialization of false consciousness inured the workers and owners to the system-sustaining demands of advanced capitalist exchange (Jacoby, 1975).

Writing in the dark times of ideological struggle from the 1920s to the 1970s (Jacoby, 1981), critical theorists at the same time recognized, as Marcuse (1964) argues, how much the perpetuation of this order rests upon the relentless and expansive exploitation of nature. Rather than embracing Habermas's dismissal of all hopes about transforming labor and technology such that nature's exploitation might be alleviated as a species of "romantic mysticism" (Habermas, 1971, pp. 43–44), an environmental critical theory hopes for realizing the "liberation of nature" (Marcuse, 1969).

Speaking out in favor of protecting the environment, guarding nature, or preserving various ecosystems means speaking out about how human society, economies, and the state presently are intertwined in a series of threatening, but also protective, actions in regard to the Earth's ecologies. Critical theory is one of the few remaining discursive traditions, like the science of ecology, that does not shrink from assuming the standpoint of the totality (Jay, 1973; Sartre, 1976; Schroyer, 1975). By taking the perspective of a holistic overview, critical theory offers a reflexive contrapuntal schematization to those advanced by big business, grand science, or national governments about what the future good life could be in all advanced industrial cultures. To undertake this critique, however, the commodity in all of its many iterations through the production of society and the reproduction of nature remains a central preoccupation for an effective critical theory.

Many critical theorists, from Lukacs (1971) to Habermas (1971, 1975), tend to place nature in a primal position prior to society. Buying into the growing prestige of the natural sciences in the early twentieth century, this stance essentially casts nature as object, and society as subject. Hence, humanity is seen as that host of agents who come after, from the outside of, and against nature. The workings of human economies and societies inside of their own subjective space of the social are, in turn, surrounded by the objective necessities of the natural. Any material advances within these artificial spaces come to be regarded as a "second nature," separate and apart from "first nature." Yet an environmental critical theory should work toward imploding this heritage of assertions. If the natural and the social are always already cultural, economic, and political constructs, then nature might be treated as "second society" just as well as society is transformed into "second nature."

An environmental critical theory, however, must return to Marcuse's, Gramsci's, and Marx's approach to critique as the "philosophy of practice." Habermas's tendency (1971) to remain caught in the antinomies of more bourgeois modes of consciousness and action, in which the subject and the object, mind and body, society and nature are regarded as useful categorical distinctions, should be left behind along with the reformist caution it inspires. A philosophy of practice, as Gramsci (1971) recognizes, would regard the environmental or the natural as always already the economic and the social. Therefore, those antinomies of abstract analysis that respect dualistic reification in order to empower "the economic" to sustainably develop "the environmental" or license "the social" to regulate "the environmental" only perpetuate existing contradictions as they struggle to tidy up around their ragged edges. To get beyond this impasse, environmental critical theory as a philosophy of practice can acknowledge how fully nature is always social, the environment is already economy, and ecologies also are activated communities of human and nonhuman life (Horkheimer & Adorno, 1972).

The Nature of Nature

Nature is an essentially contested concept, and this analysis of critical theory and the environment constitutes another expression of its constantly contested essence. The centrality of a pure, objective, unmediated Nature in the attainment of modern scientific knowledge, however, is an idea that is dying very hard, especially in the social sciences, managerial practices, and engineering science. From the vanguard of Newtonian physics in the seventeenth century to the rearguard of sociobiology in the twentieth century, many schools of modern science have assumed that their methodologies provide a privileged foundation for knowledge of what is "real" in Nature as a definitive empirically rigorous mapping of an "out there." These unsullied observations, in turn, are believed to create, once verified and validated by experiment, a true knowledge of objective reality in Nature (Adorno, 1973). This knowledge often is idealized in the mathematical proofs of physics, and its engineering applications in everyday life are widely believed to be the foundations of modernity's technological proficiency (Horkheimer, 1972). When all is said and done, humanity is believed to know how the worlds of nature work because of this disciplined application of scientific methods for observation, experiment, and verification (Popper, 1959).

Yet there also is a great deal of disquiet about these epistemological, ontological, and technological articles of faith in modernity (Mumford, 1963, 1970). Their celebrants continue to praise this system of science, and its derivative technologies, for their allegedly demonstrated ability to raise industrial output, overcome deadly diseases, speed methods of travel, and enhance a longer, richer human lifespan. Few of them, however, discuss how these same modes of scientific knowledge and technical action also generate noxious by-products, cause new afflictions, create frustrations in mobility, or perhaps detract from the qualities of life (Latour, 1993). Consequently, large social movements of concerned people—scientists and laypersons alike—have arisen to increasingly doubt, or to openly protest, these modernist formulas for legitimating scientific authority and technical power (Haraway, 1991; Hayles, 1999). Moreover, careful histories of science and technology often show that many of their advances came from artful tinkering or sheer accident rather than from some putatively pure rational knowledge of unmediated natural reality. Of course, these movements are not universally welcomed, because the cultural place, political power, and economic property of many other people are deeply embedded in preserving these modes of scientific production (Marcuse, 1955, 1964, 1969). Nonetheless, more resistances seem to develop and spread with each successive new, modern generation.

Plainly, the environmental movement has proven to be among the most ardent opponents of these fundamentalist views of science and technology. Feminists, minority peoples, and working-class groups, who rarely benefit from having scientific authority or technical power, also join environmentalists in questioning the neutral knowledge that science allegedly provides about Nature (Haraway, 1991; Longino, 1990). In its emergent days, science put forth its foundational epistemologies for dividing facts and values, theory and observation, experiments and explanations, or truth and opinion in order to challenge religious-feudal authority, whose place, power, and property in early modern society rested on other grounds. Once those traditional enemies were overcome, science and technology increasingly shifted their legitimating discourses toward operational achievement, or technical-economic performance, and away from epistemological incorrigibility, or real knowledge of Nature's inherent rationality (Idhe, 1990). Consequently, the nineteenth and twentieth centuries saw bourgeois science and industry using the technical command over the objective forms of Nature in the great "out there" to create greater wealth and knowledge in the form of new commodities for the "in here" of market economies and societies (Habermas, 1987b; Sartre, 1976).

After the twentieth century, however, everyone is dealing with postmodern conditions, which essentially are, as Jameson suggests, what prevails "when the modernization process is complete and Nature is gone for good. It has become a more fully human world than the older one, but one in which 'culture' has become a veritable 'second nature'" (1992, p. ix). Here, rogue instances of technical-economic performances, like Auschwitz, Bhopal, or Chernobyl, shake scientific technology's legitimacy, and a reflexive realization that anthropogenic changes in the Earth's climate, soils, atmosphere, waters, and biomass make any incorrigible epistemic certainty about the planet's autogenic activities very difficult, if not impossible, to maintain. On one level, the ecological opposition to modern science and technology is heartened by these recognitions, because new reservations about rampant commodification are now registered in the theory and practice of contemporary scientists and technologists (Eckersley, 1992). Accordingly, these resistance movements reason that a more self-reflexive science will be less destructive of Nature as well as more respectful of the human and nonhuman lives that dwell in the Earth's many habitats. Yet, on another level, there are no guarantees for this positive outcome, because these individuals, along with everyone else who either openly supports or does not doubt modern science, find that whatever improved cultural place, political power, and economic property that millions have attained in the twentieth century depends in some part, perhaps quite large or comparatively small, on letting science continue to amplify its technological proficiencies. Moreover, everyone continues to need the goods and services made possible by the global economy's ongoing technical-economic performance, even though this performative outcome is becoming more difficult to attain because of greater resistance to many industries' by-products and definite physical scarcities caused by resource depletion (Beck, 1992).

Environmental critical theory, then, opens all environments to transformative critique to guide new practices for change. Rather than holding society constant to improve nature, or keeping nature in check to revitalize society, environmentally aware ways of elaborating critical theory must concentrate upon reshaping nature and society together. Nature is known only through socially mediated conceptions, and society can be remade only inasmuch as relations with/in/of nature are shifted along with them.

Environmentalism and Informationalism

In the twentieth century, crisis and change became the two most overworked words in critical analysis. On a world scale, however, the history of the past fifty years in advanced industrial societies of "the West," as well as less advanced, semi-industrialized regions of "the Rest" outside of the West, clearly is one of constant crisis and continual change (Agger, 1989; Luke, 1989). During the Cold War, the comfortably centered lifeworld of industrial societies in stable, territorialized nation-states shattered as the many decentered networks of a new informational economy emerged globally from the flows and fragments produced from these implosions in the still ongoing informational revolution (Luke, 1999). With the erosion of that old industrial lifeworld, however, few social analysts have accepted the nearly total collapse of their conceptual categories, which largely were rooted in increasingly outmoded industrial forms of life, relations of power, and codes of culture (Baudrillard, 1981). A critical theory of the environment must dig out from underneath these collapsed categories, while standing up to survey what is proving to be quite new amid the rubble of these old rhetorics. Most of all, it needs to articulate a critique of how ecologies and economies coevolve in an ongoing struggle between popular local resistances and elite global authorities (Luke, 1997).

At this global turning point, it makes real sense, first, to "return to Marx," and then, next, to Western Marxism and its many derivative strands of critical theory. While attempts to decipher the still mystified futurologies of hi-tech global production out of the textual layers of orthodox Marxism will misconstrue new classes as old classes, miscode new power relations as ongoing traditional modes of power, or misinterpret the new culture as one more permutation of the old culture, the most promising path for critique must make new departures from Marx, guided by his basic desire to decipher the hieroglyphics of domination in the commodity form. From within the still inchoate upheavals of globalization, corporate capital is continuing to colonize everyday life with exchange value logics on a transnational scale, which is destroying much of what traditionally was "Nature" and "Society" in the process (Dyer-Witheford, 1999; Luke, 1989). By developing new informational modes of production, which are designed and managed by decentralized networks of professional-technical workers from a web of large complex techno-bureaucratic firms and small flexible corporate alliances, local and global capital are reconstructing the economic and political conditions of social reproduction as the ultimate guarantor of humanity's "sustainable development" and "environmental security."

While the contemporary proletariat is being disintegrated, degraded, or displaced by new investments in robotic apparatus, competing national labor reserves are divided and diluted within a transnational capital market into more and more indistinct types of increasingly underskilled work. At the same time, transnational businesses can expand, amplify, and elaborate their workings as the world's currently most important revolutionary cultural, economic, and political force (Boggs, 2000). Today the global mode of commercial production can commodify nearly everything on a planned, rational, mass scale (Harvey, 1989; Luke, 1989). Not only can the raw resources of the earth, the manufactured things of social production, and the social services of human institutions be submitted to capital's logic of reproduction, but even words, codes, memories, sounds, images, and symbols now are designed as value-added, fungible products to circulate in mass markets as efficient instruments of production, accumulation, reproduction, and circulation (Haraway, 1991).

Such developments, then, are not friction-free. Instead, as Lyotard suggests, "economic powers have reached the point of imperiling the stability of the State through new forms of the circulation of capital that go by the generic name of *multinational corporations*," and these new modes of revalorizing exchange "imply that investment decisions have, at least in part, passed beyond the control of the nation-states" (1984, p. 5). Even though it is not what many environmental activists envision when they cast ecological sensitivity as that consciousness that recognizes no organism can be entirely differentiated from its environment, no self is separate from society, and no action lacks importance, corporate powers are growing so pervasive in everyday life that the commodity form has become the most foundational mode of existence for many forms of life (Lukacs, 1971; Marcuse, 1964; Martin & Schumann, 1997). Emergent knowledges framed as digitized bits are now "circulating along the same lines as money, instead of for its 'educational' value or political (administrative, diplomatic, military) importance; the pertinent distinction would no longer be between knowledge and ignorance, but rather, as is the case with money, between 'payment knowledge' and 'investment knowledge'—in other words, between units of knowledge exchange in a daily maintenance framework (the reconstitution of the work force, 'survival') versus funds of knowledge dedicated to optimizing the performance of a project" (Lyotard, 1984, p. 6).

In the domains of transnational commodification,

> Everything has to be sacrificed to the principle that things must have an operational genesis. So far as production is concerned, it is no longer the Earth that produces, or labor that creates wealth ... rather, it is Capital that *makes* the Earth and Labor *produce*. Work is no longer an action, it is an operation. Consumption no longer means the simple enjoyment of goods, it means having (someone) enjoy something—an operation modelled on, and keyed to, the differential range of sign-objects. Communication is a

matter not of speaking but of making people speak. Information involves not knowledge but making people know. (Baudrillard, 1993, pp. 45–46)

Informationalization can turn everyone, every creature, and every thing into known quantities as bits, and knowledge on/from/with such bits easily becomes the flows of commodification and the constantly reconstructed nature-and-society that is now called "the environment."

Markets in these informational goods, then, are rendering, as Haraway claims, "thoroughly ambiguous the difference between natural and artificial, mind and body, self-developing and externally designed, and many other distinctions that used to apply to organisms and machines" (1991, p. 152). Recasting the world as bits in order to surpass, but also acquire greater control over, the world as atoms, is today's commodification project. Like all previous markets, these global informatic exchanges also are devoted to "systematizing something that is resolutely unsystematic, and historicizing something that is resolutely ahistorical" (Jameson, 1992, p. 418) by running them through the imperatives of commodification. Indeed, the informatic transformation of nature-and-society fulfills Haraway's claims that contemporary ontologies can be propounded only by seeking "chimeras, theorized and fabricated hybrids of machine and organism" (Jameson, 1992, p. 150).

Few questions for critical theory are either as interesting or as significant at this historical moment as the environmental role of informatics in reshaping the economy and society, because the *modus operandi* of so many human practices are being remade out of bits, for bits, and by bits. In part, these changes derive from the creation of new machinic collectives, like global computer and telecommunications networks, but they also reticulate, in part, the conventions of global capitalist production and consumption into everyday life, which now are colonizing time, energy, materials, and time, not only in atomic terms as matter, but also in digital forms as ones-and-zeros. This analysis also must evaluate the influence of informatics on the environment, particularly as digital technologies colonize the world's economies, governments, and societies.

On this terrain, which has been created, enforced, and sustained both by statal and nonstatal interests, new groups from all over the world are trying to reimagine human community in varied informatic terms (Anderson, 1991), while pushing their own peculiar interests in pursuit of illiberal traditions, neoliberal utopias, or antiliberal resistances. With an ironic twist to Engels' famous characterization of socialism, the flow of bits over telematic networks is moving many to think about forsaking the government of people to embrace the administration of things, which, in turn, will remediate new modes of control out of bits as a vision for digital governance over people and things expressed in many more partial, privatized, and productive practices (Luke, 1998).

The spatial reconfigurations of production and consumption in these informationalized "lifeworlds" bring "the systems" all the way home (Kellner, 1995b; Luke, 1989; Miller, 1988). Postmodernity becomes the stuff of everyday life, because, as Baudrillard observes,

The *consumption* of individuals mediates the *productivity* of corporate capital; it becomes a productive force required by the functioning of the system itself, by its process of reproduction and survival. In other words, there are these kinds of needs because the system of corporate production needs them. And the needs invested by the individual consumer today are just as essential to the order of production as the capital invested by the capitalist entrepreneur and the labor power invested in the wage laborer. It is *all* capital. (1981, p. 82)

A crude functionalism, however, is not in play here. One instead sees the informatic command/control/communication/intelligence grids of bits on the Net remediating the elective affinities of capital by drawing technologies of the self (consumer decisions to exercise purchasing power) together with technologies of production (producer choices to organize adding value) as new goods and services are recast as bits (Luke, 1998).

One of the most radical negations of today's transnational modes of production, then, is to be found in ecological or environmental resistance. Reasonable limits of resource renewability (which carry capacities in ecosphere reproduction have defined) are violated systematically on a daily basis by transnational businesses in their various programs for consolidating their corporate hold in a global marketplace. Transnational businesses, of course, are not completely monolithic, omnipotent, or evilly intentioned. Significant sectoral, national, and international divisions still hobble many of their strategies and effectiveness. Some firms do much good, but other companies do great evil in their ordinary everyday conduct of business. Consequently, it would appear that transnational corporate exchange, as it continues to develop on a global scale, serves fewer of those constructive social purposes required for maintaining truly humane forms of being. As the modern welfare state and transnational firm have become more firmly devoted to the ever more rational production of goods and services, they also spit out greater levels of waste and pollution (Beck, 1997; Boggs, 2000). And these long-term costs are piling up as death, destruction, and decay in far too many niches in the biotic webs sustaining human, animal, and plant life all over the planet.

Forging an Environmental Critical Theory

Any critical environmental discourse that is truly political in its implementation must seek the technical means to reconcile the workings of advanced economies with Nature in qualitatively new modes of production. To extend Haeckel's understanding of ecology—as the science that treats the totality of relations between organisms and their organic and inorganic environment—out to its political limits, a critical theory for environmentalism can reconfigure the practices and concepts of this still evolving science to evaluate, and then contest, the full impact of corporate capital's productive forces on Nature's ecological equilibrium (Aronowitz, 1981; Schroyer, 1975; Stokes, 1994). By finally treating "the totality of relations" between all organisms and their environments, including humans in their built environments, an environmental critical theory can go far beyond the fragmentary, specialized knowledge of more orthodox life sciences, like the discourses of zoology, biochemistry, biophysics, or microbiology that states and businesses use to conceptualize ecology for their technical needs (Eckersley, 1992; Haraway, 1991). By illustrating how the creation, circulation, and accumulation of commodities on a mass scale now mutilates the ecological order of the planet, this critical ecological sensibility should begin to present its thoroughgoing critique of contemporary society and its scientific-technical rationality (Deleuze & Guattari, 1994).

To cultivate an ecological sensibility, one must revitalize the rich traditions of critical social theory. Critical social theory implies here those diverse intellectual currents in the Western Marxist tradition, which seek to adapt Marx's insights and methods creatively to the contemporary conflicts and contradictions of mature industrialized societies by contesting ways of life rooted only in exchange value. The present-day workings of technocratic state power and corporate exchange on a world scale necessitate radical new maneuvers to redirect Marxian theory. And contemporary critical social theory, which often can be contra-Marxist, post-Marxist, or extra-Marxist in its conceptual, ethical, and political derivations, meets many of these requirements.

Critical social theory, beginning in the 1920s and 1930s with Gramsci and Lukacs or Adorno and Horkheimer, emerged at a major historical juncture, namely, the destabilizing crises of entrepreneurial capitalism in which the embattled leadership of the interventionist state and nascent multinational firm reconstituted classical capitalist forms of production in various state-corporate alliances to plan the overall levels of mass production and consumption (Galbraith, 1978; Habermas, 1975; Marcuse, 1964). For capital and a socialist revolution by labor basically shifted. Inside of what hitherto were antagonistic class relations, the development of the welfare state, the culture industry, and large integrated firms made possible an expansive production of goods and services that existing managerial and social elites could use to win class cooperation and forge social consensus (Luke, 1990). Mature corporate capital's sophisticated management of scientific-technical rationality on a global scale enabled it to dominate nature more efficiently and use the material surplus accumulated from that domination to advance its general program of social control.

In the phase of liberal entrepreneurial capitalism, Marx argued that the working classes represented the negative, transcendent opposition to the established bourgeois order. Still, an extraordinary new level of affluence under the sway of these state-corporate production alliances increasingly mollified workers with new consumer goods, commodified mass culture, and state welfare programs (Debord, 1977). Class-based sources of negativity—rooted in the practical experiences of the industrial working classes in production—dissipated in a new social regime organized around the practical experience of consumption. What is more, direct domination through instruments of police coercion and/or rigid social custom simultaneously took on far more indirect form by gatekeeping popular access to new mass-produced, but selectively distributed, goods and services (Gramsci, 1971).

The technological myths of modern production assert that the new industrial state produces abundance for all at little or no cost to anyone through technical innovation. Much of this "technical innovation," however, actually can be tied to re-organizing world trade to benefit capital-controlling regions as well as overriding the ecological balance of Nature, to produce what appears to be an unlimited or inexhaustible supply of material goods and services. Thus, the demands of markets force contemporary farms and factories to overdraw on finite renewable stocks of natural resources available now and, in effect, borrow against the future by using the yet unborn generations' potential frugal use of resources for truly profligate consumption (Schumacher, 1973). The celebrated material abundance allegedly being produced by corporate technological wizardry, in fact, might largely be only a sorry booty of resources, plundered from the future (Commoner, 1976).

Developing Ecocritiques for Today

Advocates of radical ecological change now stand to make real progress by building and maintaining new ties with an environmental critical theory. The close ties of many local cultures to the land are celebrated by American deep ecologists, nature activists, and social ecologists all around the world (Gottlieb, 1993; Harvey, 1996). And these powerful populist currents can recharge the familiar and populistic purposes of critical social theory in its environmentalist applications. Despite its intellectual contradictions as esoteric and elitist, critical theory still carries the moral rage needed for recapturing the remaining free spaces in corporate capitalist society as its devotees try to ethically inoculate those spaces against further intrusions. The practical possibilities proposed by engagé ecofeminism, environmental justice groups, radical social ecology, and deep ecology also now hold much of the vision and energies needed to build qualitatively new, ecologically rational forms of communal production and reproduction within various already existing free spaces.

By building on the critique of instrumental reason that critical theorists have leveled against contemporary capitalism, radical ecologists are articulating a new social critique closely connected to a project for the emancipation of Nature (Gottlieb, 1993). Elaborating new logics for sustainable living can defend a number of ultimate ends, which can be intellectually and organizationally counterposed to the corporate sector's continuing reliance on efficient means in the marketplace (Bookchin, 1971).

Constructing this new ecological sensibility assumes that it might not only discursively mediate the practical relation of subjective means to objective ends, but it also could help one ethically and intellectually determine, understand, and justify those ends by accommodating principles of biotic production, sustainability, carry capacity, or survivability. To accept these constraints, more fully aware, ecologically conscious agents could consent to more stringent constraints on the exploitation of the environment that could "regulate relations between man and man, and between man and nature" (Horkheimer, 1974, p. 4). Unless intrinsic limits on ecological exploitation are acknowledged to renew the planet's ecosphere, human beings will destroy the objective material basis of their own and all other lifeforms' continued survival. Such an understanding of Nature's inherent limits, in turn, could allow more ecologically cautious communities to determine and justify the moral goals served by their localized anticorporate thinking and ecological antitechnocratic action. This sort of ecologically grounded practice also could quickly begin to reorder relations between all humans as well as between humans and Nature (Adorno, 1973).

Ecological judgments are not cost-benefit analyses. Working in accord with natural reasonability is not like following administrative rationality. And transcendent ecological ends, rather than immediate managerial calculations, should emerge as a reflexive determinant of environmentally sensitive activities (Marcuse, 1969). It is the unanticipated costs incurred by society at large in serving ungratified corporate goals, as transnational corporations (Commoner, 1976; Mandel, 1978) build social hierarchy, technological complexity, political centralization, scientific domination, and cultural reification, that critical environmental theory should criticize for being too destructive of the larger balance between people in relation to Nature. By negating these tendencies, environmental critical theory could also mobilize new arguments in support of nonhierarchical social relations, technical simplicity, small-scale economies, political decentralization, reasonable science, and cultural vitality within the free spaces of present-day society. Unlike most government policies that try to favor greater market freedom through policies centered on corporate managerialism, many critical environmental theorists favor mobilizing the immediate producers and consumers to make crucial decisions about human beings' relation to Nature rather than surrendering those prerogatives to state and corporate technocrats (Eckersley, 1992).

Ultimately, this reconstruction of ecology as a new critical sensibility should renew political debate and economic struggle over the issues of who decides, who pays, and who benefits in the complex economic, organizational, and technological relations of people with nature. Renewing nature, an endless source of self-created being, promises to reorder many critical social relations: of the individual to the collective; of personality to society, and of these dual social relations to nature (Marcuse, 1964). Any critical ecological sensibility, then, must reinvest individuals with the decision-making power to order their material relations to the environment in smaller-scale, nonhierarchical, ecologically sound market ties between independent producers in local and regional commonwealths (Luke, 1999). States and businesses will not act responsibly in every instance, so environmental critical theory must reaffirm the responsibility of all individuals for preserving their ecological inheritance and passing it on with trust to future generations (Bookchin, 1971). Simply by confirming the virtues of self and social discipline in living within the renewable cycles of natural reproduction, this ecological sensibility could point to the most promising paths out of the consumerism fostered by everyday corporate growth. Rather than encouraging passivity, dependence, and purposelessness, which critical social theorists always have criticized, the discourses and practices of an environmental critical theory would stress how greater social activity, personal autonomy, and reasonable guidance are needed to preserve nature (Haraway, 1991). With these goals, the labor of competent, conscious communities could be steered toward reconstituting their social, economic, and political mediations with each other ecologically by interacting reasonably with nature (Commoner, 1976).

Furthermore, successfully embedding new social relations organized along these ecological lines could alter radically the social constructions of nature in relation to society, making it a subject, not an object; an agency, not an instrumentalist; and an equal partner, not a dominated resource. In admitting nature to animate subjecthood again, environmental critical theory also should recast human beings' image of themselves as active, equal subjects living in a respectful partnership with nature. The living and inorganic constituents of nature might even be imagined as having statuses and privileges as worthy of defense as those of humanity (Hayles, 1999). At the same time, no rationalization for nature's continued destruction could be traded in exchange for the false promise of more jobs, greater prosperity, added growth, or closer technological control (Beck, 1997; Boggs, 2000). Those guarantees of ecological security should ramify, in turn, into other opportunities for greater freedom, dignity, and reasonability for those millions of human beings whose autonomy suffers in nature's abusive indenturement to the global market's instrumental rationality.

An environmental political theory must stand for a collection of vital principles: the necessity of planning for permanence rather than obsolescence; the worth of maintaining natural and social diversity over the ill-fated design of forcing a monological instrumental uniformity on Nature; the importance of sustaining renewal, reusability, and reasonability as central principles of social exchange; and the importance of balancing past environmental destruction against both present communal utilization and future ecological renewal (Luke, 1997). In developing these principles, the new discursive representations of environmental critical theory could guide communities wanting to stick with economies subjected exclusively to narrow corporate profits to economies rooted more closely in democratic communalism. By remaining aware of all the pitfalls of instrumental reason, which aggravates the alienation of both owners and workers, experts and clients, city dwellers and rural residents in the present corporate order, an environmental critical theory could explore new forms of communal production and reproduction that could alleviate some of the destructive tendencies of transnational corporate capitalism.

Thawing out frozen relations of thinking and doing, environmental critical theory also can show how the reified commodity relations at the core of advanced capitalism come to be treated as abstract autonomous agencies, like "Technology," "Society," "Politics," "Economy," or "Culture." At the same time, the critique of technology as mystified relations of reification simultaneously shows how technologies are always working as culture, politics, and society in advanced capitalist exchange. Environmental changes, then, should be realized by reimagining how technologies create particular conventional cultural understandings in commercialized acts and artifacts, produce specific exchange-driven power effects, and generate peculiar social practices through commodification. Environmental protection should be attained by recognizing how thoroughly these conditions of association have become naturalized in capitalist commercial practices, and then realizing how nature must be protected by recontouring its protections around new social practices, power relations, and cultural understandings.

REFERENCES

Adorno, T. (1970a). Gesammelte Schriften, III, Frankfurt a.Main, Germany: Fischer.
Adorno, T. (1970b). Gesammelte Schriften, X., Frankfurt a.Main, Germany: Fischer.
Adorno, T. (1971). *Erziehung zur Mündigkeit — Vorträge und Gespräche mit Hellmut Becker 1959-1969,* Frankfurt a.Main, Germany: Fischer.
Adorno, T. (1973). *Negative dialectic.* New York: Seabury Press.
Adorno, T. (1998). *Critical models: Interventions and catchwords.* (Henry W. Pickford, Trans.). New York: Columbia Press.
Adorno, T. (1999). *Minima moralia — Reflections from damaged life.* (E. F. N. Jephcott, Trans.). New York: Verso.
Adorno, T. (2000). *The Adorno reader.* (Brian O'Connor, Editor). London: Blackwell.
Adorno, T. & Horkheimer, M. (1988). *Dialektil der Aufklärung,* Frankfurt a.Main, Germany: Fischer.
Agger, B. (1989). *Fast capitalism: A critical theory of significance.* Urbana: University of Illinois Press.
Ahmad, A. (1995). The politics of literary postcoloniality. *Race and Class* 36 (3), 1–20.
Alcoff, L. (1996). Philosophy and racial identity. *Radical Philosophy* 75, 5–14.
Aleinikoff, A.T. (1991). A case for race-consciousness. *Columbia Law Review, 91,* 1060–1123.
Anderson, B. (1991). *Imagined communities,* rev. ed. London: Verso.
Anderson, P. (1968). Components of the national culture. *New Left Review,* 50 (July–August 1968), 3–57.
Anthias, F. & Yuval-Davis, N. (1992). *Racialized boundaries: Race, nation, gender, colour and class and the anti-racist struggle.* London: Routledge.
Anzaldúa, G. (1987). *Borderlands/La frontera: The new mestiza.* San Francisco: Aunt Lute Books.
Apple, M. (1979). *Ideology and curriculum.* Boston: Routledge.
Arendt, H. (1954/1993). *Between Past and Future: Eight Exercises in Political Thought.* New York: Penguin.
Arendt, H. (1958). *The human condition.* Chicago: Chicago University Press.
Arendt, H. (1963). *On revolution.* London: Penguin.
Arendt, H. (1963 & 1992). *Eichmann in Jerusalem: A report on the banality of evil.* Harmondsworth, UK: Penguin.
Arendt, H. (1968a). *Men in dark times.* San Diego: Harcourt, Brace and Company.

Arendt, H. (1968b). *Between past and future*. London: Penguin.
Arendt, H. (1971). *The life of the mind: One volume edition*. San Diego: Harcourt, Brace and Company.
Arendt, H. (1973). *The origins of totalitarianism*. San Diego: Harcourt, Brace and Company.
Arendt, H. (1979). *The human condition*. Chicago: University of Chicago Press.
Aristotle. (1976). *Ethics* (The Nicomachean Ethics). Revised Ed. (J.A.K. Thomson, Trans.). Harmondsworth, UK: Penguin.
Aronowitz, S. (1981). *The crisis in historical materialism: Class, politics, and culture in Marxist theory*. New York: Praeger.
Aronowitz, S. (1993). Paulo Freire's radical democratic humanism. In P. McLaren & P. Leonard (Eds.), *Paulo Freire: A critical encounter* (pp. 8–24). London: Routledge.
Aronowitz, S. (2000). *The knowledge Factory*. Boston: Beacon Press.
Aronowitz, S. & Giroux, H. (1991). *Postmodern education: Politics, culture and social criticism*. Minneapolis: University of Minnesota Press.
Aronowitz, S. & Giroux, H. (1994). *Education still under siege*. Westport, CT: Bergin & Garvey.
Astin, R. (1989). Sapphire bound! *Wisconsin Law Review, 1989*, 539–578.
Astin, R. (1992). Left at the post: One take on blacks and postmodernism. *Law & Society Review, 26*, 751–754.
Ayers v. Fordice, 879 F. Supp. 1419 (1995).
Balch, S. (2000). The "civilizing mission" of academe. *Chronicle of Higher Education* (July 28, 2000), B13.
Balibar, E. (1991). The nation form: History and ideology. In E. Balibar & I. Wallerstein (Eds.), *Race, nation, class: Ambiguous identities* (pp. 86–106). London: Verso.
Balkin, J.M. (1992). What is postmodern constitutionalism? *Michigan Law Review, 90*, 1966–1990.
Barker, M. (1981). *The new racism: Conservatives and the ideology of the tribe*. London: Junction.
Baron, S. (1985). The study of culture: Cultural studies and British sociology compared. *Acta Sociologica* 1985 (28) 2, 71–85.
Baudrillard, J. (1981). *For a critique of the political economy of the sign*. St. Louis, MO: Telos Press.
Baudrillard, J. (1993). *The transparency of evil: Essays on extreme phenomena*. London: Verso.
Baudrillard, J. (2001). *Selected Writings* (M. Poster, Ed.). Cambridge: Polity.
Bauman, Z. (1987). *Legislators and Interpreters: On modernity, post-modernity and intellectuals*. Ithaca, NY: Cornell University Press.
Bauman, Z. (1999). *In search of politics*. Stanford, CA: Stanford University Press.
Beck, U. (1992). *The risk society*. London: Sage.
Beck, U. (1997). *The reinvention of politics*. Oxford: Polity Press.
Becker, C. (1995). The artist as intellectual. *The Review of Education/Pedagogy/Cultural Studies, 17*(4), 388.
Bell, D.A. (1988). White superiority in America: Its legal legacy, its economic costs. *Villanova Law Review, 33*, 767–779.
Bell, D.A. (1992). *Faces at the bottom of the well: The permanence of racism*. New York: Basic Books.
Benchimol, A. (2001). *Intellectual formations in the romantic period: A comparative study of the cultural politics and social criticism in the British public sphere, 1802–32*. Unpublished Ph.D. thesis, School of English, University of Glasgow, Scotland.

Benhabib, S. (1996). *The reluctant modernism of Hannah Arendt*. Thousand Oaks, Sage Publications.
Benjamin, W. (1969). Theses on the philosophy of history. In *Illuminations* (pp. 245–268). (Hannah Arendt, Ed., Harry Zohn, Trans.). London: Fontana.
Benjamin, W. (1972). *Gesammelte Schriften*, 1.2, Frankfurt a.Main, Germany: Fischer.
Benjamin, W. (1979). *One way street and other writings*. (Edmund Jephcott & Kingsley Shorter, Trans.). London: New Left Books.
Benjamin, W. (1983). *Charles Baudelaire: A lyric poet in the era of high capitalism*. (Harry Zohn and Quintin Hoare, Trans.). London: Verso Editions and New Left Books.
Benjamin, W. (1992). *Illuminations*. (Harry Zohn, Trans.). London: Fontana.
Benjamin, W. (1996). *Selected writings: Volume 1, 1913–1926*. (Marcus Bullock and Michael W. Jennings, Eds.). Cambridge: Harvard University Press.
Benjamin, W. (1998). *The origin of German tragic drama*. (John Osborne, Trans.). London: Verso.
Benjamin, W. (1999a) *Selected writings: Volume 2 1927–1934*. (Michael W. Jennings, Howard Eiland, & Gary Smith, Eds. Rodney Livingstone and others, Trans.). Cambridge: Harvard University Press.
Benjamin, W. (1999b). *The Arcades project*. (Howard Eiland & Kevin McLaughlin, Trans.). Cambridge: Harvard University Press.
Bennett, T. (1996). Out in the open: Reflections on the history and practice of cultural studies. *Cultural Studies 10*(1), 133–153.
Bennett, T. (1998). *Culture: A reformer's science*. Thousand Oaks, CA: Sage.
Bentley, G. (1987). Ethnicity and practice. *Comparative Studies in Society and History 29*, 24–55.
Berger, P. (1974). *Pyramids of sacrifice: Political ethics and social change*. New York: Basic Books.
Berlin, I. (1996). *The sense of reality: Studies in ideas and their history*. (H.Hardy, Ed.). London: Pimlico.
Berman, M. (1983). *All that is solid melts into air: The experience of modernity*. London: Verso.
Berman, M. (1992). Why modernism still matters. In S. Lash & J. Friedman (Eds.), *Modernity and identity* (pp. 33–58). Oxford: Basil Blackwell.
Bernstein, R. (1991). *The new constellation*. Cambridge: Polity Press.
Best, S. & Kellner, D. (1991). *Postmodern theory: Critical interrogations*. London and New York: Macmillan and Guildford Press.
Best, S. & Kellner, D. (1997). *The postmodern turn*. London and New York: Routledge and Guilford Press.
Best, S. & Kellner, D. (2001). *The postmodern adventure*. New York: Guilford Press.
Beyer, L. & Liston, D. (1992). Discourse or moral action: A critique of postmodernism. *Educational Theory 42*(4),371–395.
Bhabha, H. (1994). *The location of culture*. London: Routledge.
Bloom, H. (1998). They have the numbers; We have the heights. *Boston Review* (April/May, 1998), 27.
Bloom, H. (2000). In praise of the greats. *Brill's Content* (May 2000).
Boggs, C. (2000). *The end of politics: Corporate power and the decline of the public sphere*. New York: Guilford.
Bohman, J (2000). Participants, observers and critics: Practical knowledge, social perspectives, and critical pluralism. In William Rehg and James Bohman (Eds.), *Pluralism and the pragmatic turn: The transformation of critical theory* (Essays in honor of Thomas McCarthy). Cambridge: MIT Press.

Bollick, C. (1996). *The affirmative action fraud: Can we restore the American civil rights vision?* Washington, DC: The Cato Institute.
Bookchin, M. (1971). *Post-scarcity anarchism.* New York: Ramparts Books.
Borsook, P. (2000). *Cyberselfish: A critical romp through the terribly libertarian culture of high tech.* New York: Public Affairs.
Botstein, L. (1997). *Jefferson's children: Education and the promise of American culture.* New York: Doubleday.
Botstein, L. (1999). Making the teaching profession respectable again. *New York Times* (Monday, July 26, 1999), Op Ed Page, A19.
Botstein, L. (2000). A tyranny of standardized tests. *New York Times* (Sunday, May 28, 2000), Op Ed Page, WK, 11.
Bourdieu, P. (1984). *Distinction: A social critique of the judgement of taste.* Cambridge: Harvard University Press.
Bourdieu, P. (1990a). *In other words: Essays towards a reflexive sociology.* Cambridge: Polity Press.
Bourdieu, P. (1990b). *The logic of practice.* Cambridge: Polity Press.
Bourdieu, P. (1991). *Language and symbolic power.* Cambridge: Polity Press.
Bourdieu, P. (1996). *On television.* New York: The New Press.
Bourdieu, P. & Passeron, J. (1990). *Reproduction in education, society and culture.* London: Sage.
Bourdieu, P. & Wacquant, L. (1992). *An invitation to reflexive sociology.* Chicago: Chicago University Press.
Bourdieu. P. (1999). The social conditions of the international circulation of ideas. In Richard Shusterman (Ed.), *Bourdieu: A critical reader.* Oxford: Blackwell.
Bouwsma, W. (2001) *The waning of the renaissance 1550-1640.* New Haven, CT: Yale University Press.
Bowers, C.A. (1983). Linguistic roots of cultural invasion in Paulo Freire's pedagogy. *Teachers College Record* 84(4), 935-953.
Brah, A. (1992). Difference, diversity and differentiation. In J. Donald & A. Rattansi (Eds.), *"Race," culture and difference* (pp. 126-145). London: Sage.
Brandes, D. (1971). Education for liberation: An interview with Paulo Freire. Transcript of an interview conducted for the Canadian Broadcasting Corporation television programme *Something Else,* 18 June.
Brandt, G. (1986). *The realisation of anti-racist teaching.* Lewes, England: Falmer Press.
Brightman, C. (Ed.). (1995). *Between friends: The correspondence between Hannah Arendt and Mary McCarthy.* San Diego, CA: Harcourt, Brace and Company.
Britzman, D. (1998). *Lost subjects, contested objects: Toward a psychoanalytic inquiry of learning.* Albany: State University of New York Press.
Brown, C. (1974). Literacy in 30 hours: Paulo Freire's process in northeast Brazil. *Social Policy* 5(2), 25-32.
Brown, W.R. (1992). The convergence of neutrality and choice: The limits of the state's affirmative duty to provide equal educational opportunity. *Tennessee Law Review* 60, 65-131.
Buber, M. (1958). *I and Thou.* (R.G. Smith, Trans.) Edinburgh: T. and T. Clark.
Buber, M. (1961). *Between Man and Man.* (R.G. Smith,.Trans.) London: Fontana.
Buber, M. (1970). *I and thou.* (W. Kaufmann, Trans. and Ed.). Edinburgh: T. and T. Clark
Buck-Morss, S. (1989) *The dialectics of seeing: Walter Benjamin and the Arcades project.* Cambridge: MIT Press.

Burbules, N. (2000). The limits of dialogue as critical pedagogy. In Peter Pericles Trifonas (Ed.), *Revolutionary pedagogies*. New York: Routledge/Falmer.
Burtonwood, N. (1996). Culture, identity and the curriculum. *Educational Review 48*, 227–235.
Butler, J. (1993). *Bodies that matter: On the discursive limits of sex*. New York: Routledge.
Caglar, A. (1997). Hyphenated identities and the limits of "culture." In T. Modood & P. Werbner (Eds.), *The politics of multiculturalism in the new Europe: Racism, identity and community* (pp. 169–185). London: Zed Books.
Calhoun, C. (1993). Nationalism and civil society: Democracy, diversity and self-determination. *International Sociology 8*, 387–411.
Calmore, J.O. (1992). Critical race theory, Archie Shepp, and firemusic: Securing an authentic intellectual life in a multicultural world. *Southern California Law Review 65*, 2129–2230.
Canovan, M. (1992). *Hannah Arendt: A reinterpretation of her political thought*. Cambridge: Cambridge University Press.
Capella, J. & Jamieson, K. (1997). *Spiral of cynicism: The press and the public good*. New York: Oxford University Press.
Capper, C.A. (1999). (Homo)Sexualities, organizations, and administration: Possibilities for in(queer)y. *Educational Researcher 28*, 4–12
Cartledge, P. (2000). Boiotian swine f(or)ever? The Boiotian superstate 395 BC. In P. Flensted-Jensen, T.H. Neilsen, & L. Rubinstein (Eds.), *Polis and politics: Studies in ancient Greek history*. Copenhagen: Museum Tusculanum Press, University of Copenhagen.
Caygill, H. (1998). *Walter Benjamin: The colour of experience*. London: Routledge.
Chaloupka, W. (1999). *Everybody knows: Cynicism in America*. Minneapolis: University of Minnesota Press.
Chambers, I. (1994). *Migrancy, culture and identity*. London: Routledge.
Chang, R.S. (1993). Toward an Asian American legal scholarship: Critical race theory, post-structuralism, and narrative space. *Asian Law Journal–California Law Review 81*, 1243-1324.
Chomsky, N. (1999). *Profit over people: Neoliberalism and global order*. New York: Seven Stories Press.
Cohen, M. (1993). *Profane illumination: Walter Benjamin and the Paris of surrealist revolution*. Berkeley: University of California Press.
Commoner, B. (1976). *The poverty of power*. New York: Bantam.
Connolly, D. (2000). *Homeless mothers: Face to face with women and poverty*. Minneapolis: University of Minnesota Press.
Conroy, J. (1999). Poetry and human growth. *Journal of Moral Education 28*(4), 491–510.
Corson, D. (1993). *Language, minority education and gender: Linking social justice and power*. Clevedon: Multilingual Matters.
Corson, D. (1998). *Changing education for diversity*. Buckingham: Open University Press.
Crenshaw, K.W. (1988). Race, reform and retrenchment: Transformation and anti-discrimination law. *Harvard Law Review 101*, 1331–1387.
Crenshaw, K., Gotanda, N., Peller, G., & Thomas, K. (Eds.). (1995). *Critical race theory: Key writings that formed the movement*. New York: The New Press.
Crick, B. (1990). *Political thoughts and polemics*. Edinburgh: Edinburgh University Press.
Davis, R. (1980). Education for awareness: A talk with Paulo Freire. In R. Mackie (Ed.), *Literacy and revolution: The pedagogy of Paulo Freire* (57–69). London: Pluto Press.
Dayal, S. (2000). Introduction. In Julia Kristeva, *Crisis of the European Subject*. New York: The Other Press.

Dean, J. (Ed.). (2000). *Cultural studies and political theory*. Ithaca, NY: Cornell University Press.
Debord, G. (1977). *Society of the spectacle*. Detroit: Red & Black.
Deleuze, G. (1993). *The fold: Leibniz and the baroque*. (Tom Conley, Trans.). London: The Athlone Press.
Deleuze, G. & F. Guattari. (1984). *Anti-Oedipus: Capitalism and schizophrenia*. London: Athlone.
Deleuze, G. & Guattari, F. (1994). *What is philosophy?* New York: Columbia University Press.
Delgado, R. (1989). Storytelling for oppositionist and others: A plea for narrative. *Michigan Law Review 87*, 2411–2441.
Delgado, R. (1995). *Critical race theory: The cutting edge*. Philadelphia, PA: Temple University Press.
Delgado, R. & Stefancic, J. (Eds.). (2000). *Critical race theory: The cutting edge*. 2nd ed. Philadelphia, PA: Temple University Press.
Delgado Bernal, D. (1998). Using a Chicana feminist epistemology in educational research. *Harvard Educational Review, 68*, 555–579.
Delgado Bernal, D. (2002). Critical race theory, Latino critical theory, and critical race-gendered epistemologies: Recognising students of color as holders and creators of knowledge. *Qualitative Inquiry 8*, 105–125.
Derrida, J. (1984). On an apocalyptic tone recently adopted in philosophy. *Oxford Literary Review VI*(2), 3–37.
Derrida, J. (2000). Intellectual courage: An interview. *Culture Machine* Vol. 2, 9. Online journal at *http://culturemachine.tees.ac.uk/articles/art_derr.htm*
Descartes, R. (1931). *The philosophical works of Descartes. Vol. 1* (E.S. Haldane & G.R.T. Ross, Trans.). London: Cambridge University Press.
Deyhle, D. & Swisher, K. (1997). Research in American Indian, Alaskan, Native American education: From assimilation to self-determination. In M. Apple (Ed.), *Review of Research in Education* (pp. 113–147). Washington, DC: American Educational Research Association.
di Leonardo, M. (1994). White ethnicities, identity politics, and baby bear's chair. *Social Text 41*, 5–33.
Donald, J. & Rattansi, A. (Eds.). (1992). *"Race," culture and difference*. London: Sage.
DuBois, W.E.B. (1969). *The soul of black folks*. New York: Signet.
Dunne, J. (1996). *Back to the rough ground: Practical judgment and the lure of technique*. South Bend, IN: Notre Dame Press.
Dworkin, A. (1981). *Pornography: Men possessing women*. London: Women's Press.
Dworkin, D. (1997) *Cultural marxism in postwar Britain*, Durham, NC: Duke University Press.
Dyer-Witheford, N. (1999). *Cyber-Marx*. Urbana: University of Illinois Press.
Eagleton, T. (1981). *Walter Benjamin, or towards a revolutionary criticism*. London: Verso Editions and NLB.
Eagleton, T. (2000). *The idea of culture*. Malden, MA: Basil Blackwell.
eBay (2001a). *eBay Feedback FAQ*. Online. Available *http://pages.ebay.com/help/basics/f-feedback.html* (27 February 2001).
eBay (2001b). *Feedback Message Board*. Online. Available *http://forums.ebay.com/dws?14@1007150370092@.ee7b9c6* (11 June 2001).
Eckersley, R. (1992). *Environmentalism and political theory*. Albany: SUNY Press.

Edsall, T.B. & Edsall, M.D. (1991). *Chain reaction: The impact of race, rights and taxes on American politics.* New York: W.W. Norton.
Elias, J.L. (1994). *Paulo Freire: Pedagogue of liberation.* Malabar, FL: Krieger.
Ellsworth, E. (1989). Why doesn't this feel empowering? Working through the repressive myths of Critical Pedagogy. *Harvard Educational Review* 59(3), 297-324.
Ellsworth, E. (1994). Why doesn't this feel empowering? Working through the repressive myths of critical pedagogy. In Lynda Stone (Ed.), *The education feminism reader.* New York: Routledge.
Ellsworth, E. (1997). *Teaching positions.* New York: Teachers College Press.
Essed, P. (1991). *Understanding everyday racism: An interdisciplinary theory.* Thousand Oaks, CA: Sage.
Ettinger, E. (1995). *Hannah Arendt: Martin Heidegger.* New Haven, CT: Yale University Press.
Farber, D.A. & Sherry, S. (1993). Telling stories out of school: An essay on legal narratives. *Stanford Law Review 45,* 807-856.
Farber, D.A. & Sherry, S. (1994). The 200,000 cards of Dimitri Yurasov: Further reflections on scholarship and truth. *Stanford Law Review 46,* 647-662.
Fanon, F. (1967). *The wretched of the earth.* (C. Farrington, Trans.). Harmondsworth, UK: Penguin.
Feagin, J.R. (1992). The continuing significance of racism: Discrimination against black students in white colleges. *Journal of Black Studies 6* 546-578.
Feagin, J.R., Vera, H., & Imani, N. (1996). *The agony of education: Black students at white colleges and universities.* New York: Routledge.
Felman, S. (1987). *Jacques Lacan and the adventure of insight: Psychoanalysis in contemporary culture.* Cambridge: Harvard University Press.
Felman, S. (1993). *What does a woman want? Reading and sexual difference.* Baltimore: Johns Hopkins University Press.
Fenton, S. (1999). *Ethnicity: Racism, class and culture.* London: Macmillan.
Ferguson, H. (1990) *The science of pleasure.* London: Routledge.
Ferris, D. (1992) "Truth is the death of intention": Benjamin's esoteric history of romanticism. *Studies in Romanticism,* Vol 31, 455-481.
Fine, M. (1994). Dis-tance and other stances: Negotiations of power inside feminist research. In A. Gitlin (Ed.), *Power and method: Political activism and educational research* (pp. 129-146). New York: Routledge.
Fine, M., Weis, L., Powell, L.C., & Wong, L.M. (1997). *Off white: Readings on race, power, and society.* New York: Routledge.
Fiske, J. (1996). *Media matters: Race and gender in US politics.* Minneapolis: University of Minnesota Press.
Flecha, R. (1999). Modern and postmodern racism in Europe: Dialogic approach and antiracist pedagogies. *Harvard Educational Review 69,* 15-171.
Fonseca, C. (1973). Paulo Freire in Bombay. *New Frontiers in Education 3*(2), 92-98.
Foster, M. (1994). The power to know one thing is never the power to know all things: Methodological notes on two studies of Black American teachers. In A. Gitlin (Ed.), *Power and method: Political activism and educational research* (pp. 129-146). New York: Routledge.
Foucault, M. (1970). *The order of things.* London: Tavistock.
Foucault, M. (1975). *Discipline and punish.* New York: Vintage.
Foucault, M. (1978). *Power/Knowledge.* Brighton: Harvester Press.

Foucault, M. (1979) *Discipline and punish: The birth of the prison*. New York: Vintage Books.
Foucault, M. (1980). *History of sexuality: Vol. I*. New York: Vintage.
Foucault, M. (1984). Politics and ethics: An interview. In P. Rabinow (Ed.), *The Foucault reader* (pp. 373–390). London: Penguin.
Foucault, M. (1988a). *Philosophy, politics, culture* (I. Kritzman, Ed.). London: Routledge.
Foucault, M. (1988b). The ethic of care for the self as a practice of freedom: An interview In J. Bernauer & D. Rasmussen (Eds.), *The final Foucault* (pp. 1–20). Cambridge: MIT Press.
Foucault M. (1990). *The care of the self*. London: Penguin Books.
Foucault, M. (1991). *The Foucault effect: Studies in governmentality* (Graham Burchell, Colin Gordon, and Peter Miller, Eds.). Chicago: University of Chicago Press.
Foucault, M. (1994). Two lectures (originally written 1976). In Michael Kelly (Ed.), *Critique and power: Recasting the Foucault/Habermas debate*. Cambridge: MIT Press.
Fradenburg, L. & Freccero, C. (1996). *Pre-modern sexualities*. London: Routledge.
Franknberg, R. (Ed.). (1997). *Displacing whiteness: Essays in social and cultural criticism*. Durham, NC: Duke University Press.
Fraser, N. & Nicholson, S. (1988). Social criticism without philosophy: An encounter between feminism and postmodernism. *Communication 10*(3), 345–394.
Frege, G. (1977). *Logical investigations*. Oxford: Blackwell.
Freire, P. (1969). Cultural liberty in Latin America. *International Catholic Auxiliaries News 7*(1), 2–6.
Freire, P. (1970a). Cultural action. Lecture delivered at CIDOC, Cuernavaca, January.
Freire, P. (1970b). Showing a man how to name the world. *New World Outlook*. August, 16–17.
Freire, P. (1970c). Development and educational demands. *World Christian Education 25*(3), 125–126.
Freire, P. (1971a). By learning they can teach. *Studies in Adult Education, 2*, 1–9.
Freire, P. (1971b). Education as cultural action: An introduction. In L.M. Colonnese (Ed.), *Conscientization for liberation* (pp. 109–122). Washington: Division for Latin America.
Freire, P. (1972a). *Pedagogy of the oppressed*. Harmondsworth, UK: Penguin.
Freire, P. (1972b). *Cultural action for freedom*. Harmondsworth, UK: Penguin.
Freire, P. (1972c). The third world and theology. *LADOC*, March, 1–3.
Freire, P. (1974). Research methods. *Literacy Discussion* Spring, 133–142.
Freire, P. (1975). Oppression. *LADOC*, September–October, 16–19.
Freire, P. (1976). *Education: The practice of freedom*. London: Writers and Readers.
Freire, P. (1978). *Pedagogy in process: The letters to Guinea-Bissau*. London: Writers and Readers.
Freire, P. (1979). Letter to adult education workers. In *Learning by living and doing* (pp. 27–32). Geneva: IDAC.
Freire, P. (1985). *The politics of education*. London: MacMillan.
Freire, P. (1993). *Pedagogy of the city*. New York: Continuum.
Freire, P. (1994). *Pedagogy of hope*. New York: Continuum.
Freire, P. (1996). *Letters to Cristina: Reflections on my life and work*. London: Routledge.
Freire, P. (1997a). *Pedagogy of the heart*. New York: Continuum.
Freire, P. (1997b). A response. In P. Freire J.W. Fraser, D. Macedo, T. McKinnon, & W.T. Stokes (Eds.), *Mentoring the mentor: A critical dialogue with Paulo Freire* (303–329). New York: Peter Lang.
Freire, P. (1998a). *Teachers as cultural workers: Letters to those who dare teach*. Boulder, CO: Westview Press.

Freire, P. (1998b). *Politics and education*. Los Angeles: UCLA Latin American Center Publications.
Freire, P. (1999). *Pedagogy of freedom: Ethics, democracy, and civic courage*. Lanham: Rowman and Littlefield.
Freire, P. & Faundez, A. (1989). *Learning to question: A pedagogy of liberation*. Geneva: World Council of Churches.
Freire, P. & Macedo, D. (1987). *Literacy: Reading the word and the world*. London: Routledge and Kegan Paul.
Freire, P. & Macedo, D. (1993). A dialogue with Paulo Freire. In P. McLaren & P. Leonard (Eds.), *Paulo Freire: A Critical Encounter* (pp. 169–176). London: Routledge.
Freire, P. & Macedo, D. (1995). A dialogue: Culture, language, and race. *Harvard Educational Review 65*(3), 377–402.
Freire, P. & Shor, I. (1987). *A pedagogy for liberation*. London: MacMillan.
Friedan, B. (1981). *The second stage*. New York: Summit Books.
Friedman, J. (1997). Global crises, the struggle for identity and intellectual porkbarrelling: Cosmopolitans versus locals, ethnics and nationals in an era of de-hegemonization. In P. Werbner and T. Modood (Eds.), *Debating cultural hybridity: Multicultural identities and the politics of antiracism* (pp. 70–89). London: Zed Books.
Friedman, T. (2000). *The Lexus and the olive tree*. New York: Anchor Books.
Fromm, E. (1941). *Escape from freedom*. London: Routledge & Kegan Paul.
Fromm, E. (1961). *Marx's concept of man*. New York: Continuum.
Fromm, E. (1964a). Humanism and psychoanalysis. *Contemporary Psychoanalysis, 1*, 69–79.
Fromm, E. (1964b). *The heart of man: Its genius for good and evil*. New York: Harper and Row.
Fromm, E. (1970). *The crisis of psychoanalysis*. New York: Holt, Rinehart, Winston.
Fromm, E. (1978). *To have or to be?* London: Abacus.
Fromm, E. (1984). *The fear of freedom*. London: Ark.
Frost, G. (1997). *Loyalty misplaced: Misdirected virtue and social disintegration*. London: Social Affairs Unit.
Funk, R. (1997). Editor's Foreword. In Erich Fromm, *On being human* (pp. 9–12). New York: Continuum.
Funk, R. (2000). Erich Fromm's life and work. ww.erichfromm.de/english/life/life_bio2.html Downloaded 24/06/2001.
Funkenstein, A. (2000). Knowledge as a key for salvation. *Zemanim 73* (Winter 2000–2001), 4–9 (in Hebrew).
Gage, N. (1978). *The scientific basis of the art of teaching*. New York: Teachers College Press.
Galbraith, J. K. (1978). *The new industrial state*, 3rd ed. New York: New American Library.
Gamman, L. & Marshment, M. . (1994) *The female gaze: Women as viewers of popular culture*. Aylesbury, UK: The Women's Press.
Gasche, R. (1986). *The tain of the mirror: Derrida and philosophical reflection*. Cambridge: Harvard University Press.
Gilborn, D. (1990). *"Race," ethnicity, and education: Teaching and learning in multi-ethnic schools*. London: Unwin Hyman.
Gillborn, D. (1995). *Racism and antiracism in real schools*. Buckingham: Open University Press.
Gillett, G. (1992). *Representation meaning & thought*. Oxford: Clarendon.
Gillett, G. (1995). Humpty Dumpty and the night of the triffids: Individualism and rule following. *Synthese, 105*,191–206.

Gillett, G. (1999). *The mind and its discontents*. Oxford: University Press.
Gilloch, G. (1997). *Myths and metropolis: Walter Benjamin and the city*. Cambridge: Polity Press.
Gilroy, P. (1987). *There ain't no black in the Union Jack*. London: Hutchinson.
Gilroy, P. (1992). The end of antiracism. In J. Donald & A. Rattansi (Eds.), *"Race," culture, and difference* (pp. 49–61). London: Sage.
Gilroy, P. (1993). *The black Atlantic: Modernity and double consciousness*. London: Verso.
Gilroy, P. (2000). *Against race*. Cambridge: Harvard University Press.
Giroux, H. (1981a). *Ideology, culture & the process of schooling*, Philadelphia: Temple University Press.
Giroux, H. (1981b). Pedagogy, pessimism and the politics of conformity. *Curriculum Inquiry, 11*(3), 211–222.
Giroux, H. (1983). *Theory and resistance in education: A pedagogy for the opposition*. South Hadley, MA: Bergin & Garvey.
Giroux, H. (1985). Introduction. In P. Freire, *The politics of education*. London: MacMillan.
Giroux, H. (1988). Border pedagogy and the politics of modernism/postmodernism. In Henry Giroux, *Teachers as intellectuals* (pp. 79–114). New York: Bergin and Garvey.
Giroux, H. (1992). *Border crossings*. London: Routledge.
Giroux, H. (1996). Is there a place for cultural studies in colleges of education? In H. Giroux, C. Lankshear, P. McLaren, and M. Peters, *Counternarratives: Cultural studies and critical pedagogies in postmodern spaces* (pp. 41–58). New York: Routledge,.
Giroux, H. (1997). *Pedagogy and the politics of hope: Theory, culture and schooling*. Boulder, CO: Westview Press.
Giroux, H. (2000a). *Impure acts: The practical politics of cultural studies*. New York: Routledge.
Giroux, H. (2000b). Public pedagogy as cultural politics: Stuart Hall and the "crisis" of culture. *Cultural Studies 14*(2), 341–360.
Giroux, H. & Aronowitz, S. (1981) *Education under siege—The conservative, liberal, and radical debate over schooling*. South Hadley: Bergin and Garvey.
Gitlin, A. (Ed.). (1994). *Power and method: Political activism and educational research*. New York: Routledge.
Glazer, N. (1998). *We are all multiculturalists now*. Cambridge: Harvard University Press.
Goldberg, D. (1995). *Racist culture: Philosophy and the politics of meaning*. Oxford: Blackwell.
Goldberg, D. (1994). Introduction: Multicultural conditions. In D. Goldberg (Ed.), *Multiculturalism: A critical reader* (pp. 1–41). Oxford: Basil Blackwell.
Goldfarb, J. (1991). *The cynical society: The culture of politics and the politics of culture in American life*. Chicago: University of Chicago Press.
Gotanda, N. (1991). A critique of our constitution is color-blind. *Stanford Law Review, 44*, 1–68.
Gottlieb, R. (1993). *Forcing the spring: The transformation of the American environmental movement*. Washington, DC: Island Press.
Gramsci, A. (1967). *The modern prince and other writings*. (Louis Marks, Trans.). New York: International Publishers.
Gramsci, A. (1971). *Selections from the prison notebooks*. (Q. Hoare and G. Nowell Smith, Eds.). London: Lawrence and Wishart.
Grant, L. (1993). *Sexing the millennium: A political history of the sexual revolution*. London: HarperCollins.
Greene, M. (1978). *Landscapes of learning*. New York: Teachers College Press.
Greene, M. (1978b). The matter of mystification: Teacher education in unquiet times. In M. Greene, *Landscapes of learning* (pp. 53–73). New York: Teachers College Press.

Greene, M. (1986). In search of a critical pedagogy. *Harvard Educational Review* 56(4), 427–441.
Greene, M. (1995a). Choosing a past, inventing a future. In William Ayers (Ed.), *To become a teacher: Making a difference in children's lives* (pp. 65–77). New York: Teachers College Press.
Greene, M. (1995b). *Releasing the imagination: Essays on education, the arts, and social change.* San Francisco: Jossey-Bass.
Greene, M. (1998). An autobiographical remembrance. In William Pinar (Ed.), *The passionate mind of Maxine Greene: "I am . . . not yet"* (pp. 1–8). Bristol, PA: Falmer Press.
Greider, W. (1996). *One world, ready or not: The maniac logic of global capitalism.* New York: Simon & Schuster.
Grosz, E. (1994). *Volatile bodies: Towards a corporeal feminism.* Sydney: Allen and Unwin.
Grumet, M. (1988) *Bitter milk: Women and teaching.* Amherst: University of Massachusetts Press.
Guinier, L. (1991). The triumph of tokenism: The Voting Rights Act and the theory of black electoral success. *Michigan Law Review, 89,* 1077–1154.
Guinier, L. (1994). *The tyranny of the majority: Fundamental fairness in representative democracy.* New York: The Free Press.
Gur-Ze'ev, I. (1988). Walter Benjamin and Max Horkheimer: From utopia to redemption. *The Journal of Jewish Thought and Philosophy, 8,* 119–155.
Gur-Ze'ev, I. (1996). *The Frankfurt school and the history of pessimism,* Jerusalem: The Magness Press (in Hebrew).
Gur-Ze'ev, I. (1998). Toward a nonrepressive critical theory. *Educational Theory* 48(4), 463–486.
Gur-Ze'ev, I. (2002). Martin Heidegger, transcendence, and the possibility of counter-education. In M. Peters (Ed.), *Heidegger, education, and modernity* (pp. 65–80). Lanham & Oxford: Rowman & Littlefield.
Habermas, J. (1971). *Knowledge and human interests.* Boston: Beacon Press.
Habermas, J. (1974). *Theory and practice.* London: Heinemann Educational Books.
Habermas, J. (1975). *Legitimation crisis.* Boston: Beacon Press.
Habermas, J. (1979). *Communication and the evolution of society.* Boston: Beacon Press.
Habermas, J. (1984). *Theory of communicative action, Vol. 1.* Boston: Beacon Press.
Habermas, J. (1987a). *Theory of communicative action, Vol. 2.* Boston: Beacon Press.
Habermas, J. (1987b). *The philosophical discourse of modernity.* Cambridge: MIT Press.
Habermas, J. (1989). *The structural transformation of the public sphere.* Cambridge: MIT Press.
Habermas, J. (1993). *Justification and application.* Cambridge: MIT Press.
Habermas, J. (1994). Struggles for recognition in the democratic constitutional state. In A. Gutmann (Ed.), *Multiculturalism: Examining the politics of recognition* (pp. 107–148). Princeton, NJ.: Princeton University Press.
Hall, S. (1980). Cultural Studies and the Centre: Some problematics and problems. In S. Hall, D. Hobson, A. Lowe, and P. Willis (Eds.), *Culture, media, language* (pp. 15–47). London: Hutchinson.
Hall, S. (1992). New ethnicities. In J. Donald & A. Rattansi (Eds.), *"Race," culture and difference* (pp. 252–259). London: Sage.
Hall, S. (1996) Cultural studies and its theoretical legacies. In D Morley and K-H Chen (Eds), *Stuart Hall: Critical dialogues in cultural studies.* London: Routledge.
Hall, S. (Ed.) (1997). *Representation: Cultural representations and signifying practices.* London: Sage.

Handelman, S. (1991). *Fragments of redemption: Jewish thought and literary theory in Benjamin, Scholem, and Levinas*. Bloomington: Indiana University Press.

Handler, R. (1988). *Nationalism and the politics of culture in Quebec*. Madison: University of Wisconsin Press.

Hannerz, U. (1992). *Cultural complexity: Studies in the organization of meaning*. New York: Columbia University Press.

Haraway, D. (1991). *Simians, cyborgs, and women*. New York: Routledge.

Harre, H.R. and Gillett, G. (1994). *The discursive mind*. Thousand Oaks, CA: Sage.

Harris, A.P. (1994). Forward: The jurisprudence of reconstruction. *California Law Review, 82*, 741–785.

Harris, C.L. (1993). Whiteness as property. *Harvard Law Review, 106*, 1710–1791.

Harvey, D. (1989). *The condition of postmodernity*. Oxford: Blackwell.

Harvey, D. (1996). *Justice, nature and the geography of difference*. Oxford: Blackwell.

Hatcher, R. (1987). Race and education: Two perspectives for change. In B. Troyna (Ed.), *Racial inequality in education* (pp. 184–200). London: Tavistock.

Hauser, A. (1951) *The social history of art*. London: Routledge & Kegan Paul,

Hayles, N. Katherine. (1999). *How we became posthuman: Virtual bodies in cybernetics, literature, and informatics*. Chicago: University of Chicago Press.

Hayman, R.L. (1995). The color of tradition: Critical race theory and postmodern constitutional traditionalism. *Harvard Civil Rights and Civil Liberties Law Review, 30*, 57–108.

Heaney, S. (1966). *Death of a naturalist*. London: Faber and Faber.

Hegel, H-G. (1977). *Phenomenology of spirit*. (A. V. Miller Trans.). Oxford: Oxford University Press. From the German of 1807.

Heidegger, M. (1962). *Being and time*. (first English edition translated by J. MacQuarrie and E. Robinson). Oxford: Basil Blackwell.

Heidegger, M. (1987). *Nietzsche*. (David Farrell Krell, Trans.). 2 vols. San Francisco: Harper and Row.

Heidegger, M. (1996a). Letter on humanism. In *Basic writings* (pp. 217–265). London: Routledge and Kegan Paul.

Heidegger, M. (1996b). The question concerning technology. In *Basic writings* (pp. 311–341). London: Routledge and Kegan Paul.

Hermes, M. (1998). Research methods as a situated response: Towards a First Nation's methodology. *International Journal of Qualitative Studies in Education, 11*, 155–168.

Hicks, E. (1991). *Border writing*. Minneapolis: University of Minnesota Press.

Hill Collins, P. (1998). *Fighting words: Black women & the search for justice*. Minneapolis: University of Minnesota Press.

Hinchman, L. P. & Hinchman, S.K. (1994). Existentialism Politicised. In L.P. Hinchman & S.K. Hinchman (Eds.), *Hannah Arendt: Critical essays*. New York: State University of New York Press.

Hirsch, E. D. Jr. (1996). *The schools we need*. New York: Doubleday.

Hoffman, D. (1996). Culture and self in multicultural education: Reflections on discourse, text, and practice. *American Educational Research Journal, 33*, 545–569.

Hoffman, D. (1997). Diversity in practice: Perspectives on concept, context, and policy. *Educational Policy 11*, 375–392.

Hohendahl, P. (1995). *Prismatic thought: Theodor W. Adorno*. Lincoln: University of Nebraska Press.

Holloway, L. (2000). As poverty shifts students, getting lessons to stick proves a tough task. *The New York Times* (Thursday, May 25, 2000).

Holmes, S.A. (1996, 17 November). Bias suit harbinger. *New York Times,* sec. 1, p. 12.
Holt, L. & Margonis, F. (1992). Critical theory of a conservative stamp. *Educational Theory* 42(2), 231–250.
Horkheimer, M. (1960). Letter to Adorno 26 May 1960, Max Horkheimer Archive VI, 13, 511.
Horkheimer, M (1937/1972). Traditional and critical theory. In Max Horkheimer, *Critical theory: Selected essays*. (Matthew J. O'Connell, Trans.). New York: Seabury Press.
Horkheimer, M. (1938/1988). Montaigne und die fucktion derbSkepsis. *Gesammelte Schriften* IV (pp. 236–294). Frankfurt a. Main: Fischer.
Horkheimer, M. (1973). The authoritarian state. *Telos, 15,* 3–20.
Horkheimer, M. (1974). *The ecplise of reason.* New York: Oxford University Press.
Horkheimer, M. (1978). *Dawn & decline—Notes 1926–1931 and 1950–1969.* New York: Seabury Press.
Horkheimer, M. (1985). *Gesammelte Schriften,* III. Frankfurt a.Main: Fischer.
Horkheimer, M. (1985). *Gesammelte Schriften,* IV. Frankfurt a.Main: Fischer.
Horkheimer, M. (1985). *Gesammelte Schriften,* V. Frankfurt a.Main: Fischer.
Horkheimer, M. (1985). *Gesammelte Schriften,* VII. Frankfurt a.Main: Fischer.
Horkheimer, M. (1985). *Gesammelte Schriften,* VII. Frankfurt a.Main Fischer.
Horkheiner, M. (1985). Begriff der Bildung. *Gesammelte Schriften,* VIII. Frankfurt a.Main Fischer.
Horkheimer, M. (1985). *Gesammelte Schriften,* XI. Frankfurt a.Main: Fischer.
Horkheimer, M. (1989). *Gesammelte Schriften,* XIII. Frankfurt a.Main: Fischer.
Horkheimer, M. (1988). *Gesammelte Schriften,* XIV. Frankfurt a.Main: Fischer.
Horkheimer, M. & Adorno, T. (1972). *Dialectic of enlightenment.* New York: Seabury Press.
Horkheimer, M. & Adorno, T. (1988). *Dialektik der Aufklärung.* Frankfurt a.Main: Fischer.
Horner, B. (2000). Politics, pedagogy, and the profession of composition: Confronting commodification and the contingencies of power. *Journal of Advanced Composition* 20(1), 128–143.
Horton, M. & Freire, P. (1990). *We make the road by walking: Conversations on education and social change.* Philadelphia: Temple University Press.
Howe, S. (1998). *Afrocentrism: Mythical pasts and imagined homes.* London: Verso.
Hoy, D.C. & McCarthy, T. (1994). *Critical theory.* Cambridge: Blackwell Publishers.
Huizinga, J. (1971). *The waning of the middle ages.* (F. Hopman, Trans.). Harmondsworth, UK: Penguin.
Hune, S. (1995). Rethinking race: Paradigms and policy formation. *Amerasia Journal, 21,* 29–40.
Hunter, I. (1990). Personality as a vocation: The political rationality of the humanities. *Economy and Society* 19(4), 391–430.
Hunter, I. (1994). *Rethinking the school.* New York: St. Martin's Press.
Idhe, D. (1990). *Technology and the lifeworld: From garden to earth.* Bloomington: Indiana University Press.
Iglesias, E.M. & Valdes, F. (1998). Religion, gender, sexuality, race and class in coalitional theory: A critical and self-critical analysis of LatCrit social justice agendas. *Chicano-Latino Law Review, 19,* 504–588.
Ignatiev, N. (1995). *How the Irish became white.* New York: Routledge.
Ingram, D. (1996). Novus Ordo Seculorun: The Trial of (post)Modernity or the Tale of Two Revolutions. In L. May and J. Kohn (Eds.), *Hannah Arendt twenty years later.* Cambridge: MIT Press.

Jackson, S. (1995). Heterosexuality, power and pleasure. *Feminism and Psychology,* 5(1), 131-135.
Jacoby, R. (1975). *Social amnesia: A critique of conformist psychology from Adler to Laing.* Boston: Beacon Press.
Jacoby, R. (1981). *Dialectic of defeat.* New York: Cambridge University Press.
Jacoby, R. (1999). *The end of utopia.* New York: Basic Books
Jameson, F. (1992). *Postmodernism, or the cultural logic of late capitalism.* Durham, NC: Duke University Press.
JanMohamed, A. (1992). Worldliness–without–world, homelessness–as–home: Toward a definition of the specular border intellectual. In Michael Sprinker (Ed.), *Edward Said: A reader* (pp. 97–123). Cambridge: Basil Blackwell.
Jay, M. (1973). *Dialectical imagination.* Boston: Little, Brown.
Jay, P. (1994). Posing: Autobiography and the subject of photography. In K. Ashley, L. Gilmore, and G. Peters (Eds.), *Autobiography and postmodernism* (pp- 119–164). Amherst: University of Massachusetts Press.
Jeffares, A.N. (Ed.). (1962). *W.B. Yeats: Selected poetry.* London: Macmillan.
Jenkins, R. (1994). Rethinking ethnicity: Identity, categorization and power. *Ethnic and Racial Studies 17,* 197–223.
Jenkins, R. (1997). *Rethinking ethnicity.* London: Sage.
Jennings, M. (1987). *Dialectical images: Walter Benjamin's theory of literary criticism.* Ithaca, NY: Cornell University Press.
Jinks, D.P. (1997). Essays in refusal: Pre-theoretical commitments in postmodern anthropology and critical race theory. *Yale Law Journal, 107,* 499–528.
Johnson, A.M. (1993). Bid whist, tonk, and U.S. v. Fordice: Why integrationism fails African-Americans again. *California Law Review, 81,* 1401–1470.
Johnson, R. (1997). Teaching without guarantees: Cultural studies, pedagogy and identity. In Joyce Canaan and Debbie Epstein (Eds.), *A question of discipline* (pp. 42–73). Boulder, CO: Westview Press.
Joppke, C. & Lukes, S. (Eds.). (1999). *Multicultural questions.* Oxford: Oxford University Press.
Kalantzis, M. & Cope, B. (1999). Multicultural education: Transforming the mainstream. In S. May (Ed.), *Critical multiculturalism: Rethinking multicultural and antiracist education* (pp. 245–276). London: RoutledgeFalmer.
Kamuf, P. (Ed.). (1991). *A Derrida reader.* New York: Harvester Wheatsheaf.
Kanpol, B. & McLaren, P. (1995). *Critical multiculturalism: Uncommon voices in a common struggle.* Westport: Bergin and Garvey.
Kaplan, C. (1987). Deterritorialisations: The rewriting of home and exile in Western feminist discourse. *Cultural Critique* 6 (Spring), 187–198.
Karp, S. (1994). Lesson plans: The politics of education: An interview with Herbert Kohl. At http://zena.secureforum.com/znet/ZMag/articles/April94Krp.htm.
Kaufman, D. (1996). Notes from hell. *National Review* (September 30, 1996), 46.
Keane, C. (1994). Refiguring the body: A review of Elizabeth Grosz (1994). *Volatile Bodies: Towards a Corporeal Feminism, Australian Women's Book Review* 6(3), 16–17.
Keenan, T. (1997). *Fables of responsibility: Aberrations and predicaments in ethics and politics.* Stanford: Stanford University Press.
Kellner, D. (1989). *Critical theory, Marxism and modernity.* Cambridge: Polity Press.
Kellner, D. (1990). From *1984* to *One-Dimensional Man:* Reflections on Orwell and Marcuse. *Current Perspectives in Social Theory 6,* 223–252.
Kellner, D. (1995a). *Media culture.* New York: Routledge.

Kellner, D. (1995b). The obsolescence of Marxism? In Bernd Magnus and Stephen Cullenberg (Eds.), *Whither Marxism?* (pp. 3–30). London and New York: Routledge.
Kellner, D. (1998). Globalization and the postmodern turn. In Roland Axtmann (Ed.), *Globalization and Europe* (pp. 23–42). London: Cassells.
Kellner, D. (nd). The Frankfurt school and British cultural studies: The missed articulation. http://www.uta.edu/huma/illuminations/kell16.htm).
Kellner, D. & Cvetkovich, A. (Eds.). (1996). *Articulating the global and the local. Globalization and cultural studies*. Boulder, CO: Westview.
Kelly, U. (1997). *Schooling desire: Literacy, cultural politics, and pedagogy*. New York: Routledge.
Kennedy, R.L. (1989). Racial critiques of legal academia. *Harvard Law Review, 102*, 1745–1819.
Kierkegaard. S. (1936 & 1962). *Philosophical fragments*. (D. F. Swenson, Trans; N. Thulstrup, Intro; H. V. Hong, Revisions). Princeton: Princeton University Press.
Kierkegaard, S. (1941). *Concluding unscientific postscript*. (D. F. Swenson, Trans; N. Thulstrup, Intro; H.V. Hong, Revisions). Princeton: Princeton University Press.
Kincheloe, J. & Steinberg, S. (1997). *Changing multiculturalism*. Buckingham: Open University Press.
Kirby, V. (1997). *Telling flesh: The substance of the corporeal*. New York: Routledge.
Kirk, D. (1993). Adolescent construction of bodies: Some implications for health education and promotion. Paper presented to the XII Congress of the IAPES for Girls and Women, Melbourne, August.
Kohl, H. (1997). Herb Kohl interview. At http://www.zmag.org/sep/kohlint.htm.
Koundoura, M. (1998). Multiculturalism or multinationalism? In David Bennett (Ed.), *Multicultural states* (pp. 69–87). New York: Routledge.
Krauss, R. (1983). *The originality of the avant-garde and other modernist myths*. Cambridge: Cambridge University Press.
Kristeva. J. (2001). *Hannah Arendt*. (R. Guberman, Trans.). New York: Columbia University Press.
Kymlicka, W. (1989). *Liberalism, community and culture*. Oxford: Clarendon Press.
Kymlicka, W. (1995a). *Multicultural citizenship: A liberal theory of minority rights*. Oxford: Clarendon Press.
Kymlicka, W. (1995b). Introduction. In W. Kymlicka (Ed.), *The rights of minority cultures* (pp. 1–27). Oxford: Oxford University Press.
Kymlicka, W. & Norman, W. (Eds.). (1999). *Citizenship in diverse societies*. Oxford: Oxford University Press.
Labaree, B. (1997). *How to succeed in school*. New Haven, CT: Yale University Press.
Ladson-Billings, G. & Tate, W.F. IV (1995). Toward a critical race theory of education. *Teachers College Record, 97*, 47–63.
Ladson-Billings, G. (2000). Racialized discourses and ethnic epistemologies. In N.K. Denzin & Y.S. Lincoln (Eds.), *Handbook of qualitative research* 2nd ed. (pp. 257–278). Thousand Oaks, CA: Sage.
Lankshear, C. (1988). In whose interests? The role of intellectuals in New Zealand society. *Sites, 17*, 8–17.
Lankshear, C. (1993). Functional literacy from a Freirean point of view. In P. McLaren and P. Leonard (Eds.), *Paulo Freire: A critical encounter* (pp. 90–118). London: Routledge.
Lash, S. (1991). Genealogy and the body: Foucault/Deleuze/Nietzsche. In M. Featherstone, M. Hepworth, and B. Turner (Eds.), *The body* (pp. 59–79). London: Sage.

Latour, B. (1993). *We have never been modern*. London: Harvester Wheatsheaf.
Leder, D. 1990. *The absent body*. Chicago: University of Chicago Press.
Lessing, G. (1927). *The education of the human race*. (F. W. Robertson, Trans.). London: Anthroposophical Pub. Co.
Lévi Strauss, C. (1994). Anthropology, race, and politics: A conversation with Didier Eribon. In R. Borofsky (Ed.), *Assessing cultural anthropology* (pp. 420–429). New York: McGraw Hill.
Lipsitz, G. (1998). *The possessive investment in whiteness: How white people profit from identity politics*. Philadelphia: Temple University Press.
Lloyd, A.S. (1972). Freire, conscientization, and adult education. *Adult Education* 23(1), 3–20.
Lloyd, C. (1994). Universalism and difference: The crisis of antiracism in France and the UK. In A. Rattansi and S. Westwood (Eds.), *Racism, modernity, and identity* (pp. 222–244). Cambridge: Polity Press.
Lomawaima, K.T. (2000). Tribal sovereigns: Reframing research in American Indian education. *Harvard Educational Review, 70*, 1–21.
Longino, H. (1990). *Science as social knowledge*. Princeton, NJ: Princeton University Press.
Lopez, I.H. (1996). *White by law: The legal construction of race*. New York: NYU Press.
Löwenthal, L. (1989). *Critical theory and Frankfurt theorists: Lectures, correspondence, conversations*. New Brunswick, NJ: Transaction Books.
Lowy, M. (1992). Religion, utopia and countermodernity: The allegory of the angel of history in Walter Benjamin. In *On changing the world: Essays in political philosophy, from Karl Marx to Walter Benjamin* (pp.164–71). Atlantic City, NJ: Atlantic Highlands.
Lukacs, G. (1971). *History and class consciousness*. Cambridge: MIT Press.
Luke, T. (1989). *Screens of power: Ideology, domination and resistance in informational society*. Urbana: University of Illinois Press.
Luke, T. (1990). *Social theory and modernity: Ideology domination, and resistance*. Newbury Park, CA: Sage.
Luke, T. (1997). *Ecocritique: Contesting the politics of nature, economy and culture*. Minneapolis: University of Minnesota Press.
Luke, T. (1998). "The politics of digital inequality: Access, capability, and distribution in cyberspace." In *The Politics of Cyberspace* (Chris Toulouse and Timothy W. Luke, Eds.) New York: Routledge, 121–144.
Luke, T. (1999). *Capitalism, democracy and ecology: Departing from Marx*. Urbana-Champaign: University of Illinois Press.
Lyotard, J. (1984). *The postmodern condition: A report on knowledge*. (G. Bennington, and B. Massumi, Trans.). Manchester: Manchester University Press.
Lyotard, J.-F. (1991). *The inhuman: Reflections on time*. Stanford: Stanford University Press.
MacDonald, I., Bhavnani, R., Khan, L., & John, G. (1989). *Murder in the playground*. London: Longsight Press.
Macey, D. (1994). *The lives of Michel Foucault*. London: Vintage Press.
Mackie, R. (1980). Contributions to the thought of Paulo Freire. In R. Mackie (Ed.), *Literacy and revolution: The pedagogy of Paulo Freire* (pp. 92–119). London, Pluto Press.
Makins, V. (1972). Interview with Paulo Freire. *The Times Educational Supplement*, 20 October: 80.
Mandel, E. (1978). *Late capitalism*. London: Verso.
Mannheim, K. (1956). *Essays on the sociology of culture*. London: Routledge.
Mao Tse-Tung (1968). *Four essays on philosophy*. Peking: Foreign Languages Press.
Marcuse, H. (1936). [Epikur]. Herbert Marcuse Archive 100.25.
Marcuse, H. (1941, 1960). *Reason and revolution*. New York: Oxford University Press; reprinted Boston: Beacon Press.

Marcuse, H. (1955, 1997). *Eros and civilization*. Boston: Beacon Press; Routledge.
Marcuse, H (1964). *One-dimensional man*. Boston: Beacon Press.
Marcuse, H. (1964). Marx, Freud und der Monotheismus. Herbert Marcuse Archive 241.00 (8.6.1964), pp. 1–14.
Marcuse, H. (1968). *Negations—Essays in critical theory*, London: Penguin.
Marcuse, H. (1969). *An essay on liberation*. Boston: Beacon Press.
Marcuse, H. (1969). The realm of freedom and the realm of necessity: A reconsideration. *Praxis 5*, 1.
Marcuse, H. (1971). Nachwort. In Walter Benjamin, *Zur Kritik der Gewalt und andere Aufsätze*. Frankfurt a.Main: Fischer.
Marcuse, H. (1972). *Counterrevolution and revolt*. Boston: Beacon Press.
Marcuse, H. (1974). Marxism and feminism. *Women's Studies* 2(3), 279–288.
Marcuse, H. (1976). Art and literature in the one-dimensional society. (Oded Peled, Trans.), *Proza 10*, 18–19.
Marcuse, H. (1979a). Fortschrit—Kategorien. Herbert Marcuse Archive 564.02.
Marcuse, H. (1979b). The reification of the proletariat. *Canadian Journal of Philosophy and Social Theory, 3*, 1.
Marcuse, H. (1980). Protosocialism and late capitalism: Toward a theoretical synthesis based on Bahro's analysis. In Ulf Wolter (Ed.), *Rudolf Bahro: Critical responses* (pp. 24–28). White Plains, NY: M.E. Sharpe:
Marcuse, H. (n.d.). Culture and revolution. Herbert Marcuse Archive 406.00.
Marcuse, H. (n.d.) On pluralism, future, and philosophy. Herbert Marcuse Archive 569.00.
Marcuse, H. (2001). *Toward a critical theory of society* (Douglas Kellner, Ed.). London: Routledge.
Margalit, A. & Raz, J. (1995). National self-determination. In W. Kymlicka (Ed.), *The rights of minority cultures* (pp. 79–92). Oxford: Oxford University Press.
Martin, B. (1997). Introduction: Teaching, literature, changing cultures. *PMLA 112* (1), 7–25.
Martin, B. & Mohanty, C. (1986). Feminist politics: What's home got to do with it? In Teresa de Lauretis (Ed.), *Feminist studies/critical studies* (pp. 191–212). Bloomington: Indiana University Press.
Martin, H.-P. & Schumann, H. (1997). *The global trap: Globalization and the assault on democracy and prosperity*. London: Zed Press.
Marx, K. (1844/1961). *Economic and philosophical manuscripts* (T. B. Bottomore, Trans.). In E. Fromm, *Marx's concept of man* (pp. 90–198). New York: Continuum.
Marx, K. (1847/1967). The poverty of philosophy. In L.Easton and K. Guddat (Eds.), *Writings of the young Marx on philosophy and society*. New York: Doubleday.
Marx, K. (1859/1970). *A contribution to the critique of political economy*. Moscow: Progress Publishers.
Marx, K. (1867/1976). *Capital*, vol.1. (B. Fowkes, Trans). Harmondsworth, UK: Penguin.
Marx, K. & Engels, F. (1845/1939) *The German ideology* (C. J. Arthur, Ed.). London: Lawrence and Wishart Ltd.
Marx, K. & Engels, F. (1848/1967). *The communist manifesto*. Harmondsworth, UK: Penguin.
Marx, K. & Engels, F. (1845/1976). *The German ideology*. Moscow: Progress Publishers.
Matsuda, M.J. (1987). Looking to the bottom: Critical legal studies and reparations. *Harvard Civil Rights-Civil Liberties Review, 72*, 30–164.
May, S. (1994). *Making multicultural education work*. Clevedon, England: Multilingual Matters.

May, S. (Ed.). (1999a). *Critical multiculturalism: Rethinking multicultural and antiracist education*. London: RoutledgeFalmer.
May, S. (1999b). Critical multiculturalism and cultural difference: Avoiding essentialism. In S. May (ed.), *Critical multiculturalism: Rethinking multicultural and antiracist education* (pp. 11–41). London: RoutledgeFalmer.
May, S. (2001). *Language and minority rights: Ethnicity, nationalism and the politics of language*. London: Longman.
May, S. (2002). Multiculturalism. In D. Goldberg & J. Solomos (Eds.), *The Blackwell companion to racial and ethnic studies* (pp. 124–144). Oxford: Blackwell.
Mayo, P. (1997) Tribute to Paulo Freire (1921–1997). *International Journal of Lifelong Education* 16(5), 365–370.
Mayo, P. (1999). *Gramsci, Freire and adult education: Possibilities for transformative action*. London: Zed Books.
McCarthy, C. & Crichlow, W. (Eds.). (1993). *"Race," identity and representation in education*. New York: Routledge.
McCarthy, T. (1994). Philosophy and critical theory: A reprise. In David Couzens Hoy and Thomas McCarthy (Eds.), *Critical theory* (pp. 7–22). Oxford: Blackwell.
McCarthy, T. (2001). Critical theory today: An Interview with Thomas McCarthy. Conducted by Shane O'Neill and Nick Smith. In Rehg, W. & Bohman, J. (Eds.), *Pluralism and the pragmatic turn: The transformation of critical theory: Essays in honor of Thomas McCarthy* (pp. 413–429). Cambridge: MIT Press.
McCole, J. (1993). *Walter Benjamin and the antinomies of tradition*. Ithaca, NY: Cornell University Press.
McGuigan, J. (1992) *Cultural populism*. London: Routledge.
McIntyre, A. (1997). Constructing the image of a white teacher. *Teachers College Record, 98*, 653–681.
McKeever, M. (2000). Snakes and ladders: Ethical issues in conducting educational research in a postcolonial context. In H. Simons & R. Usher (Eds.), *Situated ethics in educational research* (pp. 101–115). London: Routledge-Falmer.
McLaren, P. (1995). *Critical pedagogy and predatory culture*. New York: Routledge.
McLaren, P. (1997). *Revolutionary multiculturalism: Pedagogies of dissent for the new millennium*. Boulder, CO: Westview Press.
McLaren, P. (2000). Reconsidering Marx in post-Marxist times: A requiem for postmodernism? *Educational Researcher 29*(3), 25–33.
McLaren, P. (2001). Wayward multiculturalists. *Ethnicities 1, 3*.
McLaren, P. & daSilva, T.T. (1993). Decentering pedagogy: critical literacy, resistance and the politics of memory. In P. McLaren and P. Leonard (Eds.), *Paulo Freire: A critical encounter* (pp. 47–89), London: Routledge.
McLaren, P. & Torres, R. (1999). Racism and multicultural education: Rethinking "race" and "whiteness" in late capitalism. In S. May (Ed.), *Critical multiculturalism: Rethinking multicultural and antiracist education* (pp. 42–76). London: Falmer Press.
McLennan, G. (2001). Can there be a critical multiculturalism? *Ethnicities 1, 3*.
McMorris, G. (1996). Critical race theory, cognitive psychology, and the social meaning of race: Why individualism will not solve racism. *University of Missouri-Kansas City Law Review, 67*, 695–729.
Meade, E.M. (1996). The commodification of values. In L.May and J.Kohn (Eds.), *Hannah Arendt: Twenty years later*. Cambridge: MIT Press.
Merleau-Ponty, M. (1968). *The Visible and the invisible*. Evanston: Northwestern University Press.

Michael, J. (2000). *Anxious intellects: Academic professionals, public intellectuals, and enlightenment values*. Durham, NC: Duke University Press.

Miklitsch, R. (1990). The politics of teaching literature: The "pedagogical effect." *College Literature* 17(2/3), 85–94.

Miller, A. (1949). *Death of a salesman*. London: Penguin.

Miller, M. (1988). *Boxed in: The culture of T.V.* Evanston: Northwestern University Press.

Miller, T. (1998). *Technologies of truth*. Minneapolis: University of Minnesota Press.

Minow, M. (1990). *Making all the difference: Inclusion, exclusion and American law*. Ithaca, NY: Cornell University Press.

Mistry, R. (1997). *A fine balance*. Toronto: McClelland & Stewart.

Modood, T. (1992). *Not easy being British: Colour, culture and citizenship*. Stoke-on-Trent: Runnymede Trust and Trentham Books.

Modood, T. (1998a). Anti-essentialism, multiculturalism and the "recognition" of religious groups. *Journal of Political Philosophy* 6(4), 378–399.

Modood, T. (1998b). Multiculturalism, secularism and the state. *Critical Review of International Social and Political Philosophy* 1(3), 79–97.

Modood, T. & May, S. (2001). Multiculturalism and education in Britain: An internally contested debate. *International Journal of Educational Research, 35*, 305–317.

Mohan, R. (1995). Multiculturalism in the nineties: Pitfalls and possibilities. In C. Newfield, and R. Strickland (Eds.), *After political correctness: The humanities and society in the 1990s* (pp. 372–388). Boulder, CO: Westview Press.

Motion of former black students of the University of Mississippi to file amicus curiae brief in support of Ayers petitioners (1990, October). No. 90–6588 and No. 90–1205, Greenwood, MS: Willie J. Perkins, Counsel of record.

Multex.com (2001). *Market Guide: Business Description. eBay Inc*. Online. Available *http://yahoo.marketguide.com/mgi/busidesc.asp?rt=busidesc&rn=A1C7E* (27 February 2001).

Mumford, L. (1963). *Technics and civilization*. New York: Harcourt Brace Jovanovich.

Mumford, L. (1970). *The pentagon of power*. New York: Harcourt Brace.

Naficy, H. (1999). *Home, exile, homeland*. New York: Routledge.

Nagel, J. (1994). Constructing ethnicity: creating and recreating ethnic identity and culture. *Social Problems 41*, 152–176.

Negroponte, N. (1995). *Being digital*. New York: Knopf.

netgrrrl ☆ (12) and chicoboy26 ★ (32), aka Knobel, M. and Lankshear, C. (2002). What am I bid?: Reading, writing and ratings at eBay.com. In Snyder, I. (Ed.), *Silicon Literacies* (pp. 15–30). London: Routledge-Falmer.

Nowak, L. (1990). Intellectuals in the age of revolutions: The case of the socialist world. *Thesis Eleven 27*, 167–72.

Omi, M. & Winant, H. (1994). *Racial formation in the United States: From the 1960s to the 1990s*. 2nd ed. New York: Routledge.

Ong, W. (1982) *Orality and literacy: The technologizing of the word*. London: Metheun.

O'Shea, A. (1998). A special relationship? Cultural studies, academia and pedagogy. *Cultural Studies 12*(4), 513–527.

Owen, D. with Doerr, M. (2000). *None of the above: Behind the myth of scholastic aptitude*. Updated Version. Lanham, MD: Rowman & Littlefield Publishers.

Paglia, C. (1995). *Sex and violence or nature and art*. London: Penguin.

Parker, S. (1997). *Reflective teaching in a postmodern world*. Buckingham: The Open University.

Parker, L. & Lynn, M. (2002). What's race got to do with it?: Critical race theory's conflicts with and connections to qualitative research methodology and epistemology. *Qualitative Inquiry 8*, 7–22.

Peters, M. (1999). Freire and postmodernism. In P. Roberts (Ed.), *Paulo Freire, politics and pedagogy: Reflections from Aotearoa-New Zealand* (pp. 113–122). Palmerston North, New Zealand: Dunmore Press.

Phillips, A. (1997). Why worry about multiculturalism? *Dissent 44*, 57–63.

Pickstock, C. (1999). *After writing: On the liturgical consummation of philosophy*. Oxford: Blackwell.

Piven, F. & Cloward, R. (1997). *The breaking of the American social compact*. New York: New Press.

Pizzaro, M. (1998). Dialogical praxis-oriented research: A response to contemporary educational methodological discourse. *International Journal of Qualitative Studies in Education, 11*, 57–80.

Plato (1974). *The Republic*. 2nd ed. (H.D.P. Lee, Trans.). Harmondsworth, UK: Penguin.

Popper, K. (1959). *The logic of scientific discovery*. London: Hutchinson.

Putnam, T. (2000). *Bowling alone: The collapse and revival of American community*. New York: Simon and Schuster.

Rattansi, A. (1992). Changing the subject? Racism, culture, and education. In J. Donald and A. Rattansi (Eds.), *"Race," culture, and difference* (pp. 11–48). London: Sage.

Rattansi, A. (1999). Racism, "postmodernism," and reflexive multiculturalism. In S. May (Ed.), *Critical multiculturalism: Rethinking multicultural and antiracist education* (pp. 77–112). London: Falmer Press.

Readings, B. (1994). *The university in ruins*. Cambridge: Harvard University Press.

Rehg, W. & Bohman, J. (Eds.). (2001). *Pluralism and the pragmatic turn: The transformation of critical theory: Essays in honor of Thomas McCarthy*. Cambridge: MIT Press.

Reitz, C. (2000). *Aesthetic education and the new sensibility in Marcuse*. Albany: SUNY Press.

Rex, J. (1973). *Race, colonialism and the city*. Oxford: Oxford University Press.

Reynolds, W.B. (1986). The Reagan administration and civil rights: Winning the war against discrimination. *University of Illinois Law Review, 4*, 1001–1023.

Rich, F. (2000). Don't worry, be happy! *New York Times* (Saturday, July 29, 2000), p. A27.

Rilke, R. (1978). *Duino elegies*. (David Young, Trans.). New York: Norton and Co.

Rizvi, F. (1993). Children and the grammar of popular racism. In C. McCarthy & W. Crichlow (Eds.), *Race, identity and representation in education* (pp. 126–139). New York: Routledge.

Roberts, P. (1994). Education, dialogue and intervention: revisiting the Freirean project, *Educational Studies 20*(3), 307–327.

Roberts, P. (1996a). Critical literacy, breadth of perspective, and universities: Applying insights from Freire. *Studies in Higher Education 21*(2),149–163.

Roberts, P. (1996b). Defending Freirean intervention. *Educational Theory 46*(3), 335–352.

Roberts, P. (1996c). Rethinking conscientisation. *Journal of Philosophy of Education 30*(2), 179–196.

Roberts, P. (1996d). Structure, direction and rigour in liberating education. *Oxford Review of Education 22*(3), 295–316.

Roberts, P. (1998). Extending literate horizons: Paulo Freire and the multidimensional word. *Educational Review 50*(2), 105–114.

Roberts, P. (2000). *Education, literacy and humanization: Exploring the work of Paulo Freire*. Westport, CT: Bergin & Garvey.

Roediger, D.R. (1998). *Black on white: Black writers on what it means to be white*. New York: Schocken Books.
Rorty, R. (1989). *Contingency, irony and solidarity*. Cambridge: Cambridge University Press.
Rorty, R. (1992). Is Derrida a transcendental Philosopher? In D. Wood (Ed.), *Derrida: A critical reader* (pp. 235–246). Oxford: Blackwell.
Rorty, R. (1999). *Philosophy and social hope*. London, Penguin.
Rosaldo, R. (1989). *Culture and truth*. London: Routledge.
Roth, P. (2000). *The human stain*. Boston: Houghton Mifflin.
Russo, M. (1994). *The female grotesque: Risk, excess and modernity*. New York: Routledge.
Rutherford, J. (1990). A place called home: Identity and cultural politics of difference. In Jonathan Rutherford (Ed.), *Identity, community, culture, difference* (pp. 9–27). London: Lawrence and Wishart.
Sacks, P. (1985). *The English elegy: Studies in the genre from Spenser to Yeats*. Baltimore, MD: Johns Hopkins University Press.
Sacks, P. (1999). *Standardized minds*. Cambridge: Perseus Books.
Said, E. (1994). *Culture and imperialism*. London: Vintage.
Sanders, T.G. (1972). The Paulo Freire method: Literacy training and conscientization. In T.J. La Belle (Ed.), *Education and development: Latin America and the Caribbean* (pp. 587–599). Los Angeles: Latin American Center.
Santer, E. (2001). *On the psychotheology of everyday life*. Chicago: University of Chicago Press.
Sartre, J-P. (1968). *Search for a method*. (Hazel Barnes, Trans.). New York: Vintage Books.
Sartre, J-P. (1969). *Being and nothingness*. (Hazel Barnes, Trans.). London: Methuen.
Sartre, J-P. (1976). *Critique of dialectical reason*. London: New Left Books.
Schama, S. (1989). *Citizens: A chronicle of the French revolution*. London: Viking.
Scheurich, J. & Young, M. (1997). Coloring epistemologies: Are our research epistemologies racially biased? *Educational Researcher* 27, 4–16.
Scheurich, J. & Young, M. (1998). Rejoinder: In the United States of America, in both our souls and our sciences, we are avoiding white racism. *Educational Researcher*, 27, 27–32.
Schick, C. (2000). "By virtue of being White": Resistance in anti-racist pedagogy. *Race Ethnicity and Education*, 3, 83–102.
Schlesinger, A. (1992). *The disuniting of America: Reflections on a multicultural society*. New York: W.W. Norton and Co.
Scholem, G. & Adorno, T. (Eds.). (1994). *The correspondence of Walter Benjamin, 1910–1940*. Manfred R. Jacobsen and Evelyn M. Jacobsen, Trans.). Chicago: Chicago University Press.
Schroyer, T. (1975). *The critique of domination: Origins and development of critical theory*. Boston: Beacon Press.
Schumacher, E.F. (1973). *Small is beautiful: Economics as if people mattered*. New York: Harper and Row.
Sears, J.T. & Williams, W.L. (Eds.). (1997). *Overcoming hetrosexism and homophobia: Strategies that work*. New York: Columbia University Press.
Sennett, R. (1998). *The corrosion of character*. New York: Norton.
Serres, M. (1995). *Angels: A modern myth*. (Francis Cowper Trans.). Paris and New York: Flammarion.
Sewell, T. (1997). *Black masculinities and schooling: How black boys survive modern schooling*. Staffordshire, UK: Trentham Books.
Shapiro, S. (1994) Re-membering the body in critical pedagogy, *Education and Society* 12(1), 61–79.

Sheets, R.H. (2000). Advancing the field or taking center stage: The white movement in multicultural education. *Educational Resarcher, 29,* 15-21.
Sherman, E. (2001). The world's largest saleyard. Online auctions: The sale of collectables is migrating to the web. *Newsweek,* March 19, 62—64.
Shohat, E. & Stam, R. (1994). *Unthinking eurocentrism: Multiculturalism and the media.* London: Routledge.
Shor, I. (1980). *Critical teaching and everyday life.* Boston: South End Press.
Shor, I. (1993). Education is politics. In P. McLaren and P. Leonard (Eds.), *Paulo Freire: A critical encounter* (pp. 25-35). London: Routledge.
Short, G. & Carrington, B. (1999). Children's constructions of their national identity: Implications for critical multiculturalism. In S. May (Ed.), *Critical Multiculturalism: Rethinking multicultural and antiracist education* (pp. 172-190). London: Falmer Press.
Showalter, E. (1999a). Presidential Address 1998: Regeneration. *PMLA* 114 (May 1999), 318-325.
Showalter, E. (1999b). The risks of good teaching: How 1 Professor and 9 T.A.'s plunged into pedagogy. *The Chronicle of Higher Education* XLV, 44 (July 9, 1999), B4-B6.
Sleeter, C.E. (1996). White silence, white solidarity. In N. Ignatiev & J. Garvey (Eds.), *Race traitor* (pp. 257-265). New York: Routledge.
Slouka, M. (1995). *War of the worlds: Cyberspace and the high-tech assault on reality.* New York: Basic.
Smaje, C. (1997). Not just a social construct: theorising race and ethnicity. *Sociology 31,* 307-327.
Small, S. (1994). *Racialised barriers: The black experience in the United States and England in the 1980s.* London: Routledge.
Smedley, A. (1999). *Race in North America: Origin and evolution of a world view.* 2nd ed. Boulder, CO: Westview.
Smith, A. (1995). *Nations and nationalism in a global era.* London: Polity Press.
Smith, P. (1990). The political responsibility of teaching literatures. *College Literature,* 17(23), 81.
Smith, L. Tuhiwai. (1999). *Decolonizing methodologies: Research and indigenous peoples.* London: Zed Books.
Soloranzo, D. (1998). Critical race theory, race and gender microaggressions, and the experience of Chicana and Chicano scholars. *International Journal of Qualitative Studies in Education 11,* 121-136.
Soloranzo, D. & Villalpando, O. (1998). Critical race theory, marginality, and the experience of minority students in higher education. In C. Torres & T. Mitchell (Eds.), *Emerging issues in the Sociology of education: Comparative perspectives* (pp. 211-224). Albany: SUNY Press.
Soloranzo, D. & Yosso, T. (2002). Critical race methodology: Counter-storytelling as an analytical framework for education research. *Qualitative Inquiry 8,* 23-44.
Southern, R. W. (1995). *Scholastic humanism and the unification of Europe Vol. 1: Foundations.* Cambridge: Blackwell.
Stanfield, J.H., II (1993). Methodological reflections: An introduction. In J.H. Stanfield & R.M. Dennis (Eds.), *Race and ethnicity in research methods* (pp. 1-14). Newbury Park, CA: Sage.
Stanfield, J.H., II (1994). Response: Empowering the culturally diversified sociological voice. In A. Gitlin (Ed.), *Power and method: Political activism and educational research* (pp. 166-175). New York: Routledge.
Stanfield, J.H., II (1999). Slipping through the front door: Relevant social scientific evaluation in the people of color century. *American Journal of Evaluation, 20,* 415-431.

Steele, T. (1997). *The emergence of cultural studies: Adult education, cultural politics and the "English question."* London, Lawrence and Wishart.
Stinson, S. (1995) Body of knowledge, *Educational Theory* 45(1), 43-54.
Stokes, K. (1994). *Man and the biosphere: Toward a coevolutionary political economy*. Armonk, NY: M.E. Sharpe.
Strati, A. (1999) *Organization and aesthetics*. London: Sage.
Swindells, J. & Jardine, L. (1990) *What's left: Women in culture and the labour movement*. London: Routledge.
Symposium. (1994). Critical race theory [Special Issue]. *California Law Review*, 82(4).
Tappan, M.B. & Brown, L.M. (1996). Envisioning a postmodern moral pedagogy. *Journal of Moral Education* 25(1), 101-109.
Tate, W.F. IV. (1997). Critical race theory and education: History, theory and implications. In M. Apple (Ed.), *Review of Research in Education* (pp. 191-243). Washington, DC: American Educational Research Association.
Taylor, C. (1984). Foucault on freedom and truth. *Political Theory* 12 (2), 152-183.
Taylor, C. (1994). The politics of recognition. In A. Gutmann (Ed.), *Multiculturalism: Examining the politics of recognition* (pp. 25-73). Princeton, NJ.: Princeton University Press.
Taylor, P.V. (1993). *The texts of Paulo Freire*. Buckingham: Open University Press.
Teilhard De Chardin, P. (1959). *The phenomenon of man*. London: Collins.
Ternasky, P. (1992). Moral realism revisited: On achievable morality. *Educational Theory* 42(2), 201-216.
Thompson, A. (1999). Colortalk: Whiteness and off white. *Educational Studies* 30, 141-160.
Thompson, E. P. (1968). *Education and experience* (Fifth Mansbridge Memorial Lecture). Leeds, UK: Leeds University Press.
Thompson, E. P. (1978). *The poverty of theory and other essays*. London: Merlin.
Todd, S. (1997). *Learning desire: Perspectives on pedagogy, culture, and the unsaid*. New York: Routledge.
Torres, C. (1994). Education and the archeology of consciousness: Freire and Hegel. *Educational Theory* 44(4), 429-445.
Torres, C. (1998). Democracy, education, and multiculturalism: Dilemmas of citizenship in a global world. *Comparative Education Review* 42, 421-447.
Torres, C. & Freire, P. (1994). Twenty years after *Pedagogy of the oppressed:* Paulo Freire in conversation with Carlos Alberto Torres. In P. McLaren and C. Lankshear (Eds.), *Politics of Liberation: Paths from Freire* (pp. 100-107). London: Routledge.
Torres, R.D. Miron, L.F., & Inda, J.X. (Eds.).(1999). *Race, identity, and citizenship: A reader*. Oxford: Blackwell Publishers.
Troyna, B. (ed.). (1987). *Racial inequality in education*. London: Tavistock.
Troyna, B. (1993). *Racism and education*. Buckingham: Open University Press.
Turkle, S. (1995). *Life on the screen. Identity in the age of the internet*. New York: Phoenix.
Tushnet, M. (1992). The degradation of constitutional discourse. *Georgetown Law Journal*, 81, 251-312.
UCLA Law Review Symposium (2000). Race and the law at the turn of the century [Special issue]. *UCLA Law Review*, 47(6).
U.S. v. Fordice, 112 S. Ct. 2727 (1992).
Valdes, F. (2000). Sex and race in queer legal culture: Ruminations on identities and interconnectivities. In R. Delgado & J. Stefancic (Eds.), *Critical race theory: The cutting edge*. 2nd ed. (pp. 334-340). Philadelphia: Temple University Press.

Venn, C. (1997). Beyond enlightenment?: After the subject of Foucault, who comes? *Theory, Culture and Society* 14(3), 1–28.
Villalpando, O. (2000, November). Symposium: Critical race perspectives, interdisciplinary implications and teaching concerns. Paper presented at the meeting of the American Educational Studies Association, Vancouver, CA.
Villenas, S. (1996). The colonizer/colonized chicana ethnographer: Identity, marginizalization, and co-optation in the field. *Harvard Educational Review, 66,* 711–731.
Vygotsky, L.S. (1978). *Mind in society*. Cambridge: Harvard University Press.
Waldron, J. (1993). *Liberal rights*. Cambridge: Cambridge University Press.
Waldron, J. (1995). Minority cultures and the cosmopolitan alternative. In W. Kymlicka (Ed.), *The rights of minority cultures* (pp. 93–119). Oxford: Oxford University Press.
Walker, J. (1980). The end of dialogue: Paulo Freire on politics and education. In R. Mackie (Ed.), *Literacy and revolution: The pedagogy of Paulo Freire* (pp. 120–150). London: Pluto Press.
Watnick, M. (1962). Relativism and class consciousness: Georg Lukacs. In L. Labedz (Ed.), *Revisionism essays on the history of Marxist ideas*. London: George Allen and Unwin Ltd.
Weber, S. (1993). Taking exception to decision: Walter Benjamin and Carl Schmitt. In Harry Kunneman and Hent de Vries (Eds.), *Enlightenments: Encounters between critical theory and contemporary French thought,* 6–16. Kampen, Holland: Kok Pharos.
Weiler, K. (1991). Paulo Freire and a feminist pedagogy of difference. *Harvard Educational Review* 61(4), 449–474.
Weis, L. (1995). Qualitative research in sociology of education: Reflections on the 1970s and beyond. In W.T. Pink & G. W. Noblit (Eds.), *Continuity and contradiction: The futures of the sociology of education*. Creekskill, NJ: Hampton Press.
Werbner, P. (1997a). Introduction: The dialectics of cultural hybridity. In P. Werbner & T. Modood (Eds.), *Debating cultural hybridity: Multicultural identities and the politics of antiracism* (pp. 1–26). London: Zed Books.
Werbner, P. (1997b). Essentialising essentialism, essentialising silence: Ambivalence and multiplicity in the constructions of racism and ethnicity. In P. Werbner & Modood (Eds.), *Debating cultural hybridity: Multicultural identities and the politics of antiracism* (pp. 226–254). London: Zed Books.
West, C. (1991). The new cultural politics of difference. In R. Fergusen, M. Geever, Trinh T Minh-ha, & C. West (Eds.), *Out there*. Cambridge: MIT Press.
Wetherell, M. & Potter, J. (1992). *Mapping the language of racism:Discourse and the legitimation of exploitation*. London: Harvester Wheatleaf.
Wicker, H-R. (1997). From complex culture to cultural complexity. In P. Werbner & T. Modood (Eds.), *Debating cultural hybridity: Multicultural identities and the politics of antiracism* (pp. 29–45). London: Zed Books.
Wilbur, R. (1988). *New and collected poems*. London: Harcourt Brace.
Williams, J. (1999). Brave new university. *College English* 61:6 (July 1999), 744.
Williams, P.J. (1991). *The alchemy of race and rights*. Cambridge: Harvard University Press.
Williams, R. (1977) *Marxism and literature*. Oxford, Oxford University Press.
Williams, R. (1979). *Politics and letters: Interviews with New Left Review*. London: NLB/Verso.
Williams, R. (1989) The future of cultural studies. In *The politics of modernism*. London: Verso.
Winant, H. (1999, August). Toward a comparative historical sociology of race. Paper presented at the meeting of the American Sociological Association, Chicago.

Wittgenstein, L. (1953). *Philosophical investigations* (E. Anscombe, Ed.). Oxford: Blackwell.
Wittgenstein, L. (1966/1978). *Lectures and conversations on aesthetics, psychology and religious belief.* (C. Barrett, Ed.). Oxford: Basil Blackwell.
Wittgenstein, L. (1967). *Zettel* (E. Anscombe and G. von Wright, Eds.). Oxford: Blackwell.
Wohlfarth, I. (1989). On some Jewish motifs in Benjamin. In A. Benjamin (Ed.), *The problems of modernity: Adorno and Benjamin* (pp. 157–69). London: Routledge.
Wojtyla, K. (1979). *The acting person.* (A. Potocki, Trans.). Dodrecht: D. Reidel Publishing.
Worsley, P. (1984). *The three worlds: Culture and world development*. London: Weidenfeld and Nicholson.
Yamamoto, E.K. (1997). Critical race praxis: Race theory and political lawyering practice in post-civil rights America. *Michigan Law Review*, 95, 821–900.
Young, M. & Laible, J. (2000). White racism, antiracism, and school leadership preparation. *Journal of School Leadership*, 10, 374–414.
Young, R. (1990). *A critical theory of education: Habermas and our children's future*. New York: Teachers College Press.
Young, R. (1995). Liberalism, postmodernism, critical theory and politics. In *After postmodernism* (pp. 13–22). London: The Falmer Press.
Young, R. (1996a). *Intercultural communication*. Clevedon: Multilingual Matters.
Young, R. (1996b). Decolonising education: The scope of educational thought. *Studies in Philosophy and Education* 15, 4: 309–322.
Young-Bruehl, E. (1982). *Hannah Arendt: For love of the world*. New Haven, CT: Yale University Press.
Yuval-Davis, N. (1997a). *Gender and nation*. London: Sage.
Yuval-Davis, N. (1997b). Ethnicity, gender relations and multiculturalism. In P. Werbner & T. Modood (Eds.), *Debating cultural hybridity: Multicultural identities and the politics of antiracism* (pp. 193–208). London: Zed Books.
Žižek, S. (1993). *Trying with the negative: Kant, Hegel, and the critique of ideology*. Durham, NC: Duke University Press.

CONTRIBUTORS

Deborah P. Britzman is Professor of Education and Social and Political Thought at York University in Toronto, Canada. Her main research and teaching interests are in psychoanalysis and education, curriculum theorizing and history, studies of social conflict and representing trauma, studies of affect in learning and teaching, and the theoretical study of social difference and ethical relations. She is author of *Practice Makes Practice: A Critical Study of Learning to Teach* (1991), *Lost Subjects, Contested Objects: Toward a Psychoanalytic Inquiry of Learning* (1998), and *After-Education: Anna Freud, Melanie Klein, and Psychoanalytic Histories of Learning* (2003). Email: *Britzman@edu.yorku.ca*

James C. Conroy is currently Head of the Department of Religious Education at the University of Glasgow and Visiting Research Fellow at Australian Catholic University. He has been a visiting lecturer/professor at universities in Australia, South Africa and Brazil, and has published widely in the fields of religious politics and education and, citizenship and moral education in the liberal state. Jim sits on a number of national and international bodies in the field of moral education. His last volume was an edited collection of papers on the politics and practices of Catholic education entitled *Catholic Education: Inside/Out-Outside/In* (1999). He is currently working on a book called *At the Threshold: Education in the Liminal Spaces*. Email: *j.conroy@mary.acu.edu.au*

Robert A. Davis is Senior Lecturer in Curriculum Studies in the University of Glasgow. He was educated at the universities of Strathclyde, Cambridge, and Stirling, where he completed his doctoral studies in Literature and Anthropology. He is a visiting lecturer in several institutions, including Fordham University, Australian Catholic University, St. Patrick's College, Dublin, and the universities of Copenhagen and Helsinki. In addition to research in literature and war, Robert Davis has written and broadcast widely on literature and myth, imagination and religion, and the cultural history of childhood. His recent publications include studies of the poetry of Robert Graves, the operas of Richard Wagner, Walter Benjamin and modernity, and the Trickster figure. He is currently completing a critical history of the English lullaby. Email: *R.Davis@educ.gla.ac.uk*

Don Dippo is Associate Dean of Education at York University in Toronto, Canada. His general academic interests include social and political organization of knowledge, critical pedagogy and cultural studies, curriculum critique and development, teaching as an occupation and teacher education. His current research interests focus on technical and vocational education and education for sustainability. He is co-author (with Roger Simon and Arlene Schenke) of *Learning Work: A Critical Pedagogy of Work Education,* and has published numerous book chapters and articles in international education journals. Email: *ddippo@edu.yorku.ca*

Grant Gillett is a Professor of Medical Ethics at the University of Otago in Dunedin, New Zealand. He is also a practicing neurosurgeon. His main philosophical work is in the philosophy of mind and psychiatry, though he also writes on topics in bioethics. His most recent books are *The Mind and Its Discontents* (1999) and he has co-authored *Medical Ethics* (2001) and *Consciousness and Intentionality* (2001). He is interested in postmodern and traditional analytic approaches to bioethics, mind and language, and psychiatry. Email: *grant.gillett@stonebow.otago.ac.nz*

Henry A. Giroux holds the Waterbury Chair Professorship and is currently the Director of the Waterbury Forum in Education and Cultural Studies at Penn State University. His most recent books include: *Channel Surfing: Racism, the Media and the Destruction of Today's Youth* (1997), *Pedagogy and the Politics of Hope* (1997), *The Mouse That Roared: Disney and the End of Innocence* (1999), *Stealing Innocence: Youth, Corporate Power, and the Politics of Culture* (2000), *Impure Acts: the Practical Politics of Cultural Studies* (2000), *Theory and Resistance in Education: Towards an Oppositional Pedagogy* (2001), *Public Spaces/Private Lives: Beyond the Culture of Cynicism* (2001), *Beyond the Corporate University* (2001); *Breaking Into the Movies: Film and the Culture of Politics* (2002), and *The Abandoned Generation: Democracy beyond the Culture of Fear.* Email: *hag5@psu.edu*

Ilan Gur-Ze'ev is a Senior Lecturer in the Faculty of Education at the University of Haifa, Israel, with particular interests in critical theory, critical pedagogy, postmodernism, postcolonialism, feminism, cyberspace, multiculturalism, Holocaust/Nakbah dialectics, and peace education. His books include *The Frankfurt School and the History of Pessimism* (1996), *Critical Theory and Education* (1997), *Philosophy, Politics and Education in Israel* (1999), *Conflicting Philosophies of Education in Israel/Palestine* (2000), and *Destroying the Other's Collective Memory* (2002). He is the author of many articles that have been published in Arabic, Portuguese, Serbian, Hebrew, and English. Email: *ilangz@construct.haifa.ac.il*

Douglas Kellner is George Kneller Chair in the Philosophy of Education at UCLA and is author of many books on social theory, politics, history, and culture, including *Camera Politica: The Politics and Ideology of Contemporary Hollywood Film* (co-authored with Michael Ryan), *Critical Theory, Marxism, and Modernity, Jean Baudrillard: From Marxism to Postmodernism and Beyond, Postmodern Theory: Critical Interrogations* (with Steven Best), *Television and the Crisis of Democracy, The Persian Gulf TV War, Media Culture*, and *The Postmodern Turn* (with Steven Best). He has just published a book on the 2000 presidential election, *Grand Theft 2000: Media Spectacle and the Theft of an Election*, and *The Postmodern Adventure. Science, Technology, and Cultural Studies at the Third Millennium* (co-authored with Steve Best). Forthcoming books include *Media Spectacle and September 11, Terror War*, and *The New Barbarism*. Email: *kellner@ucla.edu*

Colin Lankshear is a freelance educational researcher and writer based in Mexico and a parttime Professorial Research Fellow at the University of Ballarat, Australia. His recent books include *Changing Literacies* (1997), *Ways of Knowing: Researching Literacy* (with Michele Knobel, 1999), *Teachers and Technoliteracies* (with Ilana Snyder, 2000), *Maneras de Ver* (with Michele Knobel, 2001), *El Nuevo Orden Laboral* (with Jim Gee and Glynda Hull, 2002), *Social Spaces/Cyber Spaces: Culture Clash in Computerized Classrooms* (with Ivor Goodson, Michele Knobel, and Marshall Mangan, 2002), and *New Literacies: Changing Knowledge and Classroom Learning* (with Michele Knobel, 2003). Email: *colin@coatepec.net*

Timothy W. Luke is University Distinguished Professor of Political Science as well as Co-Director for the Center for Digital Discourse and Culture at Virginia Polytechnic Institute and State University in Blacksburg, Virginia. His research interests address the politics of information societies, international affairs, and ecological criticism. He has just completed a new critical study of ideological politics at a number of major museums in the United States, called *Museum Politics: Power Plays at the Exhibition* (2002). His most recent books are *Capitalism, Democracy, and Ecology: Departing from Marx* (1999), *The Politics of Cyberspace* (1998, co-edited with Chris Toulouse), and *Ecocritique: Contesting the Politics of Nature, Economy and Culture* (1997). He also is the author of *Shows of Force: Politics, Power, and Ideology in Art Exhibitions* (1992). Email: *twluke@vt.edu*

Stephen May is Foundation Professor and Chair of Language and Literacy Education in the School of Education, University of Waikato, Hamilton, New Zealand and a Senior Research Fellow in the Centre for the Study of Ethnicity and Citizenship, University of Bristol. His research interests are wide-ranging and include social theory (particularly, the work of Bourdieu), critical research, the sociology of language and education, ethnicity, nationalism, and multiculturalism. He has published widely in these areas and is particularly interested in their interconnections. Major recent publications include *Critical Multiculturalism* (RoutledgeFalmer, 1999) and *Language and Minority Rights* (Longman, 2001). He is a founding editor of the international and interdisciplinary journal *Ethnicities* (Sage). Email: *s.may@waikato.ac.nz*

Erica McWilliam is a professor in the School of Cultural and Language Studies (Faculty of Education) at the Queensland University of Technology. Her publications cover a wide spectrum, as is evidenced in her numerous publications on pedagogy, research methodology and training, leadership and management, and postmodernity. She is currently series editor of 'Eruptions' for Peter Lang, New York, and is a contributor to the *4th Handbook of Research on Teaching*. Email: *e.mcwilliam @qut.edu.au*

Mark Olssen is Reader and Director of Doctoral Programmes in the Department of Educational Studies, University of Surrey. He is editor of *Mental Testing in New Zealand: Critical and Oppositional Perspectives* (1988), author (with Elaine Papps) of *The Doctoring of Childbirth* (1997), editor (with Kay Morris Matthews) of *Education Policy in New Zealand: The 1990s and Beyond* (1997) and author of *Michel Foucault: Materialism and Education* (1999) He has published articles in Britain in the *Journal of Education Policy, The British Journal of Educational Studies, Educational Psychology*, and *Educational Philosophy and Theory*. Email: *M.Olssen@surrey.ac.uk*

Laurence Parker is an associate professor in the Department of Educational Policy Studies at the University of Illinois at Urbana-Champaign. His areas of interests are urban education policy, critical race theory, and educational policy analysis. His most recent publications include a special edited issue of *Qualitative Inquiry* (v. 8, n.1) on critical race theory and qualitative research methodology. He is joint editor (with Donna Deyhle and Sofia Villenas) of *Race Is . . . Race Isn't* (1999), and joint editor of a special issue of *The Urban* Review on critical issues in the urban education context. He has a forthcoming book for Peter Lang Publishing with Gerado Lopez, called *Interrogating Racism in Qualitative Research Methodology*. Email: *parker3@uiuc.edu*

Michael Peters is Research Professor of Education at the University of Glasgow and has a personal chair at the University of Auckland. He has research interests in education policy and contemporary philosophy with a special emphasis on educational philosophy. He has published over 100 academic articles in these fields and is the author and/or editor of over twenty books, including most recently: *Heidegger, Education and Modernity* (2002) (Ed.), *Poststructuralism, Marxism and Neoliberalism: Between Politics & Theory* (2001), *Richard Rorty: Education, Philosophy and Politics* (2001) (Eds.), *Nietzsche's Legacy for Education: Past and Present Values* (2001) (Eds.), *After the Disciplines* (2000) (Ed.), *Wittgenstein: Philosophy, Postmodernism, Pedagogy* (1999), *University Futures and the Politics of Reform* (1999), *Education Policy* (1999) (Eds.), *Virtual Technologies in Tertiary Education* (1998) (Eds.), *Cultural Politics and the University* (1997) (Eds.), *Individualism and Community:*

Education and Social Policy in the Postmodern Condition (1996), *Poststructuralism, Politics and Education* (1996), and *Education and the Postmodern Condition* (1995) (Ed.). Email: *M.Peters@educ.gla.ac.uk*

Peter Roberts is a Senior Lecturer in the School of Education at the University of Auckland in New Zealand. His teaching and research interests lie in the philosophy of education and educational policy studies. His work has appeared in a wide range of international journals, including *Educational Theory*, the *Journal of Philosophy of Education, Educational Philosophy and Theory*, the *Journal of Moral Education*, the *Journal of Educational Thought*, the *British Journal of Educational Studies*, the *Oxford Review of Education*, the *International Journal of Lifelong Education*, and the *International Review of Education*. He has published five books, including *Education, Literacy and Humanization* (Bergin and Garvey, 2000). Email: *pr.roberts @auckland.ac.nz*

Tom Steele is Reader in Adult Education and Coordinator of Postgraduate Studies in Adult & Continuing Education in the Faculty of Education at the University of Glasgow. He is the author of a number of publications in the areas of adult education and cultural studies, including *The Emergence of Cultural Studies: Adult Education, Cultural Politics and the 'English' Question* (1997) and a recent book with Richard Taylor and Jean Barr, *For a Radical Higher Education* (2002). Email: *t.steele @educ.gla.ac.uk*

Robert Young is an Honorary Reader in the Faculty of Education at the University of Sydney, Australia. He is the author of *A Critical Theory of Education* (1990), *Critical Theory and Classroom Talk* (1992), and *Intercultural Communication: Pragmatics, Genealogy, Deconstruction* (1996), and numerous articles on Habermasian critical theory. Email: *r.young@edfac.usyd.edu.au*

INDEX

action, 89–92
active nihilism, 37–45
Adams, J., 93
Adorno, T., 2, 7–9, 13, 17–23, 26–34, 68, 79, 81, 117, 132–134, 225, 229, 246
agency, 12, 22, 68, 70, 79–81, 118, 121, 124, 145–146, 161, 166, 170, 203, 209, 214, 230
Ahmad, A., 205
Alienation, 5, 8, 19, 23, 29, 33
allegory, 42–44, 46–52
Althusser, L., 230–231
altruism, 56
American Dream, 85
Anderson, P., 223–225, 229, 235
Apple, M., 125–126
Arendt, H., Ch 5, 124, 132, 134–136
Aristotle, 73, 96, 175
Aronowitz, S., 18
art, 23, 47, 49
artwork, 42–50
Ayers v Fordice, 190

bad faith, 135
Bahro, R., 78
Baron, S., 232
Baudelaire, C., 39
Baudrillard, J., 95, 244
Bauman, Z., 145–146
behavior, 89
Being (as orientation to self), Ch 3
Bell, D., 191
Benchimol, A., 232, 233

Benhabib, S., 91
Benjamin, W., 17, 22–23, 26–27, 31–32, Ch 2, 81, 225
Bennett, T., 154, 157
Berman, M., 206
Bernstein, R., 124
Beyer, L., 119
Bhabha, H., 204, 210
Bloom, H., 146–148
body, Ch 13
    as carnivalesque, 219–220
    and desire, 216–219
    female 213–220
    grotesque, Ch 13
    materiality of, 215
    normalization of, 218
    and pleasure, 216–219
Bohman, J., 12
Botstein, L., 150–152, 154
Bourdieu, P., 148, 208–210, 222–223, 226, 234–236
Brah, A., 202
Brown, W. R., 189
bureaucratization, 7–8
Butler, J., 215

Canovan, M., 97
Cartesianism, 102–103, 106
Cartledge, P., 96
Castoriadi, C., 143
Caudwell, C., 229
Chang, R. S., 192

character structure, 58
Chardin, T. de, 174
Chicano-Latino groups, 194–195
citizenship, 4–5, Ch 5, 143–145, 153–154, 160
Cobbett, W., 233
Cole, G. D. H., 228
commodification, 7–8, 59–64, 155–162
communicative action, 123
communicative reason, 80
consciousness, 19, Ch 6, 169–170, 174
consciousness raising, 133
consumption, 51, 95–96, 217
Cope, B., 201
cosmopolitanism
    as multicultural alternative, 206–208
counterculture, 77
Cremin, L., 152
Crenshaw, K., 192–193
critical pedagogy, 17–18, 20–27, 30, 33–34, 130–132, 138, 143–166
Critical Race Theory, Ch 11
    and educational research, 194–197
criticism, Ch 2
cultural hybridity, 204–206
    and creolization, 204
    and mestizaje, 204
cultural materialism, 234–236
cultural studies, Ch 14
    and adult education, 226–227
    British, Ch 14
    and Frankfurt School, 225–226
culture, 23, 27, 200–202, 225–237, 241, 249–250
culture industry, 27, 29, 33–34
cynicism, Ch 9
    culture of, 143–145

dasein, 87
Davis, N., 217
Dayal, S., 136, 139
deconstruction
    Derridean, 117, 124
    of race, 191
dehumanization, 22, 29, 178
Deleuze, G., 216
Delgado, R., 190
Delgado Bernal, D., 194
democracy, 92, 143–146, 150–152, 158–165
Derrida, J., 1, 114–119, 121–122, 124–126, 159
Descartes, R., 67, 177

Dewey, J., 123, 126–127, 152
Deyhle, D., 195
dialogue, 21–22, 176–177, 184
Disney, W., 37
Douglass, F., 166
DuBois, W. E. B., 166
Dworkin, D., 223, 230, 232

Eagleton, T., 235, 237
eBay.com 62–66
ecology, 245–250
    deep, 247
    social, 247
Edsall, T., 187
Edsall, M., 187
ego, 72
Eichmann, A., 91
Einstein, A., 27, 37
Eliot, T. S., 234
Ellsworth, E., 18, 22, 26, 154–156
emancipation, 11, 25, 28, 31–32, 76–78
    politics of, 124
empowerment, 22, 32
Engels, F., 106–107, 178, 180, 237, 244
entrepreneurial capitalism, 246–247
environment, Ch 15
environmentalism, 242–245
epistemology
    Freirean, 171–174, 186–187
equity, 123
Eros, 72, 74, 77–81
ethnicity, 208–209

Felman, S., 165
feminism, Ch 13
    and critical race theory, 192–193
    as signifier, 202
feminist politics, 213
Flecha, R., 188
Foucault, M., 1, 9, 11, 43, 69–70, 79, 114, 116–119, 121, 124, 126–127, 218–218, 222
Frankfurt School, 1–3, 7–8, 12, 17–18, 20, 22–23, 54, 67–68, 81, 132, 134, 225–226, 229, 232, 236, 238
Fraser, N., 116–117, 120
Freedom, 5–7, 12, 20, 26, 33, 68, 70–71, 74–76, 78, 88, 92–93, 95, 117, 132, 143, 145, 179, 208
Frege, G., 102
Freire, P., 17, 19–20, 22, 131, 165–166, Ch 10

French Revolution, 93
Freud, S., 49, 55, 67–72, 81
Friedan, B., 213
Friedman, J., 205
Friedman, M., 160
Friedman, T., 62
Fromm, E., 2, 13, 17, Ch 3, 79, 81, 179

Gage, N., 150
Gandhi, I., 137
Gasche, R., 46
Gates, B., 144
German Idealism, 6
Gilroy, P., 204
Giroux, H., 17–27, 125–126, 170, 172
Glazer, N., 199, 212
Goldman, L., 230, 235
Gotanda, N., 189, 192
Gramsci, A., 114, 230, 239, 246
Greene, M., Ch 8, 152
Grosz, E., 215–216
Grumet, M., 214
Grunberg, C., 3, 13
Guattari, F., 216

Habermas, J., 2, 10, 12–13, 67, 72, 79, 81, Ch 7, 134, 212, 222–223, 239
habitus (Bourdieu), 208–209
Haeckel, E., 245
Hall, S., 206, 211, 225–226, 231–232
Handler, R., 202
happiness, 70–71, 74–75, 86, 91–96, 135
Haraway, D., 244
Harris, C., 192
Hatcher, R., 200
Hauser, A., 229
Having (as orientation to self), Ch 3
Hayman, R., 191
Heaney, S., 98
Hegel, H-G., 1–2, 6–9, 24, 38, 67, 73, 87, 103–104, 112, 121, 169
Hegeliansim, 8–9
Heidegger, M., 2, 29, 42, 87, 223
Herder, G., 235
Herzen, A., 6
Hilferding, R., 5
Hill, C., 229, 232
Hilton, R., 229
Hirsch, E. D., 150
Hobsbawm, E, 229, 232

Hoggart, R., 224–225, 227–228
Holocaust, 91
Horkheimer, M., 2–4, 6–9, 13, 17–24, 27–34, 54
Horner, B., 156
Horton, M., 131
Hoy, D., 8–9
Huizinga, J., 36–37
human character orientations, 56
humanization, Ch 3, 174–176, 178, 183
Hune, S., 192
Hunter, I., 154
Husserl, E., 67

identity politics, 186
Ideology, 21, 29, 53, 88
Ideology critique, 20–22, 24, 29–30, 32, 120, 137
imagination, 76, 130, 132, 134–139
immanent criticism/critique, 24, 38–40, 42, 45, 47, 51–53, 115
indoctrination, 7, 125
informationalism, 242–245
instinct theory (Freud), 72, 81
intellectuals, 114–115, 230
  public intellectuals, Ch 9
intentionality, 106, 111, 174
interdisciplinarity, 227–228

Jameson, F., 241
Jaspers, K., 86
Jay, P., 220
Jefferson, T., 94, 152
Judaism, 31
justice, 31, 123, 125, 127, 153–154, 160, 162, 192

Kalantzis, M., 201
Kant, I., 1, 4, 6, 24, 38, 103, 112, 121
Kaufman, D., 148
Kautsky, K., 5
Keane, C., 216
Keenan, T., 159
Kellner, D., 4–5, 222, 225–226, 232, 236
Kierkegaard, S., 87
Klee, P., 40
knowledge, 149–151 153–165, 169, Ch 10, 171–174, 210, 230, 236, 243–244
  cultural knowledges, 210–211
Korsch, K., 2, 5
Krauss, R., 46
Kristeva, J., 136, 215
Kymlicka, W., 207–208

labor, 89–92
Lacan, J., 215
Ladson-Billings, G., 186
Lamarck, J-B., 113
Lane, A., 228
language, Ch 6
    and consciousness, 101, 103–105, 112–113
    and meaning, 102–103
    and rules, 110–112
    and social construction, 106
    and subjectivity, 67
Lather, P., 19, 22
Le Corbusier, C., 37
Lenin, V., 25
Lessing, E., 25, 95
Levi Strauss, C., 205
liberation, 4, 9, 68, 71, 73, 76, 79, 169, 177–181, 213–214
Liston, D., 119
Loos, A., 37
Löwenthal, L., 2
Lowman, J., 153
Lukacs, G., 2, 5–8, 229–230, 239, 246
Luxembourg, R., 123
Lyotard, J-F., 116, 204, 243

Mannheim (cont), 228–229
Mannheim, K., 4
Marcuse, H., 2, 7–8, 13, 17–18, 20–26, 29, 31–32, 55, Ch 4, 134, 239
Margalit, A., 207
Marx, K., 2–3, 6–7, 10, 24–26, 54–55, 62, 65, 67, Ch 6, 119–123, 125–126, 169–170, 175, 178, 180, 236–239, 242, 246
Marxism, 229–231
Marxist critique
    as grand narrative, 120
mass culture, 7
Matsuda, M., 189
McCarthy, T., 3, 8–12
McGuigan, J., 236
McKeachie, W., 153
McKeever, M., 195
McLaren, P., 12, 18–19, 22, 173, 202
meaning, 102, 109–110, 114
    and rules, 110
Meister Eckhart, 64
memory, 70–71
Messianism, 31–34, 39–41, 51, 53
Mikilitsch, R., 163

Miller, A., 85
Mistry, R., 137–138
Mitchell, J., 231
Modernity, 2–3
    and artwork, 40–52
    and destruction of tradition, 37
    and language, 37–38
    and mechanical reproduction, 46–52
    waning of, 40–52
moral principles
    in Freire's philosophy, 181–183
Morris, W., 234
Morton, A., 229
multiculturalism, 199–200
    critical, Ch 12

nature, 6, 29, 44, 239, 240–242, 245, 247
Nazism, 91
Negative Dialectics, 28, 32, 34
Negative Theology, 28, 31, 34
Neumann, F., 2
New Left, 77
Nicholson, S., 116
Nietzsche, F., 1–2, 37, 42, 67–68, 71, 73, 223

Offe, C., 13
Omi, M., 187
Ong, W., 46
oppression, 11, 30, 70, 75–76, 126–127, 132, 144, 169–170, 178–181, 189
optimism, 22–27
Orwell, G., 228
O'Shea, A., 156
Owen, R., 233

Paglia, C., 217–218
Paine, T., 233
pedagogy, 143–145, 153, 183
    as commodity, 158
    as a political practice, 145–148
    depoliticized, 156
Peller, G., 192
performance principle, 72–73
pessimism, 22, 26, 37
Pickstock, C., 89
Pizzaro, M., 194
Plato, 90, 172–175
pleasure principle, 71
Plekhanov, G., 5
Polanyi, K., 228, 230

politics, Ch 5, 114, 116–117, 119, 143–145, 147
  of the 'Old Left,' 119–125
  as 'the Party,' 123
  of pedagogy, 148–157
  and theory, 114
Pollock, F., 2
postmodernism, Ch 4, Ch 7, 244–245
poststructuralism, 8–9, Ch 4, Ch 7
poverty, 94
power, 30–31, 85, 90, 92, 94–96, 114, 120, 123, 147–149, 151, 156–158, 160, 162–165, 187, 201, 209–210
  as power over, 120 123
  in relation to language, 148–149
  power relations, 209–210
power/knowledge, 116, 120
praxis, 5, 14, 18–19, 22, 28, 114–115, 118, 131, 135–136, 172, 175–178, 194
private language argument, 109–110
progress, 8–9, 28, 39
proletariat, 7, 121, 125, 243
public good, 143–145
public intellectuals, Ch 9, 230
  teachers as, 149

qualitative research and critical race theory, 194–197

race, Ch 11
  social awareness of, 189
  racial harrassment, 190–191
racism, 185, 188, 192, 231
ratings (personal), 62–66
rationality, 27, 29, 67, 72, 74–76, 93, 135
rationalization, 7–8
Rawls, J., 12
Raz, J., 207
Readings, B., 160
reality principle, 72–73
reason, 4, 7, 8, 11, 19, 24, 28, 73–74, 76, 236
Reich, W., 13
Reification 5, 8
Relativism, 4
representation, 20, 30, 32, 45–47
Rex, J., 224
Rilke, R., 36
Rizvi, F., 188
Rorty, R., 12, 79, 115, 122–123, 127
Roth, P., 137
Rousseau, J-J., 6

Russo, M., 213, 218–219

Said, E., 118, 203
Sartre, J-P., 132, 230
Schama, S., 94
Scheurich, J., 186
Schiller, F., 73–74
Schmidt, A., 2
Schopenhauer, A., 73
selfishness, 56
sexism, 185, 231
Shapiro, S., 214
Sherman, C., 220
Sherman, E., 63
Shor, I., 19, 22
Showalter, E., 150, 152–154
Silva, T., 173
skepticism, 118
Smith, P., 147
social character, 55
social constructivism, 106–108
Social democracy, 5
socialization, 42–43, 69
Soloranzo, D., 194
Stanfield, J., 195
Stinson, S., 215
Strati, A., 219
subject (human), 5, 33, 67–68, 72–73, 76, 78–79, 80, 101, 181–183
  and language, 67
subjectivity, 67, 69, 70, 73–76, 78–81, 87, 125, 216–217
surplus consciousness, 78
Swisher, K., 195

Tawney, R., 228
Taylor, C., 117–118
technology, 46–52
Thanatos, 72
Thomas, K., 192
Thompson, E. P., 223–224, 227–229, 231–232, 234
Thomson, G., 228
Tillich, P., 18
Torr, D., 229
Torres, C., 171, 199, 202
totalitarianism, 27, 91
Troyna, B., 200
Tuhiwai Smith, L., 195
Turner, V., 220

utopianism, 22, 26

Villenas, S., 194
Vygotsky, L., 104–105

Waldron, J., 206–207
Weber, M., 1–2, 7, 67
Weiler, K., 17–19, 22
Werbner, P., 205
West, C., 166
Whiteness, 192–193
Wilbur, R., 36
Williams, J., 144
Williams, J., 158
Williams, P., 191

Williams, R., 166, 223–224, 226–230, 232–236
Winant, H., 187
Wittgenstein, L., 88–89, Ch 6
Wojtyla, K., 88
women's liberation, 213–214
work, 89–92
World Trade Center/Twin Towers, Ch 5

Yamamoto, E., 194
Yeats, W. B., 84, 97
Young, M., 186

Zedong, Mao, 170
Žižek, S., 28

Studies in the Postmodern Theory of Education

General Editors
Joe L. Kincheloe & Shirley R. Steinberg

Counterpoints publishes the most compelling and imaginative books being written in education today. Grounded on the theoretical advances in criticalism, feminism, and postmodernism in the last two decades of the twentieth century, Counterpoints engages the meaning of these innovations in various forms of educational expression. Committed to the proposition that theoretical literature should be accessible to a variety of audiences, the series insists that its authors avoid esoteric and jargonistic languages that transform educational scholarship into an elite discourse for the initiated. Scholarly work matters only to the degree it affects consciousness and practice at multiple sites. Counterpoints' editorial policy is based on these principles and the ability of scholars to break new ground, to open new conversations, to go where educators have never gone before.

For additional information about this series or for the submission of manuscripts, please contact:

    Joe L. Kincheloe & Shirley R. Steinberg
    c/o Peter Lang Publishing, Inc.
    275 Seventh Avenue, 28th floor
    New York, New York 10001

To order other books in this series, please contact our Customer Service Department:

    (800) 770-LANG (within the U.S.)
    (212) 647-7706 (outside the U.S.)
    (212) 647-7707 FAX

Or browse online by series:
    www.peterlangusa.com